Lightning Joe

An Autobiography

Lightning Joe *An Autobiography*

by General J. Lawton Collins

UNITED STATES ARMY

LOUISIANA STATE UNIVERSITY PRESS
BATON ROUGE AND LONDON

Copyright © 1979 by Louisiana State University Press
All rights reserved
Manufactured in the United States of America

Design: Albert Crochet
Typeface: VIP Trump Medieval
Composition: LSU Press
Printing and binding: Thomson-Shore, Inc.

LIBRARY OF CONGRESS CATALOGING IN PUBLICATION DATA

Collins, Joseph Lawton, 1896–
  Lightning Joe : an autobiography.

  Bibliography: p.
  Includes index.
    1. Collins, Joseph Lawton, 1896–   2.   United
States. Army—Biography.   3.   Generals—United States—
Biography.   4.   United States—History, Military—20th
century.   I.   Title.
E745.C64A34   355.3'31'0924 [B]   78–27375
ISBN 0–8071–0499–X

To Gladys Easterbrook Collins
with admiration and ever-growing love

Contents

List of Illustrations

ix

List of Maps

Military Map Symbols

Symbols within a rectangle indicate a military unit, within a triangle an observation post.

Military Units - Identification

⬭	Armored Command
•	Artillery
⬚	Cavalry, Mechanized
E	Engineers
⊠	Infantry
S	Signal Corps
TD	Tank Destroyer

Size Symbols

The following symbols placed either in boundary lines or above the rectangle or triangle inclosing the identifying arm or service symbol indicate the size of military organization:

•	Squad
••	Section
•••	Platoon
I	Company, troop, battery, Air Force flight
I I	Battalion, cavalry squadron, or Air Force squadron

xiii

I I I	Regiment or group; combat team (with abbreviation CT following identifying numeral)
x	Brigade, Combat Command of Armored Division, or Air Force Wing
xx	Division or Command of an Air Force
xxx	Corps or Air Force
xxxx	Army
xxxxx	Group of Armies

Examples

The letter or number to the left of the symbol indicates the unit designation; that to the right, the designation of the parent unit to which it belongs. Letters or numbers above or below boundary lines designate the units separated by the lines:

A⊠137	Company A, 137th Infantry
[•]8	8th Field Artillery Battalion
A⬭I	Combat Command A, 1st Armored Division
◭23	Observation Post, 23rd Infantry
⊠5	Command Post, 5th Infantry Division
137 –I I I– 138	Boundary between 137th and 138th Infantry

Preface

During my lifetime great technological developments in aviation, radio, television, and other means of communication have brought people and nations into closer contact than ever before, accentuating the clashes of their rival ideologies and economic systems. The United States has fought two major wars from which it emerged as a leader of the Western world. Almost at once, we found ourselves in a cold war in which we, with our concepts of personal freedom and democracy, have been pitted against the Soviet Union, intent on establishing communism's political and economic system as the dominant force in the world.

As a professional soldier, I was involved in both World Wars, and I am the sole survivor among three senior officers who commanded large combat units in the second World War in both the Pacific and European theaters. I was Chief of Staff of the United States Army and a member of the Joint Chiefs of Staff during the entire Korean War, after which I was appointed by President Dwight D. Eisenhower as Special Representative of the United States in Vietnam. During this assignment I had the personal rank of ambassador, with the mission of developing and initiating a program of military and economic assistance to the government of President Ngo Dinh Diem. On completion of this mission I reverted to my post as the American representative on the Standing Group of the North Atlantic Treaty Organization until my retirement from the United States Army, March 31, 1956.

A year later I joined Chas. Pfizer and Company as a member of its board of directors and vice chairman of its International Divisions. In the latter capacity, for the next thirteen years I traveled extensively, visiting Pfizer facilities around the world and assisting in negotiating

Pfizer trade arrangements in Turkey, India, Vietnam, and other countries of the Far East and Latin America. These tasks had diplomatic as well as business ramifications.

A large part of these memoirs deal with military campaigns that occupied the major share of my life. They require considerable details of plans and operations. I have tried to liven these accounts by pointing up the human factors that usually decide the outcome of battles. My military, diplomatic, and business experiences alike have convinced me that individual human beings, more than weapons, equipment, or group organizations, determine the fate of men and nations.

The accounts of actual fighting are based on my own field orders, situation reports, and—particularly in Europe—on daily operations memoranda, supplemented by the official histories prepared under the direction of a series of Chiefs of Military History, United States Army: Major Generals Orlando Ward and Harry J. Malony, Brigadier Generals James A. Norell, Hal C. Pattison, and James L. Collins, Jr. I am indebted to each of them and to their Chief Historians, Kent Roberts Greenfield, Stetson Conn, and Maurice Matloff. My special thanks go to the authors of the splendid histories of the campaigns in which I participated: Roy E. Appleman, Martin Blumenson, Hugh M. Cole, Gordon A. Harrison, Walter G. Hermes, Charles B. MacDonald, John Miller, Jr., Forrest C. Pogue, James F. Schnabel, and Mark S. Watson.

Edwin A. Thompson, Thomas C. Hohman, William H. Cunliffe, Edward J. Reese, John E. Taylor, Graham B. Gibson, and Timothy Nenninger of the National Archives provided invaluable assistance in documentary research. They cheerfully tackled every request I made to them and evidenced genuine interest, which I greatly appreciated. The same was true of Detmar Finke, B. C. Mossman, and especially Hannah Zeidlik of the Office of the Chief of Military History. My long-standing friends Evelyn Robinson of the Army Library and Vicki Destafano of the Army Audiovisual Center never failed to provide the proper books, reports, or official photographs to answer my many requests for information. Nannette W. Johnson, Helen Wolferich, and Ethel M. Richardson skillfully transcribed my longhand manuscript into finished type.

I am deeply indebted to Brigadier Frank Dorn, United States Army, retired, for coming to my aid on short notice and preparing half of the essential maps, the others of which were well done by Howell C. Brewer, Jr. I will never be able adequately to thank Dr. Robert H. Ferrell, Professor of History, Indiana University, who not only expertly reviewed the manuscript but made innumerable suggestions which improved its clarity and style.

Above all, I am grateful to my dear wife, Gladys Easterbrook Collins, whose cheerful tolerance, encouragement, and wise counsel account largely for any merit this book may have.

Lightning Joe

An Autobiography

CHAPTER I

EARLY YEARS

Boyhood in New Orleans

As a young boy growing up at the turn of the century in New Orleans, I had my first contact with things military at Mardi Gras time. There was a naval station not far from our house in the suburb of Algiers on the west bank of the Mississippi, and warships always took part in the gala river parade that escorted the King of Carnival up the river to the foot of Canal Street from his mystic kingdom. I once visited these ships with my father as they lay at anchor in the river. Their powerful guns and magic searchlight display at night captivated me. Though my oldest brother James attended West Point, the Navy remained my first love. So it was a shock to the family when, at the age of eight or nine, I responded one evening to a query by a visiting relative from Cincinnati that when I grew up I was going to West Point. To a family chorus demanding why I had abandoned the sea, I replied, "Because there is no home life in the Navy." The peal of laughter that followed was often repeated in later years as I was joshed about this favorite family story.

Ours was not a traditional military family, nor were we old-line southerners. My father, Jeremiah Bernard Collins, had come to America with his parents from their native Ireland in 1862, when he was fifteen years old, following relatives who had emigrated to Cincinnati during the great potato famine in Ireland in the 1840s. The Civil War was on when the Collins family arrived in Cincinnati, and my father soon enlisted, or was drafted, into the Ohio militia as a drummer boy. As far as we know, he saw no action. Family folklore has him helping to drive a herd of horses down to Texas sometime after the war. From Texas young Jerry Collins worked his way east to Louisiana, where he was hired as a deliveryman by a James Lawton, who owned and oper-

I

ated a general store on the west bank of the Mississippi below New Orleans.

Jerry Collins soon showed his good judgment, and Irish charm, by marrying his boss's lovely daughter Catherine, on December 4, 1878. Shortly thereafter the couple moved upstream to Algiers, where they set up a grocery store near the eastern terminus and maintenance shops of the Southern Pacific Railroad. The business, supported by workers at the shops and their families, gradually expanded to include such sundry items as nails, buckshot, gunpowder, imported teas and spices, animal feed, and eggs. As was the custom in those days, a beer parlor was added, which took on the air of an English village pub and served the same purpose for the workmen.

To operate this modest business required a horse and wagon, and to support both the store and a growing family we always had a cow and a hundred or more Leghorn chickens. Except for a clerk and one or two yardmen, this was a family-operated business. As it grew so did the family. I was number ten of eleven children, six girls and five boys, all sound of body and mind, and—amazing for those times—all grew to adulthood except for two tragic accidental deaths.

As with most large families of limited means, we were a closely knit, deeply loyal group, dependent on one another and strengthened by one another. We younger children all had chores. My older brother Peter worked in the store when not at the Jesuit College, and I milked and took care of the cow and the chickens and occasionally filled steins of beer at the bar. The girls helped with the cooking, sewing, and housework.

We children all studied together at the long dining room table, the older ones helping the beginners with the intricacies of the three R's. There was no kindergarten then, but I learned to read and write before going to school and skipped two grades in grammar school before entering high school at age twelve. With the urging and financial assistance of my sister Kittie, who had charge of the local library, I was privileged to take weekly instruction in "elocution" at the convent school, an early introduction to public speaking that proved of value in later life.

The most cherished periods of my childhood were our long, hot summer vacations. Barefooted, and wearing blue overalls, sleeveless cotton shirts, and soft straw hats, my younger brother Bernard and I played together incessantly, whether it was building tree houses in the back yard, playing one o'cat baseball with neighborhood kids (using a small red rubber ball and a broom handle for a bat), fishing for crayfish in a ditch alongside the "S.P." maintenance shops, or shooting marbles on the smooth-packed mud borders of the sidewalks. Few of the streets in our neighborhood were paved when we were small boys, and following the frequent heavy rains they developed wonderful mud holes. I still remember the exquisite feeling of sticky Louisiana blue clay oozing between my bare toes as we splashed through those mud holes.

Once a week Peter or I accompanied my father, whom I dearly loved, on his wagon trip to the wholesale produce markets in New Orleans to purchase supplies for the store. We delighted in helping harness "Rex" to the grocery wagon and were especially proud when we were permitted to take the reins for the drive to the foot of Pelican Avenue, where we boarded the paddle-wheeled ferry for the trip across the Mississippi. At flood level, the river was nearly a mile wide. Swirling along within its retaining levees at five miles an hour, ten feet or more above the level of the city streets, the mighty Mississippi was an awesome sight. Once safely across, we would drive up Poydras Street, Rex's steel shoes clicking over its cobblestoned pavement. We stopped and dismounted while Papa made his purchases. The pungent odor of manila hemp rope mingled with the smell of oysters and river catfish, coffee, and bananas, as we dodged our way along the sidewalks cluttered with sacks of sugar or rice, crates of fruit, casks of wine, and, occasionally, great sea turtles sprawled alive on their backs, helplessly waving their stretched-out flippers. Creole and Italian voices mixed with the shrill cries of street vendors; the stomping of horses' hoofs and the rattle of wagon wheels produced a cacophony that was music to a boy of ten. Then with the wagon loaded till its springs creaked we clomped our way back to the Canal Street ferry and on home, while my father sang some of his old Irish ditties and we talked about all sorts of things, from mice to men.

Not the least of my summer vacation pleasures, as I grew older, were, strangely enough, the afternoon tutoring sessions with Mr. Wallace Lampton, to whom my parents sent me, probably to get me out of the house. Mr. Lampton, then probably in his forties, had been blinded when eleven years old. He was standing near home plate at a sandlot baseball game when the bat slipped from the hands of the batter and struck him squarely in the eyes. He had aspired to the priesthood. Undaunted, a brilliant student, he learned braille—he could read braille or raised lettering with equal facility—completed his education, and became a teacher. He told me that the New York Public Library, from which he borrowed books for the blind, had informed him that he read more books in a year than any blind person in America. He never complained or bemoaned his fate.

For a couple of summers I was his last pupil of the day. I had not been much interested in arithmetic at school, but he introduced me to algebra and made a game of it. He quickly had me doing simple simultaneous equations, racing him for solutions on paper while he solved the problems in his head. I never beat him. Then, after an hour and a half of math, English, or history, he would bring out his books for the blind on astronomy, and read to me about the stars. Each evening after dark I would scramble up on the roof of our feed storage building and locate the summer constellations and identify the first-magnitude stars. The next afternoon I would describe them to Mr. Lampton and answer his eager questions as to their color and brightness. I obtained from our local library a nontechnical book on astronomy by the French astronomer Camille Flammarion, and read from it to Mr. Lampton. When summer was over I studied the winter constellations and often dropped by the Lampton house to describe them to him.

The second summer we read many of the Greek myths about the stars, which served to whet my interest in the universe. To this day, I get keen pleasure from a starlit night, and thrill to the exploits of our astronauts, capped for me by the flight of Apollo XI to the moon, with my nephew Mike Collins aboard. I shall be forever grateful to my friend and great teacher, Wallace Lampton. I learned much from him, not only about the stars, but, more importantly, about courage and faith.

My brother James, to whom we all looked up, entered West Point in 1903, when I was seven years old, and it was chiefly through his example and inspiration that I determined to enter the military service. My early comment about the Navy was probably picked up from one of the older Collinses, but I was not simply parroting an overheard remark. I was already drawn into the tightly spun web of our Collins family relationships. I had seen Navy warships come and go through the port of New Orleans, and perhaps sensed that their crews were away from home much of the time. I decided that home meant more to me than the Navy.

My father died in 1911. The bronchitis which had troubled him for years finally turned into pneumonia and brought a quick end. We children were summoned to join our mother at his bedside at evening time just as he quietly passed away. We said a few prayers, but there was no weeping or wailing. I remember, as if it was yesterday, that I walked directly from the bedroom out on to our upstairs porch and into the midst of a magnificent sunset. It took away all the sting of his passing.

After Papa's death, our mother quietly took over the leadership of our family. I was too young to know, but Mama had probably always been the sustaining if not the dominant factor in our lives. We feared Papa's stern standards of obedience, and Mama was the one to whom we turned for consolation when things went amiss. I can't remember receiving any physical punishment from my father, yet recall many well-deserved spankings from Mama's slipper. She became ever dearer to us as the years went by, and without lecturing us she set the standard by which we gauged our lives. As we grew older and went off to college or to work, we wrote home every Sunday. Mama circulated our letters, usually with notes or comments, to all members of the family—we were often scattered round the world—so that everyone was kept informed of our doings and family ties were kept intact. After my dear mother's death in 1924 we wrote to my eldest sister May, Mrs. Allen L. Vories, who continued to serve as our family link.

I left home in 1912, at the age of 16, for Louisiana State University at Baton Rouge, to which I had won a scholarship from Boys' High School in New Orleans. My heart was still set on West Point and an army career. However, the principal appointment to the academy from our congressional district had already been committed for the next year. Through my uncle, Martin Behrman, the mayor of New Orleans, we were able to obtain an alternate appointment, and with my usual Irish luck, which was to accompany me throughout my military career, the man who had been given the principal appointment failed the entrance examination. When my sister May telephoned me from New Orleans that I had passed and was to report to the Point, I walked on air for the next week. I entered the Military Academy on June 2, 1913.

West Point

I was one of those rare cadets who enjoyed West Point, or at least admitted his enjoyment. The academy exceeded my expectations, especially the toughness of the curriculum. I entered with the aspiration of graduating near the top of my class and joining the Corps of Engineers. But I soon realized that I would have to give up all other interests and concentrate all my time on studies if I was to have a chance of making the top ten in the class. The studies then were mostly technical, whereas my bent was toward the humanities. The academic schedule was not as crowded as now, and cadets had more time in the winter months to read and reflect. I spent many hours in the library reading Swinburne, Masefield, Lafcadio Hearn, Ibsen, and other poets and playwrights. I had been introduced to them by Lucius H. Holt, a Yale man, the only civilian professor at the Point, who, as head of the Department of English, was a refreshing and stimulating influence.

What appealed to me most about West Point, aside from its setting and tradition, was its high standard of integrity, its emphasis on duty and honor, its dedication to the service of the country. I treasured the qualities of my fellow cadets, including the diversity of their points of view which reflected that they came from every state in the Union and all walks of life. Though I loathed close-order drill, and years later devised a new drill that eliminated most of its dull routine, I never failed to be moved by the dress parades nor lost the thrill that crept up my spine as the Star Spangled Banner was played at retreat and the flag fluttered down at Trophy Point.

During my last year as a cadet, with war in the offing, my interest in tactics and the techniques of the military profession increased greatly, and I decided to request assignment to the basic service of the Army, the Infantry. I never regretted the choice. Thinking that the 22nd Infantry regiment would soon be sent overseas from New York, I requested that regiment. To my disappointment the regiment remained in the United States throughout the war. But there were compensations.

My class graduated on April 20, 1917, two weeks after our declaration of war against Germany, and two months ahead of the normal schedule. After a short furlough at home in New Orleans I returned to New York with instructions to report to headquarters of the 22nd Infantry at Fort Jay, which I understood was on an island in the metropolitan area. I took it for granted that the clerks at the Astor Hotel, where I stopped overnight, would know the location of Fort Jay. As I checked out on the morning of June 13, 1917, I casually asked the cashier how to get to Fort Jay.

"Fort Jay?—Fort Jay? It's around here somewhere. Ask the desk. They'll know."

"Fort Jay? Let me think. No-o-o. Ask the bell captain. He'll know."
"Is that the fort in Long Island Sound?"

"I don't know." I was beginning to be concerned about the nine o'clock deadline. "I'll tell you. Call a cab. The cabbie will know."

I simple said "Fort Jay" as I entered the cab. No questions asked. With a lurch and a squeal of tires we turned into Broadway and headed south. Down we careened through the theater district, dodged push carts through the garment industry area, and into lower Manhattan, the cab meter recording our progress with dismaying increases in dollars and cents. The meter seemed to increase its rate as we entered the financial district and crossed Wall Street, with my watch clicking ever closer to nine o'clock, my hour for reporting. Then abruptly we stopped alongside a subway exit marked "South Ferry" on the Broadway line from Times Square. Instead of the nickel subway fare—remember this was 1917—I paid several dollars, which I could ill afford, to the grinning taxi driver. He pointed across the street, "There's the Governors Island ferry to Fort Jay." At least we were at the right spot, and I was on time. But even now, I never pass that subway exit without smiling ruefully.

At Fort Jay I reported to Colonel John C. F. Tillson, a ramrod-straight soldier of the old school, commanding the 22nd Infantry, a fine Regular Army regiment that had just moved up from the Mexican border to the New York area following a bomb explosion on Wall Street. One battalion was at Governors Island, another at the Hoboken Port of Embarkation, and the third at Fort Hamilton on the Brooklyn side of the Narrows entrance to the port of New York. Colonel Tillson told me I was assigned to K Company, 3rd Battalion at Hamilton. Little did I dream then that this battalion was to be one of the assault units of the VII corps, under my command, on D day in Normandy, twenty-seven years later.

I reported at Hamilton to the 3rd Battalion commander Major Clifford Bluemel, later to distinguish himself on Bataan Peninsula in the Philippines in World War II. Cliff Bluemel was a slight man, with an occasional nervous jerk to his head, but with a sharp mind, and—after I came to know him—a kind disposition. Somewhat to my dismay he informed me that I was to take temporary command of M Company at once, with no other officers present. The 22nd Infantry, like all Regular Army units, had been stripped of most of its experienced officers, noncommissioned officers, and specialists such as signalmen, mechanics, and cooks, to form cadres for new units of the expanding army. To take the places of the officers thus transferred, I and my classmates were immediately given company commands. Though I was scared to my boots at Major Bluemel's announcement, I was glad for the opportunity.

I expect the Major sensed my concern, for he walked me down to the low wooden barracks of the 3rd Battalion erected in a corner of Fort Hamilton, one of the old coast artillery posts guarding New York City. On the way he said the battalion would participate next day in a parade in New York to help launch the first Liberty Loan campaign. But there was nothing to worry about. The battalion would move to New York as a unit on a special subway train from the nearby Ninety-fifth Street station and return the same way. It would leave at 9:00 A.M. for the noon-day parade. I would find a copy of the battalion order on my desk in the M Company orderly room. That was only slightly reassuring as I steeled myself for my introductory meeting with my first 1st sergeant.

Sergeant Grover C. Graham proved less ferocious than 1st sergeants are usually drawn. He was a quiet, self-assured, competent, professional, and apparently felt no need to impress me with his importance. I liked him instantly. He explained that the company had come up from the border with only one officer, who had been promoted and shifted to another regiment a few days before. The commander of L Company had been keeping an eye on M Company awaiting the arrival of a new commander.

After reviewing the parade order, inspecting the barracks, and meeting the senior noncoms, I walked back up to the bachelors quarters where I was delighted to learn that I would be sharing a small apartment with a classmate from West Point, Harold Jackson. Jack was a coast artilleryman assigned to the harbor defenses of New York.

Liberty Loan Parade, New York City, 1917

My second day at Fort Hamilton dawned bright and clear. By 7:00 A.M. I was down at M Company barracks where the NCOs were busy readying things for the Liberty Loan parade in New York. M Company was a fine, well-disciplined group of experienced men, hardened and bronzed after years on the Texas border. This was to be their first parade in the city, and they were up for it. It being wartime, we were to march in field uniforms with light field equipment, including rifles and bayonets, rather than dress uniforms. The men clearly took pride in their appearance. I was proud to be at their head, although because I was junior commander in the 3rd Battalion our company was last in the column as the battalion swung out of Hamilton and turned down Brooklyn's Fourth Avenue to the Ninety-fifth Street subway station.

The long special train was waiting and we were soon on our way. I had visited friends in Brooklyn the preceding Christmas while on holiday from West Point—New Orleans was too far away for our brief leave—but knew nothing of the intricate subway system. Since we were to return to Hamilton under battalion control, I paid little attention to the route as we rattled along. We detrained at Madison Square, where Broadway crosses Fifth Avenue. There we joined the other battalions of the 22nd Infantry, and various patriotic organizations, for the march up Fifth Avenue to Central Park. There the parade would disband and the 3rd Battalion return to Fort Hamilton.

The march began at noon as office workers poured into the street for their lunch break. They joined the crowds of shoppers and sight-seers drawn to the first wartime military parade. There were no American combat casualty lists as yet, and the crowds lining the sidewalks greeted the troops with enthusiasm. All went well until the head of the regiment reached Central Park where the parade ended. Then, to my consternation, word was passed down the column that companies would return individually to their stations, instead of under battalion control. Subway tickets were given to each company commander, but with no instruction as to how to find our way back to home stations. I hadn't the scantiest idea as to how to get to Fort Hamilton, nor did Sergeant Graham or any of the noncoms, most of whom were in midtown Manhattan for the first time.

The 3rd Battalion had halted temporarily, with M Company about opposite St. Patrick's Cathedral. I Company, next ahead, was com-manded by a Captain Slicer. I dashed up to ask Slicer if he knew the way to Hamilton. He said he did, so I decided to follow I Company. We countermarched down the avenue to Forty-second Street where, to my surprise, instead of turning east to Grand Central Station, I Company turned west past the Public Library toward Sixth Avenue. There was no opportunity to query Captain Slicer, so we followed on to Sixth Avenue (now the Avenue of the Americas). In 1917 an elevated train line ran both north and south along Sixth Avenue, with a station high above Forty-second Street, one of the busiest cross streets in New York. There our progress slowed. Forty-second Street was jammed with motor traffic, and pedestrians were scurrying around our troops, trying to get to the elevated station, which could be reached only by a long stairway, already partly filled with soldiers of I Company.

Our company started up the stairs in single file but then all movement stopped. After a few minutes I left Sergeant Graham in charge of the company and squeezed past the men of I Company to investigate. Reaching the uptown train platform, I found Captain Slicer arguing with the ticket taker that his subway tickets were valid for the elevated train that went to Brooklyn. The official insisted that the "El" was owned by a different company than the subway, and tickets were not interchangeable. It took me only a moment to realize that Slicer was going to lose that argument. There was no way to explain the situation to the men of M Company, now strung out in single file, part on the stairway, part on the street below. They could not have heard my explanation over the din of the elevated trains thundering overhead. I could only shout "Follow me!" and lead the company, still in single file, up the stairs to the train platform, across the train tracks via an overhead passageway to the downtown platform and thence down the far stairway back to Forty-second Street. With taxis honking impatiently and bewildered New Yorkers gaping curiously, I re-formed the company in columns of squads (fours) and headed east for Grand Central. The men must have thought that the young shavetail leading them, whom they had never seen before yesterday, was plumb crazy.

I knew how to get to the Brooklyn express platform at Grand Central. There was ample room for the company on the first long subway train that drew up. A helpful passenger, clutching an overhead strap next to me, explained that we would have to get off the express at Atlantic Avenue in Brooklyn and switch to a local for Fort Hamilton. He kindly volunteered to lead us through a connecting tunnel to the Fourth Avenue station. I thanked him and breathed a sigh of relief as we lined up on the platform waiting for the Fourth Avenue local. We hadn't lost a man.

My feeling of satisfaction evaporated as a single car, seemingly filled, pulled up at the platform. Only a single coach was used in the mid-afternoon slack period. The hundred and fifty men of my company, complete with rifles, could not possibly squeeze into that car. I had no other officer with me, had never seen the noncoms until the day before, and the men did not know the way. I felt I could not leave any of them behind. They had crowded into the car but there were a dozen or more left over with me on the platform as the car was about to pull out. I yelled "Get aboard!" We charged the doorways and somehow did get on, though the side walls must have bulged. This football maneuver was replayed at each subway station as we let outgoing passengers get off, then battled new incoming ones to hold our places. As a commentary on the public attitude of those wartime days, the passengers took this crowding and jostling good-naturedly, as did our men.

We got off at Ninety-fifth Street, the end of the line, where we had embarked in the morning. Then, as a final touch of absurdity, we started to march off in the wrong direction for Fort Hamilton until Sergeant Graham whispered a correction to me. When we reached the post we discovered that we were the first company back. The others straggled in until after dark, each greeted by jeers from the M Company barracks. The new lieutenant had passed muster.

Company K, 22nd Infantry

Ten days after the parade, the regular captain of M Company reported in and I was shifted to my permanent assignment to K Company. During the next month the 3rd Battalion moved by rail to the rifle range of the New Jersey National Guard at Sea Girt for the battalion's annual target practice. There I served as range officer in charge of the target pits and managed to qualify in marksmanship as an "expert rifleman." More importantly, in off-duty hours I met the family of Colonel Thomas D. Landon, the head of the Bordentown (N.J.) Military Academy and commanding officer of the 3rd Infantry Regiment of the New Jersey National Guard. The Landons had a summer cottage at nearby Spring Lake. They also had three lovely daughters, all excellent dancers, who provided welcome relief from the hot days on the rifle range. The Landons were most kind to me and several of my classmates in the 22nd Infantry. I have kept in touch with the family ever since.

Shortly after our return to Hamilton I succeeded to command of Company K, with no other officers present for duty. Fortunately, my first real command was made up of Regular Army soldiers and was staffed with a fine group of experienced noncommissioned officers. Its 1st Sergeant, Lewis A. Vinson, like Sergeant Graham of Company M, was a true professional, quiet and competent. I came to have great respect for him and depended on him greatly.

Developments came rapidly in K Company in the following weeks. First we received three new lieutenants from the first wartime officers training camps, fine men who had volunteered for service upon the declaration of war after having graduated from college. Franklin J. Peck was from Gettysburg, Samuel I. Cooper from Princeton, and Alexander H. Garnjost from Cornell. Each took command of a platoon. They were a great help, particularly as I had been appointed batallion adjutant and trial judge advocate of a general court martial. For a while I was also mess officer of the bachelor officers mess, all in addiion to my primary duty in command of K Company. We worked sixteen hours a day.

The morning I took over the company, Sergeant Vinson reported to me the disturbing news that head cook Woodward had beaten up the acting mess sergeant at breakfast and wanted to see me. I said, "All right. Have him come in." I had scarcely seated myself at the company commander's desk when not only Woodward, but two other cooks marched in, lined up in front of the desk, and saluted. Woodward, a trim-looking man, with none of the outward marks of a fighter, but with rapid-fire directness, acted as spokesman:

"I am Cook Woodward. The new Mess Sergeant doesn't know his business. I had a fight with him this morning. We can't take any more from him and are resigning."

Just like that. There was nothing in the officers training manual that matched this sudden situation. I swallowed hard as I looked the trio over, conscious of Sergeant Vinson's appraising eye as he stood in the background. I seemed to sense his saying, "Think fast, Lieutenant. Think fast." Woodward and the man next to him were neatly dressed in crisply starched cooks uniforms. They carried themselves well. But the third cook was a slovenly individual, unshaven, wearing a soiled apron. I concentrated on him.

"You man on the end. You are too dirty to be a cook in this company. You're fired. Get out of here."

"Now, Woodward, you and your assistant: I don't know what your trouble with the Mess Sergeant is, and I haven't time to find out right now. But there will be no more fighting with sergeants around here, and no resigning. As soon as I can find some new cooks, I'm going to bust the two of you. But in the meantime you are going to cook. Now get back to the kitchen." As they filed out without another word, I thought I caught an approving gleam in Sergeant Vinson's eyes. I asked him for help in solving the mess sergeant problem.

Word had gotten around through the soldiers' grapevine at Hamilton that things were looking up in K Company, 22nd Infantry. Sergeant Vinson soon persuaded an assistant mess sergeant, William F. Thompson, in one of the coast artillery batteries at Fort Hamilton, to transfer to K Company. Thompson was a big fat man who filled the role of mess sergeant both in appearance and in skill. After a brief tryout I made him our regular mess sergeant. Two experienced cooks from the same battery followed Thompson to K Company. I was now ready to make a clean sweep in the kitchen. Cook Woodward and his discontented assistant returned to the ranks as buck privates.

Sergeant Woodward

The next day happened to be a Saturday, time for the weekly inspection of barracks and the men and their equipment in ranks. The soldiers were spruced up in fine shape. But as I was inspecting the rear rank, one man brought his rifle to the port position for inspection with a snap that caught my attention. His rifle was in perfect condition, his uniform immaculate, and he stood markedly erect, looking me squarely in the eyes as if with a proud challenge. It was ex-cook Woodward, whom I had never before seen in ranks. As I passed along in rear I looked Woodward over with aroused interest. He was the best looking soldier in the company. Perhaps he was right when he beat up the acting mess sergeant.

Woodward was assigned to Lieutenant Peck's platoon. When shortly thereafter we were authorized promotions in our expanding company, Peck recommended Woodward for a corporal's warrant. I called Woodward into the orderly room and told him I had noted his fine attitude after being relieved as cook, that I intended to keep an eye on him, and that he could go as far in K Company as his interest and ability would take him. I congratulated him and gave him his warrant. As the Army expanded we were constantly being called for new sergeants. When I asked the platoon leaders for their recommendations, Corporal Woodward's name headed the list. Again I called in Woodward and presented his warrant. During the next few months Woodward rose successively to platoon sergeant and company supply sergeant, meeting each new responsibility with cool competence.

Not many weeks passed before 1st Sergeant Vinson was called to an officers training camp. This time I turned to one of our senior line sergeants, a splendid old Regular, whose name by apt coincidence was John K. Pippin. But when I offered him the position he declined, as I half expected, explaining that he had had little schooling, and would have difficulty with the payrolls and other paperwork. I asked whom he would recommend. He answered without hesitation, "Sergeant Woodward." Vinson and the platoon leaders unanimously agreed. This time, after receiving the warrant, I arranged a special retreat parade of K Company with all officers and men present, including the cooks. With Woodward standing out front, I set out the history of his rise in the company. I told the men they had a real 1st sergeant in every sense and presented Woodward his warrant as our bugler sounded the evening retreat. K Company "had it made," as the soldiers would say.

After Woodward had served for several months as 1st sergeant another call came for NCOs qualified to attend an officers training camp. I felt that Woodward had earned a shot at becoming a commissioned officer, though I was doubtful of his educational and technical qualifications—he had only attended grade school. I felt it might be better for him, and the Army, that he remain a first-class NCO rather than become an inadequate officer. I offered him the opportunity but suggested he consider it overnight. Next morning he said he had decided to stay as 1st sergeant. That it was a wise decision was proven when, after I left K Company to become regimental supply officer, my successor did send Woodward off to an officers candidate school. Woodward failed to make the grade and I later learned that he was languishing as a noncom, doing paper work, at Camp Hancock, Georgia, and wishing to get back to the 22nd Infantry. I decided to do something about this situation. Being young and uninhibited, I wrote a letter direct to the Adjutant General of the Army, outlining Woodward's history with K Company and recommended he be returned. My letter must have landed on the desk of an understanding soul in the AG's office, for, lo and behold, Woodward was ordered back to the 22nd Infantry! He ended his military career as ranking sergeant major in the regiment.

Trial Judge Advocate

While these personnel changes were taking place in K Company, I had to spend most of my afternoons and evenings on my concurrent assignment as trial judge advocate of a general court martial that sat at Fort Hamilton. The court was made up largely of retired officers recalled for active duty. Most of the cases we tried were simple cases of soldiers who were absent without leave from their units when the draft act was passed but who, when picked up by civilian police, were listed as deserters because they had no registration cards. After I had tried thirty-nine such cases, a new court was appointed consisting of National Guard officers from artillery units stationed at Hamilton. I was reappointed temporarily as judge advocate, with Major George M. Welch, a Guard officer and experienced lawyer from New York, as my assistant until Welch could become familiar with court-martial procedures. One of the fortunate by-products of my service as judge advocate was the lasting friendship that developed with George Welch when he became my successor.

George had been thwarted by his parents from attending West Point, but had enlisted in a National Guard coast-artillery unit, which in those days was mainly a social organization. He was not technically inclined and had no yen for the mathematics of artillery gunnery. Welch and a close friend, Joseph Murray, a big self-made construction superintendent with little formal schooling, were soon faced with the necessity of attending the Coast Artillery School, for which they were ill prepared. They turned to me for help, and during our "spare time" I coached them in trigonometry three or four nights a week until they went off to the artillery school. Following the war, Welch transferred to the Judge Advocate General's Corps and in World War II served on the staff of General MacArthur in the Pacific. During the same war Joe Murray, who had joined the Coast Guard, became the Commandant of the Coast Guard Academy. Following World War II we renewed our friendship while Murray was in Washington as construction superintendent for the building of the National Gallery of Art. My experience with George Welch and Joe Murray, two fine but misplaced National Guardsmen, gave me an understanding of some of the problems of the Guard that stood me in good stead in World War II and later as Army Chief of Staff.

Wartime Draftees

After a year at Fort Hamilton, K Company was transferred to Gloucester City, New Jersey, across the Delaware River from Philadelphia, to guard the Pusey and Jones shipbuilding yard. Shortly thereafter the company was brought to war strength of 250 men by an allotment of about 100 men from the draft. The system of distribution was new and there were many inadequacies. I had only a few hours notice of arrival of the draftees, who came by truck from an induction camp in New York. They were in uniform but had no equipment. K Company had just moved into a new wooden barracks in the shipyard but had no surplus cots, mattresses, bedding, or mess gear. Despite frantic calls to the Philadelphia Quartermaster Depot, it was impossible to secure supplies before the draftees arrived.

I lined up the new men, had them stand at ease, and explained our situation. I told them I was taking a blanket or pillow from each of our Regular soldiers, and would give each of the new men a cot or mattress, but some would have to sleep on the floor. Each man would receive a fork or spoon that would have to do until next day when I would send an officer with the company truck to the depot in Philadelphia. Meanwhile, I welcomed them to K Company and assured them that they would be treated on exactly the same footing as the Regulars. To my astonishment they applauded!

These men, who came largely from the sidewalks of New York and Brooklyn, were distributed throughout the company. They soon fitted into the ranks of the Texans and other southerners who made up the old company. About two weeks after they had joined, one of them asked to speak to me alone in the orderly room. He said he was the leader of a group of drug addicts from Greenpoint—he called it "Greenpernt"—the toughest section of the Brooklyn waterfront. They had brought some drugs with them but were about to run out. "You have treated us right, and we like it here," he said. "We don't want to cause no trouble, but there's bound to be trouble if we can't get our shots." I thanked him but explained that I would have to report this to regimental headquarters and that the group would probably be transferred to a rehabilitation center or hospital. He allowed as how this would be all right with them. This was done promptly, with "no trouble" as promised.

As I write this, over fifty years later, I look back with affection to my first command. Made up almost half and half of draftees from New York City and Regulars from the Deep South, Company K was an amalgam of the American youth of that day, far more representative of our democracy than any wholly volunteer army ever would be. There were some rough-and-ready spirits among them, but they were all dedicated to the well-being of their country. They would have given a good account of themselves in action.

Supply Officer, 22nd Infantry

In June, 1918, I was transferred back to Fort Hamilton to become supply officer of the 22nd Infantry. I hated to leave K Company, but Major Bluemel chided me that I would never get anywhere in the Army until I learned something about supply. While the 22nd Infantry was on the Texas border, the Supply Company delivered supplies and equipment to all units and performed other services that required transportation, for which the company employed its wagon train of twenty wagons and one hundred mules. When the regiment shifted to New York, the wagon train, complete with mules, went along by rail. This early in the war, motor trucks were available only for organizations scheduled for overseas duty. Our wagon train was my delight, and my despair, until under the tutelage of the 1st Sergeant I learned to drive a four-mule team and became familiar with the amazing capacity and idiosyncrasies of army mules and "mule skinners." The 1st Sergeant, a wonderful grizzled Texan, swore that one of his favorite mules could be kicking up its heels in the corral, only to become instantly "lame" when harnessed to a wagon. A kick in its belly, accompanied by an appropriate oath, would instantly cure the lameness.

A month after I took over the Supply Company, it was shifted, along with the 3rd Battalion, from Fort Hamilton to Syracuse to assist in operating a camp for limited-service men. The move to Syracuse was a fascinating experience. The wagon train, with its four-mule teams pulling canvas-covered wagons, accompanied by officers and NCOs on horseback as outriders, made a rare sight on the streets of Brooklyn as we marched to the Hudson River waterfront at Twenty-third Street. There we loaded on barges, which were towed across New York harbor, dodging tooting ferries and ocean liners to Weehawken. A railroad train was waiting on a dockside track. Animals were loaded into cattle cars, not to the liking of our Missouri mules, some of which balked at the insult. Bales of hay were used as ramps to get them into the cars, to the accompaniment of whooping and hollering of our mule skinners. The wagons were hoisted by cranes to the beds of flatcars where the wheels were wedged and tied in place. By dusk we were on our way to Syracuse, wagon covers flapping in the breeze, our coal-burning engine belching clouds of black smoke, and a crowd of Jerseyites cheering us on—a scene reminiscent of the early days of the Wild West.

Organizing Limited-Service Men

The tent camp north of Syracuse, which had been built in the opening days of the war, was unoccupied except for a caretaking detachment. The task of Colonel Brady G. Ruttencutter's 22nd Infantry was to reopen it, then to receive and do the housekeeping for thousands of draftees while they were being examined and reclassified for assignment to Army units throughout the East. These were men with minor physical disabilities who had been originally classified by their local draft boards as not qualified for combat. Many were artisans, carpenters, plumbers, electricians, and mechanics, or white-collar workers. There was a growing demand for such technicians to operate the supply, maintenance, transportation, and administrative services of the Army as it expanded from peacetime strength of less than 150,000 to over 4,000,000 by the end of the war. A team of doctors and personnel experts, most of whom came direct from civilian life, was furnished by the War Department to do the examining, reclassification, and assignment. In all, we processed 37,000 men.

Under supervision of the 22nd Infantry the draftees were organized into battalions of 1,000 men each. Since there were only 21 line officers, we all had multiple assignments. In addition to my responsibilities as regimental supply officer and captain of the Service Company, I was Camp Inspector and commanded one of the draftee battalions. The other battalions were commanded by captains and lieutenants, with 22nd Infantry sergeants and corporals commanding companies of 250 men. Platoon and squad leaders were selected draftees.

That this program worked smoothly was a tribute not only to our handful of Regulars, but to the willing cooperation of the limited-service men caught up in the draft, most of whom were more mature than the younger men drafted for combat service. We had no protest strikes, no antiwar demonstrations, and only a dozen or so conscientious objectors. As Camp Inspector, I investigated all of the latter in an attempt to determine the genuineness of their convictions, and I reviewed complaints of mistreatment or injustice. There was a minimum of such cases and none that required reference to Colonel Ruttencutter.

The Influenza Epidemic of 1917–1918

As autumn began to put a nip in the air, the Asian flu struck the Syracuse camp. It came in with a group of men from Camp Devens, Massachusetts. Before anyone knew what it was, six men from Devens, assigned to the same tent, came down with this virulent influenza and died. Infection spread through the camp like a wind-whipped forest fire. For extra doctors and hospital facilities we had to rely on the city of Syracuse. Fortunately, the city was spared the epidemic, which was raging throughout the country, until it had subsided at the camp. The flu put an extra burden on the officers and NCOs of the 22nd Infantry, who were already overworked. My normal good health finally gave way to the flu, and I was sent into Syracuse to the Crouse-Irving Hospital, which had been turned over to the Army. Every inch of space there, including the dining hall, nurses' quarters, and every corridor, was filled with cots which seemed to empty of soldier patients only as they died, to be refilled the same day with new patients. Nurses and doctors worked round the clock until they too began to succumb as their resistance weakened from fatigue. The lovely little nurse who did much to pull me through my illness became ill and died the next day. Her death gave a poignant note to my service at the Syracuse camp.

Battalion Command

I was promoted to the grade of major on September 9, 1918, and this probably helped speed my convalescence. My records show that I commanded the camp in the absence of Colonel Ruttencutter, who was invalided home, for its last ten days as a reclassification center. I was then given a month's leave, which I spent recuperating at home in the warm sunshine of New Orleans. Shortly after I returned to duty I took command of the 3rd Battalion, which had come down from Syracuse to Governors Island. Only a year and a half had elapsed since I first reported there. I was now all of twenty-two years of age and in command of a war-strength battalion of a thousand men.

I soon ran afoul of Colonel Tillson, who was still commanding the 22nd Infantry. He had been passed over for promotion to brigadier general, which did nothing to improve his disposition. As usual I had other duties in addition to the battalion. One of these was to serve as survey officer for the New York Arsenal, located on Governors Island. This assignment had nothing to do with engineering but involved the examination and disposition of worn-out equipment, determination of responsibility for shortages, and the like. Colonel Tillson had issued standing orders that the battalion commander was to be present on the drill field during all drill or training periods, which extended through most of the day. My difficulty with the Colonel arose from the fact that my duty as survey officer sometimes clashed with the Colonel's edict that I be present on the field during drill periods. One of the first survey investigations I had to make dealt with a box of harness needles which had been received from a manufacturer in New York City. When the box was opened at the arsenal it was discovered that, except for a top layer of heavy harness needles, the box was filled with building bricks. I had to try to determine whether this dastardly substitution had been perpetrated in the manufacturer's plant or had occurred after receipt of the box in the arsenal. This would require my visiting the plant.

Shortly after drill call one morning I was on the phone in my quarters trying to arrange an appointment with the manufacturer when Colonel Tillson's orderly appeared. He had a note for me to report at once to the Colonel at his quarters, which overlooked the drill grounds. I found the Colonel seated at his desk, with a wrathful gleam in his eyes. I saluted and stood at attention as I reported:

"Sir, Major Collins reports as directed." He demanded to know if I had been present on the drill field.

I replied "No Sir." Did I understand that his orders required me to be there throughout drill? "Yes Sir." He then raked me over the coals. He asked for no explanation for my dereliction, and I offered none, but continued to answer simply, "Yes Sir," whenever he paused for breath.

Finally he exploded: "Young man, I like your self-confidence, but if you don't obey my orders, I'll try you! Do you understand?"

I said "Yes Sir," and was dismissed. I never had another encounter with the Colonel, and as far as I remember he never checked my activities again. But I made sure I strictly obeyed his orders, unless I had an iron-clad excuse.

The Wonderful World of New York in 1917–1918

The World War ended on November 1, 1918, without my getting overseas, much to my disappointment. Governors Island was a tiny place that offered little or no opportunity for training other than close-order drill, which bored me. The only compensation was that the island was in the middle of New York harbor, with ready access to the theaters, the Metropolitan Opera, two symphony orchestras, to say nothing of a number of attractive girls I had met in the metropolitan area and nearby New Jersey.

George Welch was fond of the theater, as I was. We often met for dinner at Brown's Chop House, opposite the Old Met on Broadway, before attending a show. Our choice of plays and performers ranged from Maude Adams in *Peter Pan* to Nazimova in *The Wild Duck* and Margaret Anglin in *Electra*, and from John Barrymore in Tolstoi's *Redemption* to Al Jolson in *Sinbad*. We were lucky to see Helen Hayes in her first Broadway success, James M. Barrie's *Dear Brutus*, in which her youthful talent and fresh beauty stole the show from William Gilette. But the play I remember best was St. John Ervine's *John Ferguson*, which saved the fledgling Theater Guild from an untimely death. The Guild's initial play had flopped after only a night or two, but the Guild was able to persuade Mr. Otto Khan, the genial angel to many aspiring young artists of that era, to stake them for two performances of *John Ferguson* at the tiny David Garrick theater on Thirty-fifth Street, off Broadway. The play was an instant success. I saw one of its first performances, which rocketed Rollo Peters, Dudley Digges, Helen Freeman, and Helen Westley to stardom. I became a devotee of the Theater Guild for years thereafter.

Our sister May played the piano beautifully and had instilled in me as a boy a love of music that has remained one of the chief sources of pleasure throughout my life. The two years I spent in New York with the 22nd Infantry offered many varied opportunities for the development of my fondness for good music. Walter Damrosch was then the conductor of the New York Symphony, while Josef Stransky led the Philharmonic. I subscribed to both, and heard the great Boston Symphony under Carl Munch, and Leopold Stokowski's Philadelphia Orchestra, whenever they came to New York. I will never forget my delight at first hearing Josef Hofman play Chopin's E Minor Concerto, nor the thrill of listening to the young Jascha Heifetz, in his debut at Carnegie Hall, in the Beethoven violin concerto.

But my greatest musical thrill came with my introduction to opera at the Metropolitan on the opening night of the 1917–1918 season. Sam Cooper and I had gone over to Princeton for the junior prom that fall. One evening while there, we had dinner with an old bachelor friend of Sam, Mr. Howard Crosby Butler. After dinner Mr. Butler remarked to Sam that he would be unable to use his two tickets for the opera on Monday evening and wondered if Sam would care to have them. Needless to say, Sam accepted. He then delighted me by inviting me to accompany him.

We sat in perfect center seats in the dress circle, and heard a magnificent performance of *Aida*, sung by Caruso, Amato, Claudia Muzio, and Margaret Matzenauer. It was marvelous. Caruso was still in fine voice and I have never heard a finer mezzo-soprano than Matzenauer. Later in the season I heard the same cast in Meyerbeer's *Le Prophete*, and Caruso again in *Pagliacci*, and with Rosa Ponselle in *La Forza del Destino*. Geraldine Farrar with Martinelli and Scotti in *Carmen*, *Faust*, and *Madame Butterfly*, rounded out the old favorites, capped at the end of the season by Galli-Curci in *Dinorah*. Of course, as a young professional Army officer, I hated to miss action in World War I, but if I had to do it over again I would be tempted mightily to choose the theater and music of New York with its fabulous star performers of that era.

CHAPTER II

Overseas
at Last

Months after the armistice, in May, 1919, orders finally came directing me to report to the Hoboken port of embarkation for transportation to France. I was one of a group of Regular Army majors and colonels being sent over to replace officers due to return home. I was probably the junior man among them, but as the 3rd Battalion, 22nd Infantry was still an active unit, I retained my temporary rank of major, whereas many more senior officers who happened to be with units that had been demobilized following the armistice had returned to their permanent ranks, which were usually one or more grades lower.

We landed at Brest, the port of debarkation for General Pershing's expeditionary force, and motor busses carried us from the dock to the Hotel Continental, where we were to be billeted while awaiting our assignments. I happened to line up at the registration desk behind two well-known older officers, ex-Brigadier Generals William Bryden and Robert M. Danford, who had reverted to captain rank just before boarding the transport in New York. When the French hotel clerk noted, as they were about to register, that they were wearing captain's bars, he stopped them:

"Messieurs, the Continental is reserved for senior officers! You must go across the square to the hotel for captains and lieutenants." No amount of explanation from the ex-generals' friends in our group could budge the clerk. Greatly embarrassed, Bryden and Danford backed away while I, even more embarrassed, signed in. The day was saved for the generals when someone suggested that they buy sets of colonel's eagles from a nearby insignia store. This they did. When they checked in at the Continental a little later, they were promptly accepted.

After a couple of days at Brest our replacement group moved up by rail to Chateau Thierry, where we joined a motor tour of the American battlefields of Cantigny, St. Mihiel, and the Meuse-Argonne. This tour ended in Paris. My brother James, who had gone to France on the steamer *Baltic* with the initial contingent of General Pershing's headquarters staff, was then Secretary of the General Staff at General Headquarters (GHQ) at Chaumont. He drove to Paris to meet me. After an excellent dinner at Prunier's we walked up the Champs Élysées to the Arc de Triomphe. En route we were greeted by two demoiselles with the oft-repeated invitation to Americans in uniform, "Voulez-vous vous coucher avec nous?" Admittedly somewhat tempted, we shrugged them off.

Next day, after some sightseeing, we drove back to Chaumont in time for dinner at General Pershing's personal mess. My brother had served as aide-de-camp to Pershing years earlier in the Philippines and again in 1916–1917 during the Punitive Expedition in Mexico against the bandit Pancho Villa, following the latter's raid against Columbus, Texas. James had accompanied Pershing to Washington in 1917, where the General's secret designation to command the expeditionary force to Europe was to be confirmed by President Woodrow Wilson. The two men had traveled alone in civilian clothing, and without publicity, by rail to New Orleans, where it was necessary to change trains. Between connections they came to our house on State Street—we had moved there from Algiers after my father's death—for a short rest. I was home on graduation leave from West Point. I well remember how gracious General Pershing was to my mother and how jovially he greeted my sister Margaret, who had become a favorite of the Pershings while she was visiting James in Zamboanga in the Philippines. The General let us in on the secret of the coming assignment, which was not made public until the steamer *Baltic* was on its way to France.

Now at Chaumont, James and I joined members of the GHQ staff in the drawing room of the chateau where General Pershing was billeted, waiting for the General to make his appearance. When Pershing had visited us in New Orleans he was dressed informally. He was a handsome man even in mufti, but I was quite unprepared for his dramatic appearance, announced by an orderly, as he stood momentarily at the head of the stairs leading down from his living quarters. He was a stunning, commanding figure in his beribboned uniform, tall and erect, perfectly groomed from his iron-gray head of hair to his polished Peale boots. He had seemingly grown in stature as well as reputation since I had met him in New Orleans two years earlier. He greeted me as kindly as he had then and at once made me feel at ease. But I must have had some feelings of awe at the distinguished company because I can recall nothing of the dinner conversation.

I left Chaumont to rejoin most of our group of replacements for a tour of the Communications Zone, stopping off to visit the depots and other installations that had supported the American advance into Germany. Those of us destined for the Army of Occupation continued on down the narrow valley of the Moselle toward Coblenz-am-Rhein. We left Metz on Corpus Christi Sunday, a feast day greatly revered in this Catholic section of Germany. We passed many processions of villagers in colorful costumes winding their way up the steep hillsides, stopping for prayers and a chant at the roadside Stations of the Cross. It was a balmy June day and the terraced vineyards were bright green in their fresh spring leaves. Dark pine forests topped the hills, setting off vistas of a countryside unmarred by war.

The townspeople stared defiantly at us as we traveled through their streets, reflecting their conviction that the Wehrmacht had not been defeated in battle, even though Germany had lost the war. I thought then that General Pershing was right in his opposition to granting the Germans an inconclusive armistice, without a convincing defeat of their armies in the field. But the Americans had not suffered the heavy casualties of our French and British allies, who were understandably exhausted after four years of war.

At the junction of the Moselle and the Rhine we entered the charming little city of Coblenz, overlooked from the east bank of the Rhine by the spectacular old fortress of Ehrenbreitstein. I was glad to see an American flag flapping in the breeze atop its battlements. I learned, to my pleasure, at headquarters of the American Forces in Germany (AFG) that I was assigned to the 18th Infantry of the 1st Infantry Division. The division was then holding part of the American bridge-

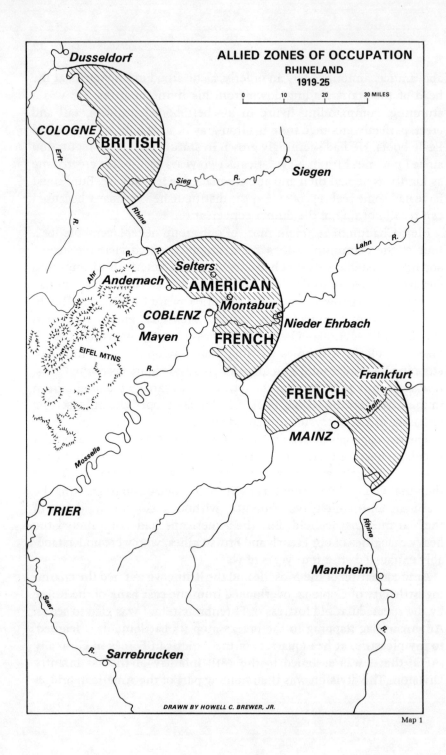

ALLIED ZONES OF OCCUPATION
RHINELAND
1919-25

0   10   20   30 MILES

Dusseldorf

COLOGNE

BRITISH

Erft R.

Sieg R.

Rhine R.

Siegen

Ahr R.

Andernach

Selters

AMERICAN

Montabur

COBLENZ

Mayen

FRENCH

Nieder Ehrbach

Lahn R.

EIFEL MTNS

R.

FRENCH

Frankfurt

Main R.

MAINZ

Mosselle

TRIER

Rhine R.

Mannheim

Saar R.

R.

Sarrebrucken

DRAWN BY HOWELL C. BREWER, JR.

Map 1

head east of the Rhine. Since the division was on an alert status, awaiting the German signing of the peace treaty at Versailles, I wasted no time in Coblenz but reported at once, on June 24, 1919, to the 18th Infantry commander, Colonel C. A. Hunt, at Baden in the Westerwald. I was surprised and delighted to be given command of the 3rd Battalion, in the towns of Meudt and Vielbach. A few days later the 3rd Battalion took over the outpost line of the regiment, which meant that if the Germans failed to sign we would lead the advance deeper into the Rhineland. With a youngster's yearning for action, I rather hoped they would not sign. But they did, on June 28. Two months later the 1st Division was ordered back to the United States and I was transferred to the 8th Infantry, which took over the division's sector. Though I had not served in combat with "The Big Red I," so called because of its shoulder patch, I was proud to have had at least a brief spell with this great division.

The Treaty of Versailles returned to France the provinces of Alsace and Lorraine, seized by Germany in 1870–1871, provided for reparations to the French and British for war damages, and placed restrictions on the size, composition, and stationing of Germany's armed forces. To ensure these conditions the Allies established three zones of occupation along the Rhine, including bridgeheads east of the river, each with a radius of thirty kilometers centered at Cologne, Coblenz, and Mainz. The British army occupied the Cologne area; the French held the Mainz sector and shared with the Americans the zone based on Coblenz.

The 8th, 5th, and 50th Infantry regiments, with the 7th Machine Gun Battalion, 2nd Battalion, 6th Field Artillery, a provisional cavalry squadron, an Army Air Corps service detachment, and various service units comprised Major General Henry T. Allen's American Forces in Germany. The 8th Infantry, 7th Machine Gun Battalion, the artillery and cavalry units all stationed in the vicinity of Coblenz, under command of Brigadier General Fred W. Sladen, was designated the 1st Brigade, AFG. The 5th and 50th regiments made up the 2nd Brigade, AFG, Brigadier General Harry G. Hale commanding. The 5th Infantry was billeted near Andernach on the Rhine, north of Coblenz, where General Hale had his headquarters. The 50th Infantry was near

Mayen, west of the Rhine. On departure of the 1st Division in August, 1919, I was placed in command of the outpost area of our bridgehead, extending from the junction with the French sector, at Nieder Ehrbach, north to the British line. My troops consisted of companies I and L, 8th Infantry and a platoon of the 7th Machine Gun Battalion. I took over the former division headquarters in Montabaur as my command post.

The American bridgehead included the rolling farmland and forests of the Westerwald. It was soft, pleasant country and the farmers were simple, honest people, much like the Germans who settled in Pennsylvania and our midwestern states. The Rhineland had been fought over since time immemorial and the Rhenish folk were accustomed to the European practice of billeting soldiers in their houses. Following the Napoleonic wars, the Conference of Vienna in 1815 awarded the Rhineland to Prussia. When Bismarck unified the loosely knit Germanic states with Prussia in 1871 to form the German empire of Kaiser Wilhelm I, the Rhineland remained a province of Prussia. Prussians were assigned as headmasters of many of the schools and controlled the administrative civil service, including the police. The relatively docile Rhinelanders were forced to accept this system, but never liked it.

At the same time I was transferred to the 8th Infantry I was appointed Superior Provost Court Officer for the American bridgehead, responsible for trying Germans charged with minor violation of American civil affairs regulations. Violations were few. The Rhenish people were instinctively law-abiding and, after becoming adjusted to our mild restrictions, were more irked by the Prussian police and administrators than by the American occupation.

This was brought home to me in the town of Selters, where I happened to be billeted when the Treaty of Versailles was signed. We began to relax our regulations that had forbidden fraternization with German civilians. To ease the monotony of occupation duties in the bridgehead, company commanders started to organize dances to which German girls were invited. The girls responded with enthusiasm to invitations to meet the carefree young American soldiers who were drawing more pay than village burgomasters and were livelier than the stolid local men. Naturally, the latter did not like this situation, which resulted in occasional conflict. After one of the early dances a group of Germans, led by the town policeman—who made the mistake of wearing his uniform—waylaid some soldiers returning to their billets and beat them up. Early next morning the readily identified policeman was arrested by the American police. Looking out my bedroom window, I saw the pompous Prussian in full-dress uniform being marched down the main street to the town jail by an American sergeant with a bayoneted rifle on his shoulder. My concern for the possible adverse reaction of the townspeople was allayed at once. Windows along the street filled with laughing women as the unique procession passed by. Village men gathered at the street corners, obviously pleased at the discomfiture of the policeman who, we were told later, had been ruthlessly lording it over the villagers for years. We had no further trouble with the dances.

Lieutenant George Bittman Barth, whose platoon was billeted in Wolferlingen—a town that became a point of interest in the American First Army's drive across Germany in World War II—forestalled any problem with dances at his location by opening them to some of the young men of the town as well as the *Mädchen*. The soldiers and the German boys alternated, dancing every other dance with the same girls. Barth attended these weekly dances to ensure order and fairness and I looked in on one of them at Barth's invitation. The scheme worked well and the dances did much to eliminate tension which might otherwise have developed with the townspeople.

As time went on, practically all of the initial animosity between the Germans and our occupying troops disappeared. During my first winter in Germany, after I reverted to the grade of captain, the company I was commanding participated in a week-long tactical reconnaissance of the Montabaur forest, in the center of our bridgehead. The company billeted at night in a village on the edge of the forest but spent the days trudging through snow-covered trails of the damp woods, as we verified the location of trails on an old German map and plotted possible defensive positions. It was bitterly cold and we returned to our billets at night wet and miserable.

I happened to be billeted in the house of an elderly German *Frau* who had lost her husband and a son in the war. She must have felt sorry for the young American captain, for her motherly instinct caused her to look after me. The first night, when I went to bed, I discovered that while I was having dinner at our company mess in the village *Gasthaus*, she had placed a hot brick, warmed in her kitchen stove and wrapped in a piece of blanket, under the covers of the foot of my bed. Thereafter, she checked every night to see that the bed was warm, and wished me *"Guten Abend."*

One Sunday evening, as she looked in, she noted that I was writing a letter. She asked, in her broken English, if I was writing to my *Mutter*. I said, "Yes." Then she cocked her head to one side as she looked at me, and said: "Vell, you tell her I have seen you and you are looking fine!"

Tears welled to my eyes and wet the letter to my *Mutter*.

I Consider Resigning from the Army

In March, 1920, the personnel section of the War Department in Washington finally caught up with me and, as mentioned, I was reduced from major to captain. Since the departure of the 1st Division, I was no longer commanding a battalion. But because of the postwar expansion of the Regular Army I had been made a permanent captain effective June 25, 1919, a rank I would not normally have reached in peacetime for several more years. Twelve years would elapse before I would again achieve the exalted rank of major, and eight more years before I became a lieutenant colonel at age forty-four.

Convinced that there would be no more large-scale wars and that, not having had command of troops in action in the World War, I would get nowhere in the Army, I gave thought to resigning from the service and studying law. I had several friends in New York, including George Welch, who were back in law practice, so I had written Columbia University and on the strength of my diploma from West Point was accepted for law school for the academic year 1919–1920. I then wrote George Welch to get his reaction, which came posthaste. He replied in effect, "Joe, you are crazy. We can hire any number of good lawyers in New York for $200 a month. Unless you marry the boss's daughter, the prospects for a young lawyer in New York are not good. Your métier is the Army. Stick to it."

Rumor must have gotten around that I was thinking of resigning, because out of a clear sky I was called in by my battalion commander, Lieutenant Colonel Charles L. Wyman, who showed me my efficiency report, which he had just made out. He had written, in summary, "The most promising officer of his length of service that I know." Colonel Wyman added orally that I was a "natural" for the army and should have "a great career."

Thus admonished on the one hand by a discerning friend, and on the other flattered by a sympathetic commander, I was in a quandary over what I knew would be a turning point in my life. Colonel Wyman's appraisal gave me pause. Except for missing combat service, I had been fortunate in having interesting and challenging assignments. I liked and respected the men with whom I had associated, and the basic business of the Army, the handling and leading of men, appealed to me greatly. In my brief service no one had asked me to say or do anything contrary to my personal standard of conduct. I was not sure this would always be the case in the legal profession or the business world. I did not know when, if ever, I would get back to Europe again, and I wanted to see more of the Continent before going home. I decided to give the Army a try for another year.

My army horizon widened soon after I had reverted to my permanent grade of captain. I had taken command of Company L, 8th Infantry, which with the 3rd Battalion had moved into Coblenz, where the battalion was quartered in a former German army barracks near the Moselle. Each morning I would march the company from the caserne out along the river or up to the Exercier Platz, a military reservation above the city. After two or three hours of field training we would return to the barracks area for a half hour of close-order drill before lunch. To give our noncommissioned officers a chance to exercise command, I frequently had the sergeants conduct these drills. One day I noticed a senior officer, a stranger, watching the drill from the sideline. I had not seen him when he arrived but I reported to him at once and explained our procedure. I recognized his General Staff insignia and saw that he was a colonel, but had no idea who he was. At the end of the drill, which had gone well, I told the 1st Sergeant to dismiss the company. The Colonel gave no sign of leaving, so I invited him to see our mess hall and kitchen, and when he still stuck around, showed him through our barracks. He seemed interested and asked a lot of questions. Finally he thanked me pleasantly and departed as unobtrusively as he had arrived, leaving me puzzled as to who he was and what his visit was all about. The following morning, June 15, 1922, I received instruction from brigade headquarters to report to General Allen's Chief of Staff, Colonel J. C. Montgomery, who turned out to be my visitor of the day before. He told me he had been looking for an officer to serve as an assistant to Lieutenant Colonel Jonathan M. Wainwright, the G-3 Operations of the AFG. The brigade commander, General Sladen, had told him I had the best company in the brigade and recommended me for the job. The assignment, which normally would have been filled by a major or lieutenant colonel, was unquestionably the best staff post for a captain in the entire AFG. My plan to retire had received its first setback.

Assistant G-3, AFG

My new boss, Colonel Wainwright, known throughout the army as Skinny because of his sparse, elongated frame, was a cavalryman, a crack horseman and polo player. I soon suspected that General Allen, also a cavalryman and devotee of polo, chose Wainwright for the key position of G-3 Operations because of Skinny's skill as a horseman, rather than for his interest in tactical planning. The war was over, and Allen, a handsome man and able administrator, probably felt, and rightly, that there was little likelihood of its breaking out again. He seemed to regard the AFG—which the troops quickly dubbed the Allen Family in Germany because of the number of relatives and close friends he assembled about him—as primarily a military showpiece rather than a combat organization. Horse shows and polo became the order of the day. When I reported to Colonel Wainwright he welcomed me kindly and casually informed me that he was leaving next day for a horse show at the Crystal Palace in London and I would be in charge of the office while he was gone. Then he added, almost as an afterthought, that there was to be a review of the 1st Brigade, in two or three days, for which I would have to do the planning. No wonder that Colonel Montgomery had been looking for an assistant G-3. I had attended a good many reviews but had never planned one.

All I knew was that as a battalion or company commander I and my troops frequently waited needlessly an hour or more at reviews for the arrival of the commanding general. I was determined that this now would not happen.

The review was to be held on the Exercier Platz, which could be reached by only two or three roads from Coblenz and Coblenz Lützel, across the Moselle, where some of the service units were located. The infantry could readily march up from the town, but the cavalry squadron would have to cross the pontoon bridge over the Rhine from its barracks at the foot of Ebrenbreitstein before moving through Coblenz, and the horse-drawn artillery would cross the Moselle from Coblenz Lützel. Different starting times had to be computed for each unit, and a coordinated schedule published in march tables attached to the review order. With help of the 1st Brigade staff we worked out these tables so that units would arrive at their places in the review line without conflict, but with minimum intervals. The last unit of artillery was scheduled to be in place just ten minutes before General Allen was to arrive. **2059297**

The morning of the review I was up on the Exercier Platz checking in the units as they arrived. I had had some qualms about our tight schedule, but units were arriving on the dot, and I was breathing easier, when word reached me that the artillery was having difficulty on the steep dirt road from the Moselle. It had rained the night before and the horses were slipping and sliding. As a tyro operations officer, I had made no allowance for such contingencies. While waiting for the artillery, with the minutes ticking away, I considered what I would say to the General in the horrendous event he should arrive before the last troops were in place. I decided to confess that, with my inexperience, I had failed to allow sufficient leeway in the march tables for unforeseen delays, but I would add that I doubted he was aware of the inordinate time troops frequently had to wait for reviewing officers because of poor staff planning, and that the effort I had made for the benefit of the troops would at least be in accord with his wishes.

Fortunately I did not have to make that speech, for just as the General's limousine, with its flags flying, came into view on the main road from Coblenz, the last artillery unit wheeled into place. There was not a minute to spare. I have sometimes wondered what General Allen's reaction would have been to my explanation of a delay. Having learned something about generals since that date, I feel sure he would have excused my failure.

Shortly thereafter two additional officers, Major Wade H. Haislip, an experienced tactician, and Major d'Alary Féchet, a machine-gun expert, were assigned to G-3. Their arrival added emphasis, on the part of AFG headquarters, to weapons training and tactical maneuvers, much to my pleasure. With the increased skill of our soldiers with all weapons, our combat field exercises—using live ammunition, planned and conducted under supervision of the G-3 division—took on a more realistic character. We violated many of the safety regulations, but never had a single accident. All infantry battalions of both the 1st and 2nd Brigades participated in the exercises.

Combat-firing exercises were followed by tactical maneuvers, conducted under the direction of the AFG Staff. The final maneuvers one year, pitting the 1st Brigade against the 2nd, culminated in a surprise attack at dawn by the 8th Infantry after a night movement of the regiment over German rail lines in the Eifel region, northwest of Coblenz. These rails were part of the system built by the Germans to facilitate concentration of their forces for the surprise attack against France in 1870. This same Eifel region was used by Hitler as the springboard of the German attack in 1944 that led to the Battle of the Bulge.

My participation in the planning of these exercises and maneuvers, particularly under such able G-3 directors as Lieutenant Colonels Timothy C. Lonergan and J. K. Herr—later the Chief of Cavalry, who succeeded Colonel Wainwright—greatly broadened my appreciation of a career in the Army and lessened my interest in the legal profession. Not the least of the benefits of assignment to G-3 was association with Wade Haislip, who became my Vice Chief of Staff almost thirty years later.

Life in Coblenz

About the time I moved from the 8th Infantry to G-3, two of my sisters, Margaret and Agnes, joined me in Coblenz. They had been members of a volunteer unit of the National Catholic Welfare Council serving with the American Army in France. When the World War ended, their unit moved up to Coblenz. Agnes, a Newcomb College graduate who had taught in New Orleans, became a teacher in the high school organized for our soldiers under the educational and vocational training program of the Army. Margaret and Agnes shared a billet with me on the first floor of a comfortable home on Mainzerstrasse, just off the Rhine Anlangen. It was owned by a retired lieutenant general of the German Army, who occupied the upper floor with his wife. The General bitterly resented our presence, though I am sure he had occupied billets in France more than once. He made life miserable for our German maid until I threatened to bring him before the superior provost court in Coblenz.

Having two sisters with me provided a homelike atmosphere to our billet and added greatly to the pleasure of my stay on the Rhine. They both loved to travel, as I did, and we made two trips to France, Switzerland, Austria, and Italy. Paris, Vienna, and Rome, with their wonderful shops, museums, great cathedrals, and music halls, were of course the chief attractions, though the mountains and lakes of Switzerland had a special appeal to me, perhaps because of my fondness at the time for the poetry of Byron and Coleridge. The latter's "Hymn Before Sunrise, in the Vale of Chamonix" led me to make a special trip to the lovely valley of Chamonix below Mont Blanc.

There was no poetry, but much historical interest, in another trip I made in September, 1920, convoying supplies from Coblenz to Warsaw for Herbert Hoover's Polish relief expedition at the time of the dreadful typhus epidemic in Poland. Rail shipments of medicine and motor maintenance equipment for Hoover's contingent in Poland were being pilfered and delayed en route to Warsaw, and it became necessary to have an officer accompany each shipment and check the sealed railway cars at every stop. I requested and drew one of these assignments. The Germans would not permit us to ship any supplies direct from Coblenz or Cologne to Warsaw. We had to go by way of Berlin to Danzig on the Baltic, thence along the valley of the Vistula via the Polish Corridor provided by the Treaty of Versailles. This roundabout way suited me fine, as it gave a chance to see Berlin and brought home to me some of the geopolitical problems of the Paris Peace Conference.

Shortly before I arrived in Warsaw, the city had been under siege by the Bolsheviks. The Polish leader Josef Pilsudski, with the help of French General Maxime Weygand, saved the city from capture, but it was flooded with almost a million refugees. Here was my first contact with the unfortunate victims of war whose counterparts I would see again in Belgium, Korea, and Vietnam. On the other hand, there were some pleasant experiences as well. After safely delivering my supplies, I spent two or three days sight-seeing, including an evening at the opera with some army friends attached to the Hoover mission. In spite of wars and typhus the opera had carried on.

Rather than returning to Coblenz via Danzig, I gambled on going back to Coblenz by rail across Czechoslovakia from Warsaw to Germany via Salzburg and Munich. I had gone to Warsaw on military travel orders, with a vaguely worded permission to return by an indirect route, but had no authority to enter or travel through unoccupied Germany. I had no passport, but only a copy of my orders and an identification card across the face of which were stamped, in French, the words "General Staff Corps, United States Army." My Army friends in Warsaw managed to have my orders countersigned, in lieu of a visa, with a rubber stamp of Pilsudski's signature authorizing exit from Poland by rail via Czechoslovakia. When my train arrived at the Czech border the Polish customs officers tried to collect a ten-dollar exit fee from me, which I was sure they would pocket, and threatened to remove me from the train when I refused to pay. I countered by showing my general staff identification card with the "Êtat Major" stamp—magic words to minor officials in Europe at that time—and said I would wire Pilsudski at once to report such treatment of a fellow general staff officer. They agreed to release me—and the train—if I would sign a paper giving my name and address, which I gladly did.

There was no trouble on the Czech side of the border. I am sure the Czech customs man did not recognize my American uniform, and I was not going to leave the train in Czechoslovakia. He passed me on without question. I still remember the look of astonishment on the face of the German customs guard in Salzburg as I brushed past him without stopping. My only belongings were in a musette bag which I carried across a shoulder, so there was no baggage to be inspected. I was gone before the guard could challenge me. I had no trouble buying a ticket and boarding the train for Munich and Coblenz.

The chaotic conditions in Eastern Europe and Germany had permitted me to get away with a fascinating trip without being thrown in jail. My only regret was that I had not been able to get to Constantinople, but an American Red Cross courier named Kelley, with whom I had traveled from Warsaw to Salzburg, and who knew all the ropes, assured me that not even my Irish luck would have carried me through the Balkans.

The opportunities for travel afforded by the Army, my improved living conditions in Coblenz, and the broadened view of the Army in its role of helping to support the foreign policy of our country, as seen from my post in the operations division of General Allen's headquarters, combined to weaken further my thought of resigning and becoming a lawyer. The last vestige of this idea evaporated on my first evening in Coblenz after I had moved there from the Rhine bridgehead in November of 1919 with Company L, 8th Infantry.

I Meet Gladys Easterbrook

I had sent Lieutenant Barth into Coblenz a few days in advance to arrange for company billets. Everything was prepared when the company arrived, which left us free to attend a 3rd Battalion officers dance that evening held in a former German officer's mess building on Kaiserin Augusta Ring. Bittman accompanied me to the dance, already in progress when we arrived. The music stopped just as we reached the entrance to the dance floor. Immediately opposite us was a lovely girl in evening dress, which enhanced her fresh beauty, in contrast to all other women present who were in Red Cross or other uniforms.

"Who is the pretty girl?" I asked Barth.

"Gladys Easterbrook. She has just arrived from the States. Would you like to meet her?"

"Would I!" Young bachelors were already converging from all directions. My luck met the challenge. I reached her side and was introduced at the moment the music resumed for the next dance. "May I

have this dance?" I asked. With a nod she accepted and we were off in
a rapturous waltz, leaving the circle of bachelors agape.

Miss Easterbrook was a wonderful dancer and we hit it off at once.
Before the evening was over we had several dances, and I had persuaded her father, Chaplain Edmund P. Easterbrook, who was chap-
eroning his daughter, to return to their apartment at his accustomed
early hour, leaving his daughter in the safe hands of old friends, Colonel and Mrs. Calvin P. Titus. Titus had won the Medal of Honor
when as a young bugler during the Boxer Rebellion in China in 1900,
he had climbed the wall of the Forbidden City in Peking, opening the
way for the American forces of the allied expedition moving to the relief of the beleaguered diplomatic colony to enter the city. I was ready
to award him a second medal when, at the end of the dance, he and
Mrs. Titus permitted me to walk Miss Easterbrook home. A full moon
shone overhead and added its magic to an enchanting evening. As we
strolled along I learned that Gladys loved to ride horseback, so before
saying good night at her parents' apartment across from the Festhalle,
we made a date for a ride the next Sunday afternoon. I walked to my
billet in a trance. Without realizing it, my last lingering thought of resigning vanished in the moonlight.

Two long years of courtship followed. Our love of the outdoors was
a common bond and the Rhineland was a perfect setting for our ro-
mance. The Germans are a nation of hikers. Their broad footpaths
climbed every hill bordering the Rhine and led always to a vantage
point with a view of the river, with grape-terraced slopes capped by
the ruins of a storied castle. These walking trails were not intended
for horse riders, but the Rhinelanders are romantic people and were
always tolerant of a young couple enjoying their countryside. This was
evident to us one bright summer day when we rode to the Molsberg
castle, overlooking the junction of the Lahn and the Rhine. We had
tethered the horses at the foot of the final steep slope below the ancient ruin and had walked to the castle with a German family who
were on a typical Sunday outing. Gladys and I climbed alone to the
top of the castle tower and stood there spellbound with the beauty of
the spot. My arm slipped around her waist for the first time and she
leaned against me. As we rejoined the German family for the walk
down the hill they smiled their blessing on us.

Had the good Pope John come along years earlier, with his broad ecumenical approach to Christianity, Gladys and I would have married shortly after that ride to Molsberg. Instead, almost two years of soul searching ensued. I was a Catholic, wedded to the faith of my Irish forebears, while Gladys was the only daughter of a Protestant minister and his devout Calvinist wife, both born in England. The one-sided barriers against Catholic-Protestant marriages, rigidly held to by the Catholic Church of that day, was the root of our problem.

Gladys and I finally decided to establish our own ecumenical accord. Brushing aside the initial opposition of her parents and some Catholic restrictions—all subsequently eliminated by Pope John and his successors—we were married in Coblenz, in three separate services, on July 15, 1921: first to make it legal, by the burgomaster; then by Gladys' father in the chapel of the Kaiserin Augusta's palace; and last in the billet of my sisters, by the understanding Catholic chaplain McNally. No wonder our marriage has lasted happily for over fifty years!

CHAPTER III

Postgraduate Schooling

Instructor at West Point

Our decision to be married in Coblenz was precipitated by orders from the War Department for me to report in August, 1921, to the Military Academy at West Point as an instructor. Major Haislip was included in the same order. We were then engaged in preparing plans for extensive maneuvers in the fall and neither of us wanted to switch from this active, creative assignment to the sedentary task of instructing cadets. We persuaded General Allen's Chief of Staff to cable the War Department that our services "could not be spared." A reply came back promptly, directing us to catch the next transport from Antwerp.

Unknowingly I was thus about to embark on a twelve-year round of assignments as an instructor or student in the Army's school system. Prior to World War I, the Army's officer educational system had developed haphazardly, from the founding of the Military Academy in 1802 to establishment of the Army War College in 1903. In between the creation of these two institutions a series of infantry, artillery, and other branch service schools had sprung up, usually on the initiative of individual, forward-looking officers. Most of the early branch schools dealt with the techniques of weapons and employment of the separate arms, with little attention to tactics, organization, or the coordination of operations. General William T. Sherman, the Commanding General of the Army in the post–Civil War era, took the first step toward integrating instruction in the combined arms when in 1881 he directed establishment of the School for Application of Infantry and Cavalry, at Fort Leavenworth, the precursor of the present Command and General Staff College.

But the individual who made the greatest contribution toward a broad understanding of military problems and the need for an integrated military educational system was Brevet Major General Emory Upton. Graduating from the Academy in May, 1861, he was sent around the world by Sherman to study the organization and methods of the armies of Europe and Asia. His resultant treatise on "The Military Policy of the United States" was not fully appreciated until long after his death in 1881. It was brought to the attention of the greatest of modern secretaries of war, Elihu Root, whose study of Upton's work led to creation of the Army's General Staff Corps and to establishment in Washington in 1903 of the Army War College, one of the objectives of which was "the direction and coordination of the instruction in the various service schools."

Thus was rounded out a military educational system unexcelled anywhere in the world. During the years 1921–1941, except for a three-year tour in the Philippines, I was privileged to have the benefit of this remarkable system and to have a part in its operations.

After returning home from Germany I reported for duty at West Point on August 25, 1921, and I learned only then, to my surprise, that I was assigned to the Department of Chemistry. I had guessed that I would teach French. Though not fluent, I had had three years of instruction in Latin and three years of French and had brushed up on my French pronunciation during several visits to France from Germany. I had scarcely given a thought to chemistry since graduation. I had done well in the subject as a cadet, and apparently my name had been recorded in the department as a potential instructor. The antiquated system of selecting teachers at the Academy has long since changed. The instructors, with few exceptions, still are junior officers of the Army, almost all West Pointers, but they are more carefully chosen now, are consulted in advance, and most are given a year or more of training in their assigned subjects at a civilian college.

We greatly enjoyed our tour at the Point. It provided stability for the early years of our marriage, at a time when conditions in the postwar Army were almost chaotic. Our son Joseph Easterbrook, whom we called Jerry, was born during our third year at the Academy, adding joy to our already happy life, and making West Point truly our first home. But in a professional sense I marked time as an instructor at the Military Academy, while the service schools out in the active Army were engaged in lively experiments in instructional methods, organization, tactics, and the techniques of weapons. The next eight years propelled me into the midst of these developments.

Student at the Infantry School

From World War I onward, West Point has laid no claim to producing 2nd lieutenants fully qualified to lead soldiers in modern combat. The introduction of aircraft, tanks, weapons with greater firepower and flexibility, as well as improved communications and transport required intensive professional training for every young officer at the service school of his branch. Upon graduation from West Point the new 2nd lieutenants are sent to their respective branch service schools before reporting for duty with troops. Rapid expansion of the Army in World War I forced me, and my classmates, to take command of troops without benefit of such training. I had acquired some professional skill through command but there were great gaps in my knowledge of the new weapons and techniques. The Army took the first step in correcting these deficiencies by sending me to the company officer's course at the Infantry School at Fort Benning. While I was a student there we lived in nearby Columbus, commuting daily to Benning, where our first daughter, named after her mother, was born at the post hospital.

At once I was struck by the competence of the instructors, the excellent methods of instruction, and the keen interest of the students, which resulted from the able leadership of Colonel Frank S. Cocheu, the Assistant Commandant, who was responsible for the conduct of the Academic Department. I was to have the pleasure of serving under him again in the Philippines. It was obvious that instructors at Benning had been selected with greater care than at West Point. All were articulate, enthusiastic, expert. They were typical of the officer corps of the Army, men who came up from the ranks, from the National Guard, the Reserve Corps, the ROTC, and West Point. In the Weapons Section there was a remarkable group of sergeant instructors, led by Sergeants Woolf and Magoni, who assisted the officers in charge of marksmanship and techniques of infantry weapons. One of the objectives of the Weapons Section was to qualify every student as an expert marksman with every infantry weapon. In this they were largely successful. I managed to reach this goal. I was especially lucky in "off-hand" rifle shooting from the standing position, at an 8-inch, bulls-eye target, at two hundred yards, which later led to an embarrassing moment for me. The year before, in the national rifle matches at Camp Perry, Ohio, the Marine Corps rifle team had defeated the Infantry team for the overall championship by outshooting the infantrymen off-hand, the most difficult section of the matches. The captain of the Infantry team, Major Courtney H. Hodges—destined to command the American First Army in Europe in World War II—determined to reverse this outcome the following year. After the Perry matches he assembled the members of my class who had done best in off-hand firing in our rifle marksmanship course. I was among them, having scored 48 or 49 out of a possible 50.

Major Hodges cited the failure to lick the Marines and his resolve to erase this blot on the escutcheon of the Infantry. He appealed to our love of the Infantry, the Army, and the country to sign up for the tryouts for the next year's team. As Hodges was speaking, my mind was racing back to the prime bit of advice my brother James had written to me when I graduated from the Point: "Don't specialize in anything." That was unique advice in those days of emphasis on specialization. James argued that specialization limited one's capacity for growth, and advised that I try to acquire a grasp of all phases of the Army's role in the national picture. This made sense.

Furthermore, I knew that I was not a natural expert marksman. I had not grown up with a rifle in my hands. And even in my short period of service I had become convinced that the Army placed too great an emphasis on training for the artificial, Camp Perry type of marksmanship, to the detriment of techniques of firing at field targets under conditions that would approximate combat. In addition, I was far more interested in organizational and tactical problems of the Army.

I happened to be end man in the semicircle of students addressed by Major Hodges. In the hush that followed his stirring appeal, he turned to me with evident expectation that I would initiate a unanimous agreement to join the team. I felt like sinking through the floor as I answered in a subdued voice, "No." To Courtney Hodges's credit he never held this defection against me. While I was serving under his command in Europe in World War II we became fast friends.

Near the end of the school year I was offered the choice of attending the Field Artillery School or the Army Air Corps Tactical School, contingent upon accepting a following assignment as an instructor at Benning. I leaned toward the air school as being newer and perhaps more challenging but finally decided to request the field artillery detail, feeling then that the link between infantry and artillery was even more basic than that between the infantry and air support. I might have chosen differently a few years later but never regretted my choice of the artillery school.

Student at the Field Artillery School

The Field Artillery School at Fort Sill was the first of the branch service schools established, in 1911. At the time I was a student, its forte was gunnery practice, which I greatly enjoyed. We spent hours out on the ranges adjusting first on a variety of targets: hill crests, clumps of bushes, edges of woods, where enemy positions were assumed to be. The instructors chose easy targets for the nonartillery "visiting firemen" like me, but gunnery tradition was said to require that no student, however experienced, would get through the course without at least one failure. Apparently no one had paid much attention to my record until after my last test, when it was discovered, to the horror of the artillerymen, that I had not had a single failure. Had the instructor known this, I am sure he could have picked a tough "lateral" target that would have stumped me.

I did not notice it at the time, but I do not recall that any reference was ever made in those gunnery exercises to the assumed location of our own troops. Firing ranges at Fort Sill were all in wide-open terrain, so that artillery observation posts could be well back of where our front-line troops would have been. This led to faulty gunnery procedures, which could not be applied with safety to our own infantry in close, wooded country such as the jungles of the South Pacific. Here was but one of the evidences of lack of coordination between the infantry and artillery of that day. The underlying cause of this disability was that, except for a single active 2nd Infantry Division, infantry and artillery units were in small, widely scattered posts. In only a few posts were they together. Funds for summer combined training were practically nonexistent. There was a tendency for the artillery to go its own way, and the infantry likewise.

I profited greatly from my year at Fort Sill and was able to put to use the knowledge I gained of the capabilities and limitations of artillery, not only as an instructor at the Infantry School but, more importantly, in combat in World War II.

Instructor—The Infantry School

Before leaving Sill for the drive to Benning, where I returned as an instructor, I had traded our six-year-old Ford for a two-door Oakland sedan, a predecessor of the Pontiac. The local dealer had been unable to sell the Oakland to any of the newly affluent, oil-rich Indians for whom a two-door car lacked the prestige of a four-door sedan. The average Indian was a ready purchaser of a second-hand Ford. Consequently, I got an exceptionally good trade.

We drove off proudly in our new car, which not only had more prestige and room than our old coupe, but rode a lot better. It was well that it did, because the last stretch of "highway" in Alabama was a pot-holed mud road, and Gladys was about to give birth to our third child. But we made it to Benning on August 3, 1927, and our second girl, Nancy, was born in the post hospital soon after arrival.

The following day, the alert auto dealer who had tried to sell us a Buick when we first reported at Benning two years before, and who had offered an allowance of $150 on our Ford, called on us. He felt certain that he could now make a sale—only to find that we had a new Oakland.

"Cap'n, what did you get for that ol' Ford?" he asked in his high-pitched, Georgia-cracker voice.

"You'd be surprised," I replied, as if reluctant to give a figure.

"Oh, come on, Cap'n, how much did you get?"

"I got only $450 for that old Ford," I said, straight-faced.

His jaw dropped as he looked at me in amazement: "My Gawd, Cap'n, you sho' ain't in need of no guardian!" he exclaimed.

It was well that our guardian angel did take care of us during the next few depression years, when our army salary was frozen and our take-home pay, after insurance, was $188 a month. Fortunately we were stationed in the South, where living costs were low and a dollar could still buy a dollar's worth of goods or services. At the salary then paid a maid, we could even afford a smart young girl, Charlene, to help Gladys with the cooking, housekeeping, and care of the children.

We lived in a small frame cottage on 1st Division Road in a grove of tall oak trees, within walking distance of the Infantry School. The cottage had no insulation. It was hot in the summer and could be freezing cold in winter when an occasional "norther" hit Benning. It was heated by a single wood stove, which used to get so red-hot that I was fearful it would set fire to the beaverboard walls. Once, while I was away on a trip to Washington during a cold spell, the water tank in the kitchen froze and burst, converting the kitchen and half the living room into a skating rink. Somehow, Gladys and Charlene managed to right things. I had always said, as a bachelor, that I hoped I would marry an Army girl. None other would have put up with the frequent moves and living conditions. Actually, we were lucky and enjoyed life at Benning.

When I reported to Benning I was disappointed to learn that I had been assigned to the Fourth Section of the school, to be in charge of editing and publishing the correspondence courses. I knew I had been asked for by the Weapons Section and had hoped to be assigned there or to the Tactics Section. Remembering how I had been stuck for four years in the Chemistry Department at West Point, I decided to ask for a change. Fortunately the head of the Fourth Section was a broad-gauge man. I went directly to him. I explained that the knowledge of artillery I had gained at Sill could better be put to use in the Tactics or Weapons Section than in the Fourth Section. He must have agreed, because in a few days I was reassigned to the machine gun committee in the Weapons Section.

Shortly before our return to Benning, Lieutenant Colonel George C. Marshall succeeded Colonel Cocheu as Commandant. My first contact with Colonel Marshall occurred when he slipped quietly into the back of a lecture hall moments after I started my first lecture, which had been postponed when I came down with a bad case of laryngitis.

To explain the postponement, I had begun a story about a visit of a Senate investigating committee to an American camp at the French port of Brest during World War I, when I spotted Colonel Marshall in the hall. All I had read or heard about him had drawn him as a grave, humorless man, all business. I had some qualms about continuing the story, which told about a visit of this committee to a model trench system used at Brest to familiarize newly arrived American soldiers with what combat trenches were like. But I was too far committed, so plunged ahead: "The senators were met at the entrance to the trenches by an officer guide. In a subdued voice he said, 'We are in a communications trench leading to the front. Follow me.' A bit farther on he stopped in a widened section of trench containing two 80-mm mortars, manned for this occasion by a section of infantrymen. 'We are now in a mortar position supporting the front-line troops,' whispered the guide as he ducked under some overhead cover. The senators followed, keeping their heads well below the parapet as they proceeded past a machine-gun nest in the front line until they came to the end of the trench where two soldiers were sprawled under a camouflage net, surrounded by loops of barbed wire. 'We are now in a listening post,' said the barely audible guide. 'How far away is the enemy?' whispered the committee chairman. 'About four hundred miles,' came the reply. 'Then what in the Hell's going on here?' roared the chairman as he straightened up. Pointing to his throat, the guide replied, 'I've lost my voice.'" When I came to the dénouement Colonel Marshall laughed as heartily as anyone in the class. This incident proved a fortunate introduction to the man who would have such a far-reaching influence on my military career.

Shortly thereafter, one Saturday afternoon while I was raking leaves in front of our cottage, Colonel Marshall, out for a walk, happened to come by. He stopped to chat, and as he seemed to linger, I invited him in for a cup of tea. I said Mrs. Collins probably was not dressed for visitors, but he accepted without hesitation. Gladys served us tea, and the Colonel sat and visited for some while in a relaxed, informal fashion. Thereafter I always felt at ease with this remarkable man.

Though his predecessors had launched the new Infantry School at Benning in 1918, the arrival of Marshall marked its coming of age. He brought a fresh outlook to the problems of the Infantry, and the Army, to which he evidently had given much thought. He came with matured judgments as to what he wanted to accomplish, which—as I came to evaluate his objective—was to shake the Infantry out of its old, conservative ways, and to develop innovative ideas and methods. Not that he advocated casting aside all doctrine and techniques that had proven sound. But he made clear to faculty and students alike that these principles and methods were all subject to challenge. He retained the system of having approved or preferred solutions to problems presented to student classes, but one of Marshall's earliest directives to the faculty was that any student's solution to a problem that differed markedly from the "approved" solution, yet made sense, would be published to the class.

Despite Colonel Marshall's seemingly forbidding appearance, he was always accessible. Anyone with a new idea, a new method or procedure, could get a hearing and was encouraged to come up with a specific project to develop his theory. Marshall frequently sat in on faculty lectures and listened in on the discussions, getting a feel for the students and instructors. As he came to know the faculty he gradually made changes. By the end of his first year he had changed the heads of the sections of the academic department, with marked improvement in several instances. He waited until he could get Lieutenant Colonel Joseph E. (Vinegar Joe) Stilwell to head Tactics. Then he shocked the infantrymen at Benning, and demonstrated his unorthodox approach, by selecting a medical officer, Major Morrison S. Stayer, who had a talent for administration, to take over Logistics. To lead Weapons, Marshall lifted Omar Bradley from the ranks of Tactics; and he rounded out his personally selected chiefs by bringing in an old friend from China days, Major Forrest Harding, to liven up the Fourth Section—History, Publications, and Methods of Instruction.

The War Department for years had looked to its schools for the development of doctrine and techniques, particularly in the period following World War I when airplanes, tanks, machine guns, and improved communications and logistics began to revolutionize combat. Under Colonel Marshall's stimulating leadership the Infantry School went beyond teaching to experimenting, testing, and writing infantry field manuals.

Faculty boards usually made the initial studies. Results were tested in the field by the 29th Infantry and an artillery battalion, which comprised the school troops at Benning. To broaden these tests—and to afford students an opportunity to exercise command—Marshall persuaded the War Department to concentrate at Benning whatever troops in the Southeast were available for summer maneuvers. The faculty prepared most of the exercises, with students participating as umpires and to some extent as commanders. After review and coordination with other branch schools and services, the War Department put its stamp of approval on the final manuals for guidance of the National Guard and Organized Reserve as well as the Regular Army. Correspondence courses conducted by the Fourth Section under Harding, with the talented assistance of Lieutenant (later Major General) Charles T. Lanham, carried the teachings of Benning throughout the Army.

After two years in the Weapons Section I was transferred to the Tactics Section, where I taught the tactical employment of infantry supporting-weapons in attack and defense. This resulted in my becoming a member of both the attack and defense committees, and brought me into close association with such men as Colonel Stilwell, Majors Omar N. Bradley, Gilbert R. Cook, Charles E. Ryder, and Captains Clarence R. Huebner and Charles L. Bolté, most of whom were destined for high command in World War II.

Colonel Marshall seemed to take special interest in Charlie Bolte and me. Additional tasks were frequently given to one or the other of us, for inquiry and oral report. We became members of an informal study group comprising most of the officers named above, reinforced from time to time by Doctor Stayer, Major Harold R. Bull, Major Bradford G. Chynoweth, a brilliant member of the Infantry Board, and others, which met occasionally of an evening at Colonel Marshall's quarters. Monitored by "Doc" Cook, one or two of the group would report on a book or subject for inquiry assigned at the previous meeting by Marshall or Cook. Subjects were seldom of a direct military nature, but ranged from geopolitics to economics, psychology, or sociology, with reference to their effect on military problems. A lively discussion always followed.

Infantry Reorganization

One of the most important problems facing the Army at that time was reorganization of its primary combat unit, the infantry division. The World War division, an enlargement of its French counterpart, totaled approximately 28,000 men. It served well for the steady, plugging trench warfare in France, but many Americans thought it too big and unwieldy for the more mobile, fast-moving fighting to be expected in any future war.

Not only was the division too large, but there was no logic back of its organization. This was especially true of its infantry component, around which the World War I division was structured, two infantry brigades of two regiments each. Each regiment had three battalions of four companies, each with three platoons of two sections of two squads. Though inconsistent in its subdivisions, this division was referred to as a "square division" because of its four infantry regiments.

At the close of World War I, General Pershing directed a study of divisional organization. Separate boards were appointed to cover the infantry, artillery, engineer, signal, and other components. A "Superior Board," headed by Major General J. T. Dickman, and including such other distinguished officers as Generals John L. Hines, William Lassiter, and Hugh A. Drum, reviewed the reports of the subordinate boards and recommended a "square" division of approximately 29,000 officers and men. Pershing held this report for evaluation before forwarding it to the Secretary of War by endorsement dated June 16, 1920. General Pershing disagreed with much of the report, and recommended a three-unit system of three regiments, with a total strength of 16,875. Meanwhile the Chief of Staff of the Army, General Peyton C. March, who disagreed with Pershing on many matters, appointed a War Department committee, which on July 8, 1920, recommended a square division of 19,217. This organization was approved by General March.

The idea of a small triangular division did not die with March's action. Unfortunately, most of the records of subsequent studies during the period 1920–1936 have been lost or destroyed, but I do know that while I was an instructor at Benning the Infantry Board and the Infantry School did make a study of infantry organization. I was appointed a member of a faculty board on reorganization of infantry units along with Major Cook and Captain Bolté. I well recall that it was Major Cook who contributed the basic analysis of a typical infantry attack in open warfare that served as a basis of the organization. This analysis indicated that there are three essential functions in an attack: the enemy must be located and held in position while the attack is launched, preferably against one of his flanks, or rear, and the attack must be brought to a conclusion by the attacker's reserve unit. These functions called for a minimum of three interchangeable rifle units plus a fire-support unit of weapons whose fire could be shifted in support of either the holding attack or the envelopment. This idea suggested that a platoon should consist of three rifle squads plus an automatic rifle unit; a company should have three platoons and a light machine-gun platoon; a battalion, three rifle companies and a heavy weapons company (mortars and machine guns); and a regiment should comprise three infantry battalions, to be supported in action by at least one battalion of artillery. Finally, a division should have three infantry regiments, supported by an artillery brigade.

We pointed out that one great advantage of linking infantry organization to the normal work of an attacking unit would greatly simplify the training of new officers in wartime, an objective constantly sought by Colonel Marshall. An officer would have essentially the same functions and comparable means with which to perform his mission as he moved up the chain of command from platoon leader to command of a division. After years of study and testing by the service schools and other War Department agencies, culminating in full-scale tests by the 2nd Infantry Division in Texas, a triangular division of 15,000 men was adopted in September, 1939, soon after General Marshall became Army Chief of Staff. By October, 1940, nine divisions of the Regular Army had been so organized, just in time for World War II.

A New Infantry Drill

One of the more important chores that Colonel Marshall turned over to me was a review of the infantry close-order drill system. Major Chynoweth had called Marshall's attention to a new French drill regulation, which Marshall asked me to study. Our old close-order drill emanated from the days when infantry marched and wheeled on the battlefield in precise, massed formations. We had modified our "extended order" combat drill to counter marchine gun and artillery fire, but there was little connection between close-order drill and combat field drill. The French regulations bridged this gap and prescribed far simpler formations for moving troops about.

I had always felt that our Army wasted an inordinate amount of time teaching soldiers the intricacies of "squads right" and "squads right about," and recommended that we modify our drill along the lines of the French regulations. Colonel Marshall decided to solicit the faculty for suggestions. Two or three drills were submitted and tested by companies of the 29th Infantry. The one I drafted was selected by a faculty board and recommended by Marshall to the Chief of Infantry. Our conservative Chief turned it down, fearing the new drill would eliminate the alleged disciplinary value of the old one. My drill, described in an article in the *Infantry Journal* of July–August, 1931, remained in limbo until resurrected by General Marshall when he became chief of staff, when he made it effective for the entire Army. Unquestionably, it saved hundreds of thousands of hours training soldiers in World War II. It is still the basis of Army drill today.

My last recollection of Colonel Marshall at Benning was a bit of advice he gave Charlie Bolté and me as we happened to be standing together watching a field exercise. The conversation had turned to the importance of duty in command of troops, and Marshall said, "If a war is ever in the offing, don't let them stick you on staff duty, as was done with me!" Ten years later that advice proved worth remembering.

Our tour at Benning was not only rewarding professionally but full of interest and enjoyment outside duty hours. I was inveigled into taking part in the post's drama club, which provided fun if not stellar performances. The reservation's 97,000 acres offered opportunity for hunting and fishing, and fine packs of hounds expertly trained by Sergeant Tom Tweed provided exciting Sunday chases of the native red foxes and bobcats, with an occasional coon hunt on foot at night. I played lots of tennis and even succeeded in winning a novice tournament. Gladys and I greatly enjoyed our cross-country horseback rides. But our chief joy came from watching our three fine children develop. In those days the Infantry School did not operate fully in the summer. We escaped the oppressive heat of Benning by vacationing in the mountains of North Carolina, where the family, accompanied by Charlene, attended Miss Ethel J. McCoy's girls camp at Lake Junaluska. I taught riding in lieu of camp fees. The children learned to swim, canoe, and ride horseback. We returned to Benning each fall refreshed in body and spirit.

We all hated to leave at the end of four years, but orders called for my attendance as a student at the Command and General Staff School at Fort Leavenworth, the next step in my military education.

Student, the Command and General Staff School

We drove from Benning to Leavenworth via Junaluska, where we stopped off for a final season at the children's camp. While there, Gladys came down with acute intestinal pains, quickly diagnosed as appendicitis. By chance a Mayo Clinic surgeon, a friend of Miss McCoy, was coming to Junaluska for a weekend visit. Miss McCoy persuaded him to perform the operation on Saturday afternoon at the Haywood County Hospital in nearby Waynesville. The Mayo man left Gladys' postoperative care in the hands of an older Waynesville surgeon, Dr. Joshua Fanning Abel, whom we had not known before. Gladys recovered rapidly under his care and was soon ready for the drive to Leavenworth. I paid the Mayo surgeon the standard fee, but received no bill from Dr. Abel. The day before we were due to leave, I stopped at his office to thank him and to settle our account. When I asked for our bill the doctor leaned back in his chair a moment and said: "Captain, you did not know that I was a reserve officer in the Army Medical Corps in the World War. While I was away in the service my daughter had to have an appendectomy. When I returned home the surgeon refused to accept a fee. And, you know," he added, as he smiled at me, "I have been waiting all these years for an opportunity to return that compliment. Now I have it." We drove off next day with lightened hearts, renewed admiration for the medical profession, and the wonderful couplet from John Masefield's "Widow in the Bye Street" singing in our memory: "Thus the love that fashioned all in human ken, works in the marvelous hearts of simple men."

I checked into Fort Leavenworth on August 29, 1931. We were assigned quarters in an apartment in a converted barracks on Pope Avenue—a big step up from our little cottage at Benning, though we missed our grove of oak trees and our backyard vegetable garden.

The Command and General Staff School, as its name indicated, was designed to give students, mostly captains and majors, tactical training with units of combined arms, *i.e.*, infantry, artillery, tanks, engineers, and supporting aircraft, so that someday they might be competent to command a division, and meanwhile be qualified to serve on the general staff of a division or higher unit. Having no troops available for practical testing and training, the school was forced to rely on theoretical map problems. The situations ran the gamut of attack and defense, with differing opposing forces, and included problems in pursuit of a defeated enemy, withdrawals, and special operations such as river crossings and amphibious landings on hostile shores.

After four years at Benning under the innovative, experimental, testing-and-proving atmosphere created by Colonel Marshall, I found instruction at Leavenworth stereotyped. I believe this was done deliberately, particularly in staff exercises. Our army had little experience in large-scale operations between the Civil War and World War I and the authorities evidently wanted to establish a pattern for staff functions dealing with personnel, intelligence, operations, and logistics. This would simplify the training of large numbers of officers, most of whom would have to come from the National Guard and Reserves in time of war.

The rigid adherence to approved solutions, carried over into the command problems, worried the Commandant, Brigadier General Stuart Heintzelman, who had served in the operations division of General Pershing's staff. Several times while I was a student, General Heintzelman, who had been listening in the back of the lecture room to an instructor's exposition of a type-solution to some tactical problem, would storm up to the platform to disagree with the patterned, school solution. He would apologize to the instructor, and would caution us to follow the instructor's guidance in any subsequent test problem. Then he would tell us what he would do under the conditions presented. He would add, "But you do what the instructor suggests, not what I say, or you will probably get a U (unsatisfactory) on the graded test." Most of us students followed his advice, and played the instructor's game, often with tongue in cheek.

When I attended Leavenworth the regular course had been expanded to two years, the second being devoted chiefly to logistics of large units, corps, armies, and groups of armies. Most of this was new to me. Though my interests leaned toward tactics and strategy, logistics were fascinating, and the instruction was first rate. For the Army as a whole, the courses at the Command and General Staff School were probably the most important in the entire system of military education, and were to prove invaluable in World War II. It was at Leavenworth that Eisenhower and Bradley and most of our senior commanders in that war, few of whom had ever commanded a combat unit larger than a battalion, learned the techniques of large units.

Near the end of my second year I was called unexpectedly to the Commandant's office. I wondered what I had done wrong. General Heintzelman asked me to be seated and said that he had been following the academic work I had been doing and had decided to send a request, which he held in his hand, to the War Department asking that I be detailed as an instructor. He must have seen my face drop, for he paused and looked inquiringly at me. I asked if he would mind if I made a statement. He nodded approval.

I said, "General, I have been teaching or being taught for twelve consecutive years at West Point, Benning, Sill, and Leavenworth. I am afraid if I were to remain here as an instructor for four more years I would lose any practical ability I might have."

He thumped his desk and exclaimed, "By God, Collins, you are right!" He tore up the letter then and there, and threw it in the waste basket.

CHAPTER IV

Service in the Philippines, 1933–1936

We were grateful to General Heintzelman for letting me go. I had not had any foreign service since our return from Germany in 1921, so was due for another tour of duty abroad. I had requested assignment to the Philippine Division, our only combat division overseas. The Islands would also offer an opportunity to travel in China, Japan, and elsewhere in the Far East. The War Department granted my request and on May 29, 1933, we left Leavenworth and headed west for the San Francisco port of embarkation.

A month's leave of absence, plus time allowance for travel, made possible a long-planned drive to the West Coast. Gladys' brother, Wilfred Easterbrook, and his family were living in Seattle, where many of her University of Washington classmates were located. I had been promoted to the grade of major while at Leavenworth, with an increase of pay which helped make the trip possible.

We drove by way of Colorado Springs, Yellowstone, Glacier National Park, Lake Louise, and the Canadian Northwest, then across the Cascade Mountains to Seattle. There we rented a cottage on Puget Sound. After the long drive from Leavenworth, we welcomed such a quiet, restful spot, though visits with Wiff and Sarah Easterbrook and their two children, as well as Gladys' many college friends, kept us reasonably busy. I and our children were delighted to get to know the West Coast branch of the Easterbrooks. We got along well together, adults and children alike.

We left Seattle reluctantly in late July. After a drive along the western slopes of the Cascades, with their snow-capped peaks towering above us, and through the fabulous giant redwoods and sequoias of California, we reached San Francisco in time to catch the Army transport *Grant*, which sailed August 4, 1933, for the Philippines.

En Route to the Philippines

The *Grant*, which could cruise at only ten knots, would take three weeks to reach Manila, including a short stopover in Hawaii. I relished the thought of such a tranquil voyage with no official responsibilities. During one of our many Cook-Chynoweth-Bolte-Collins "bull" sessions at Benning on some subject long since forgotten, Brad Chynoweth had suddenly pointed his finger at me and said, "The trouble with you, young man, is you haven't read the Bible, have you?" "No," I had to admit. "Then go read it. When you have, we will argue with you."

I took seriously Chen's admonition, but I was always too busy with other things to get past Genesis. Now the prospect of three weeks on the *Grant's* leisurely cruise to Manila afforded a welcome opportunity at least to start to fill the deep void in my education. I don't recall how far I got in those three weeks, but over the next ten years I read the Douay version of the Bible from cover to cover, enthralled with the great stories of the Old Testament and inspired by the gospels and the epistles of the Apostles. The Douay translation of the New Testament lacks much of the poetry of the St. James version, but still has a majestic sweep that I find lacking in the prosaic modern texts.

Among the passengers were Congressman John D. Dingell of Michigan and his family. They were going to Manila to visit their friend Frank Murphy, who had just been appointed Governor General of the Philippines. The Dingells had two or three children about the ages of ours, and we had other points of common interest. Dingell was interested in having a look at the Hawaiian Islands beyond Oahu during the two-day stay of the *Grant* in Honolulu. He arranged to have an Air Corps plane made available to him for the flight. He thoughtfully offered to take along any officers who might wish to accompany him. We had already arranged to have Gladys and the children stay at Schofield Barracks with the family of Major Henry Schroeder, a West Point classmate, so I accepted—the only one who did. At the last minute Dingell had to drop out. As the sole passenger, I rode with the pilot in the cockpit, which afforded a clear view of the lovely chain of islands from Oahu to Hawaii. It was a gorgeous day. I was fascinated with the infinite variety of sapphire and emerald coloring of the water along the reefs which lined the shore below us, and the varying shades of green of the island jungles, waving palm trees and fields of sugar cane, as they reflected the bright sunlight.

The plane climbed steadily as we approached Haleakala, the extinct volcano on the island of Maui. At twelve thousand feet we made a circuit of the rim of the oblong crater. Suddenly without any warning to me, the pilot sideslipped the plane below the rim and we were flying inside one of the largest volcanic craters in the world. I had a momentary eerie feeling of being trapped within the serrated walls of what was once a fiery cauldron. Ancient gas cones still showed above the floor of the crater, which seemed to be covered with yellowish pumice rather than black lava. I would guess that the longer axis of the crater would measure ten miles, with a width of about five miles. We flew around within the crater for probably five or ten minutes, though it seemed longer, before clouds began to roll in through the open end where red-hot lava once flowed out. We eased over the rim and were once again in the blue open sky, headed for Hilo on the big island of Hawaii, where the snow-capped peaks of Mauna Loa and Mauna Kea were shining in the bright sunlight.

After lunch at Hilo we flew back along the northeast coast of Hawaii, whose rampart cliffs, garlanded with dozens of gossamer waterfalls, rise abruptly from the sea. En route we circled the leper colony of Molokai, bringing back recollections of Robert Louis Stevenson's stirring defense of Father Damien. Then, to put a crowning touch on this memorable flight—the first of many such that I would have in various places around the world in later years—the sun set in a blaze of glory as we landed back in Honolulu.

After two more weeks of slow churning across the western Pacific, the *Grant* finally steamed past Corregidor Island and entered Manila Bay on the morning of August 26, 1933.

Turmoil in the Far East

We arrived in the Philippines at a time of critical ferment in the Far East. Japan was nearing the peak of its rise to power which began with the defeat of China in the Sino-Japanese War of 1894–1895. The Russo-Japanese War followed in 1904–1905, ending in the destruction of the

Russian fleet. Korea, already under Japanese control, soon was incorporated in the Japanese Empire. Then in 1931–1935 the Japanese Kwantung Army occupied Manchuria. China appealed to the League of Nations, which under pressure of world opinion, led by the United States, condemned the Japanese aggression. Japan reacted violently, and withdrew from the League. These actions were accepted, perforce, by Chiang Kai-shek in the spring of 1933, only a few months before we arrived in Manila.

While Japan was moving in Korea and Manchuria, expanding its empire in the Far East, the United States was abandoning its traditional isolationism and emerging as a world power. Following the Spanish-American War the Philippine Islands were ceded to the United States. We established, in effect, a protectorate over the Islands, which included their defense, until the Filipinos were prepared to take over their own government. Independence was authorized by the United States Congress in 1934, and a Philippine government under Manuel Quezon as president was established at that time, with complete independence to be effective in 1946.

By the time we arrived in the Islands, the American occupation forces in the Philippines had been reduced to a single under-strength division, consisting of the 23rd Brigade and service troops, stationed at Fort William McKinley on the southern outskirts of Manila; the 24th Field Artillery Regiment at Fort Stotsenberg, about fifty miles north of Manila; a separate 26th Cavalry Regiment, also at Stotsenberg; the 31st Infantry, a United States Regular Army regiment in Manila; and Coast Artillery units manning the fortifications on Corregidor and adjacent small islands guarding the entrance to Manila Bay. Except for the 31st Infantry, these units consisted of native Filipino volunteers, called Philippine Scouts, officered by a mixture of Americans and Filipinos. They were fine, well-disciplined, loyal troops.

But, as was inevitable with occupation troops in peacetime, combat training in the Philippine Division and defense planning within the Philippine Department had slackened. Training had been allowed to take second place to administration and maintenance of barracks, roads, and facilities at posts, camps, and stations. The troops were forced to spend half their time performing these essential chores with consequent deterioration of their readiness for combat. The outlook of many of the Scout officers, and the Regulars who had been there for three or four years, was illustrated to me one morning as I walked from my house to brigade headquarters. I was striding along at my customary pace when I overtook Captain Jimmie Carter, one of the abler Scout officers. "Slow down, Major, slo-o-w down," he said. "After you have been here for a while, you will learn to do the tropical g-l-i-d-e." Jimmie Carter and his fellow officers had adjusted to the tempo of the tropics but not as yet to the changing political-military situation that was building up around them in the Far East.

Japanese expansion in China and the Western Pacific, particularly after the seizure of Manchuria, forced a renewal of attention in the Philippine Department to training and defense planning. This was furthered by the arrival in the Islands of two new senior commanders, Major General Frank S. Cocheu, the former Assistant Commandant of the Infantry School, who assumed command of the Philippine Division in June, 1933, and Major General Frank Parker, an aggressive veteran of the 1st Infantry Division in World War I, who took over the Department in December, 1933. They initiated steps to correct the apparent deficiencies.

Assignment to the 23rd Brigade

These leaders found willing assistants in the group of my Leavenworth class who arrived together on the *Grant*, many of whom had served under Cocheu at Benning. During our group's two years at Leavenworth we, and our families, had come to know one another well. We all landed in top jobs in the Philippines in the fields of training or operations, for which we had been schooled at Leavenworth. I became the Brigade Executive. Major Frank H. Partridge, another Leavenworth classmate, who came on the next transport, became the G-I-4 of the Division. Though I regretted not getting a command, my assignment had the compensation of providing the family with quarters at Fort McKinley, instead of our having to live in crowded Manila.

The normal training hours in the Division were from 7:30 to 11:30 A.M. Routine parade-ground drill occupied most of the mornings, with an occasional road march off post. Afternoons were devoted to administration and to the maintenance of housing and post facilities. With the full support of General Cocheu, our Leavenworth group, now largely responsible for the preparation of training schedules, began to challenge this routine. We increased the time for weapons training, and required small-unit tactical exercises on a regular basis. Next we introduced battalion and regimental marches and maneuvers that took the troops off post overnight once or twice a month. No one among the old-timers could remember when such exercises had last been held. Our group became known as the Leavenworth "Eager Beavers." The Philippine Scouts, like good soldiers everywhere, enjoyed these field exercises, and so did their officers, once their initial reaction wore off.

The next improvement was in the coordination of training between the scattered combat units of the division. The 23rd Brigade and the 31st Infantry had to use the same firing ranges at Fort McKinley, with some resultant friction, and there was little combined training among the infantry, artillery, and cavalry units. Now a simple telephone call or visit between two or more of the Eager Beavers cleared away prior obstacles.

Philippine Defense Planning

On December 2, 1934, after a year with the 23rd Brigade, I was detailed to the General Staff Corps and assigned as the Operations and Intelligence Officer, G-2-3, of the Philippine Division. Frank Partridge, the G-1-4, and I each had a single assistant. Colonel Francis C. Endicott, an old and able friend of General Cocheu, was the Chief of Staff. The five of us constituted the entire General Staff of the Division—in contrast to the twenty-five officers authorized for a division headquarters today.

Cocheu at once set Partridge and me to work planning for the next month's maneuvers of the Division, which were to be based on the Philippine Department's plan for the defense of the Islands against possible Japanese attack. Here my experience as assistant G-3 of the American forces in Germany stood me in good stead. The Department plan derived from the War Department's plan for possible war with Japan, with the code designation of *Orange*, and anticipated

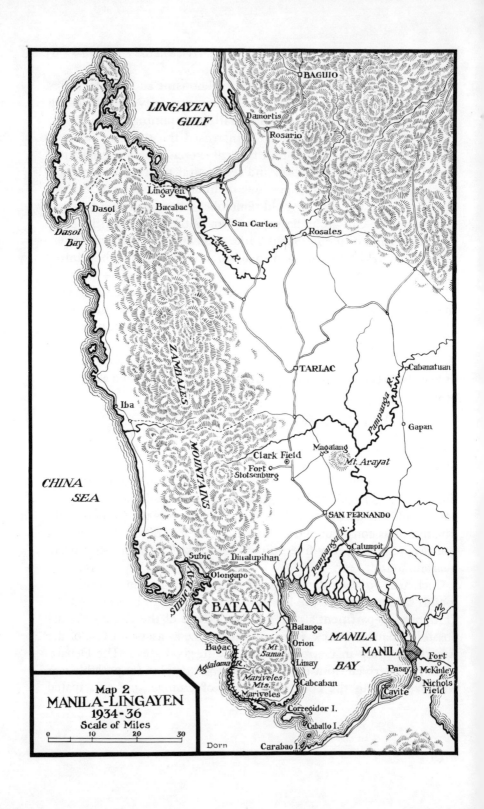

LINGAYEN
GULF

CHINA
SEA

● BAGUIO

Damortis

Rosario

Lingayen
Dasol   Bacabac
Dasol
Bay   San Carlos   Rosales

Agno R.

ZAMBALES

TARLAC   Cabanatuan

Iba   Gapan

Pampanga R.

Magalang
Clark Field
Fort   Mt. Arayat
Stotsenburg

MOUNTAINS

SAN FERNANDO

Pampanga R.

Calumpit

Subic   Dinalupihan
Olongapo

SUBIC BAY

BATAAN

Balanga   MANILA

Orion   MANILA

Bagac   Mt   BAY   Fort
Samat
Aglaloma R.   Limay   Pasay   McKinley
Mariveles   Cabcaban   Nichols
Mts.   Cavite   Field
Mariveles

Corregidor I.

Caballo I.

Carabao I.

Dorn

Map 2
MANILA-LINGAYEN
1934-36
Scale of Miles

0   10   20   30

that the main Japanese attack would be launched across the beaches of Lingayen Gulf, north of Manila, with a secondary landing to the south or southeast of Manila Bay. It was estimated that the Japanese would attack with a minimum of four divisions, supported by strong air and naval forces. It was recognized that the American forces then located in the Philippines could not be reinforced from Hawaii or the United States in less than forty-five days and might require six months.

Under these circumstances, while the "basic" plans of the Department and the Philippine Division called for the Division to meet the enemy at the beaches and prevent his landing, a more realistic auxiliary plan provided for delaying, to the maximum practicable extent, the advance of the enemy from his landing beaches until the Division was forced to withdraw to Bataan Peninsula, covering Corregidor and the sea entrance to Manila Bay. Bataan was to be held until the arrival of reinforcements.

1934 Exercises on Bataan

But details of these plans had not been worked out on the ground or tested in field maneuvers, for which funds had never been provided by the War Department or Congress. A first step to change this situation was taken in the exercises of January, 1934, plans for which Frank Partridge and I took over from our predecessors. It was too late to make any major changes in the program, which called simply for the movement of the 23rd Brigade and other elements of the Philippine Division, by barges, across Manila Bay to Bataan, after which there would be a reconnaissance of possible defensive positions in the southern portion of the peninsula.

A map study indicated that Mariveles Mountain, rising almost five thousand feet above the sea in the southern half of Bataan, was a formidable obstacle which might be incorporated in the final defensive position of the Division. Movement by barges across the bay was a slow and exposed process that boded ill for any such operation under war conditions. The troop reconnaissances turned up good defensive positions on each side of Mariveles Mountain, of which the deep crater could provide a common interior anchor, with the flanks resting on Manila Bay to the east and the China Sea on the west. Horseback was the only feasible means of transportation over the rough, narrow trails which we rode from Mariveles up and down both sides of Mariveles Mountain, checking out the defensive positions which would be manned by the 23rd Brigade. In doing so, I gained valuable knowledge of the lay of the land and some insight into the problems of organizing Bataan for defense.

General Parker joined General Cocheu at Division headquarters at Mariveles near the end of the exercises. I led them on horseback up an abandoned logging trail on the western slopes of the mountain to an observation point which had been established a few years earlier by coast artillerymen from Corregidor. From there they had a good view of the China Sea coast north to the village of Bagac.

The 1934 exercises, limited though they were, did point up the necessity of improving road communications on Bataan. The only paved road on the peninsula ran from the United States naval base at Olongapo on Subic Bay across to Manila Bay at Dinalupihan, where a graveled road branched off to the south along the east coast of the peninsula as far as Limay. Only a foot trail meandered on from there via Cabcaben to Mariveles. Another trail led from Olongapo to the village of Bagac on the China Sea and thence eastward, north of Mounts Mariveles and Samat, to Balanga on the east coast. From Bagac an abandoned narrow-gauge logging rail line ran along the west slope of Mariveles Mountain, ending at the gorge of the Aglaloma River. Another abandoned logging line climbed the western slopes of the ancient volcano from Mariveles village to the Aglaloma, where it stopped at a point opposite the end of the Bagac line.

It was obvious that if Bataan would ever have to be defended in war, these trails would have to be improved, and a road capable of carrying artillery, armored vehicles, and trucks would have to be constructed from Limay via Cabcaben to Mariveles and thence up the badly eroded western slopes of Mariveles Mountain at least to Bagac. But this would have to wait until the next dry season, when the War Department might be persuaded to allocate more funds for exercises on Bataan. The trail from Limay to Cabcaben could be cleared and widened without great difficulty, but the stretch from Cabcaben to Mariveles gave indications of real trouble. The existing foot path zigzagged steeply over grades that would have to be moderated for a motor road. An added problem was that the trail in this section crossed ancient lava flows that had disintegrated into soft, friable soil that turned into sticky mud in the rainy season, which lasted from June through November. To construct a stable roadway, capable of carrying heavy vehicles, would require more men and equipment than were available in the Division's 14th Engineer Battalion.

To solve this problem, I hit on the idea of turning the job over to the 24th Field Artillery which had tractors and other earth-moving equipment, picks, and shovels, which could be supplemented from the 14th Engineers. This proposal was not greeted with enthusiasm by the artillery, but was approved by General Cocheu for the field exercises commencing in December of 1934.

1935 Bataan Field Exercises

Again the 23rd Brigade barged to Bataan and resumed its reconnaissances for successive delaying positions. The 26th Cavalry marched down from Stotsenberg and reconnoitered the Olongapo-Dinalupihan and the Bagac-Balanga areas. The 24th Field Artillery likewise marched to Bataan and began work at once on the Limay-Mariveles road. Once on the ground, the artillerymen, under Colonel Colden Ruggles, pitched in with a will and, with technical assistance from the 14th Engineers, made good progress down to Cabcaben. As we anticipated, the section between Cabcaben and Mariveles was tough going. No bulldozers were available in those days, but scoop shovels, pulled by the artillery tractors, dug into the steep hill slope above Mariveles and widened and eased the repeated cutbacks of the new road. Every curve had to be revetted with heavy timbers cut from the adjacent forests. Meanwhile on the west coast the 14th Engineers, commanded by Major William Holcombe, assisted by Battery B, 24th Field Artillery under Captain Bryan Evans, was working on the logging line from Mariveles north to the Aglaloma River. By the end of January, 1935, a road passable for artillery and light vehicles was open all the way from Limay via Mariveles to the Aglaloma, and both slopes of Mariveles Mountain had been thoroughly explored.

A few months later the Philippine tour of General Cocheu came to an end and he returned to the States. He must have left with a great sense of satisfaction. He was largely responsible for the opening of the Bataan Peninsula, and the Philippine Division was in far better readiness to take the field than when he took command. General Cocheu gave his staff and his subordinate commanders considerable leeway in their operations, but there was never any question in anyone's mind as to who was the commander. He taught me one valuable lesson in this regard. Shortly after I became his G-2-3, some problem arose which he delegated to the Commander of the 23rd Brigade, Brigadier General Stanley Ford. "But, General," I protested to Cocheu, "this is a matter which we ought to handle at Division Headquarters." I have never forgotten his mild rejoinder: "Joe, there is one thing you must learn. The important thing is to *have* the power, not necessarily to use it." We all learned much from this wise, thorough-going gentleman. We hated to see him go, but later Gladys and I had the pleasure of his friendship and the benefit of his sage advice in Washington, where he lived in retirement, while I was Chief of Staff.

Further Reconnaissance on Bataan

One major task on Bataan remained before real maneuvers on the peninsula could be conducted. A road would have to be constructed from Bagac to tie in with the new road from Mariveles to the Aglaloma, and that deeply cut stream would have to be bridged. A preliminary reconnaissance of this route would have to be made and a site selected for the bridge. I was interested also in looking over the area just south of the Balanga-Bagac trail for a possible defensive position that would run across the peninsula in an area that I had not yet seen. Major William H. Hoge had succeeded Major Holcombe as division engineer in June, 1935. We had been in the same cadet company at West Point, where he was in the class of 1916, one year ahead of me, and we had served together for a time at Benning. As soon as the wet season was over in the fall of 1935, we took off on a fascinating trip from Limay to Bagac and thence to the Aglaloma. We had with us a platoon of Scouts from the 14th Engineers and a section of the pack train carrying rations.

The trail we followed rounded Mount Samat, north of Mount Mariveles, near its base. It was almost completely overgrown with bamboo and vicious bejuca vines, whose barbed tips could tear the shirt off a rider's back. Hoge and I on horseback were preceded by a group of Scouts on foot who cleared the trail with their long "bolo" knives. We rode through heavy stands of tanguili ("Philippine mahogony") and narra trees, buttressed with great flange-like roots. Some of the softer-wooded trees were in process of being strangled to death by balete vines, which start as air plants in the tree tops then wrap themselves in snakelike coils around the trunk down to the ground where they take root, while termites eat away the doomed parent tree.

We camped for the night at the junction where the Mount Samat trail joined the wider one that ran from Balanga to Bagac. The next morning Filipino fishermen led us to the start of the old narrow-gauge rail logging line that led south to the Aglaloma. Most of its crossties were still in place, but the jungle had almost swallowed it up. The natives warned us that there were many washed-out small bridges along its trace and they doubted that we could traverse it on horseback. We decided to give it a try.

The natives were right about the difficulty of clearing a way for our horses, but except for occasional stops to cut away trees and brush that had grown up between the railroad crossties, we made slow but steady progress up the western slopes of Mariveles Mountain. Part way up the mountainside we came suddenly onto a little village of negrito pigmies that we did not know existed on Bataan. Naked children scurried to hide in the bamboo and nipa-palm shelters that served as their homes. A few elders appeared, dressed solely in G-strings. Not even our scouts could converse with them, but they gesticulated amicably with us and chattered in a friendly fashion. They were probably an off-shoot of a group that lived in the Zambales Mountains above Fort Stotsenberg. No one knows the origin of the negritos of the Philippines, but they are thought to be the remnants of the earliest inhabitants of the southern islands, who were driven north by migrating waves of Malaysians.

After several hours we came to the end of the logging line that stopped abruptly above the narrow gorge of the Aglaloma River. We were surprised to see below us a waterfall of ten feet or more that did not show on our maps. It was not possible to cross the small but rushing stream at this point. We worked our way downstream to where we could cross and then back up till we found the old logging trail that ran from Mariveles to the Aglaloma. We had cleared this trail during the prior field exercises. Except for the crossing of the Aglaloma we had encountered no serious obstacles to our road-building project. Subsequent reconnaissance by Hoge and Captain Clay Anderson, of the 14th Engineers, staked out a bridge site just above the falls on the Aglaloma.

Philippine Division Maneuvers of 1936

The next year, Major General Charles E. Kilbourne, Parker's successor, was able to obtain sufficient funds from the War Department to extend the road building on Bataan and to conduct the first real maneuvers of the Philippine Division since the Division was constituted in 1921. The maneuvers began before dawn on January 20. In accordance with the Orange Plan, it was assumed that a Japanese convoy had appeared off Lingayen Gulf and was about to land a strong force over the beaches. The 26th Cavalry, with a battery of artillery from Fort Stotsenberg, was dispatched to Lingayen Gulf to locate the enemy and cover the advance of the Division from Stotsenberg and McKinley to Lingayen, which required four days.

Following a reconnaissance of the potential landing beaches on January 26, the division engaged in a defensive exercise on January 27 before starting its withdrawal south to Bataan. In order to familiarize the troops with the Zambales west coast of Luzon, the 23rd Brigade, preceded by the 26th Cavalry, moved from Ligayen to Dasol and thence down the coast road to Olongapo. The 24th Field Artillery, the 12th Signal Company, and the bulk of the 14th Engineers were released for necessary road and communications work on Bataan, preliminary to the division maneuvers on the peninsula.

Meanwhile the 14th Engineers, largely under the supervision of Captain Clay Anderson, proceeded with the task of opening a crossing over the Aglaloma. To stake out the grade on the steeper north side of the Aglaloma gorge, engineer soldiers had to be lowered by ropes down the side of the cliffs. Most of the work had to be done by hand, using poles, slings, bolos and shovels. The Filipino soldiers were amazingly adept with hand tools and were prodigious workers. In a matter of days they had gouged out approaches, with moderate grades, on both banks to a point where a relatively short bridge, anchored in concrete footings on a ledge just above the falls, could be built. With the completion of the Aglaloma bridge we now had a continuous vehicular road from Limay to Mariveles, north to the Aglaloma, which would be essential for the movement of troops and supplies for any subsequent defense of Bataan. It would need continual improvement and maintenance, particularly during the wet season, but the Japanese were unlikely to launch an attack in the wet months.

Successive defensive positions were reconnoitered by the 23rd Brigade, starting with one south of the Balanga-Bagac trail, and supporting artillery positions were surveyed by the 24th Field Artillery. These were recorded on maps, but not marked out on the ground, so as to avoid their being spotted by Japanese agents who were bound to be in the vicinity of Bataan, which was open to public travel.

Those of us who, during this period, worked on plans for the defense of the Islands had no illusions as to the adequacy of our planning, or the ability of the forces available to make these plans effective. General Parker, then Department Commander, wrote on February 28, 1934, to General Douglas MacArthur, then Chief of Staff of the Army, pointing out the inadequacy of the Army and Navy forces allotted to the defense of the Philippines: "There is no possibility of stopping an Orange invasion with the force that will be available in the extremely short period of preparation, in view of Orange's well known policy of beginning hostilities without warning." And, almost as a forecast of the situation that General MacArthur was to face with insufficient forces in the Philippines six years later, and again in Korea in 1950, General Parker continued: "Strategy depends directly on national policy. When this policy is lacking for a given situation there can be no strategy. Under existing conditions, a crisis will have to be met by the Army and Navy as has always been the case in our past history, by improvisation instead of the preparation which a definite policy invariably assures."

Subsequently, Admiral Frank B. Upham, Commander in Chief of the Asiatic Fleet, and General Parker, in a joint letter to the Chief of Naval

Operations and the Army Chief of Staff, asked directly if it was the policy of the United States to defend the Philippine Islands, and made certain recommendations. An answer to the above letter, signed by General MacArthur, then the senior member of the Joint Board, affirmed the policy of the United States to defend the Philippines, but promised no reinforcements.

Upon the expiration of his tour as Chief of Staff in 1935, General MacArthur became Military Adviser to the Philippine government. During the next six years, with the assistance during four of these years of Major Dwight D. Eisenhower, General MacArthur organized a Philippine Army. But neither funds nor time were available to equip fully, or train, this fledgling army before the Japanese attacked in 1941. It was possible, with the troop strength then available, to move the main defenses farther north on Bataan than we, in 1936, were able to consider. But the roads and trails we built or opened during the 1934–1936 period, extended and improved in subsequent years, provided the framework for the movement of troops and supplies during the Battle of Bataan in 1941–1942, as is attested in the Army's official history, *The Fall of the Philippines*, and John Toland's stirring story, *But Not in Shame*.

It was a source of great satisfaction to me, as I read the dispatches of the fighting on Bataan, that our work was of some help to the gallant men who fought there, including my old boss in Coblenz, Skinny Wainwright; Ned King, my chief at the Army War College (1938–1941); and my first battalion commander and mentor, Major, then Brigadier General, Clifford Bluemel, who distinguished himself in action on Bataan.

CHAPTER V

Travels in the Far East

China

One of the chief advantages of being stationed in the Philippines was the opportunity offered for travel in the Far East. The Army recognized the value of such travel, not only in broadening the outlook of its personnel but in familiarizing them with areas of potential military operations. No one at that time anticipated the conflicts on the Asiatic mainland in which we were to become involved in later years, but officers were encouraged to visit China, Japan, and southeast Asia to the extent that space could be made available on Army transports and as one's personal funds would permit. It so happened that the several trips we made to China, Japan, and Indochina—solely for pleasure and our interests in seeing new places and people—during our stay in the Philippines, were of considerable military value in my subsequent service.

China was usually the first choice for a visit. As an aftermath of the "Boxer" riots of 1900, which endangered the foreign legations in Peking, the United States, with other countries, had retained an infantry regiment in Tientsin. Army transports periodically carried troop replacements and supplies from Manila to this garrison. Space was always available for personnel on leave. After placing our two little girls in the care of American nuns in the Maryknoll convent on the outskirts of Manila, Gladys and I, with our son Jerry, sailed from Manila on March 22, 1935, on the transport *Grant* for Chinwangtao, the port of Tientsin. I had two months accumulated leave. Our close friends from Fort Benning, Charlie and Bennie Bolté, then stationed in Tientsin, met the troop train that brought us up from Chinwangtao. After a pleasant lunch with the Boltés we boarded a Chinese train, along with a group of other vacationing friends, for the three-hour ride to

Peking. We all stayed there in a guest house operated by Mrs. Chien, an American woman who had married a Chinese.

At first glance, Peking was disappointing to us. The city sits in a flat plain rendered dull and colorless in those days by the almost complete absence of greenery. Over the centuries, Chinese peasants in search of fuel to combat the freezing blasts of wintry air from Mongolia had practically denuded the plain of trees. The drabness of the countryside was carried over into the squat stone dwellings of the periphery of the Imperial City. It is within this inner city, which we approached over an avenue as wide as the Champs Élysées, that the grandeur of Peking lies. The Chien Men gate, towering above the Tartar wall which was still intact in 1935, looked down from its many-tiered magnificence on the avenue, its small arched portal untroubled by the few motor cars of those days. A sea of red-tiled roofs brightened the houses within the walled city, setting off the golden-colored tiles of the palaces of the once-restricted Forbidden City, home of the emperors.

In subsequent years, I have visited many of the great cities of more than seventy countries around the world. Peking remains the most fascinating. We spent almost three weeks there, visiting the marvelous palaces and temples of the Forbidden City, its charming parks and gardens alive with cherry and almond blossoms. The Temple of Heaven—actually a group of temples—capped by the white marble circular Altar of Heaven, open to the skies, gave us our first inkling of the great creative imagination of the ancient Chinese.

The usual mode of travel in Peking was by rickshaw, a light rubber-tired sulky, drawn by a coolie who trotted everywhere with seemingly indefatigable ease. Traveling at that pace, at street level, you were filled with the sights, sounds, and smells of the city. Chinese of all ages and descriptions, who could afford the modest fares, outnumbered the few groups of tourists like ourselves, though not all used the rickshaws. In those days, before the dull seriousness of Communist life descended upon them, the Peking Chinese, with their keen sense of humor, were quick with laughter and ever ready to joke, even at government edicts. Once, while stopped at a busy road junction, we noticed that city police were having all rickshaw coolies button the high collars of their jackets which were habitually worn open in warm weather. I asked my boy, Lie, what it was all about. He laughingly replied: "Today button-up-collar day. Tomorrow finished."

Aside from visiting the colorful temples and sights of Peking, the chief objective of our visit was shopping for rugs, jewelry, porcelain, and art objects. The temple fairs, teeming with native Chinese and a sprinkling of tourists, where items of all sorts were haggled over, were great fun. The Chinese loved to bargain and were disappointed if the unwary stranger accepted a first offer:

"You say your price."

"No! Lose money! "

"Last price 5.50."

Whispered, "For you I give special price, 2.50."

"All light, 1.75," followed by a burst of laughter.

In contrast to such street bargaining, I went alone one evening to the best shop on Jade Street, where the legitimate jade merchants were concentrated. I was courteously received by two dignified elderly Chinese men in the outer room of the store, the only furnishings of which were a few simple tables and chairs. There were no objects on display, and no other customers at the moment. I was seated at one of the tables, offered a cup of tea, and then asked what I was interested in seeing. I said I wanted to buy a pin or a similar present for my wife. The younger man withdrew into an inner room while the older one poured my tea. As he quietly gauged his young visitor, I became fascinated with a large mole on his chin, from which two long grey hairs extended down to his waist. (I learned later that such hairs were highly prized as marks of distinction.)

The younger man quickly reappeared with a modest pin containing a mottled white-and-green piece of jade. It was priced at five Chinese dollars, then equivalent to $2.50 U.S. I had been told by knowledgeable friends that the best stones are clear apple green in color. I said that I would like something better. The pin was removed and another was brought in with a clearer stone, valued at twenty-five Chinese dollars. Again I asked for another choice.

This went on for the next hour or more. As additional pieces were presented they were varied, now a brooch, next a pair of earrings, or a necklace, each lovelier and more expensive than the one before. It was soon apparent to the merchants that these items were beyond my price range, and it was equally clear to me that, while I could readily see that each successive object was lovelier and more valuable, I had no idea, no gauge, by which to estimate its increased value. But the dealers must have thought well of my taste, and became caught up in my admiration for the beauty of design of the jewelry, and the brilliance of the jade.

Long after it was obvious that I would make no purchase, the men continued to show me their most valuable pieces. The final masterpiece was a magnificent fire screen, made completely of apple-green jade. It was valued at over 500,000 Chinese dollars. As I rose to go and thanked them for the pleasure they had given me, they beamed their appreciation, and the older gentleman contentedly stroked his two long hairs.

We varied our shopping and sightseeing with two trips outside of the city, first to the Great Wall and then to the Ming Tombs west of Peking. To reach the Wall we went with a group of Manila friends by train to Ching Lung Chaio, near the Pa Ta Ling gate, through which for centuries an old caravan trail wended its way to the Gobi Desert, Mongolia, and Tibet. As we left the train there was a scramble for burros, on which we galloped off toward the Wall, led by Jerry in cowboy style, leaving behind the more sedate tourists who were carried in chairs. After a short canter we came to a bend in the trail and there before us was a long sweep of the Great Wall. Running generally parallel to the border of Mongolia, it extends 1,500 miles from Kiayukwan to Shanhaikwan on the Gulf of Chihli. It was built by labor conscripts and 3,000,000 soldiers.

We clambered up for a walk to a watch tower atop the western slope. The view from the tower was spectacular. As we followed with our eyes the course of the wall, writhing its way like a giant snake in either direction until it disappeared over the horizon or dipped into a far valley, we were awed by its immensity. I was struck with the daring of its conception and its scorn of time and space, but appalled at the pitiless disregard of the human labor that went into its construction.

Our other trip out of Peking was to the tombs of the emperors of the Ming Dynasty, who ruled China from 1368 to 1644. We drove there by car. It was the Chinese "Easter" or springtime day for visiting family

The Collins family, 1905
First row: Bernard, Joseph
Second row: Katherine Lawton Collins,
Peter, Jeremiah B. Collins, Ullainee,
Agnes
Third Row: Margaret, May, James,
Katherine

At Boy's High School,
New Orleans, 1911

Plebe camp, West Point, 1913
Joe Collins, Henley Frier

Fort Benning, Georgia, 1927
Instructor Infantry School

Home from West Point on furlough,
1915

Wedding party leaving Kaiserin Augusta Palace chapel July 15,
1921, Coblenz, Germany

Lieutenant General Delos Emmons and staff, 1942, at Fort Shafter, Hawaii
First row: Collins, General Emmons, Robert M. Bathurst, Walter C. Philips

Major General Collins, CG, 25th Division, and Major Charles Davis, CO, 3rd Battalion, 27th Infantry, confer on New Georgia, August, 1943.

General Collins and staff, 25th Infantry Division, Guadalcanal
Left to right: Lieutenant Colonel F. W. Greenough, Major General Collins, Colonel William A. McCulloch, Brigadier General Stanley E. Reinhart, Brigadier General John R. Hodge, Colonel W. P. Bledsoe, Colonel R. B. McClure

Review of the 9th Infantry Division, Southern England, 1944
Prime Minister Winston Churchill, General Eisenhower, General Bradley, Major General Collins, Major General Matt Eddy

The beachhead, Normandy, June 8, 1944

Utah Beach, June 12, 1944

Captain Robert Kirpatrick, Cleveland, Ohio, tells Major General Collins the part his unit played in the capture of Fort du Roule overlooking the city and harbor of Cherbourg, June 26, 1944.

Receiving surrender of Lietenant General Dietrick von Schlieben and Admiral Hennecke following the capture of Cherbourg

General Collins presents tricolor flag of parachute silks to M. Paul Reynaud, Mayor of Cherbourg, first city of France liberated.

Division commanders, left to right: Ira T. Wyche, 79th Division, Raymond O. Barton, 4th Division, Matthew S. Ridgway, 82nd A.B. Division, Manton S. Eddy, 9th Division, Maxwell D. Taylor, 101st A.B. Division

General Dwight D. Eisenhower, Supreme Allied Commander, congratulates Major General Collins after having awarded him an Oak Leaf Cluster to the Distinguished Service Medal following the D-day landings in Normandy.

Behind are Lieutenant General Omar N. Bradley, Commander of the U.S. First Army, and Major General Leonard T. Gerow, Vth Corps Commander, both of whom also recieved the decoration.

Tour of the Siegfried Line near Aachen in October of 1944 with General George C. Marshall, Chief of Staff, U.S. Army

The General Meets the Press
Pausing on his way to the shower to chat with War Correspondent
Bill Stoneman of the Chicago *Daily News*

With Field Marshall Montgomery and Major General Ridgway
during the Battle of the Bulge
Mean, Belgium, December 26, 1944

Checkpoint in Ardennes during the Bulge
Collins is accompanied by Jack Walsh.

Overlooking the Cologne Plain
Collins points out German positions to his nephew Lieutenant
Colonel James L. Collins, Jr., from a forward observation post near
Düren, Germany.

Cologne Cathedral with Rhine bridges
in background

Major General Maurice Rose, C.G. 3rd
Armored Division, Captor of Cologne,
on the steps of Cologne Cathedral.

Генералу Коллинс
В память, незабываемой
исторической для наших войск
и лично как, встречи в Лейпци...
1 мая 1945 г. гв. генерал-май'р Бакла...

General Collins greeting Major General Baklanoff in Leipzig, Germany, following a meeting with Russians on the Elbe, 1945

Farewell address to VII Corps

The Joint Chiefs of Staff, April 22, 1950.
Left to right: General Hoyt S. Vandenberg, General Omar N. Bradley, General Collins, and Admiral Forrest Sherman

General Collins presenting the United Nations flag to General MacArthur, Tokyo, 1950

Inspection tour in Korea, 1951

Collins, Chief of Staff, U.S. Army, stands with other Army generals after his arrival at the X Corps Airstrip to begin an inspection tour of the corps area, October 28, 1951.

Left to right: An unidentified Republic of Korea Major General; General Collins, General Matthew B. Ridgway, Commander-in-Chief, United Nations Command; General James A. Van Fleet, CG, U.S. 8th Army; Major General Clovis E. Byers, CG, U.S. X Corps; and Major General Paik Sun Yup, CG, 1st ROK Corps

Chief of Staff, United States Army, 1951

With Secretary of the Army Frank Pace
enroute to a Secretary of Defense Policy
Meeting, 1951

Conferring with Marshal Tito on military aid to Yugoslavia, Belgrade, 1951.

Prime Minister Nehru of India, Collins, Robert W. Middlebrook, and James McGee, Pfizer managers, New Delhi, India, 1958.

The Collins family with first grandchild, 1953
Left to right, second row: Caroline Gibson Collins, Lieutenant Joseph E. Collins, Nancy Collins, Gladys Collins Stenger
Seated: General Collins, with Muffy the family cat, Gladys Collins, Jerry Stenger with son Joseph

General and Mrs. Collins relaxing at their cottage "Jayhawk Rest,"
Scientists Cliffs on the Chesapeake, about 1965

graves, which are marked by mounds of earth, set in family groups, throughout the fields. We passed many families repairing the mounds, smoothing them, and placing imitation paper money atop them to appease any evil spirits who might seek to molest the graves.

After three hours of bumpy, dusty driving, we came to the fascinating avenue of giant stone animals and men, grouped in pairs on opposite sides of the road leading to the Ming tombs. It was strange to see them still standing solemnly by the roadside as if some giant boy at play had forgotten to take them home. Yet they are imposing guardians of the imperial way, and gave us some concept of the grandeur that must have marked the interment procession when one of the Mings was laid to rest.

Each of the thirteen "tombs" is actually an assemblage of palaces and pavilions, each set within its own courtyard. The principal tomb is that of Yung Lo, the third and greatest of the Ming emperors, who chose this area for the mausoleums of his successors. Yung Lo was worthy of the grandeur of the main hall of the shrine, which rivals any of the palaces in the Forbidden City. But as testimony of his greatness, he chose as the actual site of his tomb a mound of earth, three hundred yards in diameter, encircled by a high stone wall and covered with a wonderful stand of arborvitae trees.

Travels in Japan

We left Peking reluctantly on April 11 with the hope that we would return some day, which unfortunately has not yet come about. Having made reservations for a visit to Japan, we had to move on. In Manila I had obtained the assistance of Mr. Nimura, the Japanese consul, in planning our trip to Japan. Because I knew that since I was the Operations and Intelligence officer of the Philippine Division, the Japanese would be dogging my footsteps throughout the trip, I explained to Mr. Nimura that we were going to Japan purely as sightseers, with no ulterior military motives. While at Fort McKinley, I had read two histories of Japan, and as a result wanted particularly to visit Mount Hiei, above Lake Biwa, near Kyoto, seat of the Tendai Buddhist sect, one of the most powerful orders of monks at the time of the Emperor Kwammu. I was also desirous of going over the battlefield of Port Arthur, and from there would have liked to have gone to Seoul, via Mukden, and thence to Japan. We would have three weeks to spend in Japan. I would, of course, travel in civilian clothes, Mr. Nimura cooperated fully but, undoubtedly on instructions from his foreign ministry, said later that it would not be possible for us to visit Mukden, or Korea, which had been annexed by Japan in 1910.

We landed in the smoke-filled bustling port of Dairen on Saturday, April 13. After mass the following morning at the Maryknoll mission church, well attended by devout Japanese, we rushed back to our hotel only to find that our guide to Port Arthur, an employee of the local War Office, had inexplicably disappeared after leaving his guidebook to the battlefield. This was the only time during our stay in Japan that the security people seemed to interfere with us. Jerry and I drove to Port Arthur anyway and had an interesting visit to the scene of Russia's defeat that established Japanese supremacy in the Far East. The battlegrounds were as well marked as our Gettysburg.

Following the program I had arranged with Mr. Nimura, we caught another steamer to Moji-Shimonoseki at the entrance to the Inland Sea, from whence we proceeded to the charming little island of Miajima, famous for its Shinto shrine, built out over the water, and its graceful symbolic gate (Torii) standing offshore. After two restful days at Miajima we left the following morning on a small steamer for a trip through the narrow straits between islands along the north coast of the Inland Sea, a picturesque passage that is missed completely by tourists on the ocean-going vessels that run in and out of Kobe. Our combination passenger-freighter had only third-class accommodations, which would have meant our spreading out on the carpeted floor of the single large cabin, along with several Japanese families, including babies, tea pots, rice bowls, and luggage. Fortunately, the captain spotted us as we came aboard and graciously offered us the use of his personal cabin on the top deck. He was a pleasant little man of the old Japanese tradition of courtesy, who spoke good English and did everything to make us comfortable. He also waved off the busy-body police who came aboard at every little port to check on the passengers, and who otherwise would have been a nuisance. With what I was sure was a disregard of the security regulations, he gave us a map and pointed out all points of interest, including Hiroshima—which of course we did not know then would be the victim, in 1945, of the first atomic bomb—and the great naval station at Kure, the entrance to which we passed close by. It was filled with ships, giant cranes, and smoke-belching chimneys, all earmarks of Japan's feverish preparations for war with any comer. At Onomichi, where we disembarked to catch the train for Kobe, the captain went up the gangplank with us to ensure that we took the right road to the nearby railway station and waved us a cheery goodbye. His graciousness was characteristic of all the simple rural people we met throughout Japan.

We wasted no time in Kobe, before moving on to Kyoto. Unlike Kobe, a bustling commercial port, Kyoto was quieter and had a relaxed air about it as befitted the cultural center and former capital of Japan. We spent ten days in Kyoto and its environs. Its parks, lovely gardens, the old Imperial Palace, the even more impressive Nijo Palace of the Tokugawa Shoguns, and its beautiful shops filled with exquisite Chinese and Japanese antiques, made it by far the most attractive city we visited in Japan.

Our final trip in Japan was to Nikko, north of Tokyo. Upon arrival by electric train, we went at once by streetcar and aeriel cable to a high observation point from which we had a gorgeous view of the Chuzenji waterfall and the azure waters of Lake Chuzenji, above Nikko. The lake is not as intimate as Lake Louise but its setting is just as lovely. The elaborately carved and gilded temples of the mausoleum of Eyeyasa in Nikko are truly marvelous. Surrounded by giant cryptomeria trees, they are a fitting memorial to the greatest of the Tokugawa Shoguns who ruled Japan in the name of the emperors from 1603 to 1868. The exquisitely colored halls, the glistening lacquered corridors, and the famous trio of carved monkeys who hear no evil, see no evil, speak no evil, justify the Japanese adage, "Do not say *magnificent* until you have seen Nikko."

We arrived back in Tokyo in time for dinner and a fine performance of a light opera by the Takarusuka Girls Opera. The day had been a grand finale to our sightseeing in Japan. The next morning, May 8, we did our last shopping and then were off to Yokohama for our berths on the transport *Sherman* for our return trip via Shanghai and Hong Kong to Manila.

Whereas we had gone to Japan primarily for sight-seeing, our visit

did give me an insight into the character of the Japanese people and a
better idea of the capacity and limitations of the country to wage war. I
did not realize then how prophetic I was being when, in commenting
on the reverence shown by school boys and adults alike at the grave of
the Emperor Meiji, near Tokyo, I wrote in my notes at that time:

> There can be no question but that this devotion to the great men of the past
> is real and is widespread throughout Japan. Coupled with the fervent patrio-
> tism of the people, exploited to the limit by the military propagandists, it is
> the most powerful force in Japan today, and will be the greatest asset to Ja-
> pan in any future wars that she may have. It will go a long way toward over-
> coming the material deficiencies of the country, or from a tactical stand-
> point, any possible lack of originality or skill in maneuver.

Shanghai–Hong Kong

We debarked from the *Sherman* at Shanghai for a couple of day's shopping. In those days the shops of Shanghai were filled with beautiful
handwork of all kinds from "point Venice" lace and embroidery to
rugs, china, glassware, and carved chests. Our available funds were
about spent by the time we reached Shanghai, but Gladys had held
out some for special purchases there and in Hong Kong.

We wanted to see something of Canton and at least a glimpse of the
countryside and its people, so we went by train to Hong Kong. The
train ride was an experience I would not wish to duplicate. All I can
remember of it was that it was hot, and that Chinese peasants with
bundles of babies and baggage stormed on and off at every stop, with
little regard to the class of tickets they held. But all were friendly and
good humored. The countryside was flat and uninteresting and Canton, with its narrow streets and swarms of people, was stifling. We
were glad to get to the clear and orderly city of Hong Kong with its
magnificent harbor. Then, after a few days of final shopping, we boarded
the *Sherman* for the last leg of a fabulous trip that measured up to all
our expectations.

Angkor Wat

I did not want to leave the Far East without seeing the great temple of
Angkor in Cambodia, and wished also to visit Bangkok, the Malayan
peninsula and Singapore. Gladys felt that our two girls, Gladdie and

Nancy, young though they were, should see Peking. So we divided our forces before sailing for home at the end of my Philippine tour in 1936. I went off first to Indochina for almost three weeks while Gladys remained at home with the children. Then, just before we sailed for San Francisco, Gladys took the girls to Peking while I stayed behind with Jerry.

In 1936 the only way to reach Angkor from Manila was by steamer to Saigon and thence by automobile via Pnompenh, an expensive proposition. I had canvassed friends in Manila and the Philippine Division but could find no one who was interested in making the trip. Luckily, Captain Thomas J. Wells, whom I had known at Benning, passed through Manila on his way around the world, just at the right moment. He had planned a visit to Angkor en route to Bangkok, which suited me perfectly. On the Scandinavian passenger-freighter we took from Manila to Saigon we met two buxom young fräuleins, the daughters of the German consul in Honolulu, whom we persuaded to join us in renting a car for the drive to Angkor.

In Saigon, then a typical sleepy but pleasant French provincial city, with broad, tree-lined streets, we rented a big, ancient Pierce Arrow touring car, with a Cambodian chauffeur, for the drive to Angkor. We did not linger long in Saigon, which I never expected to see again. The drive up to Pnompenh, over a good gravel road, passed through extensive French rubber plantations, scene of heavy fighting in the later Vietnam War. The German girls were pleasant company and we enjoyed the ride through the flat countryside that varied from well-kept groves of rubber trees to heavy jungle and broad, open rice paddies. All went well until we entered the outskirts of Pnompenh, the capital of Cambodia. Then, with a sickening, unmistakable knock, a piston connecting-rod bearing burned out. We came to an abrupt halt several blocks from our hotel. It was in a residential section and no native boys were around. There was no alternative to pushing the car to the hotel. We thus made an inglorious entry into Pnompenh.

We found the city surprisingly attractive. The royal palaces, located on the west bank of the mighty Mekong River, though on a more modest scale than those of Bangkok, are equally colorful. We were agreeably surprised the next morning to find that native mechanics had installed a new connecting-rod bearing overnight, permitting us to resume our journey via Siem Reap to Angkor. There we stayed at a little French hotel at the edge of the ancient city of Angkor Thom, close by Angkor Wat.

Volumes have been written about Angkor. Suffice here to say that in all my subsequent travels, no monument or edifice made by man that I have seen can surpass its massive magnificence, not even the pyramids of Egypt, or the temples of Karnak or Baalbec. Completed in the twelfth century, it, and its adjacent city of Angkor Thom, was unknown to Western eyes for seven hundred years until visited in 1859 by the French naturalist Henri Mouhet. But unlike the Bayon and other monuments of Angkor Thom, the Wat had not been taken over by the predatory jungle, but has withstood the ravages of time, weather, and vandals in astonishing splendor.

On the recommendation of the manager of our hotel we drove some twenty miles from Angkor, over a road passable only in dry weather, to Banteai Srei. In contrast to the massive structures of Angkor, the buildings of Banteai Srei are like miniature pieces of carved sandalwood, but done in pink sandstone. We caught our breath in amazement as we entered a walled courtyard filled with little stone buildings, like children's play houses. It is relatively easy to carve sandalwood but how the artisans of the eleventh or twelfth century could carve sandstone so delicately without a crack or a break is a mystery, as is their perfect state of preservation after five hundred years of exposure to tropical heat and monsoons. The facades and pediments of these little buildings were beautifully carved, picturing lively scenes of tiny women dancers, or monkeys cavorting in stylized trees. We left Banteai Srei feeling as if we had been to a fairyland in stone.

The final drive in our faithful old Pierce Arrow took us to Aranyaprathet on the border of Thailand, then known as Siam. There we caught a train for the hundred-mile run to Bangkok. We arrived late on the eve of the Buddhist festival of Visakxabuja. Every male Buddhist has to serve at least three months as a monk in a Buddhist temple soon after reaching his twentieth birthday. On this day the novitiates don their saffon robes for the first time, and, with jars under their arms, walk through the streets begging food from the crowds that gather along the sidewalks. Tommy Wells, the girls, and I joined the throngs of Siamese, all in festive regalia, who filled the bowls with rice as the young men passed by in a procession led by older monks of the various congregations. They proceeded to a broad open area in front of the royal palace where a number of large tents had been erected. While the monks and novitiates lunched inside the tents, the gay crowds picnicked outside in family groups, interrupting their lunches with impromptu dances and children's games. The Siamese of those days had a fine sense of humor and a carefree outlook that was evidenced again that evening when we attended a party at the home of a Siamese classmate of Tommy's from West Point.

The young Siamese men and women who gathered there had all attended college in the United States. They had organized an informal Siamese-American social club which met from time to time at the home of one of the members. Dancing to American phonograph music was underway when we arrived. We were accepted without any ado into this jolly group, which apparently needed no alcoholic stimulant to have a good time. I soon found myself dancing with a lovely young woman who was also an excellent dancer. She was a graduate of the University of California where she had met her husband. She was part Japanese and part Scotch-Irish American, while her husband was half Russian and half Siamese. I have often wondered what their children would be like. I hope they were at least half as attractive as their mother. I was greatly impressed with the character and intelligence of these young people and happy to know that the bond that brought them together was the education they had shared in America. My own interest and participation in later years in the Institute of International Education in New York, and the Foreign Students Service Council of Washington, stemmed from that memorable evening.

We spent the next two days visiting the colorful Royal Palace, the charming Throne Hall, the Royal Museum, the Temple of the Emerald Buddha, and the Koh-si-chang Theater for a wonderful performance by a troupe of Siamese dancers. One afternoon, while the girls were shopping, Tommy and I visited a public crematory that was quite revealing as to some aspects of Siamese life. Because of the high birth and death rates in the country, and the limited amount of arable land in relation to the size of the populations, interment of the dead was frowned on, if not prohibited, by the government. Instead, cremation was the common practice. The Siamese revered their dead, and like many orientals, evidenced this reverence publicly at their cremation services by putting on as ostentatious a display as their means would permit.

Our guide at the hotel had invited us to attend the cremation of his "grandmother," perhaps in line with the custom when I was a boy, of using the funeral of a "grandmother" as an excuse for playing hookey from school. We drove out to a park where such public cremations were conducted. The more modest services were held outdoors, the bodies being cremated in wooden coffins over open grate fires, with the relatives gathered around. Several such services were in progress when we arrived. They were mostly simple, quiet, decorous, and a bit sad, though some provided a hilarious note, in order to draw a crowd of onlookers— and thus gain "face"—by showing Mack Sennett ''cops and robbers'' movies on bed sheets hung on wires between nearby trees!

We finally went inside a large shed for the cremation to which we had been invited. Members of the families of the deceased woman, dressed in semiformal native clothing, were assembled at the foot of a large artificial pyre, in the shape of a truncated pyramid, atop which the coffin was resting behind a yellow curtain. We were introduced to all present, were greeted solemnly, and offered colored curlicues of paper with which to assist in lighting a fire under the coffin. There were no monks present and no spoken service for the dead. When all was ready, the yellow curtain was withdrawn, and the relatives—we did not participate—starting with the eldest, climbed a stair in the back of the funeral pyre, and in turn started the crematory fire. As the coffin and body were consumed a functionary kept pushing the remains into the center of the fire until only ashes were left. A good draft carried the smoke and any odors out through an opening in the roof. After the ashes had cooled, fragments of bone and bits of ashes were presented to the relatives, who placed them in small urns to be taken home and kept as treasured mementos of the dead.

The entire service was conducted with great dignity and reverence.

Somber native music had been played throughout on gongs, accompanied by deep bass tones from an enormous brass trumpet that was stretched on the floor like a giant serpent. A small crowd had gathered outside, beyond a high wrought-iron fence that barred the open end of the funeral shed. The family had stationed a small stringed orchestra there to attract passersby. Despite the solemnity of the occasion, I had difficulty suppressing laughter, when near the end of the cremation, the orchestra—apparently spotting Tommy and me as Americans—broke into the refrain of the old spiritual, "Way Down Upon the Suwannee River"! Ever since, whenever I hear it, it brings back memories of wonderful Bangkok.

The remainder of our trip was somewhat anticlimactic, though I was interested from a military viewpoint, in traveling down the Malay peninsula, past the strategic Kra Isthmus where, according to rumors, the Japanese were hoping someday to build a trans-isthmian canal to avoid Singapore's dominance of the route to India. Our group parted company at Penang, Tommy and the girls to catch a steamer for India and points west, and I to continue on my way by rail to Singapore. From Singapore I would have loved to have gone on to Bali, but my leave of absence, and funds, had about run out. Indonesia would have to wait another twenty years. Reluctantly I headed back to Manila, arriving there on April 10, 1936.

CHAPTER VI

Back to School

The Army Industrial College

I had expected that when my tour in the Philippines was over I would be ordered to join the next class at the Army War College. Most of my Leavenworth classmates were on the 1936 War College list, and I was disappointed when my name was not included. I wrote to Major Ralph Huebner, then in charge of officer personnel for the Chief of Infantry, and asked, "How come?" Ralph shot back, "Keep your shirt on, Joe. We lost track of when you were coming home." He assured me that I would be given an assignment in the Washington area so that we would not have to make two household moves in one year. Near the end of the 1936 maneuvers on Bataan I had a telephone call at Mariveles from Gladys saying our orders had been received. When she told me that I was to take a course at the Army Industrial College I asked, "Where's that?" I had never heard of the school which had been started after World War I and was then located in the old Munitions Building on Constitution Avenue in Washington. Ralph Huebner had lived up to his word.

Actually he did much more for me than merely avoiding an additional change of station. Since serving as supply officer of the 22nd Infantry in World War I, I had no direct responsibility in supply matters. While engaged with the lecture series for Reserve officers in Birmingham I had gotten a glimpse of manufacturing techniques in heavy industry through my visits to plants and factories in the Birmingham area. But like most Army officers, I had little knowledge of the problems of production and procurement of munitions. The Industrial College had been established in 1924 to study and help correct the deficiencies in these fields that had developed in the military services, and in industry, during the World War, when for the first time America had to mobilize for a large-scale modern war.

The majority of the students were from the supply services of the Army, including the Army Air Corps—with a token representation from the Navy. There were a few line officers like me—later increased in numbers—who might someday have command or general-staff responsibilities that would extend beyond military strategy and battlefield tactics, and would require an understanding of the problems of industrial mobilization.

Luck plays a tremendous part in life. I certainly had my share of the breaks. Not the least of them was my assignment as a student at the Industrial College. If I had set out deliberately to qualify myself to be Chief of Staff of the Army, I should have sought a detail to the Industrial College. Instead, I lucked into it, with the help of Ralph Huebner. Not only did I learn something of the problems of industrial mobilization, I was introduced to cost and management controls that were of value not only during my subsequent tour as Chief of Staff, but during my later association with the chemical-pharmaceutical firm of Pfizer, Inc. Unwittingly, I had broadened my managerial horizon.

The most interesting phases of the course were the lectures we had from distinguished leaders of industry and our visits to the plants of Jones and Laughlin Steel, Alcoa, Westinghouse, Pittsburgh Plate Glass, and Mesta Machine Tool in Pittsburgh, the Glenn L. Martin and Chevrolet plants in Baltimore, and several Army arsenals. Of our lecturers I was most impressed with the personality and brilliant mind of Charles F. "Boss" Kettering, then head of research for the General Motors Corporation. I have often made use of Kettering's admonition to his assistants, which he had printed and hung in his laboratory for all to see who were working on any problem of the moment: THE SOLUTION TO THIS PROBLEM—WHEN IT IS FOUND—WILL BE SIMPLE.*

Near the end of the course, as at Leavenworth, I was called in by the commandant, who asked me if I would like to remain at the college as an instructor. He readily agreed, however, that I should go on to the War College if possible. He expressed the hope that after finishing the

*This is not exactly in accord with the transcribed notes of the talk on file at the N.I.C., but Kettering spoke extemporaneously, and this is my clear recollection.

latter school I would be assigned to the War Department General Staff in the G-4 Logistics Division, where the knowledge of industrial mobilization that I had acquired at the Industrial College could be put to use. I suggested that a detail in the War Plans Division might be even more suitable and important. Neither suggestion worked out. After World War II, when I joined the War Department General Staff for the first time, it was in another area even more important in rounding out my experience than logistics or war planning. But the lessons I learned at the Industrial College, including Boss Kettering's advice to keep things *simple*, were put to good use when I later held positions of high responsibility in the Army.

As forecast by Ralph Huebner, I was on the War College list for the next course commencing in the fall of 1937. In between the two colleges a fellow student, Major Alfred J. Lyon, and I took an unusual flight out to Seattle in an o-26 military observation plane. Al was an experienced Air Corps pilot. We had become fast friends at the Industrial College. The o-26 was a two-seater, open to the elements except for a plexiglass canopy that could be pulled back to cover the pilot and observer, who sat in tandem. It was an ideal plane from which to see the countryside, especially as we flew "contact," *i.e.*, navigated by visual contact with the ground, all the way.

We went out in easy stages via Kansas City to Flagstaff, just south of the Grand Canyon. Then on a bright morning we flew the length of the canyon at just below the level of its rim. I doubt that another such flight could be made today; it would be unlikely that the air controllers would permit it. It was my first view of the Grand Canyon and I can think of no finer introduction to one of the earth's most magnificent spectacles. We were awed by its great depth, the marvelous coloring of its rocks, and the fantastic shapes of its walls, sculptured by a million years of wind and water. Wary of the treacherous downdrafts that had once almost trapped him in the Snake River Canyon a few years before, Al dared not drop down too low or vary far from the center line of the gorge as we traversed the 200 miles or more to Boulder dam. Massive though the dam is, and impressive as a human engineering feat, it appeared puny in comparison to nature's masterwork.

From Boulder we headed north for Salt Lake, where we "bathed" sitting upright in the salt-saturated water before proceeding on to Pocatello, where Al had attended the University of Idaho. Another interesting geological "specimen," the extensive black lava beds west of Pocatello, publicized as "The Craters of the Moon," was on our route to the junction of the Snake and Columbia Rivers near Pendleton, Oregon. From there we had an exciting flight down the Columbia River to Portland. A stiff wind was pouring in from the Pacific and as we bucked it through the gorge west of The Dalles our light plane bobbed around like a cork. Al had made that run many times but said he had never had it rougher. However, the weather was clear and the sun setting over the Pacific added glorious color to the Cascade Mountains until we ran into fog drifting in from Puget Sound. I was grateful that Al knew this area so well as we followed a highway into Seattle, flying just above the telephone wires. We were glad to see Gladys' brother Wilfred Easterbrook and his lovely wife Sarah at the Boeing airfield to greet us.

After a couple of days' rest with the Easterbrook family and other friends on Mercer Island, we took off early one morning for the return trip to Washington in a heavy ground fog that blanketed Seattle and the Sound. We quickly climbed through it into the brilliant sunshine of a cloudless sky. There before us were five snow-capped mountain peaks soaring resplendently above the fog: Baker, Glacier, Rainier, Adams, and Hood. It was a magnificent sight. We flew just south of the Canadian border, over Glacier National Park and the Great Lakes to the locks at Sault Ste. Marie and Buffalo, then followed the Mohawk Valley to Albany and down the Hudson to New York and on to Washington. I made a second aerial survey trip with Al Lyon during the spring holiday period at the War College in 1938. This time we flew the Atlantic coast, at deck level, from Norfolk, at the mouth of the Chesapeake Bay, all the way to Passamaquoddy, noting all points of strategic interest en route. Thence we coursed south of the St. Lawrence River to Lake Champlain, and down the Hudson again to New York. Then we picked up the Delaware and followed it past Trenton and Philadelphia to Chesapeake Bay, Baltimore, and Washington.

These two flights served not only as a background for some of our strategic studies at the War College but brought home to us the beauty and the vast natural resources of our great country.

The Army War College

Thanks to Ralph Huebner's consideration, Gladys, our three children, and I were able to continue living in a rented house on 35th Place in northwest Washington while I attended the War College. I commuted daily to the college at Fort Humphreys, later named Fort Lesley J. McNair, on the Potomac River.

In 1905 when Elihu Root created the General Staff system, the War College was organized as the War Plans branch of the War Department General Staff. Following World War I, a War Plans Division had been established as part of the War Department General Staff, and the War College became the top school in the Army's educational system. Its chief mission was to round out the training of selected officers who were deemed to be the probable military leaders of the future. They came from all branches of the service, including a number of naval officers and a sprinkling of Foreign Service officers from the State Department. Unfortunately, most of the latter group would be withdrawn for active assignments abroad before completion of the course. This situation was corrected following World War II, at least with respect to the newly created National War College, when the increased military commitments of the United States around the world convinced the State Department of the value of training more Foreign Service officers at the War Colleges, and an increase in the Foreign Service made this possible.

The War College course of nine months covered the political and economic aspects as well as the military considerations involved in wartime mobilization of manpower and industry; the correlation and evaluation of political and military intelligence; the command relations between Army and Navy forces; possible interallied command relationships; as well as strategic war plans for national emergencies —a fascinating gamut of subjects to which the American public rarely gave thought prior to World War II.

I was fortunate in serving three years at the Army War College,

1937–1940, one year as a student and two as an instructor. The Commandant during most of my stay was Major General John L. DeWitt, a fine, able officer. The faculty was organized in the usual four staff groups covering personnel matters, intelligence, operations, and logistics, with a fifth "war plans" division. There were no rigid dividing lines in the faculty, the full resources of which were often pooled. I was lucky to be assigned to the war plans division under Colonel Edward P. King, a wonderful man, who later had the onerous responsibility of surrendering our forces on Bataan. Colonel William H. Simpson, who commanded the Fifth Army with great distinction in World War II, headed the G-1 division. My old confrere from Benning, Captain Bolté, was in the G-3 division. In the next three years, Charlie and I, and our families, cemented our deep friendship which lasts to this day.

I think everyone who ever attended the War College looks back on his time there as one of the finest periods of his life. As at Benning, under George C. Marshall, the students and faculty alike were interesting, able people, and the atmosphere at the college was stimulating. My year as a student merges in my memory with my years on the faculty because, except for the instructors' monitoring student studies and giving a few lectures, there was little distinction between students and faculty. No one pretended that the "instructors" knew more about a given subject than the students. The faculty simply posed questions that the War Department or the College thought were worthy of inquiry. The students worked in committees, the composition of which changed with each subject, each with a student chairman and a faculty consultant. Committees were given two weeks or so to thrash out their views. They were required to submit brief written reports in support of their conclusions and recommendations. Then the chairmen, with the assistance of any additional speakers they desired, presented oral versions of their reports to the assembled college, using such charts, maps, or other visual aids as they desired. Each presentation was followed by a free and open discussion by the student body, with no holds barred.

The same type of discussion followed the faculty lectures which introduced each new subject. The faculty spokesmen outlined the basic principles and spelled out the generally accepted doctrine and possible variations before opening the matter for general discussion. The Commandant, General DeWitt, set the tone for discussions early in my first year at the college. The subject then was the tactics and technique of the employment of fighter bombers in support of an infantry attack. Little doctrine had been developed on this subject in 1937, and there were differences of opinion between the Infantry, the Army Air Corps, and the Marines on several aspects of this important subject, particularly as to control of the bombers. The chief faculty adviser was an Air Corps officer, a somewhat opinionated man who tended to be dogmatic. He had set out in his lecture a procedure for the control of supporting aviation which was contrary to the views of many aviators. At the conclusion of his talk there was a perceptible hesitation on the part of the class before anyone spoke up. Then Captain Hubert R. "Doodle" Harmon (later the first Superintendent of the Air Force Academy) rose and said he first wanted to apologize for disagreeing with the views of the instructor. General DeWitt—who attended most lectures and discussion periods—was on his feet in an instant: "Harmon, you don't have to apologize to anyone! Say what *you* think, and don't worry about hurting anyone's feelings! "

A lively discussion followed, which became the pattern for the remainder of the year and the rest of the time I was at the college. On several occasions naval officers among the students commented to me that they were amazed at the freedom of thought encouraged at the Army War College, in contrast to the Naval War College. This right to dissent was carried over into the National War College, which was patterned generally on the Army College, largely through the influence of General Alfred M. Gruenther, the first Assistant Commandant of the national college.

The last few months of the course were devoted chiefly to war plans, or more accurately the technique of preparation of war plans. Unfortunately, we were not permitted to see any actual war plans of the War Department on which we might have based our studies. This prohibition probably dated back to an incident that occurred in the early days of World War I, prior to our entry into that war. The War Plans Branch, a component of the War Plans Division of the War Department General Staff, was located at the Army War College. President Woodrow Wilson, then dedicated to a policy of neutrality, had been infuriated by an item he had read in his morning newspaper. General Tasker H. Bliss was said to have recorded the incident in a memorandum in his own handwriting as follows:

> It was early in the autumn of 1915. I was Acting Chief of Staff. Mr. Breckinridge was, for a day or two, Acting Secretary of War. He came into my office early one morning and said that the President had summoned him a few minutes before. He found him holding a copy of the Baltimore Sun in his hand, "trembling and white with passion." The President pointed to a little paragraph of two lines in an out-of-the-way part of a sheet, evidently put in just to fill a space. It read something like this! "It is understood that the General Staff is preparing a plan in the event of war with Germany."
>
> The President asked Mr. Breckinridge if he supposed that was true. Mr. Breckinridge said that he did not know. The President directed him to make an immediate investigation and, if it proved true, to relieve at once every officer of the General Staff and order him out of Washington. Mr. Breckinridge put the investigation up to me.
>
> I told him that the law creating the General Staff made it its duty "to prepare plans for the national defense"; that I was President of the War College when the General Staff was organized in 1903; that from that time till then the College had studied over and over again plans for war with Germany, England, France, Italy, Japan, Mexico, etc. I said that if the President took the action threatened, it would only make patent to everybody what pretty much everybody already knew and would create a great political row, and, finally, it would be absurd.
>
> I think the President realized this in a cooler moment. Nothing further was said to him about the matter, nor did he again mention it. But Mr. Breckinridge directed me to caution the War College to "camouflage" its work. It resulted in practically no further *official* studies. *

In any event, we did not have access to any real plans and had to develop our own theoretical ones. They covered a possible war with Japan, in which the Philippines would be involved, a limited conflict with Mexico, and even the highly unlikely possibility of war with Canada, which would bring in the United Kingdom. These studies were of value to the students in that they learned what constituted a

---

*From Palmer's *Newton D. Baker*, Vol. I, pp. 40–41. I have sought in vain for the original of this note in the National Archives, the Library of Congress, and the files of the War Department.

war plan, the scope of military intelligence that would be required, the logistical support that would have to be provided, the combined Army, Navy, and Air operations that would have to be planned, and the political economic factors that would have to be considered.

War Clouds Gather

While we were thus peacefully engaged at the War College, the situation in Europe, created by the rise to power of Adolf Hitler and his successive violations of the Treaty of Versailles and the Locarno Pact of 1925, reached new intensity with Germany's annexation of Austria in 1938. Having been stationed on the Rhine while the Versailles Treaty was being drafted, I had been dismayed by the failure of the French government to mobilize its army when Hitler reoccupied the Ruhr in 1936, and I was further convinced of the likelihood of a major war when Neville Chamberlain and Edouard Daladier, the prime ministers of the United Kingdom and France, abjectly agreed at Munich on September 30, 1938, to the dismemberment of Czechoslovakia. Germany took over all of Czechoslovakia in the spring of 1939 and began to put pressure on Poland. Our War Department had been kept informed of the growing menace of Hitler's military power by the reports from Berlin by our able military attaché there, Major Truman Smith.

Word of these reports trickled down to us at the War College, but I can well remember the shock we all had when, in 1939 or early 1940, in a lecture at the War College, Truman Smith ran his pointer across a map of Europe from the North Cape in Norway, through the Saar Basin in France, down the length of Italy, and stated categorically that this line was Hitler's goal of German hegemony in western Europe. Few in authority in Washington would believe Truman, and when he later began to talk publicly of the threat of war he was accused by some elements of the press as being a warmonger and, ironically, pro-German.

Germany attacked Poland on September 1, 1939, the day General Marshall was sworn in as Chief of Staff of the United States Army. Britain and France declared war on Germany, in accord with their treaty obligations to Poland, on September 3. A British expeditionary force was moved to France at once and, along with the French, took positions along the fortified Maginot Line which extended from Switzerland to the Belgian frontier. Unfortunately, Belgium, relying on its policy of neutrality, never prepared its defenses north of the Maginot Line, and no integrated plan of defense was prepared with the British and French. Hitler was free to overrun Poland by the end of September, and to occupy Denmark and Norway, with only futile opposition from Britain, in the spring of 1940. He made no move against the western front during the period of the "phony war" until he launched his blitzkrieg on May 10, 1940.

Meanwhile, the Secretary of War, Henry L. Stimson, and General Marshall moved to prepare our army for possible involvement in the war. The organization of the Army was revamped, and an increase in the strength of the Army was approved by a reluctant Congress. To help train the expanding forces additional experienced Regular officers had to be made available. The Command and General Staff College was suspended in February of 1940 and the War College in early June, and their students and faculty were assigned to key command and staff positions throughout the Army.

Shortly after General Marshall became Chief of Staff I had a call from Lieutenant Colonel Orlando P. Ward, the Secretary of the War Department General Staff: "Collins, General Marshall says to get out your Benning drill regulations. He wants to put them into effect without delay. Check them over again and submit them directly to this office." In a matter of weeks the new regulations were made mandatory for the expanding Army, saving countless training hours. Despite the dire forbodings of the Chief of Infantry, the Army managed to survive.

When the War College was suspended in June, 1940, I was put on temporary duty with the Secretariat of the General Staff in General Marshall's office, where I joined Omar Bradley, Stanley R. Mickelson, Walter Bedell "Beetle" Smith, and Maxwell D. Taylor—a high-caliber group. The function of the Secretariat was to assist the Chief of Staff with his correspondence, to keep him up with his appointments, and more importantly to save time for him and his deputies in their decisions. Brigadier General William Bryden had become Deputy Chief of Staff upon the retirement of Major General Lorenzo D. Gasser, May

31, 1940. By the fall of 1940 General Marshall found it necessary to designate two additional deputies; Major General Richard C. Moore for supply matters and Major General Henry H. "Hap" Arnold for air, in addition to his duty as Chief of the Air Corps. The Chief of Staff gradually decentralized authority to his deputies to decide matters within their areas of responsibility.

Studies calling for decision by the Chief or one of the deputies were prepared in the appropriate divisions of the General Staff. Action papers based on these studies were routed through the office of Colonel Ward, who allocated them to one of his assistants for presentation to one of the deputies, or directly to the Chief. Each of us on the Secretariat was assigned from five to ten papers every day. While I was there we had no special assignment of subjects. We reviewed our papers, checked them for obvious errors, and any loose ends or unclear points which we believed would raise questions by the Chief, or Deputy, and then "briefed" a deputy, or the Chief, on each of our completed papers.

General Marshall required that all staff papers, no matter how complicated the subject, be reduced to two pages or less. The format was fairly rigid: first, a statement of the problem; next, factors bearing on the problem, pro and con; a brief discussion, if necessary; conclusions; and finally, and most important, recommended action. Aspects of the subject requiring more detailed background, discussion, or explanation, would be covered by "tabs" which could be attached to the basic papers but only briefly noted therein. The file on a very involved subject might be an inch or more thick, but the material calling for a decision had to be reduced to not more than two pages. This forced careful analysis by the staff, which led to definitive recommendations.

We on the Secretariat made our presentations orally, using the minimum of notes, restricting ourselves to the key points of each paper. We had to be prepared to answer any questions from the Chief or Deputy, or to elaborate on any point they wished amplified. Papers requiring a letter from the Chief of Staff or a major decision affecting policy would always be presented to the Chief. General Marshall had known each member of the Secretariat during our prior service and respected our judgment. We were encouraged to express any disagreement we might have with the proposed recommendations, or make any other suggestion that we felt worthwhile.

Occasionally we would be given special assignments beyond our normal duties. I was once asked to review the Ordnance Department's plans and procedures for the procurement of ammunition. This was before the powerful Chiefs of the Services, who, by acts of Congress, had considerable authority independent of the General Staff, were brought under the control of Brigadier General Brehon B. Somervell, then G-4 of the Army. The Chief of Ordnance was not enthusiastic about having an officer from the Secretariat of the General Staff inquiring into the operations of his office, but I did get the information General Marshall wanted.

A more interesting assignment was to accompany General Marshall to meetings of the Standing Liaison Committee established in 1938, to maintain liaison between the State, War, and Navy Departments. The Under Secretary of State, Sumner Welles, the Army Chief of Staff, and the Chief of Naval Operations comprised the committee. I accompanied General Marshall to one of the first meetings of this committee. On the way to the meeting I rode with the General in his car. I recall clearly his saying that he was determined to have the State Department in on our war planning in order that our military plans would be in step with our foreign policy, giving me the impression that this had not been done in the past. *

On more than one occasion while I was serving on temporary duty with the Secretariat, Colonel Ward had spoken to me about making my assignment permanent. Each time I demurred, hoping to get a command assignment with troops. Finally, in late December, 1940, Ward said that General Marshall had instructed him to have me detailed to the General Staff and assigned to the secretariat. I asked if I might speak to the General about this before any orders were issued,

---

*General Marshall's role in this matter has been questioned by Mark G. Watson in his excellent volume in the War Department's official history, *Chief of Staff: Prewar Plans and Preparations*. (See footnotes p. 90 and memo, IGS, dated Sept. 11, 1940, on file in National Archives.)

to which Colonel Ward agreed. When I went in to see the Chief, I said, "General, I understand you have told Colonel Ward to have me detailed to the General Staff and assigned here to the Secretariat." The General nodded concurrence without a word. I said, "General, do you remember the time down at Benning when you told Captain Bolté and me, 'If there is ever another war in the offing, don't let them stick you on a staff job as was done with me'?" General Marshall laughed aloud and replied, smiling, "All right, Collins, I will let you go."

A few days later I was surprised when Major General Frederick H. Smith stopped at my desk and said he had just been informed by the Chief of Staff that he was to take command of a new Army Corps being formed to supervise the training of three National Guard Divisions, and that General Marshall had suggested that he ask me to be his Chief of Staff. I swallowed hard on that for a moment, then said I had been stalling off a General Staff detail in the hope of getting a command job. General Smith said he knew just how I felt, that as a younger man he had twice refused to be executive officer for the Chief of Coast Artillery, and that he would not urge me against my wishes, though he would like very much to have me. I asked time to think it over, to which he agreed.

A little later, General Marshall called me into his office to tell me that he had suggested to General Smith—who was a Coast Artilleryman—that it might be a good idea for him to have an infantryman as his Chief of Staff, and that, along with some others, he had recommended me. He said he thought that I might be able to get a National Guard regiment, but that this job, with a corps of three divisions, might offer an opportunity even for a brigade, if the divisions should run into trouble and need help. It was a gamble that I would have to evaluate.

After a visit to the office of the Chief of Infantry, where I was informed that there was no chance, on a seniority basis, of my getting a regiment, I decided to take the job. I called General Smith's attention to the fact that I was pretty junior, but he said that as he was junior in rank to two of the division commanders he did not mind having a young staff. He went on to say that after we had gotten the Corps well on the way, if an opportunity arose for me to get a command he would be glad to let me go. On January 3, 1941, General Smith and I left Washington for Memphis to report to Lieutenant General Ben Lear, the commander of the Second Army, under whom the VII Corps was to serve. I did not dream then that three years later I would command this same Corps when it landed in Normandy.

CHAPTER VII

Chief of Staff
VII Corps

General Frederick H. Smith was a quiet, self-possessed professional soldier, with an air of natural dignity that attracted me to him at once. I had not known him, but he had served with Gladys' father, Chaplain Easterbrook, who was fond of him, as I soon became. He reminded me of General Cocheu, with the same sound judgment and lack of pretense. Having neither arrogance nor any lack of self-confidence, he was prepared to decentralize appropriate authority to me and to other members of his staff, while retaining the power of decision in all matters of major importance. He demonstrated these qualities when I told him I accepted his offer to be his Chief of Staff. He said that as a Coast Artilleryman he had been out of touch with the mobile forces of the Army and knew few of the up-and-coming younger officers of the infantry, artillery, and cavalry. He wanted to have a competent young staff, so gave me carte blanche in picking the principal General Staff members.

The War Department had already assigned as Assistant Chief of Staff, G-2, Intelligence, Lieutenant Colonel A. H. Reeves, whom neither the General nor I knew. I moved at once, from my vantage point on the Secretariat of the War Department General Staff, to secure two outstanding officers, to serve in the most important staff positions— G-3, Operations and Training, and G-4, Logistics. For G-3 we obtained Major John R. Hodge, from my class at Benning, and Major John E. Hull, who had impressed me most favorably at the War College, to be G-4. Knowing that the chief task of the VII Corps, with a limited number of Regular Army officers on its staff, would be to supervise the training of three National Guard divisions, I had suggested to General Smith, and he agreed, that we should pick men for their broad ability rather than for any staff specialty they might have, and that the three chief combatant branches should be represented in the four divisions of the General Staff. The G-2, Reeves, was a field artilleryman; Hodge and Hull were both infantrymen. I sought and secured a cavalryman for the remaining spot, G-1, Personnel, Major Thomas J. Heavey, whom I had known at West Point. The remainder of the staff was selected by the War Department in normal fashion.

With our principal staff officers confirmed, General Smith and I flew from Washington on January 3, 1941, to Memphis, where General Smith reported to Major General Ben Lear, commanding the Second Army, of which the VII Corps was to be an element. General Lear was a big, gruff cavalryman, about whom I knew little. But there was something about him that I instinctively felt boded future trouble. His Chief of Staff, Brigadier General Donald A. Robinson, was both able and likable, as was the G-3, Brigadier General Harry L. Twaddle, whom I had known slightly at Benning. They and the other members of the Second Army staff gave every evidence of being fully cooperative with our fledgling Corps.

At Second Army headquarters we learned further details of the composition, commanders, and location of the major units of the VII Corps:

> 27th Division, New York National Guard, Major General William M. Haskell, mobilized October 15, 1940, at Fort McClellan, Anniston, Alabama.
>
> 35th Division, Kansas, Missouri and Nebraska National Guard, Major General Ralph E. Truman, mobilized December 23, 1940, at Camp Robinson, Little Rock, Arkansas.
>
> 33d Division, Illinois, National Guard, Major General Samuel T. Lawton, not yet mobilized but scheduled for March 15, 1941, at Camp Forrest, Tullahoma, Tennessee.

From Memphis, General Smith and I flew down to Fort McClellan where a temporary headquarters had been set up by the Adjutant General, Lieutenant Colonel J. J. Teter, the first officer assigned to the Corps when it was activated by the War Department on November 26, 1940. General Smith had been stationed at McClellan years before. He was well and favorably known to the people of Anniston, who were anxious to have the Corps headquarters remain in Anniston. But it is never wise to impose a high headquarters on top of a major subordinate unit, and the General wanted a location more central to the three divisions of the Corps, with better road, rail, and air communications. He chose Birmingham.

As soon as the location of Corps headquarters in Birmingham was assured, I began looking there for a place for my family. Downtown Birmingham was dirty and smoky from the coal mines and steel mills, but the air was clear on the upper reaches of Iron Mountain and beyond on the south side of the city. I was lucky to find a house, at 4216 Clairmont Avenue, on the slope of the mountain, within walking distance of the school our children would be attending. I rented it before returning to Washington to pick up the family.

The family drove down to Birmingham in time to be there for the opening of Corps headquarters in the Ramsey-McCormack building in Ensley, one of the smokiest suburbs of Birmingham. The building had the advantage of being new and almost empty, affording space for our headquarters as we gradually gained our full complement of officers and men. Most of the officers came from the lists of Reserve officers in the Fourth Corps Area, the regional administrative agency, with headquarters in Atlanta, that serviced units in the southeastern United States. They were, generally, an able group of men, a number of whom remained with VII Corps headquarters throughout World War II.

Training Programs and Tests

In the summer of 1940, as the threat of war increased, the War Department had activated General Headquarters at the Army War College in Washington, as an embryonic command post for any expeditionary force that might have to be sent abroad. Meanwhile it was to supervise the organization and training of the expanding Army. General Marshall selected Major General Lesley J. McNair to be Chief of Staff of GHQ, with an exceptionally able 1917 West Point classmate of mine, Lieutenant Colonel Mark Wayne Clark, as his G-3. Clark soon moved up to be McNair's Deputy Chief of Staff for Training.

The broad program formulated by GHQ was the first integrated training program in the history of the United States Army. It was designed to develop progressively the training of individuals and small units up through battalions, divisions, corps, and field armies. It was intended principally for the National Guard and Organized Reserve units called to active duty and newly created divisions and service units of the expanding Regular Army. The Mobilization Training Program (MTP) consisted of four principal parts: first, a thirteen-week period of individual and small-unit training, later increased to seventeen weeks; second, a period of MTP tests to check progress attained in the first period; third, a post-test period to correct deficiencies developed by the MTP tests; and finally a series of division, corps, and army maneuvers. For the first time in peace, tactical corps headquarters, such as the VII Corps, distinct from the existing Corps Area service commands, were created to supervise the training of divisions and supporting units and to participate in the field maneuvers. Corps headquarters operated under the direction of the four field army headquarters established in 1932 by General MacArthur while he was Chief of Staff.

Mobilization Training Tests, 27th Division

The 27th Division had been mobilized prior to organization of the VII Corps. The MTP tests of the 27th Division, the first to be held anywhere, were scheduled for February 25 and 28, 1941. Since our VII Corps headquarters was not fully established until early February, and since we had no precedents, the Corps staff had to work overtime to be ready by the twenty-fifth.

The entire Corps staff worked under the supervision of John Hodge in the preparation and conduct of the tests held at McClellan. Colonel Hull wrote and conducted the tests of rifle units, including battalion tactical exercises; Colonel Heavey handled the heavy-weapons tests; and special staff officers checked engineer, signal, quartermaster, and other service units. Lacking an experienced artilleryman, we borrowed Brigadier General Cortland Parker from Second Army for the artillery tests. Additional testing officers were drawn from other units of the Second Army to assist the VII Corps staff; they were all carefully briefed.

In accord with GHQ instructions, General Smith had decided to check particularly for proficiency in the techniques of weapons and the tactics of small units, so that we had allotted only a little time to such items as saluting, displays of equipment, and close-order drill. We had all worked hard and were confident we had designed an excellent series of tests. General Smith had not been very well for a while and did not accompany the Corps staff to Fort McClellan for the opening days of the tests. He designated me to represent him.

General Lear and members of his staff, and observers from GHQ, arrived at McClellan on the afternoon before the tests. We had provided them all with copies of our detailed test program. Shortly after his arrival, General Lear summoned me to his office. It was apparent at once that he was in a bad humor, perhaps because General Smith was not present, though I do not know that this was the case. He was holding in his hands a sheaf of our tests which he tossed scornfully on his desk, saying brusquely that he didn't think much of them. He was especially wrought up over the fact that we had provided for only a half hour of close-order drill for each company, and comparable short periods for ceremonial inspections, and had omitted any check on the proper method of saluting. I explained that we had deliberately saved time from such formalities—in which most National Guard units were quite proficient from their hometown armory drills and ceremonies—in order to test thoroughly the skills they should have acquired at McClellan in the techniques of fire support of machine guns, mortars, and artillery, and the tactics of units up to battalions. I did not give an inch in defending our program. Lear did not order any changes, and I did not volunteer any.

But for the next two days, while Hodge and his assistants went ahead with our tests, Lear devoted his time and attention almost exclusively to close-order drill and checks of individuals in the proper method of saluting and reporting to an officer. According to reports I received from our testing officers, Lear went from company to company calling for drills, without regard to our test schedule. Fortunately, General McNair came to Fort McClellan before the tests were over, and I spent most of a day with him. He was highly pleased with what he saw and agreed thoroughly with our emphasis on the technical training of supporting-weapons crews and the tactics of small units in attack and defense. He must have so reported to General Lear, because we heard no further criticism.

At the critique following the tests, General McNair opened his remarks by stating: "I want to congratulate wholeheartedly the Army Commander for initiating the inspection tests, (and) the Corps Commander and his staff for preparing and executing the tests." After reviewing some of his experiences, he concluded: "I don't say this is the only way in which a division can be tested, but it is the best test that I have ever seen." Colonel Clark, McNair's Chief of Staff, after reviewing the reports of the GHQ observers, wrote in a memorandum for McNair: "I feel that the method used by the VII Corps in testing the results of the 27th Division's MTP training is excellent. The tests are broad in scope and cover all elements of the division." Our 27th Division test became a model, not only for tests of the 35th Division in May and the 33rd Division in July, but for other units of the Second Army.

General Richardson Succeeds General Smith

Following our MTP test of the 33rd Division in July, 1941, the last in the VII Corps, General Smith was replaced in command of the Corps by Major General Robert C. Richardson, Jr. I do not know the reason back of this change but suspect that Lear, and perhaps General Marshall, had become convinced that Smith was not in sufficiently robust health to warrant his continuance in command. We all greatly enjoyed serving under General Smith and hated to see him leave, but realized that at age sixty-two he was too old, and out of touch with developments, for even a training-corps command.

General Richardson was a cavalryman, an accomplished horseman, with a broad and varied service in command and staff positions. He was adept at languages and had taught French and later served as Commandant of Cadets at West Point; he had attended the École Supérieure de Guerre in Paris, done a tour as military attaché in Rome, and had been Director of Public Relations in the War Department. Despite the fact that as a young lieutenant he had been wounded in action fighting the Moros in the Philippines, and just prior to the outbreak of World War II had commanded the 1st Cavalry Division on the Texas border, he had the aura of a staff officer rather than a troop commander. I have often been impressed with how accurately the nickname that an officer acquires in the Army portrays his characteristics, if not his real character. While a cadet at West Point in the class of 1904, Richardson was known as Nell. This became Nellie out in the service. Richardson was unquestionably an able man, but he was also finicky, a stickler for protocol, and, at times, inordinately sensitive—characteristics that led to our crossing swords temporarily not long after he took over the VII Corps.

His method of exercising command was quite different from that of General Smith, who never hesitated to delegate authority. Perhaps we on the staff under Smith had taken such delegation too much for granted. We had become accustomed to following staff procedures as taught at the Command and General Staff College, and as I had practiced under Cocheu in the Philippine Division. When a task developed, such as a directive from the Second Army to prepare a division training test, Smith and I would discuss the matter and he would give me orally a broad outline of what he wanted to have included in the test, and generally how he wanted it conducted. He would then turn the directive over to me to initiate plans by the staff sections, which would become the basis for our tentative program. I would have informal discussions with the section chiefs as the plans developed. Smith would sometimes join our discussions. I always kept him informed of our progress and transmitted to the appropriate staff members any additional instructions from the General. This system seemed to work well and we were complimented by one of the senior inspecting groups from GHQ, which had inquired into our procedures. We naturally continued this system when Richardson assumed command.

The transition went along smoothly until one day Richardson walked into my office and discovered that I had had a large airplane mosaic map of one of our training areas mounted on the wall of the office—without consulting him as to where he might want it placed. He was furious. He said he had heard reports that I had been de facto commander under General Smith, but he wanted me to understand that *he* was in command, that *he* would make all the decisions, and added something to the effect that he would not tolerate any encroachment upon his authority.

I was dumbfounded at this wholly unexpected tirade. I told him that I had no idea where he had gotten his reports but they were not true. I outlined how General Smith did delegate authority to the staff on minor matters, under policies established by him; that the General made all major decisions; and that there was never any question in our minds as to who was commanding the Corps. I suggested that if he wished to verify these facts, he should talk to Colonels Hodge and Hull. Then, looking Richardson directly in the eye, I said, "General, if I can't decide such matters as to where to hang a map, you have the wrong man as your Chief of Staff!" At that he apparently was as taken aback as I had been at his initial onslaught. I do not recall exactly his reply, but it was to the effect that he did not want me to take what he had said quite so seriously, and that he was sure our relations would work out all right.

After this flareup we changed little if anything in our method of operating. I told only Hodge and Hull about this incident, and told them we would have to bend over backwards in keeping the General informed of our activities, but that we would proceed in the same way as in the past, unless Richardson directed otherwise. As far as I know, he mentioned our little tiff to no one, and he issued no instructions to change our operating procedure. The resultant stiffness in our personal relations gradually passed off as the period of division and corps maneuvers got under way. Richardson soon came to realize that he did have an exceptional staff. *

The Tennessee Maneuvers—June, 1941

Division maneuvers had been conducted by the Army in years past, but the size and scope of the 1941 maneuvers far exceeded any held theretofore. Never before had the War Department been able to persuade the Congress of the value of such large-scale exercises or to appropriate the sizable funds required to cover such items as the movement of troops and supplies, the rental of additional service facilities, and the settlement of claims for damages to crops and other private property caused by the movement of troops and military equipment, especially tanks. The maneuvers during the summer and fall of 1941,

* This is not an idle boast. The three key members, Hodge, Hull, and Collins all rose to four-star rank.

in which the VII Corps participated, took place in Tennessee, Arkansas, and Louisiana, areas in which there were several large military reservations and great tracts of federal or state-owned timber lands that were made available to the Army at relatively low cost.

Under the GHQ training program, after divisions had completed their MTP tests and had taken steps to correct deficiencies uncovered in the tests, they were deemed ready to participate in field exercises conducted by Corps and Army headquarters. Since VII Corps was the first such headquarters established in the Second Army, our staff did the pioneering work for the first maneuvers for divisions of that Army. These Corps exercises were held during the period June 1–15, 1941, and were followed by two weeks of maneuvers planned and conducted by Second Army. All were conducted while General Smith was in command of VII Corps.

The maneuver area included the Camp Forrest reservation and adjacent territory bounded by the towns Murfreesboro, Manchester, Tullahoma, and Shelbyville, which had been the scene of fighting in the Tullahoma and Stone River campaigns of 1862 and 1863 in the Civil War. While making our reconnaissance I had brought along my West Point Civil War history. Though we did not base our maneuver plans on those campaigns, it was interesting to check their actions on the ground. One phase of an attack maneuver we planned did follow a route frequently used by the Cherokee Indians in their early wars. It passed through backwoods towns with such fascinating names as War Trace and Bell Buckle, some of which did not show on our road maps. At one point on an old Indian trail which we had been traveling laboriously around a good-sized hill, we stopped at a crossroads where a few ramshackle houses were huddled. We asked a tobacco-chewing old gentleman to tell us where we were. His reply delighted us: "We call this place Fudge Around." There was never a more appropriate name. We duly recorded it on our map. I hope it is still there.

The Corps exercises included two command-post exercises, three controlled field exercises, and one two-sided free maneuver. A free maneuver is one that has no fixed scenario. The action develops as determined by the decisions and orders of the opposing commanders. The units involved were the 5th, 27th, and 30th Infantry Divisions, the 2nd Armored Division, the 153rd Infantry, and two bombardment squadrons of the Army Air Corps. Only one of the divisions, the 27th, had undergone training in the VII Corps. They were all inexperienced, as were the umpires. New rules were used to assess the effects of simulated artillery and tank fire and bombing. There was much confusion. We were cramming too much, too soon, in these early exercises. Nevertheless, though many deficiencies were found, especially in basic individual and small-unit training, General McNair wrote on July 16, 1941, to the Commanding General, Second Army: "These maneuvers are regarded as the best conceived, best executed and most successful witnessed by this headquarters to date."

Arkansas Maneuvers—August, 1941

The VII Corps exercises in Arkansas in August, following the MTP tests of the 33rd Division the previous month, were the first conducted under the direction of General Richardson. They were designed primarily to provide combined training for the three National Guard divisions of the Corps, only one of which, the 27th, had been through the Tennessee maneuvers. By then, Richardson had gained some confidence in the Corps staff.

The Arkansas maneuvers followed the same general pattern as those conducted in Tennessee, with two weeks of exercises conducted by VII Corps, followed by a series of maneuvers planned and directed by the Second Army. The troops involved were all from the VII Corps, including the 27th, 33rd, and 35th Divisions, the 75th Artillery Brigade, 153rd Infantry, the 107th Cavalry, three VII Corps observation squadrons, and Corps engineer, signal, quartermaster, and other service troops, totaling some 77,000 men. This time we knew all the troops and their commanders, and took a more gradual approach to the successive preliminary exercises, leading up to a final two-sided free maneuver. In addition, one battalion in each division of the Corps participated in a crossing of the Red River under assumed battle conditions, which proved of great value in the subsequent GHQ maneuvers in Louisiana

All these exercises were held in an area between the Little Missouri and Red Rivers in southwest Arkansas, centered generally around the towns of Prescott and Hope. The Prescott-Hope area had been selected by GHQ and the Second Army somewhat as a staging place en route to Louisiana, where large-scale maneuvers between the Second and Third Armies were to be held in September. The VII Corps exercises worked out well and provided excellent preparation for the more difficult two-sided maneuvers, conducted by the Second Army as the troops moved down into Louisiana, south of Shreveport.

It was in Arkansas that we first encountered problems with segregated all-Negro troops, of which there were a few in the 33rd Division. We were generally able to arrange for the use by the troops of bathing facilities in the gymnasiums of schools, most of which were closed for the summer. But several communities refused to allow the use of facilities in white schools by black troops. This caused some difficulty, because mobile bath units were new to the Army and insufficient in number. We could usually get around this problem by using Negro schools and the few available quartermaster bath units.

A potentially dangerous situation developed one day as a National Guard black company from Illinois was marching down the main highway between Prescott and Hope. An Arkansas state police car passed by with two troopers and two white women passengers who, if my memory serves me right, later investigation indicated had been picked up as vagrants in a nearby town by the police. The troops were alleged to have shouted obscenities at the women as they passed. A telephone call to Corps headquarters from a friendly townsman in a nearby village reported that a possible riot was brewing because of some trouble with a company of black troops down the road.

I reported the call to General Richardson, who approved my suggestion that I drive at once to the scene to see what needed to be done. As I passed through a small town, a little group of wild-eyed men, armed with squirrel rifles and shotguns, was gathering at a crossroad on the highway. Without stopping I proceeded a mile or so until I came upon the company, the men of which were sitting quietly on the grass to one side of the road. The company commander, a black captain, reported to me that as the police car had driven by his marching company at high speed, some of his men had called out in protest. The state troopers stopped a distance beyond the company, then drove back, and with drawn pistols, ordered the company off the road. By the time I reached the scene the police had departed without further incident, and I was unable to verify the captain's account. I told him to get his company back on the road, but suggested that he bypass the next town en route to his nearby camp. I did my best to assure him that his unit would not be further molested.

I then drove back to the town where the excited group of citizens had quieted down a bit. I identified myself to the group and, addressing myself chiefly to a responsible looking man who seemed less agitated than the others, told them the story as recounted to me by the company commander. Apparently this differed radically from the account given in the town by the state troopers as they passed through on the way to wherever they had taken the two women. I explained quietly to them that the Negro soldiers were federal troops, participating in official maneuvers, and had every right, which we intended to maintain, to move freely on the highways. I said also that General Richardson, a South Carolinian, and I from New Orleans, appreciated their sensitivity in regard to black troops, but we could guarantee that our units were well disciplined and would cause no trouble. I appealed to their common sense and suggested that they return to their homes and put up their weapons. They accepted my suggestion with no argument, offered no threats, and dispersed quietly.

I reported back to Richardson, who agreed that it was fortunate we were both southerners. The incident was duly investigated but I have found no record of it now in the official files. I did file it away in my mind where it helped years later, along with other more important events, to convince me that we should do away with segregation in the Army.

Louisiana Maneuvers—September, 1941

The culminating field maneuvers of 1941 were to be free, two-sided exercises conducted under the direction of GHQ in Louisiana. Troops of the Second Army under Lear and the Third Army, commanded by Lieutenant General Walter E. Krueger, were to be the chief opponents, supported by over 1,000 airplanes. Paratroopers, though only a single company, were to be employed for the first time. Another first was the projected introduction of an experimental Armored Corps, consisting of the 1st and 2nd Armored Divisions. In the same experimental category was to be the employment of three of the newly organized "triangular" infantry divisions of the Regular Army, operating alongside the "square" (4 regiments) divisions of the National Guard. A fair number of anti-tank units, some still experimental, were available for the first time, as was a supply of dummy anti-tank mines. All told, the troops would total almost 400,000 men. In an attempt to improve the assessment of the effects of aerial bombardment, armored action, artillery and infantry fire, GHQ had prepared a new Umpire's Manual, and an increased number of umpires had been trained. For once there would be room for maneuvers off the roads, and funds to meet claims for damages to fences and crops, so as to eliminate most excuses for troops remaining road-bound in the face of attacks from the air.

GHQ had thus created a sound basis for the largest maneuvers ever to be held in peacetime in the United States. Along with all other participants, the VII Corps looked forward to an interesting fortnight in the field. We were not disappointed. GHQ had planned the exercises in two phases. During the first period, September 14–24, the Second Army was to move southwesterly from the vicinity of Shreveport and engage the Third Army advancing from the Texas-Louisiana border west of New Orleans. Depending on how this action developed, the second phase was to require the Third Army to drive the Lear forces back north and capture Shreveport by the end of the maneuver period on September 28.

Great public interest was generated in these exercises, recognized as essential training in the event that we became involved in World War II. The press, which was well represented, naturally looked for a winner between the opposing doughty commanders, Lear and Kreuger, both of whom had come up from the ranks of the Army and had reputations of being tough competitors. The participation of an armored Corps, under the command of Major General George S. Patton, who had already become a popular swashbuckling figure, whetted the interest of the newsmen in the possibility of a "blitzkrieg." These objectives were not intended by General McNair, who was more interested in gauging the progress of the troops in their training, the development of skills in such difficult operations as river crossing, and their ability not only to exploit but to counter armored forces, and to meet the threat of aerial attacks.

At the opening gun the Second Army was northeast of the Red River near Alexandria, with the Third Army some distance to the south and southwest. The missions assigned the two Armies by GHQ required each of them to attack in a meeting engagement. The Third Army had no way, initially, of knowing the intentions of its opponent but evidently expected to find it in a defensive position north of the Red River.

Lear, perhaps influenced by a recommendation from General Richardson, decided to hold the north bank of the Red River with a light covering force and cross the bulk of his Army to the south side so as to position it on the left flank of the Third Army as the latter prepared to attack north across the river. The crossings apparently were not immediately discovered by the Third Army. The Second Army was thus favorably positioned to strike the left flank of the Third Army as it was crossing, or preparing to cross, the river. For some reason, which I have never been able to fathom, Lear did not launch his attack at once. The Third Army was able to regroup, change its front so as to checkmate the Second Army, and then, with its greater strength, force Lear's Army to withdraw.

For the second phase of the exercises, 24–28 September, the two Armies were reconstituted by GHQ. One of the chief interests of GHQ in this phase was to test the ability of anti-tank weapons to neutralize armor. The mission assigned the Second Army was to cover Shreveport. The heavily wooded terrain, crisscrossed by swampy tributaries of the Red River, was not well suited for tank operations. It favored anti-tank mines and weapons, including aircraft, in support of delaying positions back of the many streams. Not even Patton with his 2nd Armored Division could make a breakthrough, though the Third Army gradually drove the Second back. If the maneuver had been allowed to continue past its planned termination on September 28, Shreveport would have been captured by the more powerful Third Army. But the exaggerated notion of the invulnerability of armor was dissipated.

Lessons Learned

The Louisiana maneuvers provided highly valuable training, particularly for the staffs and commanders of the larger units, from divisions up to armies. Many of us were participating in large-scale, free, two-sided maneuvers for the first time under tactical situations that required coordination of infantry and armor, air and ground forces, in attack and defense. Experience was gained in two of the most difficult military operations, withdrawals and river crossings, requiring coordination between engineer and ground troops in building and demolition of bridges, erection of tank obstacles, and the laying and clearing of mine fields. Advantage was taken of the opportunity to experiment with different combinations of infantry, armor, and anti-tank units in corps and armies. The new triangular divisions proved more flexible and manageable than the square divisions, leading ultimately to the triangular organization for both the Regular Army and National Guard.

The logistical experience gained by all units participating in the Louisiana exercises was of value at least equal to tactical and organizational gains. For the first time in any American field exercises, a full-scale logistical framework had been provided by GHQ, including quartermaster, engineer, signal, ordnance, and medical troops and supplies. This offered unique opportunity in peacetime to play out the tremendous task of moving, feeding, and providing shelter and medical care for 400,000 men in the field.

The maneuvers proved of great value also in sorting out the best and the least capable leaders in the officer corps, especially in the upper echelons. Among the senior men who came to the fore were Patton, already marked for high command by General Marshall, and Colonel Dwight D. Eisenhower, the brilliant Chief of Staff of the Third Army, always highly regarded within the Army, but almost unheard of outside. But the men who impressed me most throughout the entire series of maneuvers were McNair and his deputy Clark. McNair, a man with a keen analytical mind, thorough military knowledge, great driving force, and organizing skill, had put together and supervised a training program that was well on its way to transforming the small, inexperienced American Army into a mighty, modern fighting force. Clark, who was the Deputy Director of the Louisiana maneuvers, also distinguished himself and made a major contribution to the maneuvers.

The Louisiana maneuvers turned up continuing deficiencies in the training of individuals and small units. In fact they may have added to these deficiencies. Large-scale field exercises are fine for the larger units and their commanders but are of less value to companies and battalions who get lost in the "big picture." Troops develop bad habits when no bombs are dropped, or weapons fired with live ammunition, neither of which can be done with safety in exercises involving more than a battalion. It is almost impossible to get American soldiers to take seriously attacks from planes that simply fly overhead. Troops tend to stick to the roads instead of moving in deployed formations across country, and they fail to take cover from theoretical bombardment, artillery or machine-gun fire. There are never enough umpires to assess casualties. Recognizing this condition, GHQ prescribed a four-month post-maneuver review of small-unit training in which combat firing was to be emphasized, with GHQ observers attending. Army and Corps commanders were directed to conduct field exercise tests of infantry battalions and cavalry squadrons, with artillery delivering actual overhead fire whenever feasible.

December 7, 1941

The VII Corps was well into this post-maneuver schedule when the Japanese attacked Pearl Harbor. I had just returned home from a Sunday morning round of golf at the Mountain Brook club in Birmingham when I heard a radio announcement of the Japanese attack. I called downstairs to give Gladys the startling news, adding "This means war!" We ate dinner in a daze and spent most of the rest of the day close to the radio, listening avidly to the crumbs of sad news about damage to the fleet, and wondering what effect the attack would have on the VII Corps and our family. We, of course, listened the next day as Congress passed a declaration of war, and on December 9 heard President Roosevelt address the nation and spell out some idea of our losses at Pearl Harbor. But it was not until December 12 that the war had its first direct impact on the VII Corps and our Collins family. Wild rumors of Japanese submarines off the coast of California had appeared in the press following Pearl Harbor. Finally on December 12

I had a call from Wayne Clark at GHQ in Washington saying that VII Corps was to move at once to the West Coast to take command of the defense of Northern California under General DeWitt. Then he asked how soon VII Corps could get under way.

"In two hours," I replied without a moment's hesitation. (We had practiced such a move within that time limit.)

"Oh, that won't be necessary," said Clark, "but if General Richardson, you, and Hodge can take off for Frisco tomorrow it will be fine."

I promptly informed Richardson, and we initiated our standing-operating-procedure (SOP) to get the staff and Headquarters Company under way by rail the next day. Fortunately, our staff airplane, a small four-passenger Beechcraft, was immediately available for the flight to San Francisco. We had it serviced and made ready for departure next morning.

Gladys took the news in stride like the wonderful Army wife she has always been. That evening we talked over plans for the family to join me in California when I had found a place to live and arranged for the children's schooling. The next morning I kissed Gladys and the children goodbye—then did not see them again for two years!

The weather forecast was not favorable, particularly for our light plane. A front was coming in from the west that gave indications of becoming a dangerous storm, but we took off, with Colonel Reeves, our artilleryman, who had a commercial pilot's license, at the controls. Bucking headwinds, we got only as far as Oklahoma City before dark. There we stopped to refuel and to obtain the latest meteorological forecast. It was not encouraging. We were told that if we could get up to 10,000 feet—near the ceiling for our plane—we might be able to get over a snow storm that was coming in. We tried, perhaps foolishly, but could not make it. We ran into the storm shortly after takeoff, and climbed bumpily to almost 12,000 feet through blinding snow. With the plane tossing about, and "St. Elmo" static electricity running along the wings casting a wierd light on the swirling snow, Richardson wisely decided to turn back to Oklahoma City. We landed just as the storm hit there.

The weather the following day was a bit better, though lowering clouds and stiff winds were still threatening. The meteorologist told

Reeves the storm was veering to the south and that we might be able to get around it by heading to the northwest for Reno. He did say that we would have to fly "contact"—there was no electronic guidance system to Reno—and that there was one low mountain pass en route, through which we should have a clearance of only a few hundred feet. His forecast proved accurate. We cleared the pass and made it safely to Reno by dusk. With fresh reports of bad weather to the west, Richardson decided that we had sufficiently tested our valor, and the skill of our pilot. We boarded a train for San Francisco the next morning. It was a good decision. Unbeknown to us, Major General Herbert A. Dargue, one of our pioneer Air Corps officers, flying through the same storm we had encountered, on the first leg of his journey to Hawaii where he was to have replaced Major General Walter C. Short in command of Army Forces there, was killed while trying to fly through the San Gorgonio pass east of Los Angeles. His death was to have a profound effect on my future.

After reporting to DeWitt at the Presidio on December 15, Richardson remained there to be brought up to date on the situation while John Hodge and I drove down to San Jose, designated as VII Corps headquarters. We made tentative arrangements for use of a National Guard armory, then drove back to Frisco to report to Richardson. We had a number of administrative details to look after, so it was near midnight when we turned in at the Presidio.

Richardson, Hodge, and I got an early start for San Jose the following morning. We had still not heard about the death of Dargue and there was nothing about it in the morning papers. We checked in at a hotel in San Jose, then went to the armory where we met Major General White, commanding the 7th Division, already in the area. While the two generals conferred, Hodge and I went into an adjacent office with Colonel John E. McMahon, Jr., White's Chief of Staff. We had scarcely gotten seated when a phone jingled at my elbow. Colonel James L. Bradley, DeWitt's Chief of Staff, was on the phone from the Presidio with a breathtaking message: "Joe, pack up your bags at once and return to San Francisco. You are relieved as Chief of Staff of the VII Corps and appointed Chief of Staff of the Hawaiian Department under General Delos Emmons. He is here now. You are to report to him by six o'clock and will probably fly to Hawaii tonight."

As soon as I could catch my breath, but still in a daze, I went into the next room to break the news to General Richardson. He was as amazed as I was at this sudden turn of events, and was kind enough to say that he felt as if someone had just cut off his right arm. I strongly recommended John Hodge to succeed me. He was immediately available and had earned the job. The General agreed at once. I had told Jim Bradley that I would be at his office in the Presidio by two o'clock, and as it was then almost noon, there was no time for further discussion. We said goodbye all around, and after checking out at the hotel, I was on my way. I still remember the expression on the face of the hotel clerk when I told him I was leaving. I had registered only two hours before. I am sure he was thinking, "There goes another of those crazy Army officers who doesn't know whether he is coming or going." He was right.

By the time I reached the Presidio, Emmons had left DeWitt's headquarters, and Jim Bradley told me of the death of Dargue and of Emmons's appointment to succeed him in relief of General Short in Hawaii, which would not be announced until we reached there. Emmons, whom I had never met, had left word for me to join him at Hamilton Field, just north of San Francisco, by 6:00 P.M. and that we would leave for Hawaii by 8:00 P.M. if a plane was available. Bradley told me that DeWitt and Colonel Beetle Smith, at General Marshall's suggestion I am sure, had arranged for me to talk to Beetle over DeWitt's private command line to the War Department, so that Mrs. Collins would have some word from me before I left.*

DeWitt sent me over by car to Hamilton Field where I reported to Emmons, who greeted me with a cheery smile. After a good dinner at the officers club, we boarded a B-24, a four-motored bomber, that happened to be due to leave for Hawaii that evening. We were its only passengers. At 8:00 P.M. wheels were up and we were off to the war in Hawaii.

---

*I have always credited General Marshall with having arranged for me to talk to Mrs. Collins direct in Birmingham, but that would probably have been impossible at that time. A recent rereading of a letter from me to Mrs. Collins, written that night, en route to Hawaii, confirms that my message to her had to be relayed through Beetle Smith.

CHAPTER VIII

Hawaii,
1941–1942

En Route to Hawaii

The B-24 was an ugly duckling in comparison to its predecessor, the B-17, whose graceful lines made it a thing of beauty in the sky. But the B-24 could carry a bigger bomb load, was faster, and could travel farther on its full load of fuel. We were grateful for this latter capability before this flight of 2,700 miles was over. Being a combat ship, the B-24 had no space for passengers. General Emmons and I had to sit, or stretch out, on narrow padded seats on either side of the bomb bay which, on this trip, was carrying no bombs. It was not sealed tight and cold air swirled around us as the plane climbed to cruising altitude. Fortunately, Emmons had fitted out each of us with a fur-lined flying suit at Hamilton, so that we were quite comfortable at the start.

The propeller-driven engines were noisy, and we were both too tired and absorbed in our own thoughts to do much talking. I started a letter to Gladys, but as our four big motors droned steadily onward I found myself dozing on and off. We were riding above the clouds and with no moon to light the ocean below, I could see only the stars by shielding my eyes from the overhead cabin light while peering out of a little window above my "berth." My old friend Orion looked back at me from the southern sky and pointed the way to the west. The temperature dropped gradually until it must have been near zero, but after a post-midnight snack, and while Emmons had gone forward to get warm, I drifted into a sound sleep. The first light of dawn was showing when I awoke. The General had returned to his berth.

I squeezed my way past the bomb racks and pulled myself up into the navigator's compartment to see how we were getting along. I had been told before we took off that we would not fly a direct great-circle course in order to lessen further the remote chance of interception by any element of the Japanese carrier force. Any variation from a great-circle course might make the task of navigating more difficult. When I entered the navigator's compartment I discovered, to my amazement, that he was a young Air Cadet on his first trans-Pacific flight.* He was getting a fix on our position by taking sightings on three stars through a glass window in the roof of the cramped compartment. He was using the end star in the handle of the Big Dipper, and two first-magnitude stars that I knew well, Arcturus and Vega. The navigator was having some trouble focusing on Arcturus, which I helped him identify. His arms were growing weary from holding up the heavy instrument, but he finally got through, did some rapid figuring, and announced that we were close to our plotted course.

Meanwhile we were flying along smoothly under the sure guidance of the automatic pilot. The Captain, an experienced pilot, occasionally checked dials on the instrument panel while his off-duty assistant dozed quietly in his seat alongside. Soon dawn began to break in the southeast: the sleeping pilot came to life; the crew chief responded to a word from the Captain to synchronize the two left motors better; and the General pulled up through the hatch from the bomb bay, thus crowding the compartment to capacity. By now the cloud tops above which we were flying began to reflect the growing light and to disclose holes in the gray mat of clouds below us, through which we caught glimpses of the dark blue Pacific. Soon the sun burst forth in a blaze of red and gold.

As we approached our Honolulu expected time of arrival (ETA), the Captain took over control from the gyros and spiraled the plane down through a hole in the clouds till we came out in the clear, a thousand or so feet above the water. At this elevation we could not see very far, but as our ETA came and passed there was still no sign of the Hawaiian Islands. The navigator checked the drift and there was some speculation that the head winds were stronger than predicted by the meteorologist at Hamilton Field. Because of the war, there had been no weather reports from ships at sea, and no radio beam from Hickham

---

*Emmons told me later that we had caught the first available plane leaving Hamilton Field for Hawaii and he had not checked the crew.

Field to guide us in. We had to rely on the accuracy of the plotted course, the corrections for wind, magnetic and other variations, and the skill of our young navigator to ensure that somewhere ahead of us in the low-lying clouds was the island of Oahu.

There was no real concern as we ran a half hour past our ETA, because there was plenty of gas in the fuel tanks, which would have permitted several hours of search. But as every island-shaped cloud in the distance turned out to be just a cloud, some tension began to be felt in the group of us—General Emmons, the crew chief, navigator, and I crouched behind the pilots, looking vainly past their shoulders for a glimpse of land. We all breathed easier when the sharp outline of a headland, straight to our front, took shape against a gray background of sea and clouds. It looked quite like Koko Head, on the southeast corner of Oahu, and the pilots laughingly said that they would throw the navigator overboard, like the cockswain of a winning crew, if he had hit Oahu on the nose. But as we got closer, it became clear that the island was not Oahu, though none of us could tell which it was. Then the crew chief recognized a familiar landmark and pronounced, correctly, that we were at the southeast corner of Kauai, the western-most large island of the Hawaiian group. We had slipped past Oahu, about fifteen miles off its north flank, but had not identified it because of the poor visibility. But a miss of only fifteen miles in a flight of 2,700 miles was a tribute to our navigator and we all gave him a rousing cheer. The log showed it was 9:18 A.M., December 17, 1941.

Our course was quickly changed to the southeast and a half hour later we were rounding the real Koko Head and flying along the glamorous waterfront of Honolulu, which showed no signs of war. But the blackened hulls of the battleships of the Pacific Fleet, clearly visible at Pearl Harbor, and damaged hangars at Hickham Field, were tragic reminders that the war was a grim reality, and that from the moment we landed we would share in the grave responsibility of rebuilding our defensive forces in the mid-Pacific and preparing to take the offensive against Japan.

As I recall our arrival, we were met by Vice Admiral William S. Pye, representing Admiral Husband E. Kimmel, Commander in Chief of the Pacific Fleet; by Colonel Walter C. Phillips, Chief of Staff to Lieutenant General Short; and by Major General Frederick L. Martin, Commander of the Army Air Forces in Hawaii, an old friend of General Emmons. Emmons had told me on the plane that General Marshall had hoped that we would reach Hawaii before any cable advice from Washington of the relief of Kimmel and Short, so that Emmons could personally inform Short. Unfortunately, word of the relief apparently reached Oahu before we did. For some reason—perhaps as a subtle hint of protest over the relief of Admiral Kimmel, as well as a mark of confidence in Admiral Pye and the other admirals of the Pacific Fleet—instead of rushing Admiral Nimitz out to Oahu by air, as the Army did with Emmons, the Navy sent Nimitz by train to San Francisco from Washington, where he was serving as chief of the personnel bureau of the Navy Department. From San Francisco he flew to Pearl Harbor, arriving there on Christmas Day. He then waited until December 31, 1941, before taking over command of the Fleet from Pye.

Our actions the day of arrival are hazy in my mind. I know we drove first with Martin to his headquarters, where Emmons had some private talk with Martin, after which we were briefed on the attacks on the two Army airfields, Hickham and Wheeler, and our losses and damages were outlined. After lunch we drove around Hickham, where the signs of damage were much less than I anticipated. Before departure from the United States, I had read stories in the press and had heard rumors of fabulous Japanese espionage and widespread sabotage. Neither the accuracy nor thoroughness of Japanese intelligence was borne out by what was shown us at Hickham Field. There were two rows of hangars at Hickham, the rear one of which housed repair shops and machinery, whereas the front row contained little of value. The Japanese attacked the wrong row, leaving the repair facilities practically untouched. Similarly, the main baseball diamond was heavily bombed, apparently under the mistaken impression that it contained underground gasoline facilities, while the storage tanks were untouched. Bombs were wasted in a heavy attack on the post exchange, mistaken to be an important headquarters building. The greatest damage and casualties occurred when the central mess building, crowded with airmen at breakfast, was virtually destroyed. The other serious loss occurred among the bombardment planes, lined up in

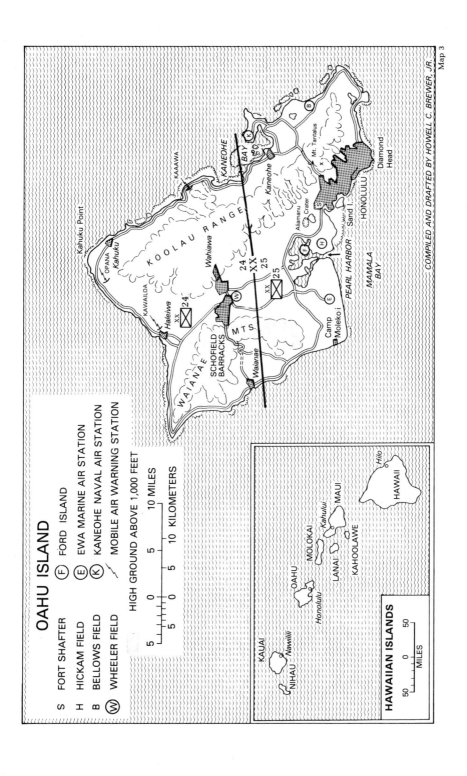

OAHU ISLAND

S   FORT SHAFTER
H   HICKAM FIELD
B   BELLOWS FIELD
Ⓦ   WHEELER FIELD

Ⓕ   FORD ISLAND
Ⓔ   EWA MARINE AIR STATION
Ⓚ   KANEOHE NAVAL AIR STATION
〰   MOBILE AIR WARNING STATION

HIGH GROUND ABOVE 1,000 FEET

10 MILES
10 KILOMETERS
5   0   5
5   0   5

HAWAIIAN ISLANDS

KAUAI
NIHAU   Newilii
OAHU
Honolulu
MOLOKAI
LANAI
Kahului
MAUI
KAHOOLAWE
Hilo
HAWAII

50   0   50
MILES

Kahuku Point
KAAAWA
Kahuku
OPANA
KAWAILOA
KOOLAU   RANGE
KANEOHE   BAY
Kaneohe
Mt. Tantalus
B
×
Diamond Head
HONOLULU
Sand I.
Crater
Aliamanu
Ⓕ
Ⓗ
PEARL HARBOR
MAMALA BAY
Ⓔ
Camp Moleko i
Waianae
WAIANAE   MTS.
SCHOFIELD BARRACKS
Ⓦ
Wahiawa
Haleiwa
24   XX
24   XX   25
XX   25

Map 3

COMPILED AND DRAFTED BY HOWELL C. BREWER, JR.

front of the hangars for security against sabotage, which never occurred. Half the bombers were destroyed or damaged seriously. Bad as the destruction was, it could have been much worse.

After the tour we drove to Navy headquarters close by Pearl Harbor. There we were given a rundown of the events of December 7 and a summary of the damage to the Pacific Fleet, to the airplanes and facilities at the Ford Island Naval Station in Pearl Harbor, at the Kaneohe Seaplane Base on the east coast of Oahu, and at the Ewa Marine Air Station, southwest of Pearl Harbor. Following this briefing, General Emmons and Admiral Pye made preliminary arrangements for subsequent meetings to iron out various procedures for the mutual cooperation of their commands which needed immediate attention. Emmons also arranged a brief call on Admiral Kimmel at the latter's quarters on a hill overlooking the harbor. I went with Emmons but remained on the porch while the General was shown into the darkened house to a room where, Emmons told me later, Kimmel was sitting alone, in total darkness. Emmons simply paid his respects and we left.

It was still light outside, so that we had a saddening view of the sunken or damaged battleships, cruisers, and destroyers caught in Pearl Harbor, and we could see something of the wreckage at the Ford Island Naval Station. But, as at Hickham, devastating as the Japanese attack was, it was not as catastrophic as it might have been. From Admiral Kimmel's quarters we drove to Fort Shafter, on the western outskirts of Honolulu, the location of Army headquarters, where General Short had his quarters. He kindly offered us the use of two guest rooms.

My Duties and Relations with General Emmons

Delos Carleton Emmons was a man of medium height and build, with an open countenance, blue eyes, and slightly curly hair that made him look younger than his fifty-three years when he took command of the Hawaiian Department. Commissioned in the Infantry upon graduation from West Point in 1909, he had been detailed to the Aviation Section of the Army Signal Corps. He had served as the Air Officer of the Hawaiian Department from 1934 to 1936, so was familiar with Hawaii and its problems. On December 7, 1941, he was Commanding General of the Air Force Combat Command at Langley Field, Virginia. He happened to be on the West Coast at the time of General Dargue's death. I assume he was picked by General Marshall to replace Dargue because of his experience, his knowledge of Hawaii, and his immediate availability. It was an excellent choice. Emmons had an astute, keen mind, was self-contained, sure of himself without being cocky, and always gave the impression of knowing what he wanted to do and how to do it, though he had no exaggerated idea of his own ability. He was easy to work with and we got along handsomely.

As soon as Emmons got his bearings after taking command, he outlined clearly to me what he wanted me to do and fixed our relationship. This he did informally in one or two relaxed sessions over highballs before dinner in our quarters. He intended to concentrate on the air defense of the Hawaiian Islands and on establishing sound working arrangements with the Navy. He was not interested in routine administration. That would be my province as Chief of Staff. I was to handle the staff and manage the business of the headquarters as I saw fit, keeping him informed of all matters which I considered merited his attention. He would make all major decisions and determine all questions of policy.

In addition to my duties as Chief of Staff, he wanted me to act de facto, but without any official announcement, as coordinator of the ground defenses of the islands, under his direction. He did this rather than constitute a separate Corps headquarters to command the two infantry divisions, the 24th and the 25th, into which the old square Hawaiian Division had been split earlier in the year. I was to supervise also the operations of the two Hawaiian National Guard infantry regiments, the 298th and 299th, called to active duty in October, 1940.

The Hawaiian Coast Artillery Command, under Major General Henry J. Burgin, would report directly to Emmons. It comprised a number of sea-coast batteries for defense against surface vessels. Its 53rd Coast Artillery Antiaircraft (AA) Brigade included two Regular Army AA regiments and the 251st AA Regiment of the California National Guard. General Burgin was responsible for the training of the AA Artillery, but it was to operate under the Interceptor Command then being established.

Nine different investigations or inquiries regarding the attack on Pearl Harbor were conducted during the period December 11, 1941, and July 20, 1946, when the Joint Congressional Committee on the Investigations of the Pearl Harbor Attack submitted its report. Neither General Emmons nor I was involved in any of these inquiries. So far as Hawaii and the military services were concerned, the chief result of these inquiries was that unity of command and responsibility was established as the guiding principle in the assignment of missions to the United States armed services in Hawaii and throughout the Pacific. This solved many problems.

General Emmons' Mission and Major Tasks

The only written instructions to Emmons from the War Department that I have been able to discover were contained in a letter from General Marshall dated December 20, 1941. It said in part:

> Instructions to the Army and Navy a few days ago assigned unity of command to the Navy in Hawaii. At the same time unity of command was assigned to the Army in Panama. . . . The efforts I have been making for over a year to secure unity of command in various critical regions have been unavailing. . . . I am giving you this information in order that you may better appreciate the problems, and, therefore, be better prepared to assist me by endeavouring to work with Nimitz in complete understanding.

General Emmons and Admiral Pye quickly established a sound working relationship. Five days after his arrival Emmons reported to General Marshall: "Unity of command here is essential, is working well, and will so continue."

Admiral Kimmel and General Short had taken command respectively of the Pacific Fleet and the Hawaiian Department in February, 1941, less than one year before the Japanese attack. They had initiated a number of measures designed to correct deficiencies in the defense of the Hawaiian Islands. Washington had been unable to meet their requests for additional support because of the shortage of funds and the higher priority given to Lend-Lease, in support of Britain in its crucial struggle with Nazi Germany. The Japanese attack on Pearl Harbor changed this. Admiral Nimitz and General Emmons were now able to obtain better results on their calls for help from Washington. The principal problems demanding Emmons' immediate attention were as follows:

1. Replacement of losses of personnel, planes, bombs and ammunition.

2. Increase in long-range planes to provide air reconnaissance in support of the Navy.

3. Completion of the radar system for the detection of enemy planes.

4. Completion of establishment of the Hawaiian Interception Command and Aircraft Warning Service.

5. Procurement of additional Army troops for the surveillance and defense of the islands of Kauai, Maui, and Hawaii.

6. Solution of Hawaiian internal security problems.

While these matters were not my responsibility, General Emmons and I discussed them frequently and I assisted in their solution.

Reinforcements

The Hawaiian Air Force consisted of the 18th Bombardment Wing, with station at Hickham Field, under Brigadier General Clarence L. Tinker, who succeeded General Martin on December 17 in command of the Hawaiian Air Force, and the 14th Pursuit Wing at Wheeler Field, under Brigadier General Howard C. Davidson. Up until December 7, the emphasis of the Air Force in Washington had been on reinforcing the Philippines, deemed to be under greater threat than Hawaii. After December 7, and even before Emmons' arrival, General Marshall decided to give highest priority to rebuilding the Hawaii defenses. By December 17 the War Department was prepared to ship to Hawaii additional troops, pilots, pursuit planes, and great quantities of bombs and ammunition. But at that time the Navy feared that the Japanese might have strong naval forces, including carriers, between the West Coast and Hawaii, and shipments were delayed until convoy escorts could be provided. But by December 21 enough B-17s had been flown out from California to build the 18th Bombardment Wing to full strength.

The Joint Chiefs of Staff (JCS) recommended, and President Roosevelt approved, a strength for the Hawaiian Air Force, redesignated as the Seventh Air Force, of 96 heavy and 24 medium and light bombers in the VII Bomber Command and 225 fighter planes in the VII Interceptor Command. Army ground troop strength was fixed at 74,000 on Oahu, 13,000 on Hawaii, and 12,000 distributed on five other islands. The 27th Infantry Division, New York National Guard, which had trained under the VII Corps, was chosen by the War Department to provide the garrisons for the outlying islands. It would not arrive until March–April, 1942. Approval had been obtained earlier for the dispatch of the 34th and 161st Infantry Regiments to bolster the defenses of Oahu. They had arrived in late December and were placed in reserve, the 34th Infantry in the North Sector and the 161st in the south.

The Interceptor Command

Of more pressing need was completion of the Army's antiaircraft warning system and Interceptor Command, not yet fully in operation on December 7. Such a system would depend on a series of radars located on high ground so as to provide 360 degrees of unobstructed screening of all approaches by air to Oahu. The stations were to be connected electrically to a central information center at Fort Shafter. There the plots of all planes, of whatever character, picked up by the radars would be shown graphically on a large board depicting Oahu and surrounding areas. In event of a threatened attack signals would be sent to all air and antiaircraft-artillery stations and a general "air alert" sounded.

Prior to December 7, 1941, only five mobile radar sets had begun operating at temporary locations around Oahu, on a training and exploratory basis. To provide full coverage many more sets would be required, their proper locations to avoid "dead-spaces" would have to be surveyed, and operators trained to man the radars and the information center. A sixth radar station had been opened at Opano near Kahuku Point, the northern tip of Oahu, by November 27, but because of a shortage of spare parts and dependable power at the sites, and a lack of trained personnel, the available radars could be kept in operation for only three or four hours a day, which, under Alert No. 1, had been set from 4:00 to 7:00 A.M. The first wave of Japanese attackers on December 7 had been spotted by the Opana station at 7:20 A.M. by a trainee operator, Private Joseph H. Lockhart, who, on his own, was working his radar overtime. By the time his report reached the information center it had closed down. An Army lieutenant, who happened to be still on duty, said that nothing need be done about the call. He knew that the Navy carriers were out and assumed that Opana had picked up a returning flight from one of them. Actually, planes from the carrier *Enterprise* did come in to the Ewa Field during the attack. This pointed out the need of full exchange of information between the Army and Navy on times of arrival and route of approach of incoming planes. I remember hearing General Davidson protest to General Emmons in the first week after our arrival in Hawaii that even after December 7 he was not kept informed as to timing and direction of approach of Navy planes, and he so testified before the Justice Owen Roberts Commission which began its hearings in Hawaii on December 22. General Emmons, in conjunction with Admiral Pye, promptly arranged a specific approach-and-identification procedure for all planes, which was to be varied each day of the week.

Internal Security

Another problem that had required immediate action by Short on December 7, and was of continuing concern to Emmons, was internal security, particularly in relation to the large part of the population on the Islands of Japanese descent. One of the missions assigned to the Army was to institute martial law in the Territory of Hawaii if there was a threat of invasion. Plans for martial law were prepared in advance.

The institution of martial law on December 7 did not satisfy everyone in Washington. The surprise attack, while the Japanese were still conducting negotiations in Washington, had caused bitter resentment and deep fear among Californians and many people in Hawaii. Secretary of the Navy Knox, supported by the President, urged that all Japanese aliens in Hawaii be concentrated on one of the islands other than Oahu. General Emmons doggedly opposed this course as both impractical and undesirable, pointing out that the "Japanese" population—20,000 aliens and 98,000 Hawaiian-born citizens of Japanese descent—provided the bulk of the labor essential to the economy of the Islands and support of the military forces. The fact that not a single act of sabotage had been discovered by either military intelligence or the Federal Bureau of Investigation strengthened the General's argument.

Under persistent pressure from Knox and the Navy Department in Washington, Emmons submitted several plans, which were debated back and forth, for evacuation of Japanese to the United States. He was finally directed in July, 1942, by the President, on the recommendation of the JCS, to which the Navy had brought the problem, to evacuate as many as 15,000 people to the United States where they were to be interned along with about 110,000 West Coast Japanese-Americans. A variety of circumstances delayed this plan. A total of 1,875 residents of Hawaii of Japanese ancestry had been evacuated to the United States by April, 1943, by which time everyone agreed evacuation should cease. The wisdom of Emmons' stand, which had been supported by Rear Admiral Claude C. Bloch, the commander of the 14th Naval District in Hawaii, was confirmed.

Coordinating the Ground Defenses

While General Emmons was devoting his attention to the above matters, I was assisting in some of the administrative details in addition to checking on coordination of ground defenses. Despite lack of any published instructions assigning this duty to me, I had no problem obtaining the cooperation of the commanders concerned. I knew both infantry division commanders. Major General Durward S. Wilson, commanding the 24th Division, and I had served together as instructors at Benning and my great friend and mentor at the Infantry School, Colonel Gilbert R. Cook, was commanding one of the regiments in the 24th. I did not know Major General Maxwell Murray, the 25th Division commander, very well, but he was a genial older man, a 1907 West Point classmate and close friend of my brother James, and kindly disposed toward me. I had been promoted to brigadier general on February 14, 1942, which also helped.

I persuaded Colonel Philips, General Short's Chief of Staff, to remain on as my deputy for administration, and, with increasing activities in the field, soon brought in a West Point classmate, Colonel Robert M. Bathurst, an exceptionally able artilleryman, as deputy for operations. We were billeted with General Emmons at Shafter but moved all operational activities to the field command post in an air-conditioned underground tunnel in the rim of Alimano crater, near Fort Shafter.

There had been nothing wrong with the Army plans for the defense of Oahu. General Short, one of the ablest tacticians in the Army, had seen to that. The island was divided into two defense sectors—approximately through its center by an east-west boundary line, with the 24th Division holding the north sector and the 25th Division the south. The plan of defense followed the classic pattern of holding the most likely landing areas with a minimum commitment of troops; with reserve forces in central locations for counterattack. The troops had moved promptly to their battle positions on December 7 following the Japanese attack and remained in the field during my entire stay in Hawaii. They had known exactly where to go, having occupied these positions on many field exercises. In May, 1941, at the time of an earlier alert, the troops under General Short's direction had constructed some pillboxes for machine guns and artillery emplacements covering likely landing places for an invader. These were not completed, because prior to the Japanese attack, there had been restrictions on barbed wire entanglements or other obstacles on the beaches, and troops were prohibited from trespassing on sugarcane and pineapple fields to emplace mortars or artillery in rear of the beaches. After the declaration of martial law these prohibitions were removed, along with restrictions on the firing of weapons from battle positions to verify and record their planned fires.

The seacoast guns were only occasionally fired in peacetime because of the danger to shipping, and the two eight-inch rifles of Battery Adams, emplaced at Black Point below Diamond Head, had never been fired because of the objections of owners of houses directly in front of the guns, who feared that the roofs would be blown off. We had the houses evacuated temporarily, windows opened, and pictures and glassware stored in basements while the guns were test fired. No damage occurred other than a few window panes.

Defense of the Outer Islands

General Emmons was greatly concerned over the defenseless state of the outlying islands where some airfields had been built which could not be protected. Emmons feared that in the event of any Japanese attempt to invade the Hawaiian Islands one or more of the outer islands would first be seized as a base for operations against Oahu. I had visited each of the outlying islands, and I accompanied General Tinker and some of his staff to examine a few temporary fields on Hawaii and Lanai that Emmons felt should be plowed up, or otherwise obstructed, if they could not be protected. While I was off on the trip with Tinker two Japanese flying boats made a futile run at Oahu on the night of March 3–4. One merely skirted the west coast of the island. The other, seeking to hit Honolulu, dropped four 500-pound bombs which, luckily, fell on a wooded slope of Mount Tantalus above the city. The planes were picked up by radar about ninety miles away. The Interceptor Command sent up four pursuit planes and alerted the antiaircraft artillery, but because of their high altitude and the thick overcast, the pursuit ships could not locate them and the antiaircraft did not fire. No general air-raid alarm sounded. It was presumed that the flying boats were refueled by a submarine at French Frigate Shoals, northwest of Oahu. Our Navy took steps to deny the Shoals area to enemy submarines, and there were no further raids.

The Japanese-Hawaiian Soldier Problem

A persistent problem for General Emmons and me was what to do about the soldiers of Japanese ancestry ("nisei") who made up a large part of the 299th Infantry, Hawaiian National Guard. The Navy had always been wary of having either regiment close to any naval installation. When, in May, 1942, our Navy learned through intercepted Japanese messages that the enemy planned to seize Midway, thus posing a serious threat to Oahu, Admiral Nimitz requested, and Emmons agreed, that the 298th Infantry, National Guard be withdrawn to Scofield Barracks in reserve, and that it be replaced by the 161st Infantry. The 27th Division had arrived from the States in March–April and took over the defense of the outer Islands from the 299th Infantry, which was also moved to Scofield.

On April 6, 1942, Emmons addressed a letter to the Adjutant General of the Army requesting that he be given authority to organize special units of nisei "with the understanding that they be sent to an

African or European theater where their physical characteristics will not serve to confuse our other troops and where they will not be opposed by Japanese. . . . It is believed that such a unit would give a good account of itself." This recommendation was turned down on May 2 by the War Department, which directed that all nisei in combat units in Hawaii be transferred to service units, other than Signal Corps or Chemical Warfare, for non-combat duty in Hawaii, or be sent to the States for assignment to service units there. General Emmons remained opposed to such action.

Fortunately, the idea of forming a combat unit in which nisei from the West Coast and Hawaii would be given an opportunity to prove their loyalty in action was revived by Mr. John J. McCloy, the Assistant Secretary of War, who was handling this recurring problem for the Secretary. McCloy, who had indicated a tolerant attitude toward the Japanese-Hawaiian when he had visited Hawaii following the Pearl Harbor attack, cabled General Emmons on November 4, 1942, suggesting that a provisional battalion of nisei be formed for employment in the European theater. The General replied the next day: "I hope project will receive approval as it will mean so much to this Territory. Am confident these men will give a good account of themselves in the European theater." This exchange ended the debate. General Emmons was directed to organize the provisional unit from the nisei in the 298th and 299th Regiments and dispatch it, without weapons or equipment, as soon as possible. I supervised its organization and chose Lieutenant Colonel Farrant L. Turner of the 298th Infantry, a Hawaiian-born National Guard officer who had served in France with the American Expeditionary Forces in World War I, to command the battalion. General Emmons had me address the assembled battalion just before it sailed for San Francisco on May 5, 1942, to assure the men that they would not be interned in the United States but would be employed in combat in some theater other than the Pacific. Upon arrival it was redesignated the 100th Battalion (Separate). After a period of training it joined the 34th Division in 1943 in North Africa and fought with great distinction at Cassino and Anzio and throughout the drive of General Clark's Fifth Army up the length of Italy until the end of World War II.

Wainwright's Philippine Surrender

Meanwhile the Japanese were winding up their campaign in the Philippines. On May 6, 1942, after almost six months of gallant fighting against overwhelming odds, Lieutenant General Jonathan M. Wainwright surrendered our forces on Corregidor. The Japanese had announced that General Wainwright would broadcast the surrender terms the following day. The War Department, anxious to verify the authenticity of the broadcast, cabled the Hawaiian Department asking if there was anyone there who knew Wainwright well enough to identify his voice. Having served as Skinny Wainwright's assistant when he was G-3 of the American Forces in Germany, I had the sad duty of listening to the broadcast and identifying his voice. I will admit I wept.

Command of the 25th Division

Major General Dwight D. Eisenhower, then head of the War Plans Division of the War Department, cabled Emmons on April 24, 1942, asking if my services as Chief of Staff of the Hawaiian Department could be spared to assume command of the 25th Division as replacement for Major General Maxwell Murray, who was being returned to the States to command the 35th Division. Emmons concurred and recommended that I be promoted to major general. Orders assigning me to command the 25th Divison came in by radio on May 6, 1942, much to my delight. I was greatly indebted to Emmons, and to General Richardson of the VII Corps, both of whom had recommended me for division command. And I expect that Assistant Secretary of War John J. McCloy had given General Marshall a favorable report on me when he returned to Washington from his visit to Hawaii. I was fortunate also in that General Marshall was then in the process of assigning younger men to command divisions.

I greatly enjoyed my service under General Emmons. I was about to write "*with* General Emmons," because, with his delegation of the role of coordinator of the ground defenses of the islands, he always treated me as if I were equal in responsibility with himself. This was far from being the case. I never presumed to exercise any authority in my own right. We consulted daily on all matters of importance, but he never interposed in any action I ever took in coordinating the ground defenses.

We partied and played golf together and became warm friends. But our tastes were somewhat different and Delos had a certain reserve about himself, so that our relationship was one of mutual respect rather than intimate friendship.

When I took command of the 25th Division it consisted of the 27th Infantry, the "Wolf Hounds," commanded by Colonel William A. McCulloch; the 35th Infantry, "Cacti," under Colonel William J. Morrisey; and the 161st Infantry, under Colonel Clarence R. Orndorff. Bill McCulloch and I had commanded adjacent companies in the 3rd Battalion 8th Infantry in Germany. Bill was a slow, quiet, deliberate man, a good sound soldier and a loyal friend; he bore no trace of resentment that I had passed over his head. Morrisey was a big, gruff older man, whom I had not known; his Hawaiian tour was about up, and he was soon returned to the States. I selected as his successor Lieutenant Colonel Robert B. McClure, who had done a fine job as G-4. Bob was a happy-go-lucky type, an athlete, with natural qualities of leadership, who as a youngster had not fitted into the pattern of a midshipman's life at the Naval Academy and had been dismissed for some breach of regulations or academic deficiency. I was glad to get him and he became a fine regimental commander.

Clarence Orndorff, the commander of the 161st National Guard regiment, was a lawyer from Washington state. He was a mild-mannered, likable man, and I imagine was quite competent in his civil profession, but like many patriotic, worthy Guardsmen had little experience with troops in the field, and was beginning to develop a paunch. The same was true of two of his battalion commanders, who, if anything, were older than Orndorff and perhaps not in as good physical condition. Remembering Ben Lear's brusque relief of General Truman from the 35th Division, I called in Colonel Orndorff for a chat after his regiment had been with the Division for a while. I told him I intended to treat him and his unit on exactly the same basis as the two Regular regiments, with no molly-coddling but with absolutely no bias. He said that was just the way he wanted it. That being the case, I said that two of his battalion commanders were too old, and inexperienced, to command battalions in the strenuous jungle fighting that might be ahead of us; but that, rather than relieve them and send them home, I would try to find administrative jobs for them within the Hawaiian Department, consonant with their civilian talents and experience. I said that he would remain in command of the regiment and I hoped he would be able to take it into action, but that if I became convinced that he was not up to it, physically or otherwise, in fairness to his men I would transfer him to an appropriate administrative post. He thanked me and replied that he agreed fully on all points. I did find suitable jobs for his subordinate commanders, who served out the war in Hawaii in responsible positions.

With my usual good luck I came up with a splendid Chief of Staff and able assistant division commander. For Chief of Staff I chose a tall, angular, raw-boned Alabamian, Major William F. Bledsoe, one of the artillery battalion commanders who had caught my eye, and ear. I had known him slightly in Germany, but had been impressed with the manner in which he commanded the field artillery in the Kaneohe Bay area. He was constantly on the go, driving his own jeep, admonishing and cajoling his troops to do a better job. He was Uncle Bill to them, and they loved him. I came to share their admiration and affection. Under his "country boy" approach was a good mind. I gave him a loose hand with the Division staff, which he managed with an intriguing mixture of firmness and finesse that was epitomized by a phrase, coined by one of its members in answer to any question that might arise with respect to procedure: "Bledsoe said so!"

I was delighted, though a bit embarrassed, to inherit from General Murray his newly appointed Assistant Division Commander, "Doc" Cook, from whom I had learned so much as a captain at Benning. I had gotten General Emmons to send a cable to the War Department supporting Durwood Wilson's and Max Murray's recommendation for promotion of Cook, who should have been selected for division command long before I was. With Brigadier General Stanley E. Reinhart as artillery commander, I had a skilled, congenial trio of top assistants, and was ready to go to work. Cook did not remain with us long. He was ordered home June 5 to take over one of the new divisions. I suspect that his name had been lost in the shuffle of early promotions in 1942, and only came to General Marshall's attention when the recommendations from Hawaii for Cook's promotion to "B.G."

came to the Chief's attention. Later in the war he moved up to command of the XII Corps in General Patton's Third Army in Europe. I asked promptly for John Hodge as Cook's replacement and General Richardson kindly released him.

Preparing the Division for Combat

The decisive victory of our Navy in the Battle of Midway, June 4–9, removed any serious threat to Oahu. This occurred one month after I assumed command of the 25th Division. I realized that the JCS would not allow two Regular Army divisions, like the 24th and 25th, to remain in Hawaii much longer, and determined that when the time came to move either of them the 25th would be chosen first, and would be ready to go directly into action.

Soon after taking command of the division, I had assembled the regimental and battalion commanders of the infantry and artillery to outline to them what I had in mind in the way of leadership, discipline, and training. In brief, I said that the success of the Division would depend largely on the quality of our noncommissioned officers and company and battalion commanders, and that every opportunity should be taken to develop their self-reliance and initiative; that we should hold to firm discipline, based on common sense and confidence between officers and men; and that our main effort in training would be to develop our infantry battalions as the key fighting units, to be closely supported by artillery and air. To achieve these ends we would spend much of our time on battalion field exercises in the Koolau and Waianae mountains, and on two combat firing ranges which I had set up on the slopes of the mountains while I was Department Chief of Staff. We would concentrate our efforts in preparing the division for offensive combat in mobile warfare, in contrast to its relatively stable defensive role on Oahu. I could tell from their eyes that the commanders were enthusiastic at the prospect.

During the next six months the Division engaged in an intensive training program. Troops were rotated from defense positions for the field exercises. Under the active supervision of John Hodge, Stanley Reinhart, and the regimental commanders, every infantry battalion, supported by its normal support battalion of light artillery and complement of 155-mm howitzers, participated in at least one tactical exercise in which all weapons were fired under as realistic combat conditions as minimum safety requirements would permit. I do not recall a single casualty.

I devoted much of my attention to developing a simple, sure method of designating targets to close-support aircraft. The Tactical Department at Benning had given some thought to this while I was an instructor there, but perhaps because of the lack of suitable aircraft had really done nothing about it, and the Army Ground Forces had not yet established any definite procedures. The standard Army–Air Force doctrine in 1941 was that fighters were not to be called on to support infantry unless the artillery was unable to destroy an enemy's dug-in position, or suppress fire that was holding up the infantry's advance. Such enemy positions are usually camouflaged or otherwise concealed, which makes them extremely difficult for a pilot in a high-speed fighter-bomber to locate. There is always the danger of bombing friendly troops who should advance as close as possible to the enemy's position so as to be able to take advantage of the bombing before the enemy can recover from its effect. Since artillery observers with the front-line infantry should have been adjusting fire on the enemy positions, they should know exactly where the positions are, and those of their own troops. I reasoned that the surest and safest way to indicate the target to the supporting aviators would be to mark it with one or two artillery white phosphorus shells, which can readily be spotted from the air. Radio communications from the ground would call in the planes, and when the planes were ready the artillery would fire a phosphorus round or two into the target, which should be bombed at once, to be followed quickly by the attacking infantry. With the co-operation of General Davidson's fighters, we proved out this scheme in numerous tests before employing it on our combat ranges, against assumed enemy positions within two hundred yards of actual troops. The system worked perfectly and became standard practice, with great success, in the division's subsequent operations in the South Pacific.

Along with such realistic training, we practiced amphibious landings through heavy surf on the Waiana beaches, using landing craft borrowed from the Navy or Marines. We had no ships from which to practice going over carrying full equipment on our backs, but we gained some experience by climbing down the walls of barracks at Scofield on landing nets strung between third-floor windows.

25th Division Firing Demonstration

There had been some curiosity among our civilian friends as to just what we were doing to meet a possible invasion, beside sitting behind barbed wire on their best beaches. I decided to put on a demonstration, not only for their benefit but to let our own men see what we could do. This would involve seacoast artillery fires against a simulated off-shore fleet, followed by dive-bombing attacks from the air; then successive concentrations of artillery and mortar fire that would meet any enemy landing force; culminating with the barrages of artillery, mortars, machine guns and rifle fire on the landing beaches and the routes-of-approach inland.

I had chosen as the site for the demonstration a sparsely inhabited area, but one of some tactical importance, along the west coast near the southern end of the Waianae range. It had a backstop of mountains that would guard against any "overs" or ricochets from the artillery, and a convenient hilltop to one side from which spectators could view the action with safety. Only the weapons actually available for defense of the area would participate, and they would be fired by the assigned troops from their battle positions. The exercise would require evacuation of a small village just north of the area and would inevitably result in damage to the railroad, highway, and power and telephone lines which ran along the shore.

When I outlined the project to the division staff I was told that nothing like that had ever been permitted, and I would never get permission from the military or civil authorities or the landowners. But after convincing General Emmons that this would not be merely a demonstration but a test of an important segment of our planned fires, he gave approval, provided I could arrange the details of evacuation and secure releases from property owners.

Through Walter Dillingham, president of the Oahu Railway, whom I had gotten to know well, I had no difficulty in getting clearance from the railroad, which owned most of the land, and from the telephone and power companies, at no cost to the Army or the government for repair of any damages. The Office of Civil Defense was happy to take over all details of the evacuation, as a test of their war emergency plans. To make this possible we scheduled the demonstration for a Sunday morning, when people would be home from work and the area could be sealed off. The villagers would be moved by plantation trucks and buses about fifteen miles to one of the planned evacuation camps, where we would arrange for a band concert and picnic lunch.

The demonstration was staged on August 9, 1942, under ideal weather, before two thousand spectators, including government officials, senior officers of the Hawaiian Department, Navy, Air Force and Marines, representative groups of civilians, members of the press and other news media, and detachments of our troops from all major units. Loudspeakers had been provided and Major Stanley R. Larsen, 27th Infantry, gave a clear explanation of each successive phase of the exercise as it developed. The bombing and artillery concentrations were impressively powerful and accurate, and the final massed fires on the beach were awesome and devastating. We had provided front-row seats for Walter Dillingham and other officials of the utility companies. The first round for adjustment of the artillery landed squarely on the hitherto sacrosanct railroad and blew up the tracks, bringing roars of approval from the troops and laughter from Walter's friends, in which he joined heartily.

At the end, to demonstrate that we did not intend to just sit and take it if the Japanese ever attempted to land, the exercise concluded with a rousing counterattack by Army troops, led by a company of tanks with guns blazing. It was quite a show. The best aspect of the exercise was that there was nothing phony about it. No one was injured; the evacuated villagers enjoyed their outing; and the railroad and utility repair crews, which had been standing by and had witnessed the exercise, pitched in at once and completed the repairs, as they would have under combat conditions. Not a word of complaint was raised by the utility companies, and even the newspapers could find no fault but lauded the troops for a convincing demonstration of their readiness for action.

Time for Relaxation

During our six-months training period we worked long hours but took time off on weekends and evenings whenever possible. Through General Emmons, who had made many friends in Honolulu during a prior tour, I met a number of wonderful people, leaders in the social and business community of the Islands, many of whom became my lasting friends. "Pinkie" Cooke, the attractive wife of J. Platt Cooke, was of tremendous help to us as head of the United Services Organization (USO) providing entertainment for our service men and women. Delos and I had many a pleasant dinner on weekends at the lovely homes of the Cookes, Louise and Walter Dillingham, "Sandy" and Una Walker, the Harold Castles, Pricilla and Al Ward, the "Andy" Andersons, and the Frank Midkiffs, even though the nine o'clock curfew and blackout curtailed the evenings. After the battle of Midway these restrictions and the pressure of our defense preparations were gradually eased.

Contacts with Admiral Nimitz

On the official side of our activities, Emmons had established cordial relations with the senior Navy commanders and I had similar close contacts with their staffs while I was Emmons' Chief of Staff. I had not seen much of Admiral Nimitz until I assumed command of the 25th Division, one month before the battle of Midway. All of the major naval installations on Oahu were in my South Sector and Nimitz took keen interest in our activities, despite his absorption in preparations for Midway.

American cryptanalysts had succeeded in breaking the Japanese code in which Admiral Isoroku Yamamoto, Commander in Chief of Japan's combined fleet, had issued his secret operations order for the attack on Midway. This attack would not only capture that strategic outpost, but would result in the final destruction of the American fleet as it came to the rescue of Midway, thus completing the work begun so gloriously on December 7 at Pearl Harbor. So thought Yamamoto, unaware of our cryptanalytic coup.

Admiral Nimitz invited Emmons and me to his operations room on the morning of June 4, 1942, to listen to radio reports of the battle. By May 27, Nimitz had known almost every detail of Yamamoto's plan for the seizure of Midway.After Admiral Chuichi Nagumo, commanding the Japanese carriers, had committed the bulk of his planes to the opening attack against Midway, dive bombers from *Enterprise* screamed down on the heavy carriers *Akagi, Kaga* and *Soryu*. One bomb exploded among the planes being rearmed on *Akagi* and another blew up her torpedo-storage compartment. Flames swept over *Akagi* and by the following morning she had sunk. *Kaga* was hit four times and sank that evening. *Soryu* was quickly disabled by *Yorktown's* dive bombers and had to be abandoned in flames; a few hours later she was torpedoed by one of our submarines. Near the end of a furious day, *Hiryu* was sunk, but the Japanese in turn crippled *Yorktown*, which in spite of valiant efforts to save her, sank on June 6. I felt almost as if I had participated in the dramatic victory which was the turning point that ended Japanese hopes of winning the war in the Pacific.

In the months after Midway I came to know Nimitz quite well and to admire him greatly. I had been impressed from the start with the quiet manner with which he had taken command after the debacle of Pearl Harbor. He restored the wounded confidence of the fleet, and established the long-overdue unity of command of all forces in Hawaii with such judicious restraint as to win the cooperation of all services. I always felt, as I did about Omar Bradley, that his approach to other men, to human problems, came from his innate modesty and simplicity that probably carried over from his boyhood in Texas. His handling of subordinates, irrespective of rank, with the same thoughtful consideration, earned their affection. Under his kindly demeanor there was unmistakable evidence of a sharp mind and a talent for making decisions. I had the pleasure of seeing the relaxed, informal side of Nimitz as I was occasionally invited to pitch horse shoes with him back of his quarters, or to join him in a stiff game of tennis, followed by highballs and dinner, in his mess. He was a tough, friendly competitor.

Farewell to Hawaii

When, as I had hoped, orders finally came from the War Department, in late October, 1942, transferring the 25th Division to General Mac-Arthur's Southwest Pacific Theater, the Admiral called me to his office. After congratulating me on the assignment he added, with a smile: "Collins, you may think you are going to MacArthur's command but I want to warn you that I am not going to let you get away. You have too fine a Divison to lose from this theater. The 1st Marines will soon be needing relief on Guadalcanal, so don't be surprised if your orders are changed while you are en route to Australia, and you are turned in there."

We gradually turned over the South Sector to the 27th Division, then under command of an old friend, Major General Ralph Smith, after which the 25th concentrated at Scofield in November to receive officers and men to bring it up to war strength, get rid of surplus equipment, and prepare guns and motor transport for shipment. The men were elated at the prospect of action and worked hard and effectively.

Before leaving Oahu, I received my first Distinguished Service Medal for duty as Chief of Staff of the Hawaiian Department. General Emmons had recommended me for this honor months before, but such top awards had to be reviewed by an awards board and approved by the Secretary of War, all of which took time. In November, Emmons cabled the War Department to speed the process, saying he wanted to present the medal. He did this at a retreat ceremony at Fort Shafter on November 24, 1942, shortly before the Division sailed. As he pinned on the DSM I was gratified and touched to have him say: "Joe, I don't know anyone that I would prefer to decorate." The Division sailed off for Australia in late November, but with destination still unknown. This time I was able to talk, circumspectly, by phone to Gladys in Washington, where she had gone with the children from Birmingham. As always, she gave me a cheerful send-off, which helped sustain me in the months ahead.

CHAPTER IX

Guadalcanal and New Georgia Campaigns, 1942–1943

Departure for Southwest Pacific

The 25th Division left Hawaii in three convoys, each comprising three or four commercial steamers. I departed November 25, 1942, with the first convoy, which carried the 35th Infantry regimental combat team (RCT) and some service units. The other convoys left at intervals of about ten days, each with an RCT, some service troops, and a quantity of food, ammunition, and other supplies, all commercially loaded, *i.e.*, not prepared to go directly into combat. As a farewll gesture Admiral Nimitz sent us the following dispatch as the first convoy sailed:

> Cincpac congratulates the 25th Division which, in addition to performing defense duties on Oahu, has made such good use of its time that it is now outstandingly fit and ready for offensive combat. Regardless of whether your active combat is in the Sopac or Sowespac area, we have high expectations of successful actions by you against the enemy. Cincpac extends best wishes to the commanding General and his division.

We had left under orders to proceed to Australia, where the Division would pass to General MacArthur's Southwest Pacific Command. On November 30, however, the Joint Chiefs of Staff acceded to the urgent request of Major General Millard F. Harmon, Commanding General, Army Forces in the South Pacific Area, and changed our assignment to the South Pacific. As Nimitz had warned me, our convoy was redirected to Noumea, New Caledonia, the base port for supply of Guadalcanal, eight hundred miles to the north, where we were to relieve the 1st Marine Division.

The Japanese 17th Army had moved into the Solomon Islands in March, 1942, in the planned extension to Australia and New Zealand of their control of the South Pacific. They had established a seaplane base at Tulagi, twenty miles north of Guadalcanal, and built an airstrip near the mouth of the Lunga River on the north-central coast of Guadalcanal. Alarmed at this advance, the JCS, to whom the United States–British Combined Chiefs of Staff had assigned strategic direction of the war in the Pacific, decided to stop the southerly advance of the Japanese. The 1st Marine Division, as part of an amphibious force under Rear Admiral Richard K. ("Kelly") Turner, had seized Tulagi and on August 7–8, 1942, landed unopposed on Guadalcanal and occupied an area between the Lunga and Tenaru Rivers, including the airstrip that the Marines called Henderson Field. For the next five months the 1st Marine Division, reinforced in the autumn by two regiments of the Army's Americal Division (for which, see below), withstood repeated Japanese attacks and extended its bridgehead east and west. But by December, 1942, it had suffered over 2,700 battle casualties, and earned its relief.

Our convoy anchored in Noumea's excellent harbor on December 10, 1942, and I reported to Admiral William F. Halsey, in command of the South Pacific Area. Halsey welcomed me to his command with his infectious grin, then shook me with word that we would sail next morning for Guadalcanal, instead of the three-day stopover I had requested in order to combat-load our transports. I had dinner that evening with the Admiral and Major General A. Archer Vandegrift, whose division we were to relieve on the "the Canal." Vandegrift's Chief of Staff, Colonel Gerald C. Thomas, and his G-3 Colonel Merrill B. Twining, were present. They were on their way to Australia in advance of their division, and presented a somber picture of conditions on Guadalcanal and warned me that we were in for a tough fight.

I flew up to Guadalcanal, via Espiritu Santo, with a small staff to prepare for arrival of our convoys, the first of which was due on December 17. We were greeted with pleasure by Major General Alexander M. ("Sandy") Patch, commanding the newly designated but still inchoate XIV Corps. I had met Patch but never served with him. He was a tall, sparse, attractive man, then in his early fifties, full of nervous energy and drive. As we entered his underground C.P., located in direct prolongation of the runway of Henderson Field, an air-raid alert

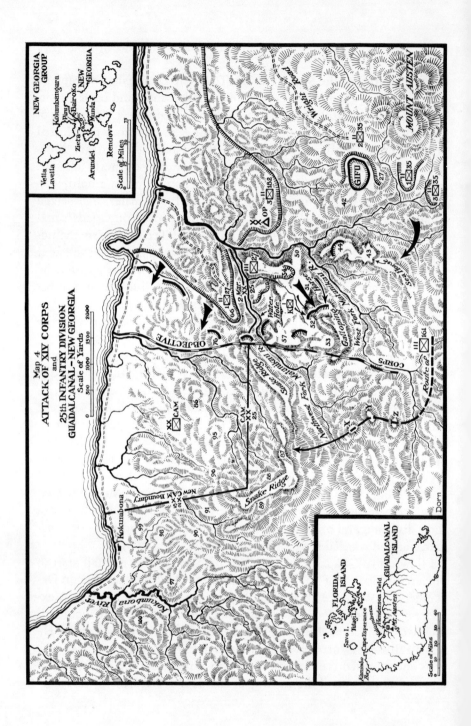

Map 4

ATTACK OF XIV CORPS
and
25th INFANTRY DIVISION
GUADALCANAL - NEW GEORGIA

Scale of Yards

NEW GEORGIA
GROUP

NEW GEORGIA

Scale of Miles

OBJECTIVE

Kokumbona

New CAM Boundary

Snake Ridge

Kokumbona River

MOUNT AUSTEN

GIFU

CORPS

Dorn

GUADALCANAL
ISLAND

FLORIDA
ISLAND

Savo I.
Tulagi I.
Cape Esperance
Kukum
Henderson Field
Mt. Austen

Scale of Miles

sounded. Sandy said, "Don't let that disturb you, Collins. Happens all the time," and nonchalantly proceeded with his briefing.

General Patch had taken command of the Guadalcanal-Tulagi area on December 9, 1942. His command included the seaplane base at Tulagi, and troops of all services in the area including the XIV Corps, which was to consist of the American and 25th Infantry Division. The "Americal" had been constituted from three separate infantry regiments, the 132nd, 164th, and 182nd, which had been lopped off three "square" National Guard divisions when they were triangularized early in the war. Two of the regiments had been rushed to New Caledonia—hence the name "Americal"—under Patch's command to secure that island as a link between Hawaii and Australia. The 164th Regiment,commanded by Colonel Bryant E. Moore, had gone to Guadalcanal on October 13 and had done well holding its sector of the 1st Marine's Lunga River perimeter during the Japanese attacks of October and again in the American attacks to extend the defensive perimeter west of the Matanikau River. The Americal was to operate on Guadalcanal for the first time as a complete division, with its full complement of artillery, engineer, and service troops. Brigadier General Edmund B. Sebree, a friend of mine, had succeeded to command of the Americal when Patch took over the XIV Corps.

Halsey had given Patch a simple mission on Guadalcanal, to "eliminate all Japanese forces." In addition to the Americal and 25th Division, Patch would have available the 2nd Marine Division, the last elements of which would arrive on January 4, the same time as the third convoy of my division. The commercially loaded 25th Division would have to be unloaded offshore into small boats and its equipment sorted out before it would be ready for action. This had an advantage in that it provided time for reconnaissance, and for personal contact by me with friends in the Americal and 1st Marine Divisions. Some elements of the latter had not yet sailed. A few years earlier I had played softball with Colonel Clifton B. Cates, commanding the 1st Marine Regiment, while we were students at the Army War College, and Bryant Moore and I had been in the same cadet company at West Point. Both of these fighting men confirmed the tough, though sometimes stupid, quality of the Japanese, and predicted a stiff fight in the coming offensive of the XIV Corps.

Preparations for First-Phase Attack

The mission assigned the 25th Division by General Patch was to relieve the 132rd Infantry on Mount Austen without delay, and upon completion of this relief to seize and hold a line approximately three thousand yards to the west, preparatory to a coordinated attack by the XIV Corps to eliminate the Japanese forces on Guadalcanal.

General Vandegrift had never had sufficient manpower to extend very far inland the line that had to protect not only Henderson Field and a fighter strip east of Henderson, but cover landing beaches and supply storage areas that extended almost twenty miles from east of Koli Point to Point Cruz. The Marines and American Division had cleared the coastal plain between these points, and the 132rd Infantry of the Americal Division had driven the enemy from most of Mount Austen, but the Japanese still held the foothills west of Mount Austen. Any attack to "eliminate all Japanese forces" on Guadalcanal would have to penetrate far enough inland to root out the enemy from these hills, which had been deeply eroded by centuries of tropical rains. A succession of streams flowed into the sea from the north slopes of the east-west mountain range that formed the central spine of the island. The stream valleys were choked with tropical jungle, but the crests of the intervening ridges were covered with tall cogan grass that showed white in the aerial photographs against the dark green of the jungle. Our air and artillery superiority had forced the Japanese to conceal their defensive positions on the reverse slopes of the ridges and in the jungled valleys.

Because of lack of maps and paucity of information on enemy positions more aerial reconnaissance of the Division zone of action was essential for planning the attack. John Hodge, Stanley Reinhart, and I, the commanders of the two assault regiments, and some of their battalion commanders, made repeated flights over the Division zone of action. This was feasible because at that stage the few remaining Japanese antiaircraft guns did not fire in daylight for fear of counterbattery artillery.

From these reconnaissances it was apparent that the rough, broken terrain would have a dominating influence on the Division plan of attack and render supply and communication extremely difficult. No southern boundary had been prescribed for the division, but the precipitate slopes above the Lunga River, south of Mount Austen, limited operations to the south. The three forks of the Matanikau River, flowing generally north through narrow, deeply eroded, and jungle-filled valleys, divided the Division's zone of action into three distinct compartments: the Mount Austen area east of the southeast fork; the area between the southeast and southwest forks that became known as the "Sea Horse" from its appearance on the aerial mosaics; and the twisting ridge between the southwest and northwest forks, which was quickly identified as the "Galloping Horse."

Mount Austen, elevation 1,514 feet, looked down on Henderson Field and the landing beaches and provided Japanese observation over all approaches to Guadalcanal from the north, until the 132nd Regiment cleared the crest in early January, 1943. The 132nd had nearly surrounded elements of the Japanese 124th and 228th infantry regiments, in an entrenched position that became known as the "Gifu" strong point. Gifu would have to be eliminated to ensure envelopment of the south flank of the Japanese positions confronting the XIV Corps.

The Sea Horse compartment was practically an island bounded by the southeast and southwest forks of the Matanikau and their tributaries. To have attacked it from the east would have required frontal movements in and out of the southeast fork, over its steep, jungle-covered slopes. Instead, it would have to be taken from the south, in connection with the southern envelopment. A similar terrain analysis applied to the Galloping Horse area in the northeast part of the Division's zone. To avoid a frontal attack across the southwest fork of the Matanikau it would be necessary to attack from the north, first crossing the northwest fork near its junction with the main stream of the Matanikau. These two movements, against Mount Austen and the Sea Horse, and the Galloping Horse, would leave a wide gap on the northwest slope of Austen, which would afford excellent positions for our artillery.

Plan of Attack

I decided to avoid all frontal attacks and go after the open ridges by flanking maneuvers, keeping out of the low jungle area. If we could clear Mount Austen and seize the Sea Horse and Galloping Horse ridges, we could trap the Japanese in the pocketed valleys of the Matanikau, where they could be forced to surrender or be destroyed by artillery and mortar fire, with minimum losses of American lives. This analysis dictated an attack by the 25th Division with two regiments abreast and the third in reserve. The 35th Infantry (McClure) was to reduce the Gifu strong point, envelop the south flank of Mount Austen, seize the Sea Horse by attack from the south, then continue the attack to the west to the XIV Corps objective. The 27th Infantry (McCulloch) was to pass through the positions of the 8th Marine Regiment and the reconnaissance squadron of the Americal Division, seize the Galloping Horse ridges, and clear the area north of the southwest fork of the Matanikau to the corps objective. The 161st Infantry (Orndorff) was to assemble in a central position as division reserve. The 3rd Battalion, 182nd Infantry, attached to the 25th Division, was to occupy an area in the gap between the 35th and 27th Regiments so as to guard their flanks and cover the division artillery.

The allotment of artillery for direct support of the infantry followed the Division's standard procedure, *i.e.*, the 64th Field Artillery Battalion supported the 35th Infantry; the 8th Field Artillery Battalion supported the 27th Regiment; and the 89th and 90th Battalions were in general support. We were also to receive some supporting fire from the Marines and the Americal Division. The only preparation fire was to concentrate on the "water hole" area in front of the 1st Battalion 27th Infantry. The 2nd Marine Division had reported this area strongly organized by the enemy. Through our liaison officer from the Thirteenth Air Force, Captain Thomas G. Lamphier, Jr., I had made arrangements for bombing the water hole and the forelegs of the Galloping Horse, following the artillery preparation. Captain Lamphier was to fly the lead bomber.

Logistical arrangements were as important as the tactical plan, and also were dictated by the terrain. The Division's 65th Engineer Battalion improved and extended Wright Trail, the one road suitable for jeeps that led up Mount Austen from the coast; it extended the jeep trails built by the Marines on either side of the Matanikau River, opened trails to the artillery positions, and assisted in establishing a supply dump up the Matanikau River. Three hundred natives were hired to carry ammunition and food and water up and over the steep hillsides from the Matanikau supply dump. The Division's Antitank Company, for which there was no tactical need, supervised the native carriers and took over some of the carrying when enemy fire got too hot for the natives.

The division command post was set up in a coconut grove on the coastal road east of Wright Road, with an observation post (OP) on hill 49, which offered a clear view of the open ridges from Mount Austen west to hills 97, 98, and 99, above the Kokumbona River. I directed much of the battle from the OP, when not with one of the regimental commanders at the front. John Hodge likewise spent most of his time at the front, while our Chief of Staff, Bill Bledsoe, remained at the CP, receiving or relaying telephone messages to and from Hodge or me, or taking appropriate action on his own whenever necessary.

The 27th and 35th Regiments moved from their bivouac near Lunga Point to their jump-off positions on January 8–9. On the north flank the 27th Infantry was prepared to pass through the lines of the 2nd Marines and the Americal Reconnaissance Squadron. The 35th Infantry had to go farther inland: the 2nd Battalion (Lieutenant Colonel Ernest Peters) relieved the 132nd Infantry on three sides of the Gifu strong point; the 1st Battalion (Lieutenant Colonel James B. Leer) was positioned eight hundred yards south of hill 27, prepared to follow the 3rd Battalion (Lieutenant Colonel William J. Mullen, Jr.) five hundred yards farther south, which was to lead the envelopment of the Japanese south flank. These two battalions were to move along the densely wooded ridge, which formed the divide between the Lunga and Matanikau Rivers, to a point south of hill 43, whence they were to attack north and seize the Sea Horse before continuing west to the Corps objective.

The 25th Division was thus poised on the morning of January 10, 1943, to launch its first attack. I had gone up to the Division OP to witness the jump off. It would be my first experience in combat, as well as the Division's, and I shared the same mixture of trepidation and confidence that ran through every man in the Division as we waited for the opening salvo, at 5:50 A.M., of the artillery preparation on the front of the 27th Infantry.

Attack of the 27th Infantry

Following a thirty-minute artillery preparation, the 27th Infantry jumped off with two battalions abreast, the 1st Battalion (Lieutenant Colonel Claude Jurney) on the right, with the mission of seizing hill 57; the 3rd Battalion (Lieutenant Colonel George E. Bush) on the left, for hill 52. The 2nd Battalion (Lieutenant Colonel Herbert V. Mitchell), in reserve, was to relieve elements of the 2nd Marine Division on hill 55.

Following the artillery preparation, P-39 fighters from the Thirteenth Air Force and Marine dive bombers dropped Navy depth charges on the area. The combined effect on the Japanese in front of the 1st Battalion, 27th Infantry, was overwhelming. Whereas the 8th Marines had encountered stiff resistance in the water hole, the 1st Battalion met almost no opposition in breaking through to the north slopes of hill 57.

This was not the case with the 3rd Battalion on the left. Hill 52, the initial objective of the battalion, was actually a ridge, which lay athwart the shoulders of the Galloping Horse, facing northeast. The cogan grass that normally covered the entire "horse" had been burned off by artillery fire, giving the Japanese, dug in on the reverse slope of Hill 52, open fields of fire covering all approaches to the hill. Colonel Bush, jumping off from hill 54, decided to attack with Companies I and L abreast in a double envelopment of hill 52. Halted by deadly crossfire, the Battalion had to throw in Company K, under cover of woods on the right of Company I, to envelop hill 52 from the north. Preceded by heavy artillery and aerial bombardment in midafternoon, K drove the Japanese off hill 52 by late afternoon and consolidated the position for the night.

The 3rd Battalion resumed the attack the following morning, January 11, but made little headway, while taking casualties throughout the day. Men were exhausted from the continuous battling uphill, the oppressive heat, and lack of water. The Galloping Horse ridges were devoid of water, which had to be hauled forward with the rations under cover of darkness. Colonel McCulloch decided to halt the attack for the night and pass the 2nd Battalion through the 3rd on January 12.

I had gone up to hill 50 on the eleventh and had discussed the situation with Colonel Bush; while I was talking with him, men of Mitchell's 2nd Battalion in reserve on hill 50 began firing indiscriminately into the woods to their right, claiming that they were receiving fire from "Jap snipers in the trees." Bullets were clipping through the tops of the trees near us, but I was convinced that this fire was coming from Colonel Jurney's battalion on hill 57 to the northwest. Mitchell was finally able to stop the firing, whereupon the "Jap" fire ceased. Thereafter, I had the regimental and battalion commanders pass the word among the men that I would pay $10 to any man who could prove he had shot down a Japanese firing from up in a tree. The offer never cost me a penny throughout my stay in the South Pacific, but it helped put down the silly claims of snipers in the tree tops.

The 2nd Battalion, 27th Infantry, relieved the 3rd Battalion on January 12 and renewed the attack at 6:30 A.M., following an aerial bombardment and artillery preparation. G Company was able to capture a ridge north of hill 52 and established contact with the 1st Battalion on hill 57, but F Company, trying to outflank the next ridge to the west of hill 52 (later designated Exton Ridge), was caught in the crossfire of machine guns from the ridge northeast of hill 53. F Company was able to occupy the first ridge, but neither F nor E Company on its left was able to advance in the face of heavy fire. During this action 1st Lieutenant Robert M. Exton was mortally wounded on the ridge that came to bear his name.

The determined Mitchell withdrew F Company from Exton Ridge and Mitchell directed F Company to outflank it from the north. This maneuver succeeded in gaining a foothold, but a concealed enemy strongpoint on the reverse slope stopped any further advance. Realizing the importance of the 2nd Battalion's attack, I joined Colonel Mitchell at his CP on hill 52, where H Company had established its machine guns and 81-mm mortars as a base of fire to support the attack. Meanwhile Mitchell had committed his reserve Company E to the left of F Company on Exton Ridge, from which it joined the attack of F Company. The two companies became intermingled. Captain Charles W. Davis, the battalion executive, in a rare display of bravery beyond the call of duty, volunteered to go forward to straighten out the companies and locate the strongpoint that was holding up their advance. We watched breathlessly as Davis, running like a half-back, dodged back and forth to avoid the fire directed against him as he advanced over open ground. He made it to the ridge beyond Exton. After untangling Companies E and F, he scouted out the Japanese strongpoint. Accompanied by Captain Paul K. Mellichamp, my former aide on Oahu, and 1st Lieutenant Weldons S. Sims, he crawled along the east side of the ridge until able to spot the location of the enemy strongpoint. But when Sims raised his head above a protecting ledge to confirm its location he was shot in the chest. His companions pulled his body back but were unable to save him. They could only honor him by giving his name to the ridge where he was killed.

Davis and Mellichamp crawled back to F Company's position, from where Davis radioed for fire from the 81-mm mortar platoon of H Company—a daring and dramatic thing to do, since not more than fifty yards separated Davis and Companies E and F from the enemy. The mortar platoon leader, Sergeant Rex P. Henry, using the bandaged head of Lieutenant Exton as a reference point, coolly drew back his fire, after an opening round well beyond Sims Ridge. Captain Davis relayed his sensings to adjust the fire until shells, exploding on the crest of the ridge and its reverse slope where the enemy was, showered Davis and our troops with dirt, rocks, and shell fragments but failed to destroy the strongpoint. Colonel Mitchell moved up to Sims Ridge, under cover of this fire, to take direct command of the operation. By this time his men had exhausted their drinking water and were on the verge of collapse. Mitchell had the companies organize for all-round defense against an expected counterattack. He and Davis remained overnight on Sims Ridge as they planned the next day's attack. I returned to my CP by jeep.

I was back on hill 52 early the next morning with Colonel McCulloch to see the windup of the attack, which had a dramatic finish. Mitchell and Davis had devised a plan to break the stalemate. Mitchell took part of E Company down the east slope of Sims Ridge over a defiladed route to the south end of the ridge and prepared to attack the ridge from the south, while Davis with four or five volunteers crawled to within ten yards of the Japanese strongpoint, covered by mortar fire hitting just beyond them. At Davis' signal to the mortars to cease firing, his party and E Company under Mitchell charged the strongpoint. Davis jumped to his feet and fired one burst from his rifle, which promptly jammed. He switched the rifle to his left hand, pulled out his pistol and began shooting the startled Japanese in the strongpoint. While still firing his pistol, Davis waved his men forward with his rifle. Spurred on by his fearless example, his party, joined by E Company, swarmed over the ridge and routed the defenders. As Davis led the charge he was in full view of us at the OP and most of the 2nd Battalion. His action had an electrifying effect on the battalion, which stormed over not only Sims Ridge but hill 53, the last Japanese stronghold on the Galloping Horse, which seemed itself to be prancing in victory.

As Colonel McCulloch and I went forward to hill 53 to congratulate Colonel Mitchell on the victory of his battalion, we found him surrounded by his exultant soldiers. But when I shook his hand and congratulated him, he replied with tears in his eyes, "It was not me, but Davis and his men that did it." Both had performed magnificently. I recommended Colonel Mitchell and his party of volunteers for the Distinguished Service Cross. Captain Davis received the Congressional Medal of Honor.

Attack of the 35th Infantry

While the 27th Infantry was distinguishing itself on the north flank, the 35th Regiment had initiated the envelopment of the Japanese south flank. Colonel Mullen's 3rd Battalion, followed by Leer, led off at 6:35 A.M., January 10, along the watershed south of Mount Austen, without firing a shot or encountering the enemy. With no trail along the ridge, it was necessary for the leading company to slash its way through the jungle with machetes and bayonets. It was difficult to gauge direction until sometime in the afternoon when patrols, advancing cautiously ahead of the company, discovered a trail crossing the ridge from the west, with a fork following the ridge toward hill 43 and another dropping down into a deep ravine to the northeast. A Japanese supply party was seen halted on the upper trail and a bivouac area spotted in the ravine. The Japanese were unaware of the approaching 3rd Battalion, which had come upon the supply line supporting Gifu and the Japanese positions on the Sea Horse.

Mullen ordered an attack at once to cut and block the supply line to the west. The supply party, caught by surprise, was wiped out. Companies K and L advanced north against sporadic resistance to the knoll south of hill 43. The Japanese in the ravine, realizing their plight, counterattacked to reopen the supply line but were driven back. By dark the head of the ravine was secured by Company I, while Companies K and L dug in on a knoll five hundred yards south of hill 43. Colonel Leer's 1st Battalion closed up on the 3rd for the night. The following morning Mullen resumed the attack and by dark, January 11, had control of the entire Sea Horse, including hill 44. Encirclement of the Japanese in the southeast fork of the Matanikau was complete.

When it became evident that the 3rd Battalion alone would capture the Sea Horse, Colonel McClure directed Leer to attack to the west to seize the XIV Corps objective overlooking the southwest fork of the Matanikau. The 1st Battalion made slow progress through the heavy jungle on the twelfth but was pinned down about a thousand yards west of the jump-off. In the interim the Japanese in the ravine launched another counterattack but were beaten back. It was not until January 16, after machine guns and 81-mm mortars had been brought forward to hill 43 to join the artillery in support of Leer's Battalion, that it was able to overrun the last opposition on the high ground above the Matanikau.

Reduction of the Gifu Strongpoint

When Bob McClure and I had first studied the Gifu strongpoint from hill 27, we discussed the possibility of sealing off its one open side on the west, which the 132nd Infantry had been unable to close. We considered a double envelopment of Gifu by attacking simultaneously from hills 31 and 27, but rough jungle-filled terrain to the west looked impassable, and we agreed not to do so. In retrospect this was a mistake. We would have saved days of fruitless frontal assaults against the north, east, and south faces of Gifu. Even after the 1st and 3rd Battalions had cut their supply line from the west, the embattled Japanese in Gifu hung on in their deep, well-concealed and well-fortified positions.

After the 27th Infantry had about completed its mission I went up again with Bob McClure to hill 27 to size up the situation on Mount Austen. No firing was going on at the time as we studied the southern flank of Gifu with our field glasses. Our men in nearby foxholes spotted us and one of them was heard to remark, "By God, there is 'J. Lightning' himself!" "Lightning" was the telephone code call for Division headquarters, and the men were familiar with my signature, J. Lawton Collins, on many orders. It was not until after conclusion of the Guadalcanal campaign that I heard of this incident, but word of it spread over the soldiers' grapevine, and "J. Lightning" had changed to "Lightning Joe," a nickname that stuck to me thereafter.

Following our survey, Bob McClure decided to put new life into the 2nd Battalion, whose commander and men alike were worn out from prolonged exertion, frustration, and malaria. He placed the battalion executive, young, vigorous Major Stanley R. ("Swede") Larsen, in command and directed him to carry out the double development of the open side of Gifu that we had earlier turned down. After a thorough reconnaissance, Larsen planned to attack on January 18 with Companies E and G, assisted by Company I, 182nd Infantry, following a heavy artillery preparation. Our lines and the enemy's were so close that McClure had our troops pull back three hundred yards while howitzers were firing their preliminary registration. I watched this firing from the OP on hill 49, which had a clear view of hills 42 and 31. Suddenly I noted shorts beginning to fall on E Company's positions and men running back to escape being hit. I immediately telephoned the fire-direction center to cease fire until corrections could be made.

When I arrived back at the command post at the end of the day, the artillery commander, Stanley Reinhart, was waiting for me as I got out of my jeep. He was furious. "General, I heard that you ordered my artillery to cease fire this afternoon. I'll have you understand that you can't do that to *my* artillery!" he said. I looked at him in amazement, and replied: "Look, Stanley, it is not *your* artillery. It is mine as well. There is only one overall commander in this division and I am it. I command the infantry, the artillery, the engineers, the quartermasters and the medicos. If you had been at an observation post, where you could have seen what was happening, you also would have ordered 'cease fire' when *our* infantrymen were endangered." Reinhart was an expert artilleryman and had trained our artillery to near perfection, but he still had some of "Bull" Ennis in his makeup. He had not quite reconciled himself to the fact that artillery has no independent role but exists solely for the purpose of supporting the division, especially the infantry. He loyally accommodated himself to my point of view and did not again question my authority.

The artillery preparation for the final assault on Gifu had been planned for the morning of the seventeenth but was held up until afternoon to allow an appeal to the Gifu defenders, in Japanese, over a loudspeaker by a psychological warfare specialist from XIV Corps, to persuade the defenders to surrender rather than force us to annihilate them.

They were allowed time to consider, but none surrendered. Two days of dogged fighting finally closed the ring around Gifu, but failed to break its tough shell until we borrowed three light tanks from the 2nd Marine Division. Two broke down on the steep climb up Wright Road but one made it to the top. Captain Teddy Deese of the 25th Division's Reconnaissance Troop, and two of his men, volunteered to man this tank. Teddy Deese—that was his full name—was a backwoods Georgia cracker of the first order. I had gotten behind him one day on Oahu during a field exercise when his tanks—which unfortunately we had not brought with us to Guadalcanal—were operating too cautiously. I said, "Teddy, get going. Let me see you rough up those doughboys a bit." He grinned back at me, "General, my boys likes to play rough!" And he was off with his troop on a wild drive that scattered the "enemy" before him.

This time he drove his tank, with a wedge of fifteen men to secure his flanks, into the Japanese position in front of G Company until its 37-mm gun was poking directly into the mouth of a machine-gun emplacement. One round knocked it out. Wheeling and churning, he charged and destroyed eight such emplacements, forming a small but important salient. Darkness in the thick jungle closed in before this break could be exploited. I doubt that any single tank was ever used more successfully or under as strange circumstances. I recommended Teddy Deese and his crew for the Distinguished Service Cross.

That night about one hundred Japanese soldiers, led by Major Inagaki, tried to break out of the trap that had closed around them. They made a "banzai" charge, throwing grenades and firing automatic weapons. Our men immediately opened up with a hail of fire that drove back the attack. When dawn broke, the Americans counted eighty-five bodies in front of F Company and the Antitank Company, including those of Inagaki, one other major, and twenty-three other officers. The remaining Japanese in the Gifu were too sick, wounded, or starved to put up much further fight. Major Larsen formed his men in a skirmish line and walked through the strongpoint with almost no resistance. By nightfall Mount Austen was free of the enemy.

Reduction of the Gifu had cost the 2nd Battalion, 35th Infantry, 64 men killed and 42 wounded. The battalion reported 518 Japanese killed. The Gifu garrison was almost wiped out. Colonel McClure reported that his troops in the Mount Austen–Sea Horse operation had killed almost 1,100 of the enemy and captured 29 prisoners, 88 machine guns, 678 rifles, 79 pistols, at least two 70-mm guns, and quantities of ammunition.

XIV Corps Attack—January 22–26, 1942

General Patch was anxious to capitalize on the 25th Divison's success east of the Matanikau River, and without waiting for the close-out of the Gifu strongpoint he ordered the planned attack of the XIV Corps to the west, to begin January 22. Apparently believing that most of the regiments of the 2nd Marine and American Divisions were too worn down for immediate action, he formed a composite division from the 6th Marine Regiment and the 147th and 182nd Regiments of the Americal Division and the Americal and Marine artillery. It was designated as the Composite Army-Marine (CAM) Division, under command of General Sebree. The CAM Division was to advance along the coastal area on a front of three thousand yards. While not specified as such, the 25th Division would make the main effort of the Corps, enveloping or turning the enemy's south flank. The attack would be preceded by a fifteen-minute bombardment by the 2nd Marine Air Wing, Naval destroyers offshore, and all available artillery.

Terrain in the 25th Division's zone of action was similar to that covered in the earlier battle. The dominant feature was the high ridge formed by hills 87, 88, and 89. (See Map 4) The best approach to this ridge lay along a lower ridge, just west of the Matanikau, that twisted through the jungle between hills 66 and 87. Its grass-covered top showed clearly on the aerial mosaic and was promptly dubbed "the Snake." Southwest of the Galloping Horse, three open hilltops designated X, Y, and Z poked up above the solid blanket of jungle in the valley of the northwest fork. This area would have to be thrashed through to ensure rounding up any enemy south of the 87-88-89 ridge.

I decided to have the 27th Infantry, well positioned on the western slopes of the Galloping Horse, attack from hill 57, to seize Snake Ridge, and then make a holding attack to the west against hill 87 to pin down any enemy there. The main effort of the Division was to be a turning movement around the Japanese south flank by the 161st Infantry under Colonel Orndorff. It was to seize hills X, Y, and Z, then attack to the northwest, capture the initial Corps objective, hill 87, and prepare to continue the attack to the northwest. This was a tough assignment for an inexperienced regiment, but I expected it would meet little opposition until it approached hill 87. Its hardest job would be to traverse the deep jungle and hold to a proper compass bearing on hill 87.

The 35th Infantry was still cleaning out the Gifu when the 25th Division jumped off in the XIV Corps attack at 6:30 A.M., January 22. I had gone up to the OP on hill 49 to witness the attack of the 27th Infantry, led by Colonel Jurney's 1st Battalion. Preliminary patrolling had penetrated unopposed to the Snake, but drawn fire from hill 87, indicating it would be held in strength. Following a short but intensive bombardment of hill 87, Jurney moved out in column of companies along the Snake. As Company C started to climb 87F, it was halted by machine-gun fire from hill 87. Mortars and 37-mm guns of the battalion silenced the enemy fire as the battalion deployed to assault the hill. I watched with my field glasses and was amazed to see the assault waves storm over hill 87. The enemy had evidently withdrawn. I notified Colonel Bledsoe at our CP, jumped into my jeep, and headed for the Snake to ensure we would capitalize on this break. Fortunately I ran into General Patch's Chief of Staff, Brigadier General Robert L. Spragins, on hill 66. I explained the situation and, in accord with Patch's instructions not to stop at the Corps' initial objective of hill 87, obtained permission to push our attack to Kokumbona. We would have to cut across the front of the CAM Division after capturing hills 89 and 91, which would require a change of boundary between the two divisions so as to place hills 91, 98, 99, and Kokumbona in the 25th Division zone. Spragins approved and notified Corps and CAM headquarters so we would not be caught by friendly artillery fire.

I proceeded on a trail that ran along the Snake to a point on hill 87 just below its crest, and there met Colonel Bill McCulloch, who had moved up to the front on his own, as he should have. I outlined the change in boundary and directed him to take over the main effort of the Division from the 161st Infantry. He was to continue the attack via hills 88, 89, and 91, and, if possible, seize hills 90 and 98 before dark.

I advised our CP that I would remain on the Snake trail awaiting the leading battalion of the 161st Infantry, which had not yet had time to hack its way through the jungle from hills X and Y. It reached the trail below hill 87 about midafternoon, having encountered only scattered rifle fire. I had it assemble south of hill 87 in reserve and sent word to Colonel Orndorff, who had remained at his CP near hill 53, to assemble his 1st and 3rd Battalions in that area in reserve. Worn down by the heat and a bout of malaria, Orndorff had been unable to make the strenuous trek through the jungle with the 2nd Battalion.

I then followed along in rear of the 3rd Battalion, 27th Infantry, until I caught up with Bill McCulloch on hill 89. Jurney's 1st Battalion had already reached hill 91, with little opposition. McCulloch and I studied hills 90 and 98 with our glasses and could see no signs of enemy. We decided there should be time for Jurney to occupy those hills in daylight, if he moved out at once. McCulloch and I agreed that he would push into Kokumbona the following morning with his 1st Battalion, with the 3rd Battalion on the northeast slope of hill 99 blocking escape of any enemy caught in the ravine east of Kokumbona in front of the CAM Division. Mitchell's 2nd Battalion was to continue the attack westward. Leaving McCulloch to complete these arrangements, I returned to the Division CP. McCulloch established his CP for the night on hill 89.

Next day, January 23, while the 27th was advancing into Kokumbona, I went up with Bob McClure to Mount Austen to see the windup of the Gifu battle. (See Map 4) It was raining hard and we had to leave our jeep at the head of Wright Road. We went forward on foot to a point above the ravine on the west side of Gifu, where Swede Larsen's 2nd Battalion, 35th Infantry, was still clearing out the few Japanese who refused to surrender. We could see nothing in the jungle, but as the sporadic firing ended we went down into the ravine to meet Larsen's men assembling there. By this time we were muddied from head to foot and indistinguishable from the men. Officers in the South Pacific did not have their insignia of rank painted on their helmets, as we did later in the European Theater, and most wore no insignia, for Japanese marksmen had a bad habit of picking off officers. Before leaving Hawaii, I had a friend in the Navy's shops at Pearl Harbor make a tiny set of silver stars, which I wore on the collar of my two-piece green jeans, the latter being the common uniform of officers and men. We joined the men assembling in a hollow as they came in from all directions, jubilant over their success, boasting of the number of bronze-star souvenirs they had collected from dead Japanese. In the Japanese army a private soldier wore a small bronze star on a cloth tab sewn on the collar of his tunic. A private 1st class had two bronze stars, and a superior private 1st class wore three. Our men had torn these tabs from the collars of the dead Japanese soldiers and were counting them off as proof of their prowess.

As the men began to move out to return to their bivouacs, I tagged on the tail end of a column in single file going up a steep slope. It was still raining and the trail was slick with mud. The man ahead of me slipped. I grabbed his arm to keep him from falling. He turned and for the first time noticed the small stars on my collar.

"Gee! *Silver* stars! Where'd you get 'em!"

I said, "Son, don't you know what this insignia is?"

"Nope," came the reply. Evidently he was one of the new men who had joined the Division just before we left Hawaii.

"Well, this is the insignia of a major general. I happen to be General Collins, your division commander."

That stopped him cold. He looked me over from head to feet, then shrugged his shoulders in disbelief as he resumed his climb: "Wa-a-l, I hope you're right! "

Occupation of Kokumbona

On the morning of January 23 the 27th Regiment occupied Kokumbona without a fight; but as the 3rd Battalion was moving into position on hill 99 to block escape of any enemy in front of the CAM, that division opened up with machine guns and artillery fire on the Japanese trapped in the stream bottom east of hill 99. Overs began to zip into the 3rd Battalion. A hurried telephone call from Bill McCulloch to me at the Division CP was quickly relayed to CAM headquarters, which managed to lower the CAM barrage without damage to our battalion. South of Kokumbona the 2nd Battalion, after outposting the hills 90–97 ridge, fought its way across the Kokumbona River against a group of diehard Japanese.

During the next two days the 27th Regiment continued its attack to the west until it attained the XIV Corps' objective of the Poha River. To our deep regret the Division was halted there by the Corps because of a reported Japanese threat to try to recapture Guadalcanal. The Division was withdrawn by XIV Corps, to take over beach defenses east of the Lunga River. The rumored Japanese attack never developed.

The CAM Division was directed to pass through the 25th Division on January 26 and continue the attack "to effect the kill through aggressive and untiring effort," but in nine days the front advanced only four miles, and General Patch on February 6 called on the 161st Infantry to relieve the worn-out 147th Regiment of the Americal Division and press the pursuit. Under its new commander, Colonel James L. Dalton II, a young aggressive West Pointer, who had succeeded Colonel Orndorff, the 161st put new zest in the drive. In three days it advanced over ten miles as the remnants of Japanese forces were completing their evacuation from the Cape Esperance area. To forestall such an evacuation General Patch landed the 2nd Battalion, 132nd Infantry on the west coast of Guadalcanal on February 1, with the directive to march on Cape Esperance. Its advance was slow, and by the time it reached Kamimbo Bay on February 8 the last Japanese were gone, evacuated from Marovovo and Kamimbo Bay by destroyers on the night of February 7–8.

The 161st Infantry and the 2nd Battalion, 132nd Infantry, met in the village of Tenaro on the afternoon of February 9, thus ending the fighting on Guadalcanal, except for rounding up scattered Japanese stragglers. Postwar interviews of Japanese commanders, as well as published Japanese studies, indicate that the Japanese 17th Army began withdrawal to Cape Esperance on the night of January 22–23, and evacuation by destroyers was carried out at night during February 7–8. Their reports of the numbers evacuated range from nine to thirteen thousand. The XIV Corps estimate was three thousand.

There is no doubt in my mind that the shift of the 25th Division from pursuit to a defensive role against a possible Japanese counteroffensive against Guadalcanal was a mistake. The 25th Division had the Japanese on the run from January 23 on. It had demonstrated ability to maneuver quickly over the rough terrain of Guadalcanal. Had the division been permittd to maintain its attack, little if any of the Japanese 17th Army would have gotten away. In postwar interviews Japanese commanders commented that the Americans had moved on Cape Esperance too slowly and stopped too long to consolidate positions. The commander of the 17th Army, General Hyakutake, stated that resolute attacks would have destroyed his army.

General Patch was most generous in recognizing the decisive role of the 25th Division in driving the Japanese from Guadalcanal, as indicated in his citation for the Division, dated March 7, 1943.*

---

*Citation for the 25th Infantry Division

"1. I personally and officially commend the officers and enlisted men of the 25th Infantry Division for their outstanding performance of duty in action on Guadalcanal, Solomon Islands, during the period 10 January–9 February 1943.

2. The 25th Infantry Division making the main effort of the XIV Corps attacked through dense tropical jungles and over mountainous terrain against well organized positions manned by tenacious enemy whose mission was to hold to the last man. This division by its rapid advance and skillful maneuver encircled and pocketed enemy centers of resistance and finally broke the enemy's power to offer further effective defense by fighting its way into Kokumbona.

It was largely through the sustained drive of the 25th Infantry Division that the last vestige of organized resistance on Guadalcanal was crushed and possession of this stra-

Aftermath of Combat on Guadalcanal

It was quite a comedown for the men of the 25th Division, who now regarded themselves as combat veterans, to revert to the guarding of beaches they had done for so long in Hawaii. Worse yet were the chores of clearing the beach areas of the jumble of surplus equipment, ammunition, and other supplies that the Marines and early Army units had no time to sort out and store before moving into combat. Much of this material had already sunk in the mud immediately back of the beaches.

I was anxious to maintain the fighting edge we had honed so well in Hawaii and sharpened in combat and decided to take time from the stevedoring to hold a thorough critique of our Guadalcanal operations while they were still fresh in the minds of officers and senior noncoms. Each regiment and battalion commander prepared a written account of actions of his unit including frank appraisal of things that went wrong. These accounts were presented orally in a series of outdoor conferences attended by the bulk of officers of the Division and at least two noncommissioned officers from each company or battery. Our G-3 staff produced a large-scale map of the island showing sufficient detail of the terrain so that speakers could point out the highlights of operations. Assisted by members of the staff, I first outlined each phase of the operations of the XIV Corps and the 25th Division, followed in subsequent meetings by accounts of the infantry and artillery commanders and commanders of service units.

I summed up each phase of the action, pointing out mistakes—including at least one mistaken judgment on my part in reduction of the Gifu strongpoint—and extolling praiseworthy performance of units or individuals, like the exploits of Major Charley Davis. The critiques were reproduced in a mimeographed volume, along with a map and several aerial mosaics, and distributed to units for further study. Copies went to appropriate higher headquarters. Entitled *Operations of the*

---

tegically important Island, so vital to projected operations, finally wrested from the hands of the Japanese on 9 February 1943.

3. The splendid results obtained are attributed directly to the superb leadership, fighting spirit and eagerness for combat inherent in the 25th Infantry Division."

Alexander M. Patch
Major General, U.S. Army

25th Infantry Division on Guadalcanal, the volume drew high praise from the office of the Chief of Military History, Department of the Army.

To get troops back in fighting trim, we resumed combat training as soon as it became apparent the Japanese would not be able to mount a counteroffensive against Guadalcanal. With approval of Major General Oscar W. Griswold, who succeeded Patch in April of 1943 in command of the XIV Corps, I selected an area east of Koli Point, unoccupied by copra plantations or native villages, as a combat range, where we could conduct battalion exercises comparable to those held in Hawaii. The area offered training in heavier jungle than in Oahu and included extensive swamps as well as some open ground. Again we fired all supporting weapons close to front-line troops, and with cooperation of air units on the island perfected our technique of close aerial support.

Health conditions on Guadalcanal were almost as much a hindrance to operations as were the Japanese. The swampy streams were breeding grounds for the Anopheles mosquito, which transmits malaria. Before the Japanese occupied the island they were probably infected and passed the infection to the Marines and Army troops. The atabrine or quinine we took daily as a suppressant of the disease was not a preventative. All that was needed to receive the disease was a bite from an infected mosquito. I received one or more such infections within twenty-four hours of my arrival on the island, even though I slept under a net. My experience was typical of many members of the division. By June, 1943, battle casualties and illness had reduced the Division's strength by about 250 officers and 2,500 men.

Atabrine kept me on my feet until the fighting was over, when I promptly came down with estuvo autumnal malaria, one of the more serious varieties of the disease. Confined to my screened tent rather than going to the hospital, I took the "cure" of thirty grains of atabrine daily for a week, followed by thirty grains of quinine a day for a second week, then a lesser amount of plasmochin for a week. Later on the island of New Georgia I had a relapse, coupled with a violent attack of gastroenteritis in the middle of a night in a tropical rainstorm—the low point of my military career.

Malaria, fungus infections, and diarrhea, combined with the heat, humidity, and ever-present mud, wore down many of the men. It was not until the Navy's Seabee construction units cleaned, drained, and oiled the coastal streams that the mosquitoes and leeches were brought under control. By that time the 25th Division was beginning to move up to New Georgia, two hundred miles north.

Meanwhile, important changes of personnel had occurred: John Hodge was promoted to major general and took command of the Americal Division. Bill McCulloch became a brigadier and Hodges' assistant commander, and our G-3 was promoted colonel and transferred to a regiment in the Americal Division, giving that division an infusion of 25th Division experience. Stanley Reinhart got his second star and one of the newly organized infantry divisions in the States. I selected Colonel Bob McClure as replacement for John Hodge and Bill Bledsoe as my new artillery commander. Colonel William W. Dick, Jr., Field Artillery, took over from Bledsoe as chief of staff. Three new colonels, all first class, now commanded the infantry regiments: Douglas Sugg, the 27th; Everett Brown, the 35th; and Jim Dalton, the youngest of the lot, whom I selected over the heads of some seniors, to succeed Clarence Orndorff in the 161st Infantry. We still had a fine group of leaders.

With the Division back in trim, I took advantage of an opportunity offered by General Harmon for a three-week recreational leave of absence in New Zealand, where the Army had a rest center.

The New Georgia Campaign

Having checked at Guadalcanal the Japanese advance toward New Zealand, the Allies in the south and southwest Pacific areas now sought to capture the Japanese air and naval base at Rabaul, on the island of New Britain, in the Bismarck Archipelago. The prior capture of the airstrip of Munda on New Georgia was essential. But Major General Noboru Sasaki, the tough commander of Japanese Army and Navy forces in the New Georgia group of islands, which included Vella Lavella, Kolumbungara, Arundel, and a host of islets around the main island of New Georgia, was determined to protect Munda. (See Map 4)

The capture of Munda was expected to be difficult but was made more so by Rear Admiral Richmond ("Kelly") Turner in command of Task Force 31, designated by Admiral Halsey to clear New Georgia. In addition to discounting the fighting qualities of the Japanese, Turner had a penchant for complicated command arrangements and the mixing of units in various task forces. The configuration of New Georgia with its surrounding reefs prevented a direct amphibious landing close to Munda; establishment of a base on Rendova, off the southern coast, would be required prior to an attack on Munda.

Instead of placing General Griswold in command of land operations and using the XIV Corps staff to coordinate the supporting administrative and logistical arrangements, Turner gave this responsibility to Major General John H. Hester—in addition to the latter's command of the 43rd Division, which was to make the attack on Munda. The 43rd Division, constituted in the States from three New England National Guard regiments, was an untested outfit, in action for the first time. Turner designated a second major task force, the Northern Landing Group, commanded by Colonel Harry B. Liversedge, U.S. Marine Corps, to land northeast of Munda, seize Bairoko Harbor, and prevent reinforcement of Munda by Japanese from Kolumbangara. Instead of assigning this task to a regimental combat team of the 37th Division, he formed Liversedge's task force from a mixture of the 1st Marine Raider battalion and three Army Infantry battalions, each from a different regiment of the 37th Division. What a jumble! These troops had never worked together and their capabilities and limitations were unknown to Liversedge, as he was unknown to them. As if to ensure a poor result, Turner gave Liversedge's force no artillery. The remainder of the 37th Division, Ohio National Guard, under Major General Robert S. Beightler, which had been occupying the Fiji Islands, was staged up to Guadalcanal but was to be employed only on Admiral Halsey's orders. At the outset the 25th Division was to remain on Guadalcanal, for possible use on Bougainville.

After some initial success in a landing near Munda, the 43rd Division quickly ran into trouble as it hacked its way through the sodden jungle. The debilitating heat and humidity sapped the energy of the poorly conditioned Americans, and the wily Japanese, who seemed to melt into the jungle by day only to harass the inexperienced Americans by local counterattacks at night, created psychological hazards that undermined the morale of the badly disciplined troops. By the time the Division reached the outer defenses of the Munda airfield, which General Sasaki had skillfully organized, the attack was hopelessly stalled. General Harmon, who from the start had been unhappy with Turner's command setup, felt that Turner "was inclined more and more to take active control of land operations" from his CP on Guadalcanal, two hundred miles away. With Admiral Halsey's approval, Harmon sent General Griswold up to Rendova on July 11 to check on the progress of the 43rd Division. It did not take Griswold long to size up the situation. He urged that the 25th Division and the remainder of the 37th Division be sent into the battle at once.

When shown the cable from Griswold, Halsey informally appointed Harmon as his deputy to "assume full charge of and responsibility for ground operations on New Georgia." Harmon promptly had Griswold take over command of the New Georgia land campaign from General Hester, whose sole responsibility would be to command the 43rd Division. Harmon moved up the 37th Division from Guadalcanal and assigned it to the XIV Corps, along with the 161st Infantry regiment of the 25th Division. Thus reinforced, the XIV Corps launched its attack to capture Munda on July 25. By the twenty-ninth, after a grueling fight in which Jim Dalton's 161st Infantry played a major role, the airstrip was almost surrounded. It was abandoned by the Japanese on August 5.

The 25th Division Resumes Control of the 27th and 161st Regiments

The Munda fighting took a heavy toll of casualties in the 37th and 43rd Divisions, both of which were now far under strength. The only source of reinforcements available to General Harmon to meet Griswold's urgent calls for fresh troops was the 25th Division, which Admiral Halsey had planned to use for the invasion of Bougainville. Reluctantly, Halsey agreed to Harmon's request to release the 25th Division to the XIV Corps, but held out the 35th Infantry Regiment in reserve.

With the 27th and 161st Regiments already committed on New Georgia, I moved my headquarters there on August 1, 1943. Following the capture of Munda, the 161st Infantry and the 27th returned to my command. Griswold now directed me to pursue Sasaki's troops, which were believed to be withdrawing in two columns, one to the north toward Bairoko, the other toward the village of Zieta northwest of Munda. (See Map 4) I assigned to the 161st Infantry the mission of pursuing the force moving on Bairoko, hoping to trap it between the 161st and Liversedge's command; the 27th RCT was to pursue the Zieta force. I established my CP on a hill overlooking the Munda airstrip and the junction of the Bairoko and Zieta trails.

We had no maps of the jungle-covered area of New Georgia beyond Munda, and our airplane mosaics showed little below the treetops. A faint trail ran north from Munda. After a short distance it forked, with one fork leading toward Zieta and the other toward Bairoko. The 25th Division moved out from Munda on August 4 in a column of regiments with the 27th Infantry in the lead. It ran into its first resistance a short distance north of Munda, which it overcame next day. During the fighting the leading battalion, commanded by Lieutenant Colonel Joseph F. Ryneska, had gone past the trail junction leading off toward Zieta. I had joined Ryneska's 1st Battalion on August 6. To avoid backtracking his battalion, I attached it to Dalton's 161st Infantry, which continued north to a junction with Liversedge's force east of the Bairoko River on August 9.

For the next three weeks, Dalton's and Liversedge's forces, pushing through heavy jungle over almost impassable trails, gradually closed in on Bairoko. Light Japanese forces withdrew ahead of them, finally evacuating Bairoko by barges on the nights of August 23 and 24.

While the 161st advanced on Bairoko, the 27th Regiment (less 1st Battalion) pursued the bulk of Sasaki's forces to the northwest along a trail that led to the village of Zieta. The regimental commander, Colonel Douglas Sugg, had been hospitalized on Guadalcanal with a severe case of fungus infection, shortly before the 27th left for New Georgia, and Lieutenant Colonel George E. Bush was temporarily in command. Bush had done a fine job on the Canal, but this was the first time he had responsibility of a regiment, so I went along with his CP most of the daylight hours, interposing to the minimum extent. We had good telephone communication back to the division CP and, through the switchboard there, forward along the Bairoko trail to Dalton's 161st Infantry. The swampy terrain in between was covered with almost impenetrable jungle.

An incident on the Zieta trail remains in my memory as an example of the fidelity and courage of our infantry officers and men who, day after day, bear the brunt of combat, in rain, heat, and mud, as in no other branch of the service. Late one afternoon we received word from a friendly native that a shortcut led off to the left to Zieta from the trail we were following. Bush decided to send a platoon cross-country through the jungle to intercept any Japanese who might turn off on the shortcut. As I watched the platoon move out, on a compass bearing, in the gathering dusk, I marveled at the integrity and bravery of its young leader and the men who followed him with such discipline and loyalty. The platoon could easily have halted for the night after moving a half mile, then returned the next morning with a report that they could not intercept the Japanese party. No one would ever have known the difference. Instead they found the shortcut to Zieta, established an ambush, and when a large body of Japanese walked into it during the night they mowed it down before the remainder slipped by, through the jungle. I passed the spot the following morning and saw the results of their mission. It was the last resistance along the way to Zieta.

The Piru Plantation

From Zieta the 27th Infantry pushed across a broad swamp, filled with cypress trees, carrying food, ammunition, and weapons, to the Piru Plantation, along the banks of the Diamond Narrows, which separated the island of New Georgia from Arundel Island. On August 23, accompanied by an aide, I followed on foot the advance of the 27th Infantry to the edge of the swamp, after having left our jeep some distance back where the trail became impassable for vehicles. We stopped at noon when we reached the swamp, where we met a couple of signalmen who had just laid a light telephone line across the swamp to link the 27th Regiment to the Division CP. We shared our C rations with these men as they brewed some coffee in a helmet.

When I had left the CP in the morning I had no intention of hiking so far in rubber boots with only heavy socks, but no shoes; nor had I expected to walk across the swamp. It was a long way back to the jeep, so I decided to go on and spend the night with Colonel Sugg, who had returned from the hospital to command his regiment. As we separated after lunch, I asked one of the linemen just how deep the water in the swamp was. He replied: "Well, I'll tell you, Gen'rall. The way to cross this swamp is to step from one of those cypress knees [roots] to the next. But if you slip off, you'll go right up to your ass hole!" I soon found that he was precisely accurate. Crossing that swamp was the toughest physical test I underwent during the war. Those cypress knees were not only slippery but hard and sharp. By the time we reached the Piru Plantation, after two hours of slipping and sliding, in and out of the swampy muck, under the oppressive heat, the only thing that revived me was word from Sugg that the 27th Infantry had driven the last Japanese from the plantation; they had withdrawn to Arundel Island. For the 25th Division the New Georgia campaign was virtually over. After spending the night with Sugg and his men, I returned the next morning by boat to my CP, proud that the Division had again accomplished its mission.

During the remainder of the campaign the Division was not employed as a unit. Kolumbangara was bypassed while the 35th Infantry regimental combat team, under General McClure, did an expert job driving the Japanese from the island of Vella Lavella, between August 15 and September 24, enabling the Seabees to construct an airfield there for use against Rabaul. While the 35th RCT was securing Vella Lavella, General Griswold called on Colonel Sugg's 27th RCT to assist the 43rd Division in clearing the last of General Sasaki's troops from Arundel.

Bob McClure returned to the States shortly thereafter, was promoted, and given a division. He was succeeded as my assistant division commander by Charles L. ("Love") Mullins, a classmate of mine from West Point, who had been sent over from the States.

Near the end of the New Georgia campaign Generals Harmon and Griswold and Colonel Godwin Ordway, a friend who was then an observer from the War Department, came up to my CP for a round of visits to some of my troops. While accompanying them, I had jokingly remarked to Miff Harmon that in light of the number of observers the Department was sending out to look us over it was about time for one of us to go back to Washington to "observe" the War Department. I said I had no ulterior motives, but that my family was in Washington and I had been away from home for two years. Miff laughed that one off, but the seed bore fruit a few months later.

The 25th Division Moves to New Zealand

Following the windup of the New Georgia campaign the 25th Division was staged through Guadalcanal to New Zealand for rest and rehabilitation, as was sound practice in the South Pacific. The movement of the Division by ship convoy began in early November and was completed November 5, 1943. I had flown down in late Ocotber to arrange for billeting and a command post. With help of Colonel James Boyers, in charge of the U.S. Army Service Command in New Zealand, I looked over and decided on locations formerly occupied by other American troops. As a billet for Bill Bledsoe, "Love" Mullins, Bill Dick, and me, I was pleased to find the spacious country home, Manurewa House, of the English Earl and Countess of Oxford, who were away in England.

The Division began its medical overhaul at once. Many men had residual effects of malaria, fungus infections, and intestinal parasites. The 39th General Hospital had been set up early in the war in Auckland as part of a far-sighted prewar medical plan. It was staffed by doctors from the medical school of Yale University, all of whom were members of an affiliated Reserve Corps unit, and by nurses from a New Haven hospital. The 39th General was commanded by Colonel Don W. Longfellow and the Chief Nurse was Esther Butt. It did a wonderful job helping take care of the sick and wounded in the South Pacific. I have wondered since if the Yale authorities who did away with the ROTC program in the wake of the war in Vietnam knew of the contributions of their medical unit in World War II.

Finding training areas, especially for artillery firing, was most difficult. The New Zealanders were rightly concerned about protecting their "bush," as they called their sparse forests. Bill Bledsoe and I looked at all areas offered, but could find nothing resembling a tropical jungle and only very limited wooded areas where we would be permitted to conduct combat-firing exercises with live ammunition. It was not that the New Zealanders were uncooperative, but having escaped the ravages of war they naturally were loath to subject their lovely countryside to practice shelling, the need for which they could not understand. We found them friendly and hospitable, welcoming our officers and men into their homes with an informality that belied their British ancestry.

Bill Bledsoe and I had returned to Manurewa House on December 1, 1943, after having been away on a three-day reconnaissance trip looking for training areas. I was pretty tired and did not pick up the stack of accumulated official mail until after dinner. It was nearing midnight and I was half asleep when I opened a letter from Al Barnett, General Harmon's Chief of Staff. I came to life in a flash as I read the startling sentence, recalling my joshing remark to Harmon en route to New Georgia: "Miff says to tell you that if you are really serious about wanting to get home for a visit, it is all right to go." After some hurried telephone calls, frantic packing, and a little sleep, I left the following morning at 5:30 A.M. I was lucky to catch a direct military plane to Washington. I did not know that I was leaving for good my Tropic Lightning Division, which I dearly loved. There was no time for farewells as I was anxious to get home for Christmas. I made it on December 23.

CHAPTER X

Off to England to Command VII Corps

Gladys met me at the National Airport in Washington. Not knowing until the day before that I was coming home for Christmas, she and our younger daughter Nancy had gone up to West Point, where our son Jerry was a plebe at the Military Academy, to spend the holidays with Jerry and our older daughter, Gladdie, a freshman at nearby Vasser College. Gladys had returned to meet me. She was a joy to behold.

Gladys and I were anxious to join the children at West Point, so we flew at once to New York where an Army car met us for the drive to the Academy. We had a grand reunion. Jerry looked fine in his cadet uniform, and Gladdie and Nancy had developed during my absence into handsome teenagers. As we sat down for a family dinner at the Thayer Hotel, together for the first time in two years, we thanked the good Lord for our manifold blessings.

After a wonderful Christmas at the Point, Gladys, Nancy, and I returned to Washington. Gladys had moved the family to Washington while I was away, and had found a place to live on 31st Place, N.W. After tramping the halls of Congress she had finally secured an appointment for Jerry to West Point; and then packed Gladdie off to Vassar. Meanwhile she did Gray Lady work at Walter Reed Hospital.

Back in Washington, I called on General Marshall in his office in the Pentagon, and found him fit, relaxed, and confident. He had clearly overcome the strain of the Pearl Harbor days and showed no sign of disappointment that Eisenhower, and not he, had been chosen by the President as Supreme Allied Commander Europe (SACEUR) for the invasion of France, announcement of which had been made by President Roosevelt on Christmas Eve. He received me cordially, saying that while flying home from Australia, where he had stopped off to see General MacArthur following the Cairo-Teheran conferences, he had tried to make connections with me when he learned that I was flying up from New Zealand at the same time. He had radioed a message to me which I received too late to join his plane at one of the way stations leading to Hawaii. He congratulated me on the performance of the 25th Division and had me tell him briefly the highlights of our operations. I reminded the General that I had commanded the Division for over a year and felt that I could manage a Corps. He replied, "I am sure you could."

General Marshall told me he had raised with MacArthur the question of my getting a Corps. He said, with a chuckle and a rare twinkle of his eyes, that MacArthur had replied, "But Collins is too young!" As I was leaving, I said, "And General, I would like to have a crack at the European Theater." He answered with an enigmatic smile, "Maybe you will." Then he advised me that General Eisenhower would shortly be returning to Washington from North Africa on a secret visit, and that he was having a stag dinner at the Alibi Club the following Monday in Eisenhower's honor, to which I would be invited. He added that he had arranged for Mrs. Collins and me to fly down to White Sulphur Springs, in the mountains of West Virginia, where the Army had taken over the Greenbrier Hotel as a convalescent hospital. He enjoined me to forget about the war for a week or ten days and hoped I would relax and enjoy the stay with my wife.

The Alibi Club had been established years before as a private eating club at 1806 I Street, N. W., in Washington, and through the courtesy of Robert Woods Bliss the facilities of Alibi were made available to General Marshall, who took advantage of the occasional presence in Washington of senior field commanders by introducing them to congressional leaders and other prominent Americans at informal dinners. I attended the one in honor of General Eisenhower on January 2, 1943. Present in addition to Eisenhower were Secretary of War Henry L. Stimson; James F. Byrnes, Director of War Mobilization; Senators Warren Austin and Wallace H. White; Representatives Andrew J. May, Walter G. Andrews, and R. Ewing Thomason; Robert P. Patterson, Undersecretary of War; Assistant Secretary John J. McCloy; Bernard Baruch; Admiral Harold R. Stark; Generals Henry H. Arnold, Brehon B. Somervell, Joseph T. McNarney, and George Kenney.

Marshall and Eisenhower greeted the guests as they arrived. I had not seen Ike since the Louisiana manuevers, and he looked well and was in fine fettle. He gave me a grin and a cherry "Hello Joe," but with the onrush of arriving guests there was no time or opportunity for any further exchange. I knew most of the other guests and visited with them before we sat down at one large oval table for an informal dinner. After the meal General Marshall called on each of the overseas guests to speak. He named me first to cover the highlights of the 25th Division's operations on Guadalcanal and New Georgia; Kenney described the airborne attack in the Markham Valley on New Guinea and operations in New Britain in the South Pacific; and Admiral Stark, former Chief of Naval Operations, outlined naval problems in the North Atlantic. General Marshall then called on Ike to talk about recent operations in the Mediterranean. Despite all that was written in later years about Eisenhower's broken syntax, Ike was one of the most effective extemporaneous speakers I have ever heard, particularly when talking about military matters. He was, of course, on top of his subject that evening and made a tremendous impression.

White Sulphur Springs

Gladys and I left the following day for White Sulphur Springs, where we were assigned one of the white cottages set off from the main building at the Greenbrier in a grove of old oaks. We had been there only a day or two when we were invited to dinner at the house of the commander of the hospital, Colonel Clyde McK. Beck, at seven o'clock that evening. Mrs. Beck said it would be just a small, informal party, then puzzled us by suggesting that we be sure to be on time. This caution was explained shortly after our hosts had greeted us and one other couple, when the front door was opened and in walked General and Mrs. Eisenhower. The General was as surprised to see me as I was at his and Mamie's appearance. He stopped short and exclaimed: "Why Joe! I didn't know you were down here. I understand you are coming over to join us!"

That was how I learned that I was to be transferred to the European Theater. I simply said, "Thank you very much!" Knowing the security dangers involved in cocktail and dinner talk, Ike volunteered no further information. I took it for granted that when he had seen General Marshall in Washington, Marshall had recommended me as a corps commander. Ike offered no hint of this, and I asked no questions, content in the knowledge that I would not return to the Pacific.

Much as I had enjoyed the privilege of commanding the 25th Infantry Division there, I realized that the decisive battles would be fought in Europe and I wanted to participate. I was confident that after defeating Hitler and his legions, the Allies could finish off the Japanese, who had neither the economic nor military resources to withstand alone the mighty forces we were creating. But that evening at the Greenbrier we did not discuss the war, engaging only in the usual dinner small talk, chiefly about mutual friends. Ike and Mamie left early. I did not see Ike again until I reported to him in England.

Orders assigning me to the European Theater were issued January 19, 1944; but before I could leave I had to pass a physical examination, a sound requirement of the War Department covering all officers going overseas. The exam was held a few days before clearance for departure, followed by a final brief check within twenty-four hours of takeoff. I easily cleared my exam on a Friday morning, went home for lunch, then suddenly was hit with chills and fever, sure signs of a recurrence of malaria. Fortunately I had brought with me from the South Pacific the drugs necessary for a "cure" and started taking quinine at once. Gladys was off shopping. When she returned I was in bed, with the covers up to my ears and an ice bag on my head. Her face turned white when she saw me. We both could envision my orders being canceled, but I was not going to let that happen if I could help it. I took thirty grains of quinine each day, Friday, Saturday, and Sunday, and got by the final check on Monday without a trace of fever. I never mentioned my "cure" to the checking medical officer, kept up the quinine at reduced dosages for some while, and never had a recurrence.

On January 26, 1944, I kissed Gladys and Nancy goodbye and headed off by air for the great adventure in Europe. Weather was foul over the North Atlantic, so we were routed on a southerly course, developed during the war, via Miami-Trinidad-Natal-Dakar-Marrakesh to Prestwick, Scotland, stopping off in Natal and Dakar. We were scheduled to remain overnight at Marrakesh while waiting for a weather clearance to Prestwick. I was billeted in the sumptuous Villa Taylor, built by some wealthy gentleman and taken over during the war by our Army as a guesthouse. It had all the tappings of an *Arabian Nights* castle. I was intrigued by a gilt-mosaic sunken bath, in which I was about to luxuriate before dinner, when I received a hurry-up call that I was to be at the airport within an hour so we could take advantage of a break in the weather at Prestwick. I was told later that no matter how bad flying conditions were elsewhere in the British Isles, planes could always get in to Prestwick. It was a dark and stormy night when we landed. A train ride through the Bobby Burns country brought me into London in the forenoon of February 2. I checked in at the Dorchester Hotel, adjacent to Hyde Park, where I was to be billeted, and reported at once to Eisenhower's headquarters at 20 Grosvenor Square.

When I met Eisenhower and Bradley I learned that no decision had been made on my assignment. They asked a good many questions about my experience in the Pacific. I emphasized that I had always gone after high ground in attack. At that, Brad turned to Ike and said, "He talks our language." That conversation may have been the clincher that decided Eisenhower to assign me to command the VII Corps, replacing Major General Roscoe B. Woodruff, who had succeeded General Richardson and brought the Corps to England. Neither Woodruff nor Major General Leonard T. Gerow, commander of the V Corps, the other assault corps for Operation OVERLORD, had any combat experience in the Second World War, which concerned Bradley and Eisenhower. Bradley recommended and Ike approved my taking over the VII Corps. On February 12 orders were issued confirming this assignment. While I was happy to assume command of the corps that I had helped organize in Birmingham, I had great sympathy for Woodruff, a West Point classmate of Eisenhower and Bradley who had been cadet First Captain when I was a yearling. Woodruff later commanded a division in the Pacific and a corps in the Japanese occupation. I was just lucky to be in the right place at the right time.

I had not really known Eisenhower or Bradley as cadets, except by reputation; Ike had been a halfback on the football team until injured, and Brad a crack baseball player. I had come to know Ike in the Philippines, but not intimately. Brad and I had served together at West

Point in the twenties and later as instructors at the Infantry School under the then Colonel Marshall. I got to know him well there and to admire him greatly. His rough-hewn features bespeak a deep-seated integrity, along with an uncommon feeling for his associates and the men under him, and a rare ability to gauge their fine qualities as well as their human frailties. He is one of the most genuinely modest men I have ever known, but back of his somewhat retiring nature is a keen mind and a toughness in making decisions that engenders confidence. I was delighted to be part of his American First Army.

The VII Corps was not included in the OVERLORD plan as originally drafted in 1943 by a British-American staff, called COSSAC, under British Lieutenant General Frederick E. Morgan. That plan envisaged an allied landing on the coast of Normandy, in the vicinity of Caen, with an assault force of only three divisions, a limit imposed by the number of available landing craft. The assault area did not include a major port, essential to sustain the invasion. Eisenhower had been shown a draft of the COSSAC plan before he had been designated SACEUR, but had no time to study it. He had commented informally that the plan provided for a front that was too narrow, and should be expanded to include five to six divisions in the assault. After his appointment he had sent his deputy, General Bernard L. Montgomery, ahead to London with instructions to present his views. But so far as can be determined, Montgomery was given no instruction with respect to landing a corps on the Cotentin (Cherbourg) peninsula nor was any mention made of the necessity for early capture of the port of Cherbourg.

Before Eisenhower arrived in London, Montgomery, his Chief of Staff, Major General Francis de Guingand, and Eisenhower's Chief of Staff, Major General Walter Bedell Smith, studied the plan, and all agreed that the assault should be strengthened and broadened to include the Dunes of Varreville on the east coast of the Cotentin peninsula and extend east of the Orne River. When Montgomery met with Eisenhower on January 21, 1944, he emphasized the desirability of the early capture of Cherbourg. In the ensuing weeks, at the insistence of Eisenhower, Montgomery, and Bradley, additional landing craft and air troop carriers were made available; the assault forces were increased to five infantry and three airborne divisions; and the VII Corps was added to the command structure.

A few days before my assignment was announced I was invited to accompany Eisenhower and Bradley on a trip through an area of Devonshire where some of the VII Corps troops were billeted and from which we would leave for Normandy. It was an interesting reconnaissance. Of even more value to me, it gave the three of us a chance to talk. I met old friends among the commanders of troops that would be in the VII Corps. Though a newcomer to the theater, I was greeted warmly and accepted as an equal by those who had served in North Africa and the Mediterranean.

General Bradley outlined the mission assigned to the VII Corps: land on the east coast of the Cotentin peninsula between Varreville and the mouth of the Douve River; seize the beach; link with the V Corps west of the Douve; capture Cherbourg as early as possible.

The 4th Infantry Division, commanded by Major General Raymond O. Barton, a friend from Coblenz days, was to be my assault division, followed by the 90th Division and possibly the 9th Division. It would be the first action in the war for the 4th and 90th Divisions; the 9th Division under Major General Manton S. Eddy had done well in the African and Sicily campaigns. Drops by the 82nd and 101st Airborne Divisions in support of the 4th Division were being planned by First Army. These divisions would pass to my command after landing. In addition, the VII Corps included the 4th Cavalry Group, and a full complement of corps artillery, tank and antitank battalions, engineers, and other supporting and service units.

Most of the combat troops were billeted in Devonshire or Hampshire, but other elements were scattered from Wales to Chichester, southeast of London. It took hours of driving on the narrow roads of southern England to visit all units of the Corps, which I did as soon as possible. On these visits I spent most of my time with the troops in the field, witnessing their training and meeting and observing the commanders, down to battalions. The 4th Division initially drew most of my attention. While a Major in Germany, General Barton had established himself as a first-class trainer. He was not a brilliant man but was thoroughly versed in the tools of his trade, and had matured

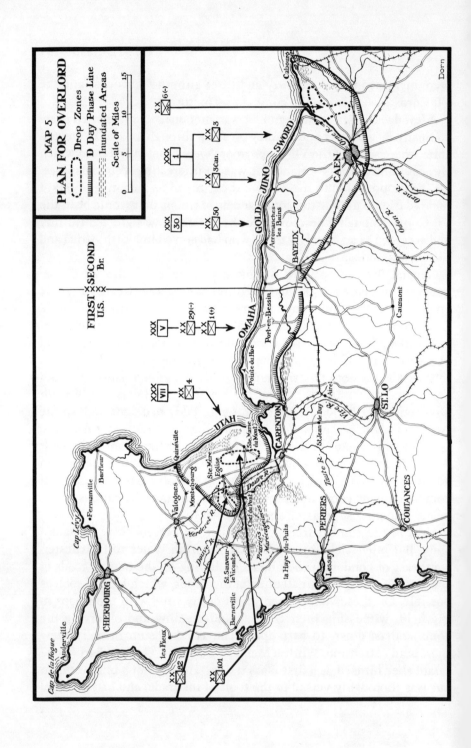

MAP 5

PLAN FOR OVERLORD

◌ Drop Zones
▬▬ D Day Phase Line
▨▨ Inundated Areas

Scale of Miles
0   5   10   15

Dorn

into a dependable division commander. I was fond of him personally and so were his men. The division was in splendid shape, sharp and eager to get under way.

Whenever possible at these troop inspections I would address the officers and men in convenient groups, outlining my concepts of discipline, proficiency in the techniques of fire and movement, the high standards of performance that I expected of them, and my confidence that they would meet these tests.

I was particularly impressed with the 8th Infantry, my old regiment in Germany, and its commander, Colonel James A. Van Fleet, a classmate of Eisenhower and Bradley in the outstanding class of 1915 at West Point. I had known him slightly as a cadet, chiefly as one of the toughest and most versatile backs in an era of fine Army football teams, and had seen something of him at Benning. The trouble was that General Marshall, while Assistant Commandant at Benning, unfortunately had gotten Van Fleet confused with a man with almost the same name, for whom the then Colonel Marshall had only slight regard. Van Fleet had done well over the years, but each time during the war when he had been recommended to be promoted to brigadier, General Marshall had turned him down. After thoroughly inspecting the 8th Infantry, I called General Bradley and told him we were wasting Van Fleet as a regimental commander, that he should be commanding a division. Bradley said, "Well, Joe, he is in your Corps. Do something about it." I replied, "If Van does as well on D day as I feel sure he will, I will recommend him at once to be a BG." That was to be only the first of Van Fleet's promotions for which I would recommend him during his distinguished career.

The command post of the VII Corps was in the little village of Braemore, south of Salisbury in Hampshire. I drove down from London through the lovely countryside of Devon, untouched by the war except for the fact that the farms were being tilled and the cattle cared for by women, members of the Women's Land Army Corps. I was charmed at once by quiet little Braemore, with its thatched-roofed houses, some of the thatch two to three feet deep. It seemed an unlikely place for a corps CP, except for a large and stately Tudor mansion on its outskirts. This provided billets and office space for most of the staff and had the advantage, rare in England, of central heating and plumbing, which the owner had installed prior to the war.

Returning to VII Corps was like coming home, though except for the Deputy Chief of Staff, Howard S. Searle, and the G-1, John D. Higgins, the principal staff officers had all changed since I left the Corps in 1941. Colonel Leslie D. Carter had taken over as G-2, and Peter C. Bullard, G-3. But such stalwarts as Mason J. Young, the Engineer; Arthur H. Luse, Ordnance; Paul Warfield, Quartermaster; Jack W. Sawyer, Signal Officer; Lawton Butler, Adjutant General; John W. Nicholson, Inspector General; James R. Fancher, Surgeon; Richard A. Welch, Judge Advocate; and Dell B. Hardin, Civil Affairs Officer: these mainstays of the excellent Special Staff I had helped organize while Chief of Staff of the Corps were still on the job and had matured with experience.

There were three important vacancies that had to be filled. General Woodruff had taken his Chief of Staff with him, and the former G-4 had been invalided home and not yet replaced, while the artillery commander had been transferred to the 12th Army Group shortly after I rejoined the Corps. General Bradley arranged to have Colonel Richard G. McKee, who had been Chief of Staff of the Third Army in the States, and Colonel James G. Anding, an experienced logistician, made available to me. Both officers had fine reputations and I was glad to get them. An artilleryman, Brigadier General Charles R. Doran, whom I did not know, was en route from the States to join the Corps.

Although it was a competent staff, in the ensuing months of training and preparing for the invasion of France there were changes in two key posts. Peter Bullard, the G-3, was a graduate of the French École de Guerre and had been an instructor at the Command and General Staff School at Leavenworth. He had little or no command experience with troops to temper his theoretical knowledge. One of the fetishes of Leavenworth doctrine of his day was that boundaries between units in an attack should run along ridge lines, so that attacking units generally should move along the valleys in between. My experience, which coincided with Bradley's in North Africa, was that units controlling the high ground would dominate any troop movements in the valleys. The axis of advance of attacking units should follow ridge lines wherever possible. This meant that boundaries between units should follow the stream lines, leaving no doubt as to what unit was responsible for any piece of high ground. Steeped in the Leavenworth doctrine, Bullard could not bring himself to accept my decision as to how I intended to fight the VII Corps. I finally had to ask General Bradley to replace him with a man who would conform to my wishes. Brad sent me a younger officer, Colonel Richard C. Partridge, a graduate of the German Kriegsakademie and a West Pointer, who was in the operations division of Bradley's First Army. Partridge was an immediate success.

The other change was in command of the corps artillery. It came about for much the same reason as the G-3. If I had learned one thing in the Pacific that I was sure of, it was that artillery had to conform to the needs of the infantry. This meant that thoroughly competent artillerymen, not mere observers, had to accompany front-line infantry troops, and should be competent to place concentrations of fire within one hundred to two hundred yards of those troops, with safety. I soon discovered that the artillery commander, Brigadier General Doran, an artilleryman of the old order, still clung to the outmoded routine of depending on observers on hilltops, often well to the rear of the front lines. After watching one of his training exercises conducted in this fashion, I instructed Doran to outline the location of troops he was supposed to be supporting in every firing exercise and to have the battery commanders, or other experienced observers, adjust fire from within or close to our own front lines. In succeeding exercises I found that Doran was not complying with my wishes, whereupon I had him relieved. This time Bradley furnished a top-notch replacement, Brigadier General Williston B. Palmer, who gave the VII Corps expert artillery support throughout the war. I had no further problems with artillery.

We Establish Contact with the Navy

My opposite number in the Navy, the Commander of Task Force V, which would land VII Corps on beach "UTAH," was Rear Admiral Don P. Moon, United States Naval Academy class of 1916. His headquarters was in Plymouth, close by his landing craft and supporting ships, which were located in the ports and southern coastal waters of Devonshire. I drove down with my aide, Captain John Walsh, to call on the Admiral soon after taking command of VII Corps. As I traveled the 130 miles from Braemore to Plymouth, I realized that the Corps CP was much too far away from Moon's headquarters for the two of us, and our staffs, to get to know one another and work out the myriad details of an amphibious operation. I decided to move my CP to Plymouth as soon as accommodations could be arranged.

I found the Admiral's headquarters in a badly bombed area of the city near the waterfront. Moon and his top staff officers occupied a damaged stone building across Fore Street from an open space, from which some bombed-out houses had been removed. Several corrugated-iron Quonset huts had been erected in this area, to house headquarters personnel. The whole place was ringed with barbed wire and well guarded.

Admiral Moon was an attractive, friendly man and I liked him right off. Our paths had never crossed before but we had several mutual friends in the Navy, and he knew of my service in the Pacific. I told him I wanted to move down to Plymouth and asked if he would have his people locate accommodations for my CP. He said he would do better than that. He would have one or more Quonset huts added to the group across the street and provide the necessary communications to link our staffs. He would also make arrangements for me to be billeted at the Grand Hotel, which had been taken over by the military. I thanked him, and we then toured his establishment and had lunch with his staff. After a drive around the city, which as a major port had been severely damaged by German bombardment early in the war, I left Plymouth assured that we had made a good start toward sound and friendly relations with our Navy counterparts. The operations part of Corps headquarters moved to Plymouth in mid-March. The rear echelon administrative headquarters remained at Braemore until shortly before D day.

After visiting all major units of the Corps, I initiated a series of battalion combat exercises within the 4th Division comparable to those that had proved so valuable in the 25th Division. The areas in crowded England were very limited where such exercises could be held, involv-

ving as they did the firing of all infantry weapons and supporting art-
tillery. The British Army training area at Woolcombe in Devon was
made available to us, as was a British range on the River Clyde in Scotland. Landings from the sea could be made at both places, leading directly into the combat-firing ranges. Extensive areas, large enough for
regimental combat team maneuvers, were available on Salisbury Plain,
but no firing could be done there. To correct that situation the British
government had taken over the village of Slapston Sands and adjacent farmland on the coast of Devon, near Dartmouth, for large-scale
amphibious exercises. The villages and nearby farms were evacuated so that all types of fire support, including aerial bombardment
and naval gunfire, could be emloyed in close support of attacking infantry, and the new-fangled amphibious tanks could be tried out under battle conditions. A series of regimental combat-team exercises
had been conducted by the 4th Division in March, 1943, at Slapston
Sands and on the Clyde River.

I could see great value in the amphibious tanks but was skeptical of
their seaworthiness. These thirty-two-ton medium tanks were made
amphibious by attaching dismountable canvas collars around their
waists to provide flotation—somewhat like those used in recent years
to float astronauts' modules. A dual drive system was added, with
twin propellers for swimming and normal track drive for land movement; hence their name, "DD tanks." To check their operation during
one of our Slapston Sands exercises I put off in a small boat from our
command ship *Bayfield* with our G-3 and went forward with the line
of LCTs (landing craft, tank) carrying the DDs of the 70th Tank Battalion, attached to the 4th Division. Good-sized waves were pitching
the LCTs about as we approached the shore and lowered the gangplanks to put off the DDs. From close alongside I watched the tanks
drive off the ends of the gangplanks, their canvas collars barely avoiding gulps of water as they plunged overboard. Once the DDs settled
down they rode very well. But I decided that I would insist that the
Navy take the LCTs with our DDs as close to shore as possible on D
day before dumping them off, a provision that proved both a lifesaver
and a DD saver on D day.

By the time this particular exercise was over the waves were whitecapping as my LCVP (landing craft, vehicle and personnel) returned to the *Bayfield*. Our boat would have to be hoisted aboard the *Bayfield*. The ship swung out a boom and lowered a cable with a big, heavy hook at its end. Our LCVP was equipped with three steel cables fastened to the framework of the boat and joined at their ends to a heavy steel ring. The tricky task now was for two seamen, balancing themselves on the pitching deck, to catch the ring on the hook as it swung back and forth like a pendulum. I could foresee that when they did catch the ring, the three cables would pull dangerously taut. I cautioned everyone to flatten himself against the deckhouse. The men finally caught the hook just as a large wave pitched the boat sharply to one side. As the full weight of the boat was thrown suddenly on the cables they snapped taut. In a flash my head was caught between the deckhouse and one of the cables. Fortunately my steel helmet protected my left eye as the cable drew across my forehead and cheek. Fortunately also, the wall of the deckhouse against which my head was pinned was made of light plywood, which gave way from the pressure of the cable against the helmet, freeing me in a moment. As the boat lurched to level itself, my feet slipped from under me, my helmet rolled away and I skidded across the deck, spouting blood from my forehead. For a moment I was not sure that the top of my head was in place. Actually a few stitches in my forehead and an overnight stay in a British naval hospital fixed me up in time to conduct a critique of the exercise the next day, albeit looking like a battered prize fighter.

A full-scale dress rehearsal of our D-day landing, Exercise "Tiger," was held at Slapston Sands on April 28, under the watchful eyes of General Bradley. All went well, except for a few casualties, none fatal, from naval gunfire. Far more serious was an attack by German E-boats, small fast craft comparable to our PT boats, on one of our convoys carrying engineer-support troops in Exercise "Tiger." Two LSTs (landing ships, tank) were sunk and one damaged, costing over seven hundred casualties, most of whom drowned. The loss was heavier than that suffered by the VII Corps on D day.

A companion exercise, "Eagle," involving a night drop by paratroopers of the 101st Airborne Division under its commander, Major General Maxwell D. Taylor, was conducted shortly after "Tiger." It was not possible to stage this second exercise in the vicinity of Slapston Sands, but an area resembling the planned drop zone back of UTAH beach was selected in Berkshire. No comparable night training exercise had ever been held. It went well, with a minimum of casualties and no fatalities, though paratroopers crashed through the roofs of houses in the drop zone. Many valuable lessons were learned that were put to good use in the D-day drop. I watched this exercise with keen interest, and, I will admit, with some trepidation, as the troopers poured out of the skies and rained down around a group of observers, of which I was one.

Final air support exercises to confirm our techniques of designating targets for close support by means of colored smoke shells, which I had helped introduce, were conducted in May.

Mixed in with my schedule were some diversions. Gladys' parents had been born in Devonshire, her father in Torquay and her mother in Newton Abbot. She still had several uncles and aunts living in Devon. After we were married in Coblenz in 1921, we had no time to visit any of them before sailing for home. But we had met her father's brother, Herbert Easterbrook, and his wife Edith when they came to Washington to attend a convention of international lawyers. Uncle Herbert practiced law in Torquay, where the Easterbrooks lived in an attractive house on a hillside overlooking Tor Bay, one of the beauty spots of southern England. At the first opportunity I looked up Herbert and several Sundays thereafter had the pleasure of having dinner with his family, including daughter Fern and her husband, Arthur Waycott, who lived in nearby Paignton. The Easterbrooks were great travelers, had cosmopolitan tastes, and were interesting and amusing company. They were also gourmets of the first order. Despite the rationing of meat, they managed to dig up a good roast whenever I came to dinner and added fresh vegetables from their garden. To top the menu, Uncle Herb would always produce a fine bottle of claret from his well-stocked cellar. Our headquarters mess was good, but could not match the Easterbrook cuisine. This was all the more welcome to me because what seemed to be standard British boiled dinners left me cold.

While at Braemore, I had many pleasant contacts with the townspeople. Lady Amy Normanton, who had taken our staff under her wing, Dr. and Mrs. Wilson, the Reverend Mr. Workman, D.D., who was Vicar of the little Saxon church, and several others had us to tea or dinner and did their best to make us feel at home. But the most interesting people we met were Mr. and Mrs. Hewitt, the land agents for the nearby estate. Mr. Hewitt, an amateur archaeologist, had discovered the entrance to what appeared to be a Roma villa buried under a large mound in an open pasture. The Hewitts had Jack Walsh and me to a Sunday picnic lunch in the field. We looked on, fascinated, while the Hewitts carefully troweled aside bits of turf, exposing the bright-colored Roman tile walk leading to the still-buried villa. As I watched this couple, in the middle of a war that threatened the very existence of Britain, actively interested in uncovering a relic of former conquerors centuries before, I thought what a remarkably stable, wonderful people the British are.

This was brought home to me more strikingly when I had the privilege of spending most of a day with the Prime Minister, Winston Churchill, during one of his several visits to our troops in the field. On these inspection trips Churchill traveled from London on the special train the government had arranged for General Eisenhower, and which carried Ike's limousine. Each evening Ike provided dinner on the train for the senior commanders of troops visited during the day. I was invited to one such dinner during an inspection of the 9th Division, and happened to draw the seat to the left of the Prime Minister. The party was small and informal and, as there were no reporters, we were all relaxed. In addition to Ike and Churchill, Bradley, Manton Eddy, commanding the 9th Division, Sarah Churchill, then a WAAC, Ike's British aide Colonel James Gault, Kay Summersby, Ike's attractive chauffeur, and I made up the company.

When I saw him that evening Churchill had had two strenuous days of inspections and had ridden for miles perched on the tonneau of an open command car so that he could better see and be seen by the troops. Despite a recent illness he had insisted on getting out of the car to walk around the honor guards and examine the weapons displayed. That day he had stood through a review of our regiments and delivered a stirring address to the men. In one of the towns through which we passed he had gotten out of the car to walk with General

Eisenhower for a couple of blocks through throngs of cheering towns-people, who pressed about him in their enthusiasm, many with tears streaming down their cheeks. Yet that evening he was as fresh as we were, and held forth after dinner until eleven o'clock, dominating the conversation, alternately regaling us with stories or stirring us as he spoke feelingly of our common ideals and endeavors. He ended the evening with passages from Kipling and from Bret Harte's *The Reveille*, to each verse of which he added extemporaneously, "The drums! The drums! The drums!," which he rolled forth with obvious relish. The evening was a fitting end to a memorable day.

When Eisenhower was appointed Supreme Commander, General Montgomery had been designated as his Deputy. Monty also was appointed to command the 21st Army Group comprising British and Canadian forces in the United Kingdom. Admiral Sir Bertram Ramsey had been assigned Commander in Chief of the Allied Naval Expeditionary Force and Air Chief Marshal Sir Trafford Leigh-Mallory as Commander in Chief of the Allied Expeditionary Air Force. No comparable commander for the allied land forces had been designated. Initially the British and Canadians were more experienced and probably would have the preponderance of troops; it was arguable that the ground commander should be a Britisher. The Americans knew that ultimately they would be furnishing the bulk of the Army forces, and that American public opinion would insist on an American Commander in Chief, if one were to be designated. Eisenhower solved the dilemma by asking Montgomery to act temporarily in that capacity, which would include operational control of the American First Army as well as command of the 21st Army Group, until the First Army under Bradley could expand on the Continent into a complete Army Group.

Review of Invasion Plans

Montgomery therefore supervised the joint planning for the assault and initial operations in France. As plans began to firm up, he scheduled an oral presentation of them at his headquarters in St. Paul's School in Kensington, London, on April 7, 1944. A large relief map of Normandy, in color, showing all the landing beaches and reaching inland beyond early objectives and north to include Cherbourg and all the Cotentin peninsula, was spread on a tilted platform on the floor of a school lecture room.

While waiting for the audience to assemble, I witnessed a first sign, but not the last, of Bradley's irritation with Montgomery. Brad had told me that in earlier discussions of OVERLORD with Montgomery, he had refused to agree to setting any phase lines for expansion of the initial bridgehead that should be reached by certain days. He thought that Montgomery had accepted his objection, at least for the American sector. When we arrived at St. Paul's School we discovered that Monty's map showed such lines. Brad insisted that the times shown, by which the phase lines were to be secured by the Americans, be removed. Monty, somewhat petulantly, finally agreed.

The audience included Churchill, Eisenhower, the Commanders in Chief of the Allied Naval and Air Forces and some distinguished visitors, and sat in semicircular tiers of chairs looking down on the map on which Monty stood, clearly relishing his role of impresario. He first outlined the plan of attack, striding across the beaches, hills, and streams as he indicated objectives and salient features of the terrain with a long pointer. The British Second Army, Lieutenant General Miles C. Dempsey commanding, consisting of the British I Corps and XXX Corps, was to land west of the Orne River on beaches JUNO and GOLD between the mouth of the Orne and Arromanches. The American First Army under General Bradley would land Gerow's V Corps on OMAHA, to the west of the British, and the VII Corps on UTAH west of the Douve River. (See Map 5)

Corps commanders, in turn, starting with the British I Corps on the east flank, outlined their plans for the assault. Most of them read prepared statements, standing on the floor below the map with an aide pointing out key features. The VII Corps being on the extreme west flank, I spoke last. I stood on the map, as Monty had done, and spoke extemporaneously, using a pointer myself as I outlined the Corps plan for linking up the 4th Division with the 82nd and 101st Airborne Divisions, and driving north on Cherbourg. As I sat down, Bedell Smith, who was sitting behind me, leaned over and whispered, "Joe, done in the best tradition of Benning!" In any event Monty must have been impressed, because thereafter he seemed to take a special interest in what I was doing.

Tension Mounts as D Day Approaches

As D day approached, preparations for our takeoff gradually increased in intensity, and tension began to build. Our relations with Admiral Moon and staff grew closer as together we worked out the final details of loading and landing tables, signal communications, naval gunfire support, and the many other joint arrangements involved in an amphibious operation. I became a bit concerned about Don Moon's working overtime and his tendency to do too much himself instead of giving some of his responsibilities to his staff. Occasionally I tried to get him to leave his office early and join me in a walk or a game of tennis, but was never able to do so. I thought also that I detected a certain lack of firmness and a tendency to be overly cautious, which worried me. It was a small thing, but I wrote Mrs. Collins on May 17: "He is the first Admiral I've ever met who wears rubbers on a mere rainy day, but he is all right. He is certainly pleasant to do business with and is genuinely cooperative in every way."

I am still amazed that the Germans did not discover the concentration of Allied forces along the south coast of England in the last week before D day. Every port from Portsmouth to Plymouth was jampacked with landing craft, and every road for miles back of the ports in the staging areas—nicknamed "sausages" by the troops, from their appearance on map overlays—was loaded to the hedgerows with troops, guns, tanks, jeeps, and trucks. Some of the narrow backroads had to be widened to accommodate the larger vehicles by bulldozing down the hedgerows, with their bright flowers, so precious to every Englishman, who raised not a word of complaint. The "sausages" would have made deadly targets for German bombers or V bombs, if they had ever been discovered. That they were not discovered was a tribute to the Allied air forces, who had nearly annihilated the Luftwaffe and rendered ineffective what was left of it.

Another factor that helped conceal Allied preparations was the elaborate plan of deception organized by the British. From the first the Germans seemed to have convinced themselves that any invasion would come in the Pas de Calais. To strengthen that conviction the British created a phantom force, "Army Group Patton," complete with inflatable rubber landing craft, tanks, and artillery, supposedly located near Dover. Some of these locations were discreetly camouflaged poorly. Bogus messages were passed back and forth, sometimes in the clear, from one nonexistent command post to the other. The Germans swallowed this deception whole and neglected to check the unlikely areas opposite the Bay of the Seine.

But to me the most remarkable element in preserving the concealment of Allied concentrations was that there was not a leak, intentional or accidental, in the newspaper press or through private channels of information in England, despite the fact that over 250,000 troops were cooped up in the farms and hedgerows of southern England for a week or more. In addition, the people living in the vicinity of the "sausages" were not permitted to enter or leave the area. But, toughened by the reality of the threat to their freedom and by the possibility of a German invasion in the early days of the war, the people of Devon accepted the restrictions on freedom of movement and communications, and kept their mouths shut, while the British press cooperated fully. I wonder if it could ever happen again—certainly not in America.

On the evening of June 2, Admiral Moon and I moved our Command Posts to the USS *Bayfield*, moored in Plymouth Harbor, which had been fitted out as a command ship and troop transport. General Barton and his 4th Division headquarters came aboard, along with the 3rd Battalion, 8th Infantry, one of the assault battalions. Under joint Army-Navy regulations, Admiral Moon was in command of Task Force UTAH until the VII Corps would be established ashore.

D day was originally scheduled for June 5, when tide and light would be most favorable. The Germans had embedded steel obstacles along the broad flat beaches. Demolition engineers would have to clear passages through the obstacles at low tide so that landing craft could pass on a rising tide and proceed close to the low seawall before beaching. Engineers needed some light to set their demolitions, while infantry wanted to approach as far as possible under cover of darkness. Landing time, H hour, was set for thirty minutes after dawn, June 5.

General Bradley, accompanied by key staff officers, had driven down from his CP in Bristol to Plymouth on the morning of June 3. I met them in the outskirts of Plymouth and led them to a quay where the barge of Rear Admiral Alan R. Kirk, commander of the Western Task Force (which included Task Forces OMAHA and UTAH), was waiting to take them to Kirk's command ship, the cruiser *Augusta*, moored in Plymouth harbor.

Weather had been unsettled, and the forecast was discouraging, but a decision by Eisenhower whether we would go for a landing on June 5 would not be made until a meeting of Eisenhower and the Combined Commanders in Chief with the Meteorologic Committee, headed by Group Captain J. M. Stagg of the RAF, scheduled for that evening, Saturday, June 3. The meeting was held at 9:30 P.M. at Southwick House, Admiral Ramsey's headquarters north of Portsmouth. Stagg forecast that June 5 would be overcast, with a cloud base of five hundred feet to zero, accompanied by high winds. He added that any prediction more than twenty-four hours in advance was highly undependable. But the long period of unsettled conditions was beginning to break up. After some discussion General Eisenhower decided to postpone final decision until 4:30 A.M. the following day, meanwhile letting elements of Task Force UTAH farthest away from Normandy get underway. By the time of the 4:30 meeting Sunday morning the weather had improved slightly, although not enough to permit air operations. Full air support, including airlift of the paratroopers, was essential for the assault. General Eisenhower decided to postpone the operation for twenty-four hours. Prearranged signals were sent out and vessels already underway turned back. None had left Plymouth, and Admiral Moon and I turned in for a few hours of sleep.

The weather on June 4 in Plymouth showed slight signs of the expected break. Admiral Kirk had invited Major General Ralph Royce, Deputy Commander of the Ninth Air Force, who had joined Bradley on the *Augusta*, and General Bradley to meet with him ashore in the headquarters of the British naval command in Plymouth, in the late afternoon of the fourth to consider alternatives if the landing had to be postponed past June 6. After much discussion it was agreed that Admiral Kirk should recommend to Admiral Ramsey that we should chance a landing as late as June 8 or 9, rather than face delay of two weeks before the tide would again be favorable. Assault troops had already been briefed on the OVERLORD plan and knew their exact destinations. Further postponement would have required them to be incommunicado within their barbed wire enclosed "sausages" as well as necessitating continuation of the restrictions already in effect on the movement of civilian residents of the staging areas. It would have been almost impossible to maintain secrecy.

Eisenhower had scheduled another senior commanders' meeting in Portsmouth at 9:30 that Sunday evening, June 4. This time Meteorologist Stagg reported a new weather front that gave hope of improvement throughout June 5 and until the morning of the sixth, but there was a chance the forecast might be wrong. As the conferees mulled this over, Admiral Ramsey interrupted to insist, "Admiral Kirk must be told within the next half hour if OVERLORD is to take place on Tuesday."

Don Moon and I remained ashore in the damp underground naval headquarters in Plymouth until about midnight, when a message was received from Ramsey that, subject to final confirmation after the 4:00 A.M. commanders' meeting June 5, Eisenhower had decided to go for the June 6 landing. That final decision was made at 4:15 A.M., June 5.

That evening, after we had set sail for Normandy, I wrote Mrs. Collins from the *Bayfield*, in part as follows:

> Generals Bradley and Kean, Admirals Kirk, Moon and Wilkes (U.S. Navy Base Commander, Europe), I and several Britishers, were none too optimistic as we assembled last night for the word as to whether or not we would get under way again. It was with a mixture of relief and misgiving that we received the decision to go ahead, subject to final confirmation early this morning. . . . We were greatly relieved when we came out from our meeting to find the moon breaking through scattered clouds, the wind down and the sea appreciably quieter. Don Moon woke me from a sound sleep this morning to give me the final word that we were definitely on the way. Perhaps it was because I had a sense of unreality about this thing that I was able soon to go back to sleep again. It was scarcely believable that the Germans would permit the assembly and departure of this tremendous force with only a few sporadic and ineffectual air raids. . . . This morning as our particular convoy formed up (at 9:30 A.M.), the crew of a passing British cruiser gave us three rousing cheers, much as they would at a football

game, and we responded in kind. Whether our confidence and seeming nonchalance is unwarranted we will know in a few hours. The tension, I am sure, will at least be on us.

I thought of you all most keenly yesterday morning, as I do each Sunday, as mass was celebrated in the main mess hall aboard ship. The hall was packed with soldiers, sailors, officers and men alike. I am sure the thoughts of everyone were more on our families at home than they were on the service, though the seriousness of the project on which we were embarked was to me, for the first time, clearly in the air. This dual feeling was reflected in the frank whole-heartedness with which the men joined in the singing of hymns that most of them had rarely sung since they were boys. As I offered a soldier next to me one of the hymn books being passed about, he answered me almost scornfully, "I know them hymns!" And he did, from the grand "Holy God We Praise Thy Name" to "God Bless America." The latter song, no matter what its musical qualities are, unquestionably epitomizes more nearly than any other the simple love our men have for home and the America for which we will soon be fighting.

CHAPTER XI

Normandy—D Day to the Capture of Cherbourg

D Day

The night was almost pitch black when the anchor chain of the *Bayfield* rattled out at 2:30 A.M., June 6, 1944. Except for the fact that we were twelve miles out, off the coast of Normandy, its sudden clanking might have alerted the German defenders whose radars evidently had failed to detect the approach of the vast armada of ships and planes that was about to attack the east coast of the Cherbourg peninsula. Because of the foul weather over the English Channel on June 5, German naval patrols had been canceled and the Luftwaffe grounded. Their meteorologists had not picked up the break in the weather front that led to Eisenhower's decision to proceed with the June 6 assault. The weather thus provided a better cover than anything man could devise.

Even before the *Bayfield* anchored, parachutists of Max Taylor's 101st Airborne Division began dropping behind UTAH beach at 1:30 A.M., to seize the exits of four causeways over an area that the enemy had flooded just inland from the beach and south of the town of Ste. Mère-Église. (See Map 5) Matt Ridgway's 82nd Airborne Division commenced its drop an hour later astride the Merderet River, west of Ste. Mère-Église, to seize that road center and block any German reinforcements that might advance against our 4th and 101st Divisions from north or west.

Don Moon and I looked up as we heard the roar of our air transport planes returning from the drop. A shiver of apprehension ran up my spine as the first planes approached from the west, almost at masthead level. I recalled that in Sicily, a few months before, many air transports had been shot down by friendly Army and Navy antiaircraft fire. Plans called for our planes to avoid the ship transport area by swinging to the north after dropping their loads. The discipline and good judgment of our troops and naval gunners, however, saved the situation, and not a shot was fired as the transports lumbered overhead.

A new fear beset me as I realized that at least some of these planes had dropped their paratroopers outside the prescribed drop zones. This later proved to be the case, particularly in Ridgway's 82nd Airborne. Scattered drops made it tougher for the 82nd and 101st Divisions to protect the landing of the 4th Division on UTAH and assist its advance inland. Still, the widespread dispersion of the paratroopers added to the confusion of the Germans, slowing their reaction to the principal drops and to the seaborne landing.

Meanwhile troops of the 3rd Battalion, 8th Infantry* on the *Bayfield*, heavily laden with rifles, machine guns, mortars, and other gear, moved quietly over the side of the ship, climbing down the rope mats and into the small landing craft (LCVPs) circling below. They were to have a long, wet ride through six-foot waves to the beach, which was to be hit at H hour, 6:30 A.M., about one hour after first light. Brigadier General Theodore Roosevelt, Jr., who after having been relieved as assistant division commander of the 1st Division had persuaded Bradley to attach him to the 4th Division for the Normandy attack, accompanied the assault wave.

At 5:52 A.M. the bombers of Major General Hoyt S. Vandenberg's Ninth Air Force began their bombardment of the German coastal batteries. We could hear nothing from their motors or the bomb blasts, but could follow the pin-points of flame that seemed to run rapidly after one another in the darkness where the beach must have been. There was no evidence of enemy counter air action, but off in the distance, toward Cherbourg, there were bursts of antiaircraft fire, probably directed at stray planes, following the airborne assault.

As the sky grew lighter, the array of ships began to loom around us. First the other troop transports and LCIs (landing craft, infantry); then the bulky LSTs, crammed with tanks, artillery, and motor vehicles, which were to follow the LCVPs ashore; next the ghostly outlines of

*By chance, I had commanded in World War I the 3rd Battalion, 22nd Infantry and Companies K and L of the 3rd Battalion, 8th Infantry, two of our D-day assault battalions. The men of course had changed, but I thus had special interest in these units.

cruisers and destroyers, which were to furnish fire support for the assault; finally, off toward shore, the long, thin lines of bobbing LCVPs, which looked awfully small and powerless as they approached the beach.

The infantrymen in these craft, on whom the success of the entire operation depended, were now receiving powerful fire support from seventeen combat ships of Navy Task Force 125, commanded by Rear Admiral Morton L. Deyo, which fired, over the heads of the assault craft, against known locations of German batteries and strongpoints. The fire was lifted on signal when the LCVPs were a few hundred yards from the beach, and shifted farther inland. At this moment, direct fire was taken over by Army artillery specially mounted in LSTs in the rear assault waves and by rocket ships.

This fire-support display was awe inspiring. Salvos from the heavy naval guns belched yellow flames, followed by rolling waves of black smoke that gradually obscured the entire debarkation area; but not before we could see from the *Bayfield*, through field glasses, the streaking arcs of hundreds of rockets that saturated the landing beaches, raising clouds of sand and smoke until the beaches themselves and the assault waves of troops were lost to view. We on the bridge of the *Bayfield* prayed that none of this fire was hitting our troops, but we couldn't tell, and there were queasy feelings in our stomachs until the first reassuring radio reports began coming in. Things were off to a good start on UTAH beach.

Not everything goes as planned in war. Because of the smoke, wind, and tides, the assault waves of the 4th Division landed almost two thousand yards farther south than planned, leaving exit No. 4 over the inundated area uncovered, requiring adjustment in the tasks of the assault troops. As with the scattered parachute drops, this proved an advantage, in that it avoided a heavily defended area, with many beach obstacles, east of St. Martin-de-Varreville. By 9:30 A.M. the engineers had cleared all obstacles and blown wide holes in the low seawall; amphibious tanks of the 70th Tank Battalion had landed with only four losses; assault battalions of the 8th and 22nd Infantry were moving across the causeways to a junction with the 101st Airborne, against only sporadic artillery fire from the Varreville area.

I would like to be able to say that I went ashore on D day, but I knew I would have better communication with the Airborne Divisions, and General Bradley, from the command center on the *Bayfield*. This proved to be the case. Paratroops had only light radio sets, many of which were lost or damaged in the drops. It was late in the night of June 6–7 before we had word through the 4th Division that the 82nd Airborne had control of the crossing of the Merderet west of Ste. Mère-Église and had seized the northern outskirts of that key town. It was well that I had remained aboard the *Bayfield* because that afternoon Admiral Moon became agitated over loss of a few vessels from mines and gunfire and by a report from Navy Lieutenant Mark Dalton, who had been sent ashore by Moon's Intelligence Officer, Commander Robert H. Thayer, to check beach conditions. While listening to Dalton's report, Moon suddenly suggested suspension of landing operations. I had to put my foot down hard to persuade the Admiral not to do so.

By the end of D day, General Barton and his 4th Division were established ashore and the bridgehead had expanded to west of Ste. Marie-du-Mont and les Forges, but little progress had been made to the north and an enemy pocket of resistance existed south and east of Ste. Mère-Église. Confident that Admiral Moon would remain steady, but not altogether satisfied with the Corps progress, I decided to go ashore the following morning. I sent ahead a small party under the Deputy Chief of Staff, Colonel Searle, to locate a command post near the 4th Division CP.

The VII Corps Plan of Attack

The VII Corps plan of attack had been based on study of the terrain of the Cotentin peninsula and possible reaction of the Germans. The peninsula juts into the Atlantic from the north coast of France, and measures about twenty-five miles from Cherbourg to the swampy Prairies Marécageuses at its base, thirty miles from the mouth of the Douve River to Carteret on the west coast. Cherbourg lies in a bowl near the center of the north coast, surrounded by hills cut by the narrow valley of the Divette River. South of these hills the peninsula is drained by the Douve and Merderet Rivers, which flow south, generally parallel to one another until the Douve turns east below St. Sauveur-le Vicomte and the Merderet empties into the Douve near the village of Beuzeville-la-Bastille. The Germans had created a serious obstacle to the inland advance of the 4th Division by damming the irrigation ditches that water the cultivated meadows bordering the east coast, inundating this area. A good net of graveled roads crisscrossed the peninsula, connecting the principal towns, chief of which were Carentan and Valognes, with Cherbourg. A rail line ran from Cherbourg through Valogne and Carentan and on to Paris.

Cherbourg was protected from sea invasion by heavy concrete fortifications, with long-range guns. The Germans had completed a ring of field emplacements on the hills south of the city to guard the landward approaches. After Hitler appointed Field Marshall Erwin Rommel to strengthen the coastal defenses of Europe, Rommel directed construction of an "Atlantic Wall" of concrete strong-points covering all beaches, and emplacement of beach obstacles, wire entanglements, and mine fields. He feared that overwhelming air superiority would preclude traditional reliance on counterattacking reserves to drive the invaders into the sea. He planned to use his few reserves close at hand, but hoped to destroy an invading enemy largely by fire from his "wall."

Defenses of Cotentin were under command of Colonel General Friedrich Dollmann's Seventh Army, also responsible for Brittany. The 243rd and 709th Divisions of the Seventh Army's LXXXIV Corps, stationed on the Cotentin peninsula, were reinforced in mid-May, 1944, by the 91st Division, along with the 6th Parachute Regiment and the 17th Machine Gun Battalion. The 709th Division had a goodly number of non-German, anti-Russian troops, mostly Georgians of doubtful reliability. The 709th Division, commanded by Lieutenant General Karl von Schlieben, with headquarters near Valognes, was responsible for the east coast, and the 243rd was generally along the west coast.

Montgomery and Bradley had put great emphasis on early capture of Cherbourg, the mission of the 4th Division, which was to be assisted, as required, by the 90th and 9th Divisions as they came ashore. My plan was to drive on Cherbourg via the corridor between the sea and the Merderet and the upper Douve, while blocking possible counterattack with the 82nd and 101st Airborne Divisions along the Douve and at Carentan. If Cherbourg could be seized quickly, it might not be necessary to seal off the peninsula in a time-consuming attack across its base to the west coast.

Ashore on D + 1

As my LCVP pounded toward the beach I could tell from shell bursts on OMAHA and the hill slopes back of it that Gerow's V Corps was still meeting stiff opposition. Sometime before D day the Germans by chance had moved an additional division, for training, into the V Corps sector. This reinforcement, coupled with the dominant terrain, made the task of V Corps more difficult than ours. I could see also that our Naval Task Force was still receiving sporadic gunfire from enemy positions north of Varrville, though little was coming in on UTAH. As we landed I kept thinking how unreal it seemed coming ashore in France with such light resistance. Rommel's plan to destroy us on the beach had failed and I felt confident of our victory in the war.

Howard Searle's party met us opposite causeway Exit 2 and, after checking to see that supplies were coming in satisfactorily, I drove in an armored car via Exit 2, past one of our knocked-out DD tanks, to the Corps CP, which was being organized on the farm of M. Cotelle in the tiny village of Audouville-la-Hubert. But first I walked across the road to General Barton's CP, in a small grove of trees.

On entering Barton's command tent I found that an officer of the 82nd Airborne had just arrived from Ste. Mère-Église with a message from Matt Ridgway that he was expecting an imminent attack by a column of German armor moving down on Ste. Mère-Église via the main road from Cherbourg. Ridgway urgently requested help from tanks he knew were attached to the 4th Division. Company C, 746th Tank Battalion, was parked under cover not far from the CP, but Barton was loathe to release it. Barton admitted that though his progress to the north was slower than expected, he had no immediate need for the tanks. Checking with the officer from the 82nd who knew exactly where General Ridgway was, I directed Barton to turn the tank company over to this officer who would lead it cross-country to Ste. Mère-Église for attachment to the 82nd Airborne. I learned later that the

tanks reached there in the nick of time to knock out the enemy column, which turned out to be lightly armored vehicles. I saw their
burned-out hulks when I joined Matt Ridgway shortly thereafter.

I congratulated Tubby Barton on the success of his landing but told
him I was concerned about the slow movement on the north flank. I
urged him to check personally to see what was needed to speed the attack. Leaving him, I returned to M. Cotelle's farm. Sections of our
headquarters were being set up in the stone house of the Cotelle family, which had taken refuge in the cellar, and in the several stone-
walled barns. As soon as I had checked with G-2 and G-3 on our situation and the enemy's, and learned that the German position south of
Ste. Mère-Église had been cleaned out by the 8th Infantry, I left in our
armored car with my aide, Captain Walsh, via Ste. Marie-du-Mont
and les Forges for Ste. Mère-Église, which had been taken by the 82nd
Airborne.

We met Colonel Jim Van Fleet, commanding the 8th Infantry, near
the southern outskirts of the town. His troops were still mopping up
the German position there. He offered to take me to Ridgway's CP,
which he had already visited on the northwest edge of Ste. Mère-Église.
Van joined me in the armored car, suggesting that we close the hatch
as we drove through town, with German artillery knocking tiles from
the roof tops. I found Matt, who had parachuted with his troops, in an
apple orchard on a knoll looking down on the bridge over the Merderet
near la Fière. The bridge had been the scene of heavy fighting, as indicated by dead Germans and American paratroops still lying along the
road crossing it. Matt, in fine spirit, thanked me for the tank assistance
and said he now had the situation on either side of the Merderet under control, but had not yet heard from all the scattered elements of
his division between the Merderet and the Douve to the west. His
325th Glider Regiment had landed earlier in the morning in the vicinity of les Forges with not too many casualties from the hedgerows and
the barbed stakes that the Germans had implanted in the open fields.
The regiment had moved to help secure the crossing of the Merderet
at Chef-du-Pont.

From Ridgway's CP, I moved south to the CP of the 101st Airborne
at Hiesville and found Max Taylor at a lookout post in an open field
near Vierville, from which we could see Carentan and the lock over

the Douve at la Barquette, which had been seized on D day. Max also had landed by chute and was in fine shape. The drop of his troops was not as scattered as the 82nd, though it took three days to assemble all his men, and most of the parachute artillery was lost. The 327th Glider Infantry, which landed partly by glider and partly by LCTs over the beach, brought in antitank and antiaircraft weapons, a powerful radio, and medical supplies. The hedgerows and implanted stakes took a toll among the gliders, including the Assistant Division Commander, Brigadier General Don F. Pratt, who was killed when his glider crashed against a hedgerow.

The Capture of Carentan

Taylor told me he had designated his Chief of Staff, Colonel Gerry Higgins, to take Pratt's place, with which I concurred. He outlined his plans for the capture of Carentan and a linkup with the V Corps. Eisenhower and Bradley were concerned that this linkup had not been made by D + 1, but I was confident that Max Taylor and his paratroopers would soon close the gap between the V and VII Corps. I was more concerned with the progress of the 4th Division toward Cherbourg, the main objective of the VII Corps. During the next few days I devoted most of my attention to the attack of that division to the north, assisted by the 82nd Airborne, while General Bradley kept an eye on the Carentan area. He sent his Deputy Commander, Lieutenant General Courtney H. Hodges, to check on Taylor's closing drive on Carentan, which was held by the German 6th Parachute Regiment and elements of the 91st Division. This attack by the 501st and 506th Parachute Infantry Regiments and the 327th Glider Infantry was under the direct command of Brigadier Anthony J. McAuliffe, who first showed here the mettle that distinguished him later at Bastogne. Heavily supported by naval gunfire, artillery, and mortars, the attack jumped off at 2:00 A.M. on the night of June 11–12. After some tough fighting the city was cleared of the enemy by early morning, June 12, and the flanks of the V and VII Corps were secured.

Expanding the Bridgehead to the North

The terrain in the 4th Division zone east of the Merderet was relatively flat but was crisscrossed by small streams and hedgerows, which provided the Germans with good delaying positions, which were strengthened by the heavily fortified areas of Crisbecq, Azeville, and Ozeville, and points along the beach. The ground rose gradually past these strongpoints to the Quineville–Montebourg–le Ham ridge, which had been part of the 4th Division's D-day objective, and which Lieutenant General Karl von Schlieben, the defender of Cherbourg, had strongly organized.

To put more impetus behind the drive to expand our bridgehead to the north, I directed a coordinated attack by the 4th Division and the 505th Parachute Regiment of the 82nd Division on June 8. The attack was launched with regiments abreast: Colonel Harvey A. Tribolet's 22nd Infantry along the coast; Colonel Russell P. "Red" Reeder's 12th Infantry next; then Van Fleet's 8th Infantry and Colonel William E. Ekman's 505th Parachute Infantry west of the Ste. Mère-Église–Montebourg road. The objective was the Quineville ridge.

The 8th and 505th Regiments made good progress initially, but it was not until June 12, after stiff fighting, that the Montebourg–le Ham road was reached. The 8th Infantry was ordered to dig in short of Montebourg until the VII Corps was ready to begin its final drive on Cherbourg.

Realizing that Cherbourg could not be quickly captured, General Bradley on June 9 directed me to give top priority to sealing off the Cotentin peninsula, so as to prevent the enemy from reinforcing the city's defenses. This required a temporary change in direction of the main effort of the Corps from the north to an attack across the base of the peninsula to the west coast. But before such an attack could be successful, the north flank of the Corps would have to be secured by capture of the Quineville ridge through action of the 4th Division then under way.

The 12th Infantry, under the inspired leadership of "Red" Reeder, a crack athlete at West Point, had made a clean breakthrough after a deadly fight west of Azeville, and bolted up to the highway east of Montebourg. Unfortunately Red was severely wounded leading his regiment on June 11 and had to be invalided home. I pinned a Distinguished Service Cross on his tunic at an evacuation hospital on the beach. He was succeeded by Colonel James C. Luckett.

Farther east the 22nd Infantry had the toughest nuts to crack in the concrete fortifications of Crisbecq and Azeville. It required two days of severe battling by Tribolet's men, supported by heavy artillery and naval gunfire, culminating in a dramatic assault on the last of four concrete blockhouses at Azeville, led by Private Ralph G. Riley, whose flamethrower set off explosives in the blockhouse, leading to surrender of the position. Crisbecq held out against three successive attacks, the last by a task force under the Assistant Division Commander, Brigadier General Harry A. Barber, a gallant soldier who had won a DSC in World War I. I had followed this attack with General Barton. We realized that Barber had burned himself out, along with the regimental commander, and much of the 22nd Infantry.* We decided to suspend the attack on Crisbecq and give the 22nd Infantry a rest. On June 12, I attached the 39th Infantry of the veteran 9th Division to the 4th Division, with the mission of clearing the fortified beach positions east of Crisbecq. Led by the redoubtable Colonel Harry A. "Paddy" Flint, the 39th Infantry fought past Fort St. Marcouf and outflanked Crisbecq. After a respite, the 22nd reduced the fortifications of Oze-ville and joined with the 39th Infantry in attack on Quineville, eastern anchor of General von Schlieben's ridge-line defenses. Quineville fell to Paddy Flint on June 14.

The north flank of the VII Corps bridgehead was now secure and I could turn full attention to sealing off the peninsula. I had made a quick trip out to the *Bayfield* on the night of June 8 to bid Admiral Moon and staff goodbye and thank them for their fine cooperation.

Expanding the Bridgehead to the West

While the 4th Division was struggling to the north, Matt Ridgway's 82nd Division was having difficulty linking two shallow bridgeheads over the Merderet opposite la Fière and Chef-du-Pont, in the face of counterattacks by the German 91st Division. The 82nd showed mettle in consolidating its Mederet holdings by the afternoon of June 8.

The attack of the Corps to the west was initiated June 10 by the 90th

---

*General Barber was evacuated to a hospital in the States in late June, and was succeeded by General Roosevelt. Barton replaced Colonel Tribolet on June 26 with Colonel Robert T. Foster.

Division, under command of Brigadier General Jay W. McKelvie. I directed McKelvie to pass his 357th and 358th Regiments through the 82nd Airborne and seize the north-south stretch of the Douve River north of St. Sauveur-le Vicomte. It was the 90th Division's first action. Its attack went badly from the start. After two days of lackluster fighting the Division made little progress through the hedgerows, taking heavy casualties from mortar and artillery fire. Determined to find out what was holding up the attack, I went forward on foot into the 90th Division's zone on June 13 with my aide, Captain Walsh. After checking in with the Division CP, we could locate no regimental or battalion headquarters. No shelling was going on, nor any fighting that we could observe. We soon found ourselves practically in the front line north of Orglandes, without seeing any officers until we ran into Lieutenant Colonel William L. Nave, a battalion commander of the 358th Infantry. He was the only commander who seemed to be operating in the field. He was killed in action two days later.

On the way back to the Division CP, we came upon a group of men, including a sergeant, well back of the front, in a ditch alongside a main road. I stopped and asked the sergeant what they were doing. He made some evasive reply. It was obvious they were malingering. I tried to appeal to their pride in the 90th Division, citing its great record in the Meuse-Argonne battle in World War I and the fine work of the 82nd Airborne through which they had passed. They were not interested and said so. I ordered them back to the front, but could not stay to see if they complied. I reported the incident to General McKelvie and described the situation at the front as I had observed it. He made no excuses, but seemed at a loss as to what to do about the lack of fight in his division.

When I got back to my CP, I called General Bradley and told him what I had found. I said the basic trouble with the 90th was inadequate training and lack of leadership, but that I thought McKelvie, who had been the artillery commander and inherited the Division only a few months before it sailed from the States, should not be held responsible for its poor condition and lack of will to fight. I blamed the former commander who clearly had not toughened the troops to meet the grim realities of war. I recommended that McKelvie be replaced by Major General Eugene M. Landrum, an experienced infantryman. I knew Landrum only slightly, but reports from the Pacific indicated that he had done well in the occupation of Attu and he had been attached to the VII Corps by the War Department as a spare, potential division commander. I suggested that McKelvie be relieved without prejudice to his career and that he be given another artillery assignment. I urged Bradley to permit me to employ Matt Eddy's 9th Infantry Division, along with the 82nd Airborne, for the drive to the west coast of the peninsula, and replace the 90th Division with the 79th Division when the latter unit came ashore. Brad quickly approved all my proposals.

I discussed the situation with Gene Landrum and advised him to change commanders of the 357th and 358th Regiments, which had done so poorly in three days of action. He agreed. We had no spare regimental commanders available, but our G-3, Dick Partridge, who had been present during my discussion with Landrum and who was anxious to get a command, volunteered for one of the regiments. Though he was not an infantryman, I knew he had received good basic training at West Point, had attended the German Kreigsakademie just prior to the war, and had impressed me most favorably since joining the Corps staff. Landrum was glad to get him and assigned Partridge to the 358th Infantry. For the other regiment I suggested Colonel George Bittman Barth, then Chief of Staff of the 90th Division. Bittman, like Partridge, was an artilleryman, but also a West Pointer, had been one of my lieutenants in the 8th Infantry in Germany before transferring to the field artillery, and had seen combat with the 9th Division in the Mediterranean. With Landrum's concurrence I called Matt Eddy and asked if he would release Barth, if the latter would be willing to take over the 357th Infantry. He and Barth promptly agreed.

These changes were the beginning of the conversion of the 90th Division from a spiritless outfit to one of the finest fighting units in the European Theater. There was nothing basically wrong with the men of the Division. What they needed was leadership. Partridge and Barth began to supply it, setting an example for their juniors by getting out of their command posts and leading their troops in combat. As with so many brave men, each was soon severely wounded in action and had to be evacuated.* Unfortunately, Landrum did not quite measure up. General Bradley relieved him in August and assigned Major General Raymond S. McLain, a National Guardsman from Oklahoma who had distinguished himself in Italy. Under McLain, and later under Van Fleet, whom I had recommended for his first star at the end of the Cherbourg campaign, the 90th Division reached its top rating.

The VII Corps Seals Off the Cotentin Peninsula

With Bradley's approval I revamped my plan to seal off Cotentin and issued oral instructions directly to Generals Landrum, Eddy, and Ridgway on June 13 for an attack the following morning with the initial objective of seizing the line of the Douve River south of Terre-de-Beauval. The 9th and 82nd Divisions after passing through the 90th would attack abreast, with the 9th Division on the right. The 9th was to drive on Ste. Colombe and prepare to cross the Douve to the southwest and block the peninsula west of the Prairies Marécageuses. The 82nd Airborne was to seize St. Sauveur-le Vicomte and protect the south flank of the Corps west of Baupté. When passed through, the 90th Division was to pivot to the northeast of Beauval and establish a defensive line between le Ham and Beauval. The 101st Airborne was to continue to protect the south flank of the VII Corps east of Baupté.

Considerable shifting of troops proved necessary for the changed plan so that only slight progress was made on June 14. The attack of the veteran 9th and 82nd Divisions really got underway on June 15.

---

*When I learned that Partridge had been wounded I went to the evacuation hospital on Utah beach to see him. I checked with the surgeon in charge and was told that Dick had been hit by a sniper's bullet, which had cut across the muscles of his back, missing his spinal cord by a fraction of an inch. He assured me that Partridge would not only survive but could return to duty in a few weeks. I decided then and there to offer Dick the post of Chief of Staff of the Corps. I found him in some pain and low in spirit, as he feared he was through for the duration of the war. I had brought him a bottle of scotch, which cheered him somewhat. After assuring him that the doctor said he would be all right, I asked:

"Dick, how would you like to return to the Corps as Chief of Staff?"

His eyes brightened, "Do you mean it?"

I replied, "I certainly do!"

Dick grinned from ear to ear. "General," he said, "I am well already." The doctors said later that I had speeded his recovery immeasurably.

Despite enemy reinforcement of the Douve front by the 265th Division from Brittany, the 82nd advanced to within one thousand yards of St. Sauveur, but the 60th Infantry under Colonel Frederick J. de Rohan—the only regiment of 9th Division thus far engaged—was hit by a counterattack supported by tanks, and its advance checked until late in the day when Colonel George W. Smythe's 47th Infantry was inserted on the right of the 60th, as the left flank of the 90th pivoted to the north. The 47th Infantry made rapid progress and by dark had taken the high ground west of Orglandes.

I had followed closely the attacks of June 15, shifting back and forth on visits in the field with Ridgway and Eddy, both fine front-line commanders. Ridgway complained that the 9th Division was not keeping up with the 82nd, but I told him not to worry about his right flank, as I was returning Paddy Flint's 39th Infantry to the 9th Division and was confident the 9th would not falter. I directed Ridgway to drive hard to the Douve on June 16, irrespective of what happened on his right, while Eddy was to attack with his three regiments abreast, along with the 359th Infantry of the 90th Division, which I placed temporarily under Eddy's command.

This tactic worked. Ridgway's 325th Glider Infantry and 505th Parachute Regiment reached the Douve across from St. Sauveur, where it joined the 508th Regiment. Ridgway spotted the enemy pulling out of St. Sauveur. He promptly requested, and I granted, permission to cross the Douve and establish a bridgehead on the west bank. I instructed Ridgway to push a bridgehead across the Prairies Marécageuses south of St. Sauveur, and initiate reconnaissance south toward la Haye du Puits.

It appeared that the enemy was shifting from a north-south line west of the Douve to an east-west position. I therefore directed Matt Eddy to speed the attack of the 60th and 47th Regiments to the Douve between Beauval and Ste. Colombe, with the 39th Regiment remaining east of the Douve to protect the Division's north flank until it could be relieved by the 359th Infantry. The 9th was to cross the 60th Infantry over the Douve in the vicinity of St. Colombe and seize the high ground west of Nehou, while the 47th Regiment was to pass through the bridgehead of the 82nd west of St. Sauveur-le Vicomte and attack to the southwest to plug the gap between the Prairies Marécageuses and St. Lô-d'Ourville.

While these moves were getting under way the 2nd Battalion, 60th Infantry, under Lieutenant Colonel Michael E. Kauffman, supported by a company of tanks of the 746th Tank Battalion, made a wide sweep cross-country, avoiding enemy contact, and drove into Ste. Colombe in one of the most brilliant actions I know of in the entire war. With scarcely a pause, Kauffman pushed his leading Company E over two of the three branches of the Douve at this point. The bridge over the third branch was out and the battalion came under direct artillery and infantry fire from the high ground on which Nehou sits. The tanks had to turn back, but Company E crossed the last stream branch, held on to the hill slopes below Nehou, and was reinforced during the night by Company G and the 3rd Battalion of the 60th Infantry.*

Anticipating the early severing of the German position on the peninsula, I was anxious to capitalize on the breaks of the 9th and 84th Divisions west of the Douve, so stayed behind them, particularly the 9th, throughout the seventeenth. Progress in the morning was rapid on the fronts of both the 60th and 47th Regiments but was slowed by enemy delaying actions in the afternoon and early evening.

The going was a bit tougher in front of the 60th Infantry, partly because initially it was all up hill out of the valley of the Douve. But by early evening the 3rd Battalion, leading the attack, had reached St. Jacques-de-Néhou. I arrived there with Captain Walsh at about dusk. Fighting had apparently stopped for the day. I found the commander of the 3rd Battalion in the central square of St. Jacques, opposite the church. He was dead tired, almost out on his feet from lack of sleep. He said the Germans had just withdrawn from the town and he had lost contact with them. I had Jack Walsh clip our telephone, which he always carried, across the battalion line back to the regiment and Division, and get General Eddy on the phone. For once Matt Eddy was not out in the field. I described the situation in St. Jacques to him and told him I wanted him to meet me there as soon as possible.

As the Germans pulled out of St. Jacques they had fired an 88-mm

---

*I personally saw to it that Colonel Kauffman received the D.S.C. for his exploit.

shell through the face of the clock in the stone church tower. The wooden supports of the clock and church bell had caught fire and black smoke was pouring from the belfry when we arrived. Waiting for Eddy to come up, Jack Walsh and I helped organize a water-bucket fire brigade of townspeople, who had begun to appear from their cellars. They closed the heavy inner doors leading from the tower into the nave of the church and began dousing the burning debris falling from the belfry.*

Shortly before Eddy arrived the brass bell crashed to the floor of the tower in a shower of sparks, without hurting anyone, and I turned my attention to Eddy. I pointed out that the way appeared open to the west coast, and I wanted him to put fresh troops into the attack of the 47th and 60th Regiments, and have them drive all night if necessary to cut off the peninsula. He happily took steps at once to comply. We were operating on double daylight-saving time and there were still a few hours of light at that latitude before nightfall. By the time I was back at my CP at Ste. Mére-Église, about 10:00 P.M., I had word that George Smythe's 47th Infantry had cut the Barneville-sur-Mere–la Haye du Puits road. Meanwhile de Rohan's 60th Infantry, led by Company K of the 3rd Battalion riding on tanks and other armored vehicles, drove on Barneville throughout the night, against only light resistance. At 5:00 A.M., June 17, the battalion reached the hill overlooking Barneville and sent a company into the town, deserted except for a few surprised German MPs. The fate of Cherbourg was sealed by the 9th Division on the night of June 17–18.

German Reaction

With an American breakthrough across the base of the Cotentin peninsula in sight by June 14, Field Marshal Rommel sought to save the LXXXIV Corp's best division, the 77th, from being bottled up in the peninsula and directed the LXXXIV Corps to reorganize its forces into two Kampfgruppen. The order, a copy of which was captured by the

---

*When I returned to St. Jacques in June, 1974, on the occasion of the 30th Anniversary of D day, I was delighted to learn that the church had been saved and the old bell recast and replaced in the tower along with a new clock. I had the pleasure of talking with two of the townspeople who had participated in the bucket brigade.

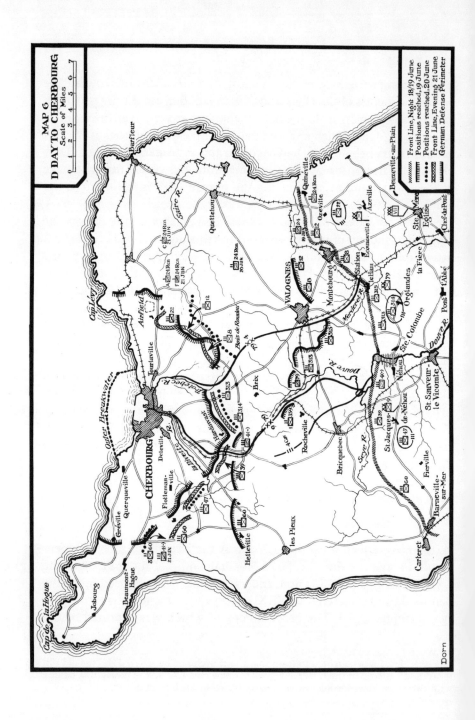

MAP 6
D DAY TO CHERBOURG
Scale of Miles
0 1 2 3 4 5 6 7

Front Line, Night 18/19 June
Positions reached, 19 June
Positions reached, 20 June
Front Line, Evening 21 June
German Defense Perimeter

9th Division, placed the 709th and 243rd Divisions in one group under General von Schlieben, which if the peninsula were cut off would withdraw to the south. Hitler overruled his generals—as he was to do often thereafter, usually to the advantage of the Allies—and directed them to hold fast. By July 17, when the German Seventh Army under Colonel General Friedrich Dollman finally ordered the 77th Division to withdraw south to the vicinity of la Haye du Puits, it was too late to escape the trap set by the 9th Division.

The situation was made more difficult for the Germans when General Hellmich was killed on June 17 while rearranging his forces, and General Rudolf Stegmann, commanding the 77th Division, was killed the same day by a fighter-bomber attack while Stegmann was trying to break his division out of the clutches of the 1st Battalion, 39th Infantry, attached to the 60th Regiment. This battalion had followed the 60th to St. Jacques-de-Néhou and was blocking to the north in that vicinity. In a bitter night fight the battalion was forced to give some ground, but after daylight on June 18 it counterattacked and drove the Germans back with heavy losses. The only point where the enemy was able to penetrate American lines was in the southwest corner, near St. Lô-d'Ourville, after the 357th Infantry of the 90th Division had relieved the 47th Infantry. A battalion of the 1050th Grenadier Regiment of the 77th Division captured over a hundred Americans of the 90th Division—still an ineffective unit—and opened a way for about 1,400 men of the 77th Division to escape to the south.

During the period June 15–19 the VIII Corps under Major General Troy H. Middleton had relieved the VII Corps of responsibility for operations south of the line Ste. Mère-Église–Orglandes–Ste. Colombe–Barneville. The VIII Corps took control of the 82nd and 101st Airborne Divisions and the 90th Infantry Division, and this freed my VII Corps, now consisting of the 4th, 79th, and 9th Infantry Divisions, for the drive on Cherbourg.

Advance to Outer Defenses of Cherbourg

Following my customary practice I discussed with General Bradley and then with the division commanders on June 17–18 my plan for a coordinated attack on Cherbourg, to be launched June 19. Oral instruc-

tions issued during this period were confirmed in Operations Memorandum No. 17 and recorded in Field Orders 2. As usual I based my scheme of maneuver on an analysis of the terrain and what we knew of the enemy's plans and potential. A relief map of the Cotentin peninsula that Mason Young, our Corps Engineer, had prepared for me, *
showed that the Divette River and the upper reaches of the Douve divided the northern half of the peninsula into two broad compartments. The eastern compartment, in which the 4th Division had been fighting, contained two small cities, Montebourg and Valognes, whose solid stone houses could become strong enemy redoubts. The compartment west of the Douve was more open country, with fewer natural obstacles, and was not being held in strength. Ground rose steadily in both compartments to the hills ringing Cherbourg, broken only by the narrow Trotebec and Divette streams, both of which flowed into Cherbourg harbor. We knew from aerial photographs that the Germans had organized this ring of hills, cresting four to five miles from the city, with a formidable series of mutually supporting strongpoints consisting of concrete machine-gun, antitank, and 88-mm gun emplacements, and tank barriers. Our able G-2, Colonel Leslie D. Carter, estimated that the enemy would fight stubborn delaying actions until he withdrew within his ring defenses. This was confirmed by capture of orders of the LXXXIV Corps and the 77th Division. The total enemy force, including coastal defense, antiaircraft, and naval personnel and organized labor battalions, was estimated at from twenty-five to forty thousand.

I decided to hit the enemy with three divisions abreast, in order from the east: 4th, 79th, and 9th. The major effort of the Corps would be in the form of a double-pronged attack by the 4th and 9th Divisions, cutting in against the Cherbourg defenses from east and west, with the 79th Division and the 4th Cavalry Squadron serving as a link between the two prongs.

VII Corps Attack of June 19

The VII Corps attack was initiated by the 4th Division under cover of darkness at 3:00 A.M., June 19, without an artillery preparation. The

*This map I carried with me in the field and consulted throughout the Cherbourg Campaign; it is now in the military museum in Fort du Roule overlooking Cherbourg.

enemy had strengthened his positions on the Montebourg front during the four-day lull while we concentrated on sealing the peninsula, and the 4th Division made little progress until after daylight. A well-executed double envelopment of Montebourg by Van Fleet's 8th Infantry forced evacuation of that city and assisted the advance of the 12th Regiment on its right, and by midnight of the nineteenth both regiments were closing in on Valognes. Thereafter the enemy offered little resistance. Valognes was abandoned and on June 20 von Schlieben's forces withdrew within the outer-ring defense of Cherbourg. The 4th Division followed up on June 20, and on the twenty-first the 8th and 22nd Infantry Regiments developed cracks in the German perimeter. Similarly the 79th Division met only light initial resistance. Since this was the Division's first combat, I was anxious to have it avoid the experience of the 90th Division, so followed it during most of the first day. But the 79th was well trained and well led by Major General Ira T. (Billy) Wyche, a 1911 West Pointer whom I had known in Coblenz. As with the 9th Division at St. Jacques-de-Néhou, I did have to press the division to continue its attack well into the night as the Germans began to withdraw to the north. This uncovered an uncompleted V-bomb launching site in a wooded area near the village of Brix, northwest of Valognes. It was one of several such sites overrun by the Corps on the Cotentin peninsula. Fortunately they were captured before they could do damage to the ports of England.

Over on the front of the 9th Division the going was easier still, at first. As soon as Matt Eddy discovered after the jump-off at 5:00 A.M., June 19, that his advance was unopposed, he put the 39th and 60th Regiments in road-march formation. By 7:00 A.M. an old fortress town where resistance had been expected, Bricquebec, was overrun without a shot by Paddy Flint's 39th Infantry. De Rohan's 60th Infantry had a longer distance up the road along the west coast to les Pieux but by late afternoon the Division, with the 4th Cavalry Squadron on its right, reached the line Helleville–Coville–St. Martin. There it began to run into fire from Cherbourg's outer-ring defenses.

The need for early capture of the port city was dramatized by a four-day storm that hit the Normandy beaches beginning June 19. By the twenty-first the ships and barges sunk or moored offshore to form artificial harbors began to break up, and unloading of ammunition and other supplies had to be suspended. Combat operations ashore as well as the landing of additional troops would be gravely threatened if capture of the port facilities was long delayed.

The Final Drive on Cherbourg

As a prelude to the final assault planned for June 22, I requested General Bradley to arrange a saturation bombing of the German defensive perimeter, the objective being primarily to weaken the already failing morale of the defenders and possibly induce them to surrender. With Bradley's approval Major General Elwood R. (Pete) Quesada, commanding the IX Tactical Air Command, consulted with Brad and me and drafted the outline of the bombing plan, which was relayed to England, where the final plan was worked out by the IX Bomber Command. Bombing was to concentrate on the front of the 79th and 9th Divisions. Starting at H hour minus eighty minutes, antiaircraft positions would be hit by four squadrons of RAF Typhoons, after which RAF squadrons would strafe the area. During the last hour before jump-off, twelve groups of U.S. Ninth Air Force fighter-bombers would hit strongpoints within the perimeter. When our attack moved out, it was to be preceded by eleven groups of the IX Bomber Command, which would bomb ahead of the troops, like a rolling artillery barrage.

Oral instructions for renewal of the Corps attack were given to division and major unit commanders on June 21 and confirmed in Field Orders 3. No changes were made in the missions of the divisions, but they were advised of the aerial bombardment and instructions were issued for marking front lines with yellow smoke and—for the near edges of targets to be attacked by the Ninth Air Force—with white phosphorous artillery shells.

On the night of June 21–22 the hopelessness of the German situation was called to the attention of the garrison of Cherbourg in a multilingual broadcast, and I made a personal appeal for its surrender, warning that if I did not have word of capitulation from General von Schlieben by 0900 the following morning, we would proceed with its annihilation. I really did not expect a reply. None was received. H hour was set for 2:00 P.M., June 22.

I went up to observe the bombing from a hedgerow about a half mile back of the front line of Billy Wyche's 79th Division on the Valognes-Cherbourg highway. With me were Pete Quesada and Brigadier General Richard E. Nugent of the 9th Air Force, who had come over from England to witness the air attack, which went off exactly on time. Its accuracy was not as precise. The first we knew of it was when a flight of British fighters strafed the next hedgerow in front of us, not more than a hundred yards away, behind our front lines. We could see the yellow smoke clearly marking the front, but the pilots must not have seen it. I was glad to have Dick Nugent with me to observe this incident firsthand, as we flattened ourselves against our hedgerow while several successive flights roared by. Fortunately we received no reports of anyone being injured in this attack, which continued in other areas for twenty minutes.

Then for the next hour wave after wave of American fighter bombers, 375 in all, plastered six principal targets marked with white phosphorus. Destruction caused by the mass bombing was not very great, but judging from the interrogation of prisoners it did serve its major purpose of helping to undermine the morale of the German troops. The heavy artillery shelling that followed the bombing probably did more real damage.

Despite the bombing and shelling, the Germans clung tenaciously to their dug-in positions. Penetrations of limited depth were made at points along the perimeter but there was no clear breakthrough anywhere on June 22. There were some signs of crumbling German defenses. Evidently even Hitler realized that the situation was desperate. Unknown to us, he had sent orders to von Schlieben: "Even if worse comes to worst, it is your duty to defend the last bunker and leave to the enemy not a harbor but a field of ruins. . . . The German people and the whole world are watching your fight; on it depends . . . the honor of the German Army and your own name." Such exhortations were no substitute for the reinforcements which von Schlieben requested, but which could not be furnished either by air or by sea.

On June 22 all three divisions of the VII Corps, with excellent close support from Pete Quesada's fighter bombers, penetrated the perimeter defense and on the twenty-fourth closed in on the city from all directions. I was concerned that von Schlieben might try to break out to the west-northwest and attempt a last stand in the Cap de la Hague, and instructed Matt Eddy on June 24 to complete seizure of the high ground overlooking Cherbourg but not to become involved in street fighting in the city. He was to continue blocking the area northwest of Flottemanville-Hague and contain the enemy in the Cap de la Hague peninsula. Similarly on the east flank the 4th Division was to seize Tourlaville and contain any enemy in the Cap Levy peninsula, including the city airport.

We Ready the Last Blow

General Bradley came up to visit me on the twenty-fifth to discuss final plans for reduction of the inner defenses of Cherbourg. As always he was helpful. He had arranged with Admiral "Mort" Deyo to have Task Force 129, including three battleships and four cruisers, shell the coastal batteries covering the seaward approach to the city. He also told me with a chuckle: "Joe, you will love this. Monty has just announced, 'Caen [not yet taken by the British army] is the key to Cherbourg.'" I said: "Brad, let's wire him to send us the key." In the interest of Allied amity we did not do it.

For a summary of events on June 25 I can do no better than quote from the letter I dictated to my sergeant-secretary, Robert G. Ruth, for Mrs. Collins on June 26, 1944:

> Yesterday was one of our great days. The evening before we had ringed around the city and I was confident that we would be able to enter Cherbourg proper sometime on Sunday. Despite the fact that I was up until 1:30 in the morning, I got up in time for 9 o'clock mass which was held in a stable formerly occupied by some German artillery. Brad came over to see me to discuss future plans which occupied the rest of the morning.
>
> Right after lunch, I started out on my usual round visiting the divisions. Mr. Stoneman, of the Chicago Daily News, rode along with us in an armored car that has been my rolling CP.
>
> First, we went out to see Tubby Barton's division. Teddy Roosevelt acted as our guide and led us to a captured German position overlooking the city from the east. This point had just been taken by the 12th Infantry, and a short distance off to our right in another German position, we could see hundreds of Boche prisoners being rounded up by our troops. The view of Cherbourg from this point is magnificent. Off to the left were the steep

cliffs of the highlands that run right up to the back door of the city. Another of our divisions was rapidly closing in on this area from the south and we could see smoke from the fires being directed into Fort du Roule, which is the central bastion of the German defenses, on a high bluff overlooking the city. Over to the right were the inner and outer breakwaters with their old French forts guarding the entrance from the sea. Beyond the haze of smoke, we could see part of our battle fleet engaged in the shelling of the seacoast batteries west of the town. Within this frame, the city itself lay as in a bowl from which billows of smoke poured up in spots where the Germans were demolishing stores of oil and ammunition. As we watched, one of our heavy batteries fired a perfect concentration onto a German position just west of the Fort des Flamands. It was a thrilling and, in a sense, an awe-inspiring sight. I knew definitely then that Cherbourg was ours and directed Tubby to push one of his regiments into the eastern section of the city before that night.

From there, we drove around to Billy Wyche's CP. After discussing the situation with Billy, who had just come back from the central front, we worked our way forward to another hill overlooking Cherbourg from the south near the Fort du Roule. Scattered rifle fire kept us from going as far forward as I would have wished. Some litter bearers carrying back a wounded man warned us to go no farther, and as there was no point in doing so, we turned back. I had given Billy Wyche instructions to push two of his regiments into the city from the south and they were already on the way.

We then circled back to the south and up to the western sector where Matt Eddy has been doing a bang-up job. He was quite jubilant that one of his left regiments, commanded by George Smythe, had entered the city proper at 12:50 in the afternoon against only light resistance. However, his right regiment, under the redoubtable Patty Flint, had run into a hornet's nest just south of the city and had drawn considerable shelling from the German positions which had been broken through much farther west. I was anxious to see just what the situation was on this front, as the major part of the city lay in this sector. Matt Eddy took us up to a former German anti-aircraft position which had been pulverized by a dive bombing attack the day before. This place was exposed to view from a German position farther to the east in Billy Wyche's sector which we had by-passed the day before. We soon drew fire from an 88mm gun which was located in this by-passed area, but we were able to duck down into a German communication trench and made our way forward to a secure concrete observation post from which we had another fine view of the city. While we were there the Germans were shelling in the area in which Patty Flint was operating and as we left some of these shells landed so close that Matt and I had to take cover faster than I have yet had to do. Fortunately, our counter-battery soon brought this German fire to an end and we were able to return unmolested to the jeeps we had left farther back under cover. I directed Matt to push his two regiments into the city, and before dark one of them had broken through to the sea, effectively cutting the last route of withdrawal of the Germans to the area they still hold in the Cap de la Hague to the northwest.

Capture of General von Schlieben

Two events highlighted the stirring day of June 26: capture of General von Schlieben and Admiral Walther Hennecke, commander of Cherbourg naval arsenal, and the fall of Fort du Roule.

The 2nd Battalion, 39th Infantry, under Lieutenant Colonel Frank L. Gunn, advanced toward the Cherbourg docks and discovered two or more tunnels leading to a cave near St. Saveur on the outskirts of Cherbourg, and word had reached the battalion that von Schlieben's headquarters was in such a cave. Captain Preston O. Gordon, commanding Company E, sent a German prisoner into the cave to demand its surrender. He received no response, whereupon the battalion maneuvered tank destroyers into position to fire into its entrances. On hearing of the cave's discovery General Eddy and Colonel Flint had come up. General Eddy described in his diary what followed, as quoted in part in the 9th Division history, *Eight Stars to Victory*:

> After half a dozen shots from the TD's three inch gun into the rear entrances, which apparently played havoc, a loud voice called out in German from the front entrance to cease fire. After much difficulty we were able to get all of the battalion quiet.
>
> I then directed a soldier who could speak German to call and tell them that we would give them two minutes to come out. Instantly, a German with one of the largest white flags I have ever seen ran out . . . followed by a young typical German lieutenant who, I swear, all but goose stepped. . . . The lieutenant asked to see the ranking officer present. . . . He informed me that the Commanding General of the 709th Infantry Division was in the cave and wished to surrender. He requested that I send a staff officer down with him to escort the General to me.
>
> In the meantime, the tank-destroyer's projectiles had caused so much dust and fumes in the tunnel that the German soldiers, once finding that the white flag had been raised, began to pour out. By actual count later there were 842 of them. These Germans were in such a rush that they denied the General his wish for a formal surrender. As he was standing near the entrance, the avalanche of soldiers carried him and his party with it.
>
> When the General came up out of the pit to me and told me he was von Schlieben I damn near died. When he introduced me to Admiral Hennecke, I thought I was dead.

General Eddy led his captives to his own headquarters, where he tried to persuade von Schlieben to surrender his forces in order to save soldiers' lives, German and American alike, but von Schlieben refused, whereupon Matt sent the two prisoners on to me. I was up at Fort du Roule when a radio message reached me that they were on the way. I hurried back to my CP at the Chateau de Servigny, Yvetôt Bocage, near Valognes, and demanded of the big, hulking von Schlieben that he surrender all forces under his command. When he refused I asked how he could justify having his soldiers fight on when he saved himself by giving up, and he answered weakly that he had learned from the Russians that even small, scattered units could put up considerable resistance. He said that even if he wanted to surrender his troops he could not reach them all because of his disrupted communications. I offered to furnish the necessary communications, but he still refused. I permitted him and the Admiral to wash up a bit, then started them back under an armed guard to First Army. After they left I had no compunction about instructing our psychological section to make maximum use of the charge that von Schlieben had saved his own skin while requiring his men to continue fighting.

Fall of Fort du Roule

Meanwhile the 314th Regiment, 69th Division, was winding up its seizure of Fort du Roule, the last formidable bastion of Cherbourg's defenses, built into the solid stone bluff above the city. Heavy artillery on the lower of its several levels was still menacing our troops entering the city down below, while machine guns and 88-mm cannon in concrete emplacements on the upper levels covered the approaches from the rear. It took heroic actions on the part of individuals and small groups to break into these upper levels. First Lieutenant Carlos C. Ogden, despite a head wound, and in the face of enemy fire, personally disabled an 88-mm gun, while Corporal John D. Kelly crawled up the hill slope under machine-gun fire from a pillbox. After two futile attempts he succeeded in blowing open the rear door of the pillbox with a pole-charge, forcing the crew to surrender. Ogden and Kelly each received the Medal of Honor. Even after the upper levels were occupied, the enemy held out below until holes were dynamited in the floors and demolition charges dropped through them. This was still being done when I entered the back door of the fort at ground level on the afternoon of the twenty-sixth, just before I was called back to my CP to receive von Schlieben.

Resistance in the city ended on June 27 at the naval arsenal in the port area. Surrounded by a high wall, partly protected by a moat, and mounting antitank and antiaircraft guns on its parapets, the arsenal could have been tough to crack. But after two of its guns had been knocked out by tank fire, and its commander apparently persuaded by one of our broadcasts that von Schlieben had surrendered, white flags appeared. A costly assault by George Smythe's 47th Infantry was avoided.

Though the city was in our hands, the two promontories east and west of Cherbourg, which we had bypassed, were still held by the enemy. The 4th Division had been continuously in action since D day and was responsible for the Cap Levy area to the east. In order that this excellent division might have a part in the capture of Cherbourg, I authorized General Barton to send one of his regiments into the city on June 25. He chose the 12th Infantry, a fine regiment, the nearest available. I was a bit sorry he had not picked our D-day assault unit, the 8th Infantry. As I had forecast, the regiment and its commander, Jim Van Fleet, had performed admirably. Van Fleet was given his first star shortly thereafter. The 22nd Infantry, with the 24th Cavalry attached, which had been blocking off the Cap Levy promontory, was now assigned the task of clearing this region. This was accomplished by midnight, July 27.

Cleaning up the Cap de la Hague peninsula required some heavy fighting by the 9th Division. The 60th Infantry had been blocking this area while the battle for Cherbourg was in progress. After the fall of the city General Eddy regrouped his forces, and on June 29 jumped off with the 47th and 60th Regiments abreast, 47th on the right, 60th in the middle, and the 4th Cavalry Squadron on the left. The country here was open and the Germans had studded their commanding ground with gun emplacements and tank barriers comparable to the Cherbourg outer ring. It took all of the skill of the veteran 9th Division in combined infantry, artillery, tank, and fighter-bomber operations to break through this position. German resistance began to give way on the thirtieth. Auderville, at the tip of the peninsula, was secured by 5:00 A.M., July 1.

I did not wait until quite the end of the campaign to return the city of Cherbourg to French civil control, for I wanted to have present the commanders of all divisions that had made its capture possible. The 69th Division was slated to move south to join the VIII Corps and the 82nd and 101st Airborne Divisions would shortly return to England. At the suggestion of one of my staff officers, we made a French tricolor from colored parachutes of our Airborne divisions. On the afternoon of June 27 in a moving ceremony on the steps of the city hall I presented the tricolor to Paul Reynaud, the venerable Mayor of Cherbourg, in the presence of the city council and our division commanders— Ridgway, Taylor, Barton, Eddy, and Wyche—and before a gathering of French citizens in the Place Napoléon. Speaking in halting French, I said simply that we Americans were proud to return to our sister republic its first city to be liberated by the Allies.

Reynaud replied eloquently, in his polished native tongue, expressing the gratitude of his townsmen at being free from Nazi control, and pledged eternal friendship of France for America. He invited us into the council hall for a glass of champagne, which he assured me he had never offered the Nazis. On the way in, Billy Wyche provided a break in the relative solemnity of the occasion.

"Joe," he said, "I didn't know you spoke French. I could understand every word you said!"

"That's bad news, Billy," I replied, "because if the Americans could understand me, the Frenchmen could not."

It was excellent champagne.

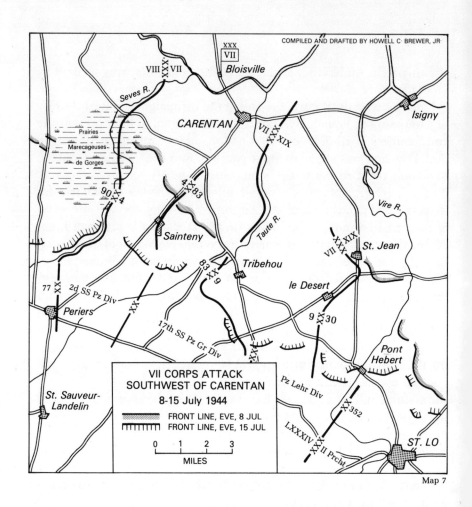

VII CORPS ATTACK
SOUTHWEST OF CARENTAN
8-15 July 1944

FRONT LINE, EVE, 8 JUL
FRONT LINE, EVE, 15 JUL

0   1   2   3
MILES

Map 7

CHAPTER XII

Breakout from Normandy

Change of Fronts

Even before the fall of Cherbourg, General Bradley stopped at my CP to check our progress and discuss the next phase of operations—a breakout from Normandy. I was to turn around the VII Corps, that is, the 4th, 9th, and 83rd Divisions, and position it southwest of Carentan for a drive across the Cotentin peninsula toward Coutances, in conjunction with the VIII Corps. The 79th Division would join the VIII Corps and be replaced by the 83rd, which was already in the area of Carentan.

Following the German reverses in Normandy, there was a general shake-up of their command on the Western Front. Hitler replaced Rundstedt as commander in chief with Field Marshal Günther von Kluge, who had commanded a corps against the Russians. Rommel remained in command of Army Group B, which had tactical control, under von Kluge, of troops manning the English Channel coast north of the Loire River. The Seventh Army, which had met the Allied invasion, was now commanded by General Paul Hausser. It comprised two corps, the II Parachute on the St. Lô front opposite the American XIX and V Corps, and the LXXXIV opposing the VIII and VII Corps. Lieutenant General Dietrich von Choltitz was shifted from Italy to command the LXXXIV Corps, leaving Rommel the only senior commander with experience against the Allies on the Western Front. In the area southwest of Carentan, Choltitz had the 17th SS Panzer Grenadier Division and 6th Parachute Regiment, both understrength, but tough and experienced.

By July 1 we had moved our CP down to Bloisville, north of Carentan, and the following day I took over the 83rd Division, which was holding a position astride the Carentan–Périers road, three miles south-west of Carentan. The road ran along a low, narrow isthmus, three miles wide, between the swamps of the Prairies Marécageuses Gorges and the flooded banks of the Taute River. The flat land between was soggy from incessant rain and crisscrossed by a series of hedgerows, fifty or so yards apart, which marked off the small fields of Norman farms. The saplings that grew in the mud walls of these hedgerows were cut back periodically for firewood, which resulted in a heavy, matted root growth that made the hedgerows formidable barriers even for tanks. Where adjoining properties met, the hedgerows were double, with a passageway in between that resembled a communications trench and provided concealment for enemy machine guns and mortars. While the VII Corps was advancing on Cherbourg, the Germans had penetrated between the V and VII Corps, but had been driven back from Carentan by the 101st Airborne Division; they had time to organize a series of defensive positions across the isthmus. The flanks of these positions, which rested on the swamps to the west and Taute River on the east, were covered by machine-gun fire, and their fronts were protected by mine fields.

When I studied the terrain on the Corps front I knew we were in for tough sledding. Any commander worth his salt hates to make frontal attacks, but there was no alternative here. Furthermore, the isthmus was so narrow that there was room for only one division, and that was a new unit, the 83rd Infantry Division, in action for the first time. The 4th and 9th Divisions were still moving down from Cherbourg.

The 83rd Division was commanded by Major General Robert C. Macon, a tough, able soldier, who had done well in command of a regiment in North Africa. I had reinforced his division with additional tanks, tank destroyers, chemical mortars, and antiaircraft. The fires of the 83rd Division Artillery would be augmented by the 9th Division Artillery.

The 83rd Division jumped off at 4:45 A.M., July 4, with two regiments abreast, Colonel Martin D. Barndollar's 331st Infantry on the right of the Carentan–Périers road, and Colonel Ernest L. McLendon's 330th Infantry on the left. The Division at once ran into trouble, for the tanks became bogged down in the spongy soil, and poorly laid communications were cut, resulting in loss of contact with front-line units and almost nullifying the powerful artillery support that was available. Poor small-unit leadership and discipline showed up in lack of tank-infantry coordination and failure to employ local flanking maneuvers effectively. Casualties and stragglers increased as the enemy brought in heavy mortar fire from hidden hedgerow positions, which at the time we had no electronic means of locating. One hedgerow looked just like another. The morale of the troop sagged. Colonel Barndollar, perhaps the ablest regimental commander, was killed by small-arms fire in midmorning.

By the end of the day the Division had lost almost 1,400 men and failed to reach its initial objective of Sainteney, where the isthmus broadened enough to permit employment of the 4th Division alongside the 83rd. The second day was a repeat of the first. Despite the severe pressure that I put on General Macon, and which he passed on to his subordinates, little progress was made in the face of adverse weather, difficult terrain, and the stubborn resistance of Colonel Friedrich von der Heydte's 6th Parachute Regiment. Von der Heydte showed a touch of compassion by sending back some of the 83rd's captured medical personnel with a note saying he thought General Macon needed them. He added that if the situation was ever reversed, he hoped Macon would return the favor.

When it became evident that the 83rd Division alone would not break the enemy front, I decided to have General Barton pass his 12th Infantry through the 331st Regiment early on July 9 and have the 4th Division take over the zone west of Périers road, but even the more experienced 4th Division made little headway. Hoping to get the attack moving, I arranged with Pete Quesada's IX Tactical Air Command for an unusual preliminary mass bombardment by three groups of over 100 fighter bombers over a period of forty-five minutes, commencing at 6:00 A.M. To avoid dependence on frontal attacks the 4th Division was directed to send one regiment across a swampy stream west of the Périers road under cover of darkness on the night of July 6–7, to outflank the enemy. Corps Artillery was to support the night attack. The 4th Division was to jump off at 6:30 A.M., July 7, and the 83rd at 6:45 A.M.

I had high hopes for this attack, but they were dampened, literally, when a drizzly rain settled in early on July 7, forcing cancellation of the dive-bombing. The 8th Infantry, then commanded by Colonel James S. Rodwell, was able to get only one battalion across the stream west of the highway before being stopped by German machine-gun flanking fire. Unable to receive bombing support, it withdrew after suffering heavy casualties. Forced to depend on frontal attacks, the 4th Division again bogged down in the hedgerows.

The 83rd Division fared no better, though the Division was showing signs of settling down. Tank, artillery, and infantry coordination was beginning to improve and command control was tightening up, particularly in Colonel Edwin B. Crabill's 329th Infantry.

During the next few days some progress occurred. General Barton was finally able to get room on the edge of the Prairies Marécageuses to insert his third regiment, the 22nd Infantry under Colonel Charles T. Lanham, on July 8. At the same time the VII Corps zone was widened on the east to include part of Corlett's XIX Corps zone east of the Taute River. This would permit employment of the crack 9th Division to assist the 83rd, still struggling down the soggy isthmus to the west. The 22nd and 8th Regiments of the 4th Division made some advances east of the 83rd on July 9 and 10, but the 9th Division in its first encounter with the combination of hedgerows and swampy ground on July 9 was checked initially, as its predecessors had been.

German Counterattack

As the XIX Corps advanced toward St. Lô, von Kluge and Rommel realized that if this road and rail communications center was lost it might unhinge the German defenses in the Cotentin peninsula facing the American VII and VIII Corps. They decided to shift the Panzer Lehr Division, commanded by Lieutenant General Fritz Bayerlein, from the Caen sector for a counterattack in the area west of the Vire, generally at the junction of the American VII and XIX Corps, a favorite German tactic. Bayerlein planned to attack with two regimental combat teams abreast, one in the XIX Corps zone astride the Pont-Hébert–Carentan road, the other in the VII Corps zone, with the le Désert–St. Jean-de-Daye road as an axis. The two groups were to converge on the high ground at St. Jean, which dominated the crossings of the Vire River and the Vire–Taute canal. Under pressure from Rommel, Bayerlein moved his division during the night of July 10–11 and, without pause, launched its attack before dawn on the eleventh.

In the VII Corps zone two small penetrations were made on the front of Paddy Flint's 39th Infantry near le Désert, and some confusion and slight withdrawals occurred before veteran subordinate commanders rallied their men and began to check the German armor, which could do no better in the soggy ground than the Americans. Tanks and self-propelled guns became bogged down and separated, in small groups. With the coming of daylight the reaction of the 9th Division was swift, disciplined, and effective. Communications were restored to all units and a coordinated defense took shape almost automatically. Small groups of infantry and bazooka teams cut in behind the German armor, sealing off routes of withdrawal, while machine guns, mortars, and artillery pounded the accompanying German infantry. Tank destroyers swarmed around isolated groups of Tiger and Panther tanks, attacking them on their vulnerable flanks. Artillery struck a stalled column of tanks west of le Désert, and fighter bombers flying other missions were called in to attack rear elements of Panzer Lehr. Comparable actions were taken by the 30th Division and by a Combat Command of the 3rd Armored Division in the XIX Corps zone west of the Vire.

By midafternoon the attack of Panzer Lehr was stopped cold, and General Eddy was able to renew his attack and eliminate the German penetrations. The following day I went forward with Eddy to see some of the carnage near le Désert—destroyed German tanks, self-propelled guns, abandoned equipment. One column of six or eight Mark IV medium tanks apparently had been trapped in a half-sunken road and knocked out by our tank destroyers, their burned-out hulks in some instances still carrying on their decks the charred bodies of crew members. Extravagant claims of tanks destroyed in a battle are always made, but there is little question that Panzer Lehr lost about a quarter of its combat strength. Von Kluge thereafter was able to obtain Hitler's approval to move elements of the 6th Parachute Division and the 275th Infantry Division from Brittany to bolster Panzer Lehr in opposing the advance of the VII Corps toward the St. Lô–Périers road.

Though we did not know it then, the Panzer Lehr counterattack marked the end of the worst phase of the hedgerow-swamp combat for the VII Corps. Except for the later Hürtgen Forest, it was the deadliest, most difficult fighting I experienced in France, with the concealment afforded the enemy by the hedgerows and the tenacity of the Germans making it much like the jungle fighting in the Pacific against the Japanese.

General Bradley Reviews the Situation

It was about this time that General Bradley first mentioned to me an idea he had for breaking the near-stalemate in the Cotentin peninsula. He said he was considering asking for a saturation bombing on a section of the front as soon as we could reach firmer ground. He would use the VII Corps to break through this section and wanted me to study the situation and recommend an area for the breakthrough. He said some planning along these lines had been done by his staff. I have no written record of our conversation or my recommendations, but know that I recommended the firm ground between Marigny and St. Gilles.

In any event, on July 12, 1944, in a conference at his CP back of OMAHA beach, Bradley outlined to his staff and corps commanders his tentative plan for a breakthrough by the VII Corps following saturation bombing of a section of the front west of St. Lô. Present at the conference in addition to the four corps commanders of the First Army— Gerow, Corlett, Middleton, Collins—were Deputy Army Commander Hodges, Pete Quesada, and Major General Leroy H. Watson, commander of the 3rd Armored Division. Bradley pointed out on a large map the salient features of the plan, after which he asked for comments and suggestions. Discussion followed, with expressions of accord from all commanders. The only question raised was the weight of bombs to be dropped. British armor reportedly had been held up by cratering of the ground in an earlier heavy bombing. To avoid this Quesada suggested 250-pounders. I said I would take a chance on the cratering and favored the greater blast effect of 500-pound bombs with instantaneous fuses. This conference was typical of the method of Bradley and the American Army: developing an attack plan whenever time permitted. I followed essentially the same system throughout our campaigns in Europe.

The following day an outline plan was published by First Army for operation "Cobra." The VII Corps, to consist initially of the 9th and 30th Divisions, was to continue its current offensive to drive the enemy back to his main defensive position, expected to be along the Périers– St. Lô road. When this position was located, an area in advance of it would be saturated by medium and heavy bombers, following which the VII Corps, reinforced to include the 1st, 9th, and 30th Infantry Divisions and the 2nd and 3rd Armored Divisions, was to drive through the bombed area, seize Coutances and the crossings of the Sienne River to the southwest and the town of Brehal (five miles south of Coutances), and prevent any enemy reinforcement from the south. The VIII Corps, to the right, was to continue its effort to reach the Lessay–Périer road, and the XIX Corps on the left was to seize St. Lô prior to the commencement of Cobra; both corps were to tie down enemy forces, which might otherwise move to seal off the Cobra penetration.

Bradley rearranged corps boundaries and division assignments. The 83rd and 4th Divisions were transferred to the VIII Corps along with responsibility for the Carentan–Périers isthmus. VII Corps retained the 9th Division and acquired Major General Leland S. Hobbs's 30th Division. My new zone of action was now on firmer ground. We would be advancing along three low ridges rising gradually toward the Périers –St. Lô road, between the Lauson River and the Vire. The changes were to be effective July 16.

VII Corps Plan for the Breakthrough

As was his practice, Bradley gave me considerable leeway in the outline plan for Cobra, in adapting it to the terrain, in choosing troops made available to the VII Corps, and in the bombing plan as the latter developed.

During the July 12 conference I persuaded Bradley to let me have the 4th Infantry Division to bolster the forces in the breakthrough and exploitation. The addition would permit me to employ the 4th, 9th, and 30th Divisions in the breakthrough area between Marigny and St. Gilles, and then to protect the flanks of the penetration with the 9th and 30th, both of which had suffered heavy casualties in the hedgerow fighting. The 9th Division, after clearing the Marigny–St. Gilles gap,

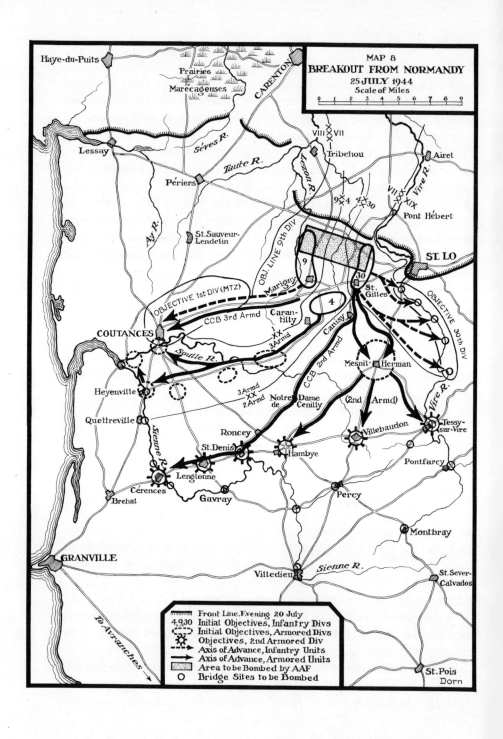

MAP 8
BREAKOUT FROM NORMANDY
25 JULY 1944
Scale of Miles

Front Line, Evening 20 July
4,9,30 Initial Objectives, Infantry Divs
Initial Objectives, Armored Divs
Objectives, 2nd Armored Div
Axis of Advance, Infantry Units
Axis of Advance, Armored Units
Area to be Bombed by AAF
Bridge Sites to be Bombed

was to swing to the northeast and seize the ridge west of the Lozon River. The 30th Division, after clearing its zone in the gap, would protect the left flank of the Corps and seize the crossings of the Vire River south of St. Lô. The 4th Division, following its attack in the center of the penetration, was to protect the center of the Marigny–St. Gilles gap from counterattack from the south, and be available as Corps reserve.

The First Army Outline Plan divided Cobra into three phases: breakthrough, exploitation, consolidation. The VII Corps operation plan made important changes in the scheme of maneuver during the two latter phases. Army had approved my selection of the Marigny–St. Gilles front for the breakthrough, and I decided to make the principal effort with the redoubtable 1st Infantry Division, motorized, reinforced by a combat command, CC "B" of the 3rd Armored, in a direct drive on Coutances. The 1st Division, a veteran of the North Africa and Sicily campaigns, was commanded by Major General Clarence R. Huebner, in whom I had great confidence. The 3rd Armored, less CC "B," would follow a roundabout route from Marigny to Coutances. The 1st Infantry and 3rd Armored would join in destruction of any enemy troops caught between the VIII and VII Corps.

The 2nd Armored Division, under Major General Edward H. Brooks, with the motorized 22nd Infantry Regiment attached, would follow the 30th Division and seize the area LeMesnil Herman–St. Sampson to cover movement of the 1st Division and 3rd Armored through the Marigny–St. Gilles gap. The 2nd Armored would push a combat team to the southwest via the St. Gilles–Canisy road, prepared, on my orders, either to seize points along the Brehal–Hambye road between Cérences and St. Denis-le-Gast to prevent any reinforcements moving north through this area; or to move on Coutances in support of the 3rd Armored; or to move to the southeast to reinforce the main body of the 2nd Armored in its mission.

The above scheme of maneuver was developed during the week following publication of the First Army's Outline Plan on July 13, after several informal discussions with General Bradley and with the division commanders, and almost continuous collaboration between the staffs of First Army and the VII Corps. As approved by Bradley the plan was embodied in the VII Corps Field Orders 6, dated July 20.

Martin Blumenson in his excellent official history of the Cobra operation, *Breakout and Pursuit,* makes quite a point as to whether Cobra was planned simply as a breakthrough of the German defenses on the Cotentin peninsula or intended as a breakout from Normandy into Brittany. While pointing out that Bradley and I worked together in developing the Cobra plan, he gives me undue credit for having changed the concept of Cobra so that it was "no longer a plan designed primarily to encircle Coutances after penetration; it had become a plan to encircle and secure Coutances, disrupt the German defenses of the Vire River, and set up a situation suitable for exploitation, presumably by the VIII Corps." Blumenson's point is largely academic. It is hardly conceivable that the tremendous effort by Allied Air Forces in the saturation bombing, and the commitment of four infantry and two armored divisions to the ground attack, was intended merely to break through the German position on the Cotentin and capture a single town. The senior commanders of the First Army knew, or at least surmised, that General Patton was assembling a large force north of VIII Corps. In the interest of secrecy Bradley did not tell me in the early planning phase of Cobra that this force under Patton would be used to break out of Normandy; he indicated this to me shortly before the attack, when he confided, "Joe, if this thing goes as it should, we should be in Avranches in a week."

We had high hopes of speeding the ground attack not only because of the expected disruption of the German defenses resulting from the massive bombardment, but because of a hedgerow cutting device developed by Sergeant Curtis G. Culin, Jr., of the 102nd Cavalry Reconnaissance Squadron. Tanks normally rose up in front on hitting a hedgerow, exposing their unarmed bellies to enemy fire. Sergeant Culin invented a hedgerow cutter in the form of several tusk-like prongs, made from scrap steel, welded to the front of a tank. Culin's "Rhino" bored into the mud base of a hedgerow, holding down the front of the tank while it crashed through the hedge. After witnessing a demonstration of the device, Bradley ordered Rhinos for all assault tanks participating in Cobra. First Army Ordnance, working secretly, thereupon converted many of Rommel's beach obstacles into these valuable hedgerow cutters, which would permit our tanks to speed cross-country through the remaining hedgerow terrain.

Final Preparations

General Bradley had set July 18 as the tentative date for the start of Cobra, but it became clear that this date was too early, as four days of laborious fighting by the 9th and 30th Divisions were required before the Périers–St. Lô road was reached on July 20, and the XIX Corps's 29th Division did not enter the battered city of St. Lô, the eastern anchor of Cobra, until the nineteenth. On that date Bradley flew to England to arrange details of the saturation bombing with Air Chief Marshal Leigh-Mallory, commander of the Allied Expeditionary Air Force, responsible for coordination of tactical air support of ground operations. Present at this conference, in addition to Leigh-Mallory, was Air Chief Marshall Arthur Tedder, Eisenhower's Deputy; General Carl "Tooey" Spaatz, commander of the United States Strategic Air Force in Europe; Lieutenant General Lewis H. Brereton, commanding the American Ninth Air Force, who was to arrange the detailed bombing plan; and General Quesada, who accompanied Bradley. Leigh-Mallory heartily approved the plan and promised 2,246 heavy, medium, and fighter bombers, many more than Bradley had hoped for.

General Bradley and I agreed that the area to be bombed would be a rectangle seven thousand yards wide and five thousand yards deep, immediately south of an arrow-straight section of the Périers–St. Lô road, which showed up clearly from the air against a background of trees. We had fought hard to seize this stretch of road so that it could serve as an ideal bomb-safety line, from which we would pull back our troops about a mile just before the bombing and cover their withdrawal with artillery concentrations. Admittedly this was a narrow safety margin, but Bradley and I had specifically requested that the bombers coming over from England make their turn to the left over Périers, then make a straight run, just south of and parallel to the Périers–St. Lô road, to the target area.

The bombardment was to commence eighty minutes before the troops jumped off, with a twenty-minute strike by 350 fighter bombers of the United States Ninth Air Force, chiefly against enemy positions just south of the Périers road. Following immediately, 1,800 heavy bombers of the American Eighth Air Force were to blast the rectangular target area, after which 350 fighter-bombers were to cover the advance of the 9th, 4th, and 30th Divisions back to the Périers–St. Lô jump-off line, while 396 medium bombers of the 9th Air Force were to hit the southern half of the rectangular bombing area for forty-five minutes as troops attacked south from the Périers–St. Lô road. Throughout the bombardment 500 American and Royal Air Force fighters were to fly air cover.

It was the mightiest air armada ever planned in support of a ground attack. As with D day, Allied weather experts would fix the date and time of attack. After a week of waiting, the forecasters predicted favorable weather for ground operations on July 24 and 25, and moderately satisfactory for air activity. Leigh-Mallory set H hour as 1300 24 July 1944.

False Start

Unfortunately the weather did not follow the forecast, and unfortunately also Leigh-Mallory did not fly to Normandy to observe the operation until midmorning of the twenty-fourth. He found the sky overcast, with thick clouds that would make the bombardment hazardous. He decided to postpone the attack, but his message did not reach England until a few minutes before the scheduled H hour. Except for the medium bombers, all the planes had taken off. Three of the six fighter-bomber groups received orders to turn back before dropping their loads; the others, operating below cloud level, made their attacks without endangering the front-line troops, which had withdrawn north of the Périers–St. Lô road on schedule. Inadequate emergency communications to the heavy bombers delayed word of the cancellation, but the first formation of 500 planes found visibility so poor on arrival over the target area that it dropped no bombs, while only a few planes in the second formation dropped their loads, with unknown results. Over 300 heavy bombers in the third formation, with slightly better visibility, let loose their bombs before further bombing could be stopped. Some of these bombs fell 2,000 yards north of the Périers–St. Lô, killing 25 men in the 30th Division and wounding 131. Enemy antiaircraft artillery destroyed three of our heavy bombers.

At about noon, only minutes before the first heavy bombs fell, word of Leigh-Mallory's postponement reached me at my CP at the village of Goucherie, about five miles north of the bombing area. Since our front-line troops had withdrawn about 1,500 yards, leaving a vacuum in that area north of the Périers–St. Lô road, I directed the 30th, 4th, and 9th Divisions to attack at 1:00 P.M. to regain their original lines. Enemy troops had followed up the withdrawal of the 9th Division on the right. A tough fight ensued, in which the 39th Infantry suffered 77 casualties, including the death of its revered commander, Colonel Paddy Flint, thus adding to the tragic losses caused by the short bombing.

Bradley, Quesada, and I were greatly upset when we learned that the heavy bombers had approached the target area from the north, perpendicular to the Périers–St. Lô road instead of flying parallel to the road, as Bradley understood had been agreed at the July 29 conference with the Allied Air Commanders. Apparently there had been no clear agreement at that conference. Quesada's fighter-bombers had made a parallel approach. In a telephone call to Bradley after the aborted attack Leigh-Mallory stated that, if Bradley insisted on a parallel approach, the attack, rescheduled for the twenty-fifth, could not take place. Bradley feared that the Germans might have been alerted to the planned area of attack by the bombing on the twenty-fourth and did not wish to give them any additional time to shift reserves and reorganize their defenses. Reluctantly he accepted the fact that the complicated details involved in such a massive attack could not be changed in the short time remaining before the bomber crews would have to be briefed for an early morning takeoff on the twenty-fifth. The attack had been rescheduled for 11:00 A.M., July 25, when the weather was forecast to be favorable.

Bombing Attack of July 25

Bradley arrived at my CP on the morning of the twenty-fifth about a half hour before the heavy bombers began their runs at eleven o'clock, and remained until the massive bombardment was over. We sat in a little cafe partly destroyed in earlier fighting, in Goucherie, adjacent to the command post. Starched lace curtains hung in the open windows. The roar of our incoming heavy bombers was terrific as, once again, they passed overhead, and the "carumps" of the bombs shook the cafe as they exploded.

The initial loads seemed to land on target, but some bomb loads began to drop short as the area became obscured by dust and smoke. We could tell this because the blast from such short clusters would perceptibly blow in the lace curtains in the windows. We sat helplessly, fearing that these intermittent shorts, which followed no pattern, were landing among our troops.

It was not until the bombing was over and some ruptured communications were restored that the full extent of casualties from the short bombings were reported. Units on the flanks, particularly in the 30th Division, were hardest hit; this division had 61 killed and 374 wounded. The 47th Infantry Regiment of the 9th Division, on the right, suffered 14 killed and 33 wounded. In all, VII Corps had a total of 601 casualties, including 111 killed. Among the killed was Lieutenant General Lesley J. McNair, former commander of Army Ground Forces, who was acting commander of the phantom Army Group supposedly assembled in England opposite the Pas de Calais to deceive the Germans as to our main landing area in France. Unknown to me, McNair had joined an assault battalion to observe the bombing firsthand.

The initial effect of the short bombing was demoralizing to the units hardest hit by the haphazard concentration of shorts. The entire command group of the 3rd Battalion 47th Infantry, except for its commander, was wiped out. Even in the central zone of the 4th Division all four assault companies of the 8th Infantry were hit. The fire direction center of the 957th Field Artillery Battalion was obliterated, and all wire communications between the 9th Division Artillery Command post and the firing batteries were cut. Aside from the deadly physical damage, the shock effect was truly awful. The 30th Division reported 164 cases of combat exhaustion resulting from repeated shorts.

Despite the disrupting result of the bombing errors, only minor delays occurred in the jump-off of front-line infantry troops in the three assault divisions—a tribute to the discipline of the troops and the steadfast leadership of commanders of all infantry units from battalions down to platoons and squads and their supporting artillery. Order was soon restored, communications repaired, and the dead and wounded cared for in truly admirable fashion. But as could be expected under the circumstances, the attack got off to a wobbly start.

Effect of the Bombings on the Enemy

The premature bombing of July 24 alerted the Germans to the possibility of further activity in the vicinity of St. Lô, but the fact that the bombing was not followed up with a strong ground attack misled General Hausser, the Seventh Army commander, and Bayerlein of Panzer Lehr, as to American intentions. Both felt they had withstood a major effort by the Americans, and Hausser made light of Field Marshal von Kluge's worried call about the situation west of St. Lô. Panzer Lehr had lost about 350 men and ten or more tanks, but received 200 replacements on the twenty-fourth. Expecting a renewal of the ground attack and confident that he could repulse it, Bayerlein thinned his outpost north of the Périers road and moved additional troops into the area south of the road, directly into the zone that would be struck by the real Cobra the next day.

The full-scale bombing on the twenty-fifth set back the VII Corps ground attack initially, but raised havoc on the enemy side. As the bombs rained down, defensive positions were churned into mounds of upturned dirt, burying their defenders in tons of debris. Tanks were overturned or blown up, and communication lines and radio equipment blown to bits. As was the case with American troops caught in the short bombing, the psychological and morale effect on the Germans was even worse than the physical damage. VIII Corps intelligence reported that many prisoners captured following the bombing were wandering around in a daze, babbling incoherently. They spoke with awe about the hell of la Chapelle en Juger, a key road and command-post center in the middle of the target area, which was almost leveled.

The attack of the 9th, 4th, and 30th Divisions, nonetheless, was met with surprisingly dogged resistance from the infantry troops of Panzer Lehr, and by the fanatic young Nazi soldiers of the 5th Para-

chute Division, on the right of Panzer Lehr, which had escaped most
of the bombing. Matt Eddy's 9th Division moved quickly through the
German outpost area but made slow progress south of the Périers
road. With uncharacteristic caution Eddy halted his troops for the
night, short of Marigny. The 8th Infantry, the assault regiment of the
4th Division in the center, which had suffered heavily from the short
bombing, meanwhile moved out in good order and by nightfall had
penetrated the main German defenses. On the left the 30th Division,
hardest hit by the bombing errors, recovered rapidly but was hit again
by strafing fighter-bombers and checked by Mark V tanks south of the
Périers highway. By fighting until midnight the division captured part
of its first day's objective.

Perhaps expecting too much from the massive bombing, and shocked
by their own unexpected casualties, the divisions were discouraged
that they had not been able to break through the main German defenses. I had not planned to employ the 1st Division and the 2nd and 3rd
Armored Divisions until this was done, but noting a lack of coordination in the German reaction, particularly their failure to launch prompt
counterattacks, I sensed that their communications and command
structure had been damaged more than our troops realized. Before the
enemy could recover I decided in the late afternoon of the twenty-fifth
to throw in the 1st Division on the morning of the twenty-sixth, with
Colonel Truman E. Boudinot's combat command (CC) "B" attached,
and Ted Brook's 2nd Armored, with Colonel Charles T. Lanham's
22nd regimental combat team attached. Watson's 3rd Armored Division, less CC "B," would remain in concealed bivouacs in reserve.
The Infantry divisions were to continue their attacks to open a gap
between Marigny and St. Gilles, but the mission of seizing Marigny
was shifted to the 1st Division, and the 9th and 30th Divisions were
directed to facilitate passage of the 1st Division and the 2nd Armored
through their zones. The mission of the 2nd Armored to drive to the
southwest remained unchanged.

This decision proved timely. Though the enemy fought tenaciously
in and around Marigny for the next two days, Ted Brook's 2nd Armored,
given a good start by Hobbs's 30th Division, and sparked by the slash-
ing drive of Colonel Maurice Rose's CC "A," scattered the enemy de-

fenses hastily thrown up against it, and by midafternoon rolled through St. Gilles, opening the exploitation phase of Cobra.

I was disappointed with the slow progress of Huebner's 1st Division. I have always said that an order is but an aspiration, a hope that what has been directed will come true. The enemy has something to say about that. In this case Choltitz, the LXXXIV Corps commander, withdrew along the west coast during the night of July 26–27 and established a north-south line facing eastward against the 1st Division. By now the advance of the 2nd Armored seemed to assure that no substantial German reinforcements would get through from the south. Meanwhile Barton's Infantry Division had cleared a small gap in its central zone. I decided to launch Watson's 3rd Armored toward Coutances on the twenty-seventh, hoping to pry loose Huebner for his drive on Coutances.

The First Army plan had called for Middleton's VIII Corps to pin down the German forces north of the St. Lô–Coutances road, while the VII Corps enveloped these forces from the south. But the VIII Corps had its troubles with the terrain, extensive mine fields, and the tough 2nd SS Panzer Division, and was unable either to prevent the shift of the 17th SS Panzer Grenadier division to the north-south defense line facing the 1st Division, or to stop the escape of considerable German forces south through Coutances. Watson's 3rd Armored Division, showing signs of inept leadership, was slow to unravel itself when confronted by stubborn German resistance. It made little headway and when, on July 28, it ran into the defensive line of the 17th SS Panzer Grenadier Division, was unable to break through to Coutances. The escaping Germans, however, were not "home free," for in the original VII Corps plan Ted Brook's 2nd Armored Division was to fence off the south side of the Cobra area along the road from Cérences to Tessy-sur-Vire, to prevent German reinforcements moving north to aid the enemy we expected to trap between the 1st Division-3rd Armored drives and the VIII Corps. The 2nd Armored now was equally well positioned to block escape of the German forces moving south from the Coutances area. While Maurice Rose's CC "A" was moving on July 27–28 to block any enemy advance between Hambye and Tessy-sur-Vire, I directed Brigadier General Isaac D. White's CC "B," which had followed "A" to Canisy, to continue on July 28 to the southwest to block any escaping enemy between Cérences and St. Denis. Only now was "B" reinforced on the night of the twenty-eighth by Colonel Sidney R. Hinds reserve CC and a battalion of the 4th Infantry Division, and would have to face north while keeping a lookout to the south.

During the next two days and nights, in some of the wildest melees of the war, elements of the LXXXIV Corps and the II Parachute Corps tried to break through the 2nd Armored Division barrier. After dark on the twenty-eighth a force of tanks and infantry overran an outpost on the road southwest of Cenilly manned by a company from the 4th Infantry Division, forcing it back into the firing positions of the 78th Armored Field Artillery and the 702nd Tank Destroyer Battalion. With part of the cannoneers fighting as infantrymen, they turned their guns and fired directly into the oncoming enemy. Some Germans managed to get through but counterattacking armored infantry reestablished the roadblock. At dawn they counted seven destroyed Mark IV tanks and over 125 enemy dead.

A bit farther down the road, another group of enemy tanks and infantry, led by a self-propelled 88-mm gun, struck a 2nd Armored force guarding a road junction two miles south of Roncey. Rifle shots killed the driver and gunner of the 88-mm gun, leaving it astride the junction, blocking the enemy tanks, while German infantry, crawling along the roadside ditches, tried unsuccessfully to open the way. A few Germans were able to get through, but at dawn the bulk of the enemy withdrew, leaving 17 dead and 150 wounded. This action caused a tremendous backup of German armor and motor vehicles in the vicinity of Roncey. Drivers of these vehicles, parked bumper to bumper and triple banked, fled on foot as Pete Quesada's fighter-bombers and our Corps artillery blasted the massed and immobile target.

During daylight of the twenty-ninth, General Brooks reorganized and strengthened his positions along the Cérences–St. Denis-le-Gast road in anticipation of further German efforts to escape. That night saw a repetition of the previous night's action, this time largely centered in the triangle Lenglonne–Cambry–St. Denis. At Lenglonne some 150 Germans found themselves caught in the bivouac area of the 62nd Armored and surrendered after a short fight. A force of about a thousand enemy and a hundred armored vehicles made a determined attack at St. Denis-le-Gast; some got away in the confused fighting in the dark, but the Americans held and in the morning counted 130 Germans dead, over 500 prisoners, and numerous vehicles destroyed, including seven tanks. In a larger skirmish near Cambry about 2,500 Germans made a strong attack and almost succeeded in getting through, but again point-blank artillery and tank fire greatly aided the armored infantry in breaking up the attack. After six hours of confused fighting, illuminated by burning vehicles, the 2nd Armored held fast. About 450 Germans were killed, 1,000 taken prisoner, and about 100 vehicles destroyed. Ted Brook's 2nd Armored Division had done a magnificent job. The division had killed an estimated 1,500 of the enemy and captured about 4,000, while sustaining a total of almost 400 casualties, of whom less than 100 were killed.

VII and VIII Corps Meet in Coutances

General Bradley on July 28 issued his Field Orders No. 2, transferring to the XIX Corps the 30th Division and Rose's CC "A" with its attached 22nd Infantry, both of which had turned east toward the Vire River. The VII Corps was to "continue present operation to isolate enemy forces north of Coutances and at the same time continue to push rapidly to the south." Anticipating difficulties as the VII and VIII Corps neared Coutances, the order stated that "When VIII Corps is prepared to advance south of Coutances, CG, VII Corps [will] adjust right boundary with CG VIII Corps." As I had noted the fumbling efforts of the 3rd Armored Division to coil up off the roads when checked south east of Coutances, I realized that there would be a horrendous traffic jam in that city between the VIII Corps's 4th Armored Division, coming down from the north, and the 3rd Armored when it finally broke into Coutances from the east. There was no way of telling which division would get there first. I headed for Coutances on July 28, arriving in the afternoon almost simultaneously with the leading elements of the 3rd and 4th Armored Divisions as they reached the city's outskirts. I found the wild confusion that I had anticipated. Both divisions were trying to get on the Gavray road, which was originally in the VII Corps sector. I clipped in my portable phone to a line leading through VII Corps headquarters to First Army, and when Bradley came on I described the situation. He promptly, and properly, decided that the 4th Armored, already headed south, would have the right of way, confirmed later in the day when the boundary between the VII and VIII Corps was shifted to the east of the Coutances-Cérences road.

As tanks and troopers of the two armored divisions swirled around a main road junction on the edge of Coutances, neither General Watson nor any senior officer of the 3rd Armored was in sight. Again I had my aide, Captain Jack Walsh, clip in our phone, this time to Watson's CP where Watson still was at midafternoon, instead of being at the crucial point up front. I directed him to proceed at once to Coutances to unscramble his division from the 4th Armored. I waited until he arrived, then returned to my CP, a short distance north of Marigny. This time I got Bradley on the phone and asked that he replace Watson. I told him Watson was a fine man and a good soldier but out of place in an armored division. Though Watson was a West Point classmate of both Bradley and Eisenhower, Bradley agreed, and promised to send me an experienced tanker as soon as one was available. With his typical fine judgment of men he selected Maurice Rose. Then engaged in some tough fighting near Tessy-sur-Vire under the XIX Corps, Rose could not be released until August 7. Watson was transferred to the 12th Army Group on August 6, later given an infantry division, and I understand that he did well with it.

Meanwhile the 1st Infantry Division was assembling northeast of Coutances, while CC "B" from the 3rd Armored Division reverted to control of the 3rd Armored on July 29. The 9th Infantry Division was to assemble in concealed bivouacs southwest of Marigny in Corps reserve.

I now turned my attention to reorienting the VII Corps to the south, to participate in the Cobra exploitation. Units most readily available were the 4th Infantry Division, already moving south through Notre-Dame-de-Cenilly, and the 3rd Armored near Coutances. On July 28, I directed the 4th to relieve the 2nd Armored east of Hembye and prepare to attack south on July 30 in the eastern half of the VII Corps zone with the mission of capturing Villedieu-les-Poëles. The 3rd Armored was to move south early July 30, pass through elements of 2nd

Armored between Lenglonne and Hamby, and attack south in the western half of the Corps zone to seize crossings of the Sienne River west of Villedieu. When passed through, the 2nd Armored was to assemble in the vicinity of Cenilly.

With the new commander of the 3rd Armored not available for several days, and traffic problems between the 3rd and 4th Armored Divisions persisting along the Lenglonne–Gavray road, I decided on July 30 to bring General Huebner down to take command of the forces in the western zone including his 1st Infantry Division, to which I attached CC "A" (General Hickey) from the 3rd Armored and additional artillery. Similarly, I placed General Barton in command of the east zone of action with his 4th Infantry Division, to which I attached CC "B" (Colonel Boudinot) from the 3rd Armored Division. I thus prepared to push the attack of VII Corps on July 31 with two balanced infantry-armored forces, each under an experienced commander in whom I had confidence.

When General Rose reported for duty on August 7 to take command of the 3rd Armored Division, less Combat Commands "Hickey" and "Boudinot"—designations I now adopted for morale reasons to identify the commands with their leaders—he objected forthrightly to this separation of his division, for which I respected him. I explained that it was only a temporary expedient and that as soon as he had time to become acquainted with the personnel and operating procedures of the Division, which I felt needed correction, I would reassemble the Division as a unit and fight it as such, under his direct command. Meanwhile he was to follow closely the operations of the two combat commands while administering and supplying them. He responded faithfully and loyally, and became my top division commander.

About this time I was summoned for instructions to General Bradley's CP, in an apple orchard near the village of Colombières fifteen miles northeast of St. Lô. When I arrived I found General Patton there waiting to see Bradley. It was the first time I had seen Patton since the incident on Upatoi Creek at Fort Benning in 1941. We chatted for a few minutes before Patton went in to see the General.

"You know, Collins," said Patton, in that high-pitched voice of his, "you and I are the only people around here who seem to be enjoying this goddamned war!" Then, pausing as his face clouded momentarily, he added, in reference to the incident in a hospital in Sicily when Patton had slapped a soldier he thought was malingering, "But, I'm in the doghouse! I'm in the doghouse! I've got to do something spectacular!" And he did, rampaging across France and Germany.

I have always thought that the way in which Eisenhower and Bradley handled that inexcusable incident was a mark of their own great human qualities, their intuitive ability to judge the real worth of a man—beyond his petty foibles. Lesser men than Ike or Brad would have relieved Patton of his command, and the American press and public would have applauded. Fortunately, Eisenhower and Bradley, who shared the responsiblility, saw the overriding drive of the man that might someday prove invaluable. They were right—and a great, though fault-ridden soldier, was saved, for the benefit of his country.

VII Corps Runs Interference for Patton's Army

With Combat Commands Hickey and Boudinot spearheading the attacks of the 1st and 4th Divisions, Huebner and Barton made good progress on August 30–31. I had stayed behind the attack of CC Hickey on the thirty-first, and when I learned that an infantry-armor task force (TF) under Lieutenant Colonel Leander L. Doan, after cutting the Villedieu–Granville highway, was about to bivouac for the night, I directed Hickey to have Doan continue the attack across the See River south of Brécy. Doan, who became one of the sparkplugs of the 3rd Armored, "made a Hollywood entry into the center of Brécy, taking pot shots with his pistol at the surprised enemy soldiers lounging along the curb." Driving hard across the See River, he did not stop until his men seized the ridge above the crossing.

Doan had been greatly aided by the close machine-gun support of twenty P-47s, which flew air cover for the task force on this crystal clear night. This system of air cover, in which air controllers rode in leading tanks, with radio communication to fighter bombers overhead, had been instituted in the First Army by General Bradley and Pete Quesada, and we employed it in the VII Corps whenever possible, with wonderful results. *

---

*A German military commentator later wrote: "While the pattern bombing and concentrated artillery fire were the decisive factors on 25 July, 26 July was characterized by low-flying aircraft. Their cooperation with American ground forces was exemplary."

By August 1, one week after the beginning of Cobra, the VII Corps had advanced more than thirty miles south of the Périers–St. Lo jump-off line. The move of Doan into Brécy had outflanked the German defensive front that the Seventh Army Commander, Hausser, was trying to establish southwest of Vire while, unknown to us at Corps level, preparing to counterattack toward Avranches.

Field Orders No. 3 First Army, August 1, directed all units of the First Army, except V Corps, to attack to the southeast. General Courtney Hodges on August 1 took over First Army from Bradley, when the latter assumed command of the 12th Army Group, and I must have received oral instructions from Hodges on that date to change direction of the VII Corps to the east to exploit our breakthrough at Brécy. Confirmation of such instructions was in First Army Field Orders No. 4, August 4, which directed the VII Corps "to continue to change its direction to threaten the enemy left rear."

VII Corps Turns East to Mortain

I issued Field Orders No. 7 on August 1, confirming the oral instructions earlier in the day, to envelop the enemy's left flank and exploit the breakthrough south of Villedieu. The 1st Division, with CC Hickey, 4th Cavalry Reconnaissance Squadron, and additional tanks, tank destroyers, antiaircraft and artillery, was to turn to the east and seize the high ground west of Mortain. The 4th Division, with CC Boudinot, 83 Reconnaissance Battalion, and additional tanks, tank destroyers, antiaircraft, and artillery, was to seize St. Pois–Chérencé-le-Roussel. The 9th Division, which I had brought down from its position in reserve near Marigny, was to attack on the left of the 4th Division and seize the high ground and road centers in the vicinity of Gathemo–Perriers-en-Beauficel.

I had met General Huebner in the afternoon of August 3 at a crossroads south of Brécy, after the 1st Division had turned east, and pointed on my map to hill 317, above Mortain, which dominated the countryside for miles to the east.

—From Manuscript B-723, The Campaigns in Northern France, Vol. II, Chap. 2, "The American Breakthrough in the Direction of Avranches," on file, Office Chief of Military History, Department of the Army, Washington, D.C.

"Ralph," I said, "be sure to take hill 317."

"Joe, I've already got it," he replied with a grin.

As Major General Wade H. Haislip's XV Corps, the left flank corps of the Third Army, on the right of VII Corps, advanced east toward Laval, a gap began to develop between the XV and VII Corps, and to cover this gap General Hodges directed me on August 6 to move the 1st Division to the southeast. Anticipating such an order, I had instructed Huebner on August 4 to initiate reconnaissance in the area Domfront–Mayenne north of Laval, and the following day I sent a regimental combat team of the 1st Division to occupy Mayenne and secure a crossing of the Mayenne River north of that town. Huebner was to push reconnaissance to the north, east, and southeast.

To take over the role of the 1st Division in the Mortain sector required considerable shifting and rearrangement of First Army troops facing the German Seventh Army, and Hodges on August 5 passed control of Hobbs's 30th Division from the XIX to the VII Corps to replace the 1st Division. I had Hobbs at once send CC Hickey to secure Barenton along with a crossing of the Varenne River at Domfront. The 9th Division was to continue its attack on the left of the 4th Division, which would be pinched out between the 9th and 30th Divisions, when it would assemble near St. Pois in Corps reserve. CC Boudinot reverted to control of the 3rd Armored Division in reserve, as there was no room as yet to employ the 3rd Armored as a unit.

The Germans Counterattack via Mortain

The German counterattack early on August 7 was not unexpected. We now know through publication of F. W. Winterbotham's *The Ultra Secret* that the British in 1940, with the help of the Polish resistance, had broken the top-secret German code, and that by 1944 the Allied high command was receiving full information of all important top-secret communications between Hitler and his senior commanders in the West. When the First Army collapsed the German front west of Avranches as a result of Operation Cobra, and both the First Army and the newly constituted Third Army (Patton) began their exploitation to the east, Hitler and his generals recognized the threat to the entire German position in France. Hitler personally took over direction of the war in the West and on July 2 ordered von Kluge to counterattack to close the gap between Mortain and Avranches. The order was intercepted and passed to Churchill and the very limited number of British and American political and military leaders privy to the "Ultra" secret. Corps commanders were not included. But as early as August 1, when I issued VII Corps Field Orders No. 2 and cautioned General Huebner to be sure to seize hill 317 west of Mortain, I—and General Bradley I am sure—foresaw the possibility of a German counterattack from the Mortain area to capture Avranches, which if successful would have cut off the Third Army.

What did surprise us was the strength and exact timing of the attack, which caught the VII Corps in the process of shifting the 1st Division from Mortain to Mayenne and replacing it with the 30th Division. American air had noted German armor north of Mortain on August 6, and around midnight I had warned Huebner and Hobbs of a possible counterattack in the vicinity of Mortain.

Shortly after midnight of August 6–7, without an artillery preparation, the Germans attacked between Chérencé and Mortain, with the XLVII Panzer Corps. General Hans von Funck commanded the Corps, which consisted of four Panzer divisions brought down from the British front. The attack met little opposition initially except on the north flank, where Matt Eddy's 9th Division was in course of an attack toward Chérencé. The 116th Panzer Division, opposite the 9th Division, never got started. The 2nd Panzer, attacking in two columns south of the 116th, was delayed getting off but did achieve surprise. Its right column came under heavy fire from the artillery of the 4th Division, which was in Corps reserve at St. Pois, in position to stop any advance north of the See River. The left column, after some early success, was slowed by well-organized antitank positions at St. Barthelemy and checked by the 117th Infantry of the 30th Division east of Juvigny. With his main effort stopped short of its initial objectives, Funck committed his reserve 1st SS Panzer Division through the 2nd Panzer Division in the already congested central zone where it, along with the 2nd Panzers, were brought under heavy artillery and air attack. Funck halted the attack before noon and had the two divisions dig in, short of their objectives.

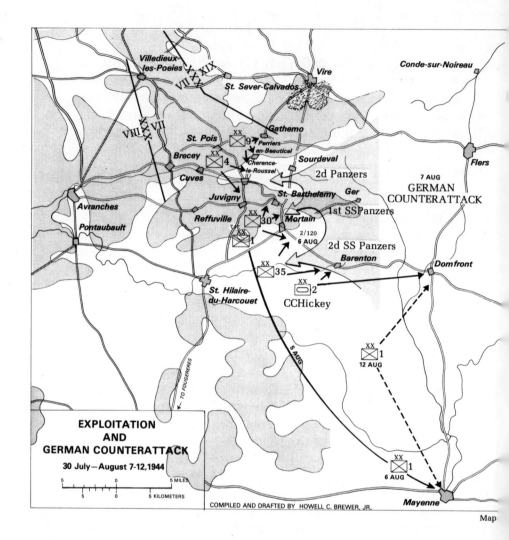

EXPLOITATION
AND
GERMAN COUNTERATTACK

30 July—August 7-12, 1944

5 MILES
5 KILOMETERS

COMPILED AND DRAFTED BY HOWELL C. BREWER, JR.

Map

The Germans had better luck with the 2nd SS Panzer Division on the south flank. It overran elements of the 120th Infantry of the 30th Division in Mortain, captured the town, and set up blocking positions on the St. Hilaire road to protect the south flank of the XLVII Corps. The one critical thing it failed to do was to capture hill 317, held by the 2nd Battalion 120th Infantry, the CP of which had been overrun in Mortain and its command group captured as the officers tried to join the companies isolated atop 317. There Captain Reynold C. Erichson assumed command of the battalion. Two forward observers, 1st Lieutenant Charles A. Barts and 2nd Lieutenant Robert L. Weiss of the 230th Field Artillery Battalion, trapped on the hilltop, coolly brought accurate observed artillery fire on the several enemy tank columns of the 1st and 2nd SS Panzer Divisions, clearly visible below them.

The Great Defensive Battle of Mortain

As I reviewed the situation on the morning of the seventh, I was satisfied that the enemy would be unable to break through the 9th and 4th Divisions, but I was concerned about the situation at Barenton, six miles south of Mortain where there was only a battalion of the 30th Division and CC Hickey of the 3rd Armored Division to protect that important road center covering the approaches to St. Hilaire and thence to Avranches from the southeast. To strengthen the Barenton force I attached to the 30th Division the only unengaged unit available, CC Boudinot, which had been detached from the 4th Division the afternoon before. But Hobbs had a more immediate threat north of Mortain and had to use Boudinot in that area, still leaving a dangerous situation in the Barenton–St. Hilaire area.

When General Hodges, on August 6, directed me to move the 1st Division to the southeast between Mayenne and Domfront, he released the 2nd Armored Division (less CC "A") from the XIX Corps and started it moving via Villedieu-les-Poëles and St. Pois toward Mayenne, where it was to support the 1st Division in any advance to the east. By good fortune the 2nd Armored was held up by shellfire near Chérencé on the morning of August 7. I seized the opportunity to ask First Army to employ the 2nd Armored (less CC "A") in the vicinity of Barenton. Hodges agreed and passed Brook's division to my command effective at 10:00 A.M. that date. I directed it to move to Barenton.

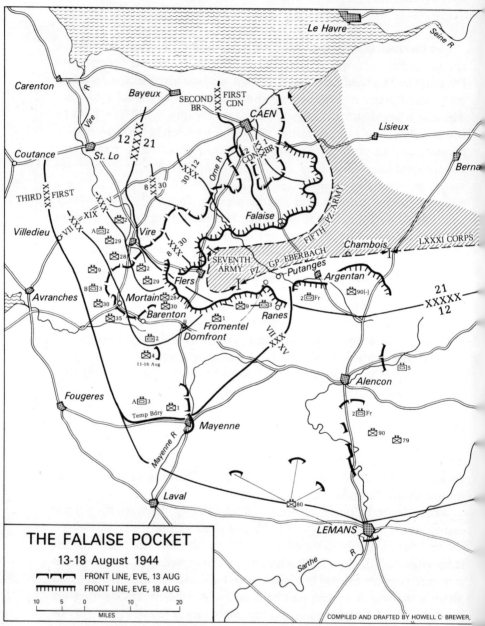

THE FALAISE POCKET

13-18 August 1944

FRONT LINE, EVE, 13 AUG
FRONT LINE, EVE, 18 AUG

10 5 0 10 20

MILES

COMPILED AND DRAFTED BY HOWELL C. BREWER,

Meanwhile the gallant 2nd Battalion, 120th Infantry, surrounded on hill 317, held out against almost continuous attacks from the 17th SS Panzer Grenadier Division. Defensive artillery fires were made available to forward observers on the hill. Some food and ammunition was parachuted from cargo planes, and in a unique employment of artillery the 230th Field Artillery Battalion and other units fired smoke-shell cases, filled with bandages, morphine, and other medical supplies, to the beleaguered battalion. French farmers on the broad hilltop shared their chickens and vegetables, as well as the common danger. Fortunately Allied air held off any German aircraft that might have been available to bomb the hill, while Quesada's fighter-bombers and ten squadrons of the Royal Air Force helped check and destroy the Panzer armor. On August 11 the 35th Division drove the Germans from their positions southwest of Mortain, and next day stormed the south slopes of hill 317 while the 30th Division surged into Mortain.

The defense of hill 317 by the 2nd Battalion 120th Infantry was one of the outstanding small-unit actions of World War II. The battalion was given a presidential unit citation and each of the four company commanders received the DSC. Of the nearly seven hundred men in the battalion, three hundred had been killed or wounded. According to German reports they had been a "thorn in the flesh" that helped paralyze enemy movements in the area. The disruptive attacks of the 2nd Armored Division against the lines of communications and supply of the XLVII Corps added to this paralysis.

On August 12 the Germans gave up on their ill-fated attempt to cut off the Third Army and withdrew their Panzer divisions, leaving behind close to one hundred abandoned tanks.

It was apparent to Bradley as soon as the Germans were checked at Mortain that their counterattack would not break through the VII Corps. Eisenhower had come over from England to follow the action, and while he was at Bradley's CP the latter telephoned Montgomery, still in control of the land battle in France, pointing out that the German Army was now vulnerable to encirclement from south and north. Monty approved Bradley's suggestion that the First and Third Armies pivot on Mortain and wheel to the north, with the First Army heading between Argentan and Flers, twenty-five miles to the west, and Haislip's XV Corps, on the left flank of Patton's Third Army, moving via Alençon toward Argentan and Falaise. The British and Canadians would attack from the north, with General Henry D. G. Crerar's First Canadian Army closing the upper jaw of the Allied pincers at Falaise. Haislip's XV Corps, and my VII Corps, would drive north to seal the southern half of the "Falaise pocket."

VII Corps Moves Against the South Flank of Falaise Pocket

In preparation for the move of VII Corps, I reassembled the 3rd Armored Division under General Rose's command, with the 60th Infantry attached, on the outer flank of the Corps northeast of Mayenne, to the east of the 1st Division. On August 13 the VII Corps drove over twenty miles against light resistance. Over 1,600 prisoners were taken. The 26th Infantry, 1st Division, captured la Ferte-Macé. As the front broadened I moved the 9th Division in line between the 3rd Armored and Huebner's 1st Division. Heavy fighting developed all along the front, but by evening of August 16, CC Hickey had fought its way into Fromenthal north of Ranes. On the 17th contact was made by the 1st Division with the 11th Armored Division, XXX Corps of the British Second Army, in the vicinity of Briouze. Falaise was occupied the same date by elements of the British XII Corps and the First Canadians.

The 3rd Armored had been halted at Fromenthal by First Army orders, to avoid any firing into the Canadians. But when no contact was made north of Fromenthal on the seventeenth, and after clearance from Hodges, I telephoned Bradley and secured permission to send part of the 3rd Armored north to the outskirts of Putanges on the Orne River. Contact was made there on August 18 by CC Boudinot with elements of the British Second Army, ending the VII Corps's participation in reduction of the Falaise pocket.

Retrospect

Falaise marked the end of the Normandy phase of the war, during which the VII Corps had borne a major share of the fighting of the First Army, including the Cherbourg campaign, the Cobra breakout from the Normandy bridgehead and the subsequent pursuit, and the great defensive battle of Mortain. The Corps staff had shaken down into a smooth-running, well-integrated group. The Corps Artillery under the leadership of General Palmer had developed superbly, as had the Corps Engineers under Mason Young, while the service units kept pace with the combat elements. Historians will probably debate for years the failure of the Allies to destroy the German Seventh Army in the Falaise pocket, a goal which, though not spelled out in so many words, was clearly implied in General Eisenhower's appeal transmitted on August 13 to major elements of the Allied Command. The failure resulted from slowness of the Allies in closing the open eastern end of the pocket. When Patton's XV Corps under Wade Haislip on August 12 had reached the east-west boundary line between the British and American forces, just south of Argentan, the first Canadian Army was still some distance north of Falaise, moving slowly against stiff opposition. An eighteen-to-twenty-mile gap existed between the Canadians and the XV Corps, through which the Panzers and SS troops of von Kluge's Seventh Army were already beginning to escape to the east. It was not until August 19, six days after Haislip's XV Corps had reached Argentan, that Montgomery's Polish Armored Division linked up with the Third Army at Chambois.

General Bradley estimated that seventy thousand enemy were killed or captured by the Allies in the Falaise pocket, and that 19 German divisions had been decimated. German reports indicated that the six armored divisions that escaped totaled no more than two thousand men, sixty-two tanks, and twenty-six artillery pieces. Though the Allied victory was not quite as great as Eisenhower had hoped, it resulted in German evacuation of France. Elements of the Seventh Army and the Fifth Panzer Army that had escaped were harassed by the British Second Army and the American First Army as they retreated to the north. And the VII Corps was destined to have another hard crack at them as we surged into Belgium, after crossing the Seine, following the fall of Paris.

CHAPTER XIII

On to Germany and the Siegfried Line

Even before the Falaise pocket was closed, General Bradley had authorized Patton to turn two divisions of Haislip's corps toward the Seine. They joined the rest of the Third Army, which broke through the Paris –Orleans gap between the Seine and the Loire and by August 25 had seized bridgeheads over the Seine at Melun and south to Troyes. Meanwhile the First Army assisted the British and Canadians in cleaning out the pocket. On August 24 the First Army, now comprising the XIX, V, and VII Corps, commenced its move to the Seine between Melun and Paris.

The advance of the VII Corps was a route march, against no opposition, with the 4th Cavalry Group screening the advance, followed by the 3rd Armored and then by the 1st and 9th Divisions. We had been informed that Major General Jacques Philippe Leclerc's French 2nd Armored Division would be marching on Paris over some of the same roads as the VII Corps. In order that the French Army might participate in the liberation of Paris, Leclerc's division was to have priority on the roads. His troops, however, moving in small groups, were having too gay a time receiving the plaudits of the French villagers to be greatly concerned about pressing on to Paris. They stopped in each town en route while the demoiselles climbed on their tanks, decking them with flowers and plying the men with vin rouge. We had trouble getting by the halted vehicles in the narrow streets, and by the time we reached Chartres we were well behind schedule. At the western entrance to this city we ran into a company of Leclerc's tanks, laden with troops and girls, going round and round a large traffic circle, the riders waving gaily to the cheering crowds while blocking all traffic. I found an American MP officer and instructed him to let each succeeding French group go around the circle twice, then send them on their way.

We reached the Seine southeast of Paris on August 25, the day the German commander in Paris, General Dietrich von Choltitz, surrendered to Leclerc's forces. The following day the 4th Cavalry Group and the 3rd Armored Division crossed the river at Melun into a bridgehead established by the Third Army. The 1st and 9th Divisions continued their march to the Seine.

Allied Plans for Operations East of the Seine

In determining the allied plan of attack beyond the Seine, General Eisenhower faced a dilemma, for the American-British Combined Chiefs of Staff in their basic directive to the Supreme Commander had simply designated "the heart of Germany" as the objective of operations in Western Europe, leaving to Eisenhower the choice of intermediate objectives, subject to the overriding considerations of destroying the German Army and Air Forces there and crushing the German capacity and will to continue the war. Eisenhower favored an attempt to destroy the Wehrmacht west of the Rhine, then to make his major effort to reduce the industrial heart of Germany, the Ruhr basin east of the Rhine.

Montgomery in mid-August had proposed a single massive thrust north of the Ardennes region toward the Ruhr by the Canadian Army, the British Second Army, and the American First Army, under his command. Bradley was agreeable to supporting Montgomery's effort with one American corps, but countered with a plan for an American drive by his First and Third Armies south of the Ardennes to the Rhine on the front Mainz–Mannheim, through the coal-producing basin of the Saar, an essential complement of the iron and steel manufacturing complex of the Ruhr.

After some wavering Eisenhower decided essentially on Montgomery's plan: to send the Canadian and British Second Army to the northeast to clear the Channel ports and Antwerp, capture the V-1 sites and airfields west of the Rhine, and destroy the German Fifteenth Army. Hodge's First Army was to support Montgomery's main effort north of the Ardennes. Patton's Third Army with reduced allotments of gasoline would drive south of the Ardennes on the Saar and the Mainz sector of the Rhine.

The VII Corps in the center of the First Army prepared to attack to the northeast across the Seine on August 27. The 4th Cavalry Group was to continue to screen the advance of Maurice Rose's 3rd Armored Division, which was to be followed by the 1st and 9th Divisions. On the morning of the twenty-sixth, the day after Paris fell, I flew in a Piper Cub plane to each of our divisions and there issued oral instructions for the next day's advance. As we were returning to my CP near Melun, the pilot suggested that we take a swing over nearby Paris. It was a beautiful sunny afternoon, and as far as I could see, ours was the only plane in the skies. I quickly agreed to the pilot's suggestion. Again I quote from a letter to Mrs. Collins:

> We had a wonderful ride that I'll never be able to duplicate. We flew in from the south west at an elevation of about a thousand feet to have a clear view of all that was going on. . . . There were still one or two pockets of Germans holding out on the outskirts, but I was delighted to find that the city had been practically untouched by the war . . . still the loveliest city in the world. . . . We didn't fly *under* the Eiffel Tower but couldn't resist the temptation to circle round it. Then below us I spotted Les Invalides with the dome of Napoleon's tomb, and my mind flashed back to the time (in 1919) I had stood in awe above the catafalque illumined in a golden light from the stained glass windows. The Place de la Concorde lacked only its usual stream of taxis and drays, though small groups of people were gathered about the statues. The Louvre was undamaged, at least from the outside, and a fountain was still playing in the immaculate Tuilleries Gardens.
>
> Up the Champs Élysées we flew, watching a parade of French armored cars which I assumed carried de Gaulle or General Leclerc round the majestic Arc de Triomphe, which we also circled. A great French tricolor hung inside the Arc over the grave of the Unknown Soldier. The Avenue was strangely not crowded, though this could be accounted for by the lack of gasoline and power to run the buses, cabs and subway, and perhaps partly by the fact that this staged parade was somewhat of an anticlimax to the spontaneous joyful reception that had been given, in genuine Parisian style, to the first troops that entered the day before. . . . I couldn't see if the book stalls along the Seine were still operating, but there was Notre Dame in all its glory.

VII Corps Attacks Across the Seine

The advance of the VII Corps early on August 27 met with no opposition, until at Meaux it hit the flank of a position the Germans were trying to organize between the Oise and the Marne. The 3rd Armored quickly drove the enemy from Meaux and sped on toward Château-Thierry and Soissons, scenes of American victories in World War I. As we had approached the Seine, I remembered that Ralph Huebner, when a captain in the 1st Division in World War I, had been wounded in action near Soissons. As a gesture of respect for my old friend and an added incentive for the 1st Division, I moved it up on the left of the 9th in order that Huebner's division might pass through the same area again.

By the end of August the 3rd Armored, which Rose had transformed into a great fighting machine, had reached Montcornet and Rethal, a hundred miles beyond the Seine. It had not been necessary to employ the 1st and 9th Divisions except in light mopping-up operations. The Allies had the Germans on the run. As we neared the Belgian border General Bradley realized that Hodges' army had a chance of intercepting the German Seventh Army, then withdrawing to the northeast toward Brussels, and decided to turn the First Army to the north. As I waited in my CP on August 31 for an expected routine visit of the Army Commander, the phone at my elbow rang. General Hodges was on the line:

"Joe, you've got to change direction at once toward Mons to help cut off the German Seventh Army." For the VII Corps, the right-flank unit of the First Army, that would require a change of direction of almost 90 degrees and would pull the Corps away from the Third Army, with which I had been required to maintain contact. I asked:

"But who will fill the gap that will develop between my right and the Third Army?" Courtney's reply was blunt, and to the point, as he hung up: "Joe, that's your problem!"

I thought for a moment of dropping off the 9th Division, but not knowing what we might run into at Mons, I wanted to keep the bulk of the Corps together, so decided instead to form a special task force to do the job. Colonel Joseph M. Tully had done well in command of the 4th Cavalry Group. I had known him as a tough, aggressive end on the 1916 football team at West Point, and had confidence in his ability to handle a semi-independent command.

I called him in and explained his mission. He was to command a

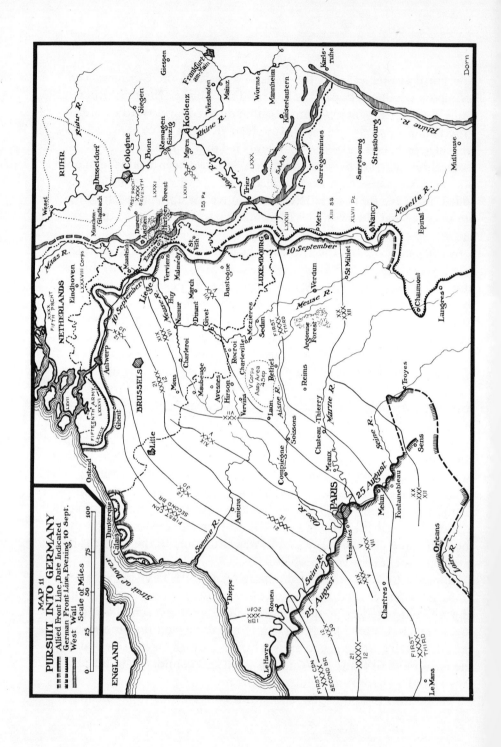

MAP 11

PURSUIT INTO GERMANY

▬▬▬ Allied Front Line, Date Indicated
▬▬▬ German Front Line, Evening 10 Sept.
▬▬▬ West Wall

Scale of Miles

0   25   50   75   100

Dorn

task force consisting of the 4th Cavalry Group, the 759th Tank Battalion, and a detachment of engineers. He was to reconnoiter toward Laon –Verviers, protect the east flank of the VII Corps, and maintain contact with the Third Army—no small task even for a Joe Tully. Later his reconnaissance mission was extended to the Mouse between Dinant and Givet and he was given a motorized infantry battalion, a tank destroyer battalion, and a field artillery battalion.

The VII Corps Turns North on Mons

I got word as quickly as I could to our three divisions, and the 3rd Armored veered promptly toward Mons. By the evening of September 2 leading elements of Rose's division had entered Mons, where they were halted on First Army orders because of the shortage of gasoline. We were beginning to feel the pinch caused by the distance from our Normandy supply bases. The 1st and 9th Divisions were several miles back, as was the V Corps, on our left, which had already run out of gasoline.

Though the V and VII Corps had encountered few escaping Germans, we did not know how large a remnant of the German Seventh Army might still be back of us. I was concerned about the gap that had developed between the V Corps and the 3rd Armored Division, particularly when we began to get reports from the 1st Division of small German groups on its left flank.

Late in the afternoon of September 2, I drove up to Rose's CP just south of Mons. He also was beginning to get reports of enemy coming up on his left rear. He had set up road blocks between Avesnes and Maubeuge while the 1st Division attacked to the northwest from Avesnes into a confused mass of retreating Germans. I was interested in checking on the situation in Mons to see if any enemy was getting through there. Rose warned me not to linger, as he expected to be hit shortly. I found Mons strangely quiet, with no enemy movement through the town but with few townspeople in sight, always a danger signal. I went back to Rose's CP, told him to hold tight, and informed him that I was proceeding to the 9th Division near Charleroi to ready it for movement to the east, in accord with instructions from First

Army. Shortly after I left Rose, I got word that his division, along with the 1st, was engaged in a wild melee reminiscent of the 2nd Armored's experience during the breakthrough in Normandy. On September 2–3 close to 10,000 prisoners were taken, a number that reached nearly 25,000 by the end of the Mons action on September 5. We had dealt a crippling blow to the German Seventh Army.

When General Hodges turned the VII Corps to the north on August 31 he initiated a movement that thrilled me, not only because of the opportunity for another crack at the German Seventh Army but because I could see that we were about to reenact, *in reverse*, the advance through Belgium of the right wing of von Kluck's First Army in the opening campaign of World War I. While a cadet at West Point, and later at Benning, I had studied that campaign in detail and had become familiar with the terrain while stationed in Germany. The VII Corps was destined to capture in succession Maubeuge, Mons, Namur, Liège, and Aachen, all key points along the invasion route of von Kluck's army.

The VII Corps had begun its historic move to the east even before completion of the Mons battle, and by September 5 had reached the Meuse from Namur to Givet. I caught up with the 3rd Armored just as Combat Command Boudinot entered Namur. Retreating Germans had blown the main bridge and were holding the opposite bank. The small "place" near the bridge was swarming with cheering Belgians, oblivious of the danger of possible enemy fire from across the Meuse. We had difficulty persuading them to disperse, even when an 88-mm shell passed overhead. Farther to the right Combat Command Hickey, clearing Charleroi, was likewise impeded more by welcoming citizens than by scattered enemy resistance. Still farther to the right on the VII Corps' thirty-five-mile front, the 9th Division was about to cross the Meuse astride the town of Dinant. To cap a remarkably fine job by his task force, Joe Tully had seized a small bridgehead beyond the Meuse at Malmédy, which he turned over to the V Corps. General Hodges had shifted the V Corps to our right after it was pinched out at Mons.

During the next two days the 3rd Armored advanced along both sides of the Meuse, seized two bridges intact at Huy, and on September 7 captured the important city of Liège, where the Meuse turns north, parallel to the German frontier. There they found all bridges destroyed.

Meanwhile the 9th Division in its crossings near Dinant ran into its first real opposition since the Seine. Elements of the 2nd SS and 12th Panzer Division, which had escaped from the Falaise pocket, held dominating heights on the east bank of the Meuse looking down on the ferry and foot-bridge sites by which the 9th had managed to seize shallow footholds north and south of Dinant. Fire from the German positions prevented construction of ponton bridges to bring tanks across. When word of this situation reached me I directed Rose to send a tank task force from the Namur bridgehead up the east bank of the river to aid the 9th Division. Later I joined General Craig at a high point opposite Dinant, where we had grandstand seats as we watched the task force from the 3rd Armored, under Lieutenant Colonel Rosewell King, rout the SS Germans, house by house, from in front of Craig's division. The 9th Division cleared Dinant the following morning, bridged the river, and began moving east to join the 3rd Armored and the 1st Division south of Liège.

As the VII Corps was preparing to cross the border between Belgium and Germany, I wrote Mrs. Collins:

> In many ways we will be sorry to leave Belgium. We have all been impressed with the enthusiasm, initiative and energy of the Belgian people. There can be no question as to the sincerity of the welcome they have accorded us. While the French in many cases apathetically stood by and watched our men repair bridges and roads, the Belgians have often pitched in and actively assisted. We moved so fast after our victory at Mons that . . . in some instances the public utilities were untouched. Street cars were still running in some localities, and where the wires had been damaged the Belgians were out fixing them the next day.

I went forward to Liège on September 8 to review the situation there with General Rose, whose engineers were completing a bridge over the Meuse, for a move on Verviers the next day. With our field glasses we searched the open ridge, jutting out menacingly toward Liège, up which climbed the main road to Aachen. We could see no signs of trenches or emplacements. The Germans would certainly have organized that ridge as part of a river-line defense east of the Meuse if they

had the time or troops. Instead Field Marshal Model, who had succeeded von Kluge after Falaise, was forced by the speed of the American advance from the Seine to withdraw within the West Wall, or Siegfried Line, inside Germany. Unlike the outmoded Maginot Line in
France that did not extend along the Belgian–French border, and consequently could be outflanked there by the Germans in 1940, the West
Wall was a more modern complex of reinforced-concrete antitank obstacles and gun emplacements that ran continuously from Switzerland to the Rhine River on the border of Holland. Built in 1936–1938,
it had not been kept up in recent years but was still a formidable barrier, especially in critical areas such as Aachen, where a double row of
obstacles barred the historic route of invasion to and from Germany. I
directed Rose, Huebner, and Craig to push on to the east with the hope
that we might crack the West Wall before it could be fully manned.

The border country between Liège and Aachen (Aix-la-Chapelle)
had been fought over from the time of Charlemagne, and the boundary between what is now France and Germany had changed back and
forth. It was still an area of divided loyalties. I was a bit fearful after
we entered Germany that we might run into fanatic groups of Nazi
youth who might engage in guerrilla operations. In the light of subsequent fears of the possible establishment of a German "national re-
doubt" in the Bavarian Alps, and the conjectured organization of diehard groups of Nazi "werewolves"—neither of which developed, but
which did have some effect on Eisenhower's strategy in the closing
days of the war—an excerpt from a letter I wrote Mrs. Collins in September 1944 is relevant:

> *Somewhere in Germany!* . . . How is that for a heading? . . . So far we have
> received no resistance from the civil population. In the first German town
> we occupied [Rötgen] . . . the acting burgomeister told our Civil Affairs
> people that the Nazis had all fled; that the people who lived there were pri-
> marily interested in their homes; that we were there as a conquering army;
> and that they were ready to receive orders. Many homes had white towels,
> undershirts or pillowslips stuck up on poles in the yards or hung from win-
> dows in token of submission. The Nazis had told the people that we would
> burn their homes, though returning German soldiers had assured them
> that we would not. They are so relieved that we are not molesting them
> that I feel sure that this side of the Rhine, at least, we will have no real

worries about guerrilla warfare behind us. . . . Thus far, we have had no sniping and no acts of sabotage, and I am hoping that no underground resistance will be attempted. As many prisoners here have said, the Germans are accustomed to obedience and guerrilla tactics do not fit the national character.

Logistics Calls a Halt

As the American First and Third Armies neared the German border they had outrun the capacity of the logistical system of the 12th Army Group to keep them supplied with gasoline and ammunition. Nearly all American supplies in northern Europe were still in depots close to Cherbourg and the Normandy beaches and had to be hauled over three hundred miles to the front, largely by trucks of the extemporized "Red Ball Express" system. The Red Ballers did a wonderful job, but until the badly bombed rail lines could be reopened, on which Army engineers worked around the clock, Hodges' and Patton's armies would be limited by supplies of gasoline and ammunition.

Faced with the prospect of hard fighting to break through the West Wall, General Hodges on September 10 called a halt of a couple of days while additional ammunition could be brought forward. I was anxious not to lose our momentum, so I requested Courtney to authorize a reconnaissance in force of the German position to our front. Somewhat reluctantly the Army commander agreed and gave the same authorization to Gerow's V Corps, while Corlett's XIX Corps, which had come up on our left, halted short of Aachen.

VII Corps Probes the West Wall

As the VII Corps turned east from Mons our assigned zone of advance was on a front of thirty-five miles, too broad a front on which to assault the West Wall looming ahead of us. Consequently I kept the striking power of the Corps, consisting of the 3rd Armored and the two infantry divisions, concentrated in the critical northern third of the zone along the axis Liège–Aachen–Düren, with Tully's 4th Cavalry Group covering the remainder of the front and maintaining contact with the V Corps.

Upon reaching the German border we recognized two major obstacles ahead of us in the active third of our zone, in addition to the dou-

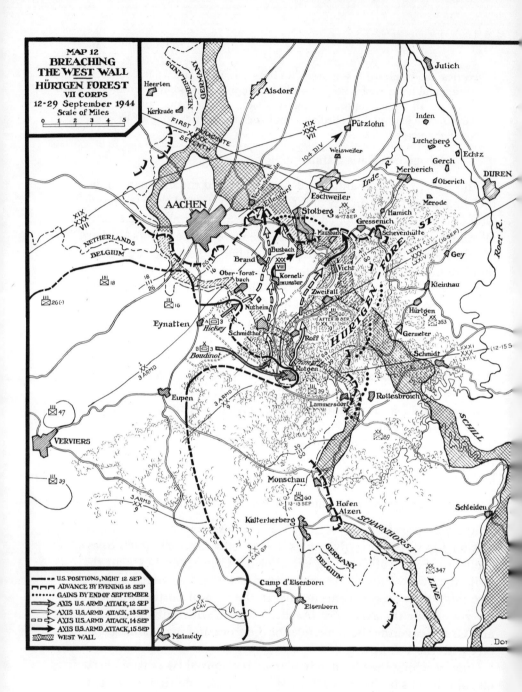

MAP 12
**BREACHING
THE WEST WALL**
HÜRTGEN FOREST
VII CORPS
12-29 September 1944
Scale of Miles
0 1 2 3 4 5

Jülich

Heerlen
Kerkrade
Alsdorf
Inden
Pützlohn
Lucheberg
Echtz
104 DIV
Weisweiler
Gerch
Merberich
Oberich
DUREN
AACHEN
Eilendorf
Eschweiler
Merode
Stolberg
Hamich
12
16-17 SEP
Gressenich
Schevenhütte
Mausbach
(16 SEP)
Gey
NETHERLANDS
BELGIUM
Brand
Busbach
Vicht
Roer R.
Ober-forst-bach
Korneli-munster
18
26
Zweifall
Kleinhau
16
Nütheim
AFTER 18 SEP
9
Hürtgen
353
Eynatten
Hickey
Schmidthof
Roff
Germeter
Boudinot
Rötgen
Schmidt
3 ARMD
Eupen
3 ARMD
9
39
Rollesbroich
47
Lammersdorf
89
VERVIERS
39
Monschau
13-18 SEP
Hofen
Alzen
Schleiden
3 ARMD
9
Kalterherberg
347
4 CAV GP
Camp d'Elsenborn
9
4 CAV
Elsenborn
Malmedy
Dor

U.S. POSITIONS, NIGHT 12 SEP
ADVANCE BY EVENING 18 SEP
GAINS BY END OF SEPTEMBER
AXIS U.S. ARMD ATTACK, 12 SEP
AXIS U.S. ARMD ATTACK, 13 SEP
AXIS U.S. ARMD ATTACK, 14 SEP
AXIS U.S. ARMD ATTACK, 15 SEP
WEST WALL

ble band of the West Wall: the city of Aachen on the north and the
dense Hürtgen Forest about ten miles to the south. The corridor in between, the only area that would normally lend itself to armored operations, was blocked by one of the most formidable sections of the West
Wall, a double row of continuous "dragon's teeth," tank obstacles of
reinforced concrete, covered by fire from concrete gun emplacements
on a ridge east of the industrial town of Stolberg. Looking ahead to the
attack that would follow our reconnaissance, we faced an intriguing
tactical problem: should we first seize and clear Aachen in order to
get more maneuver room to attack the West Wall, or should we try
for a quick, sharp break through the Stolberg corridor?

The capture of Aachen would be the exclusive task of the 1st Division, and I discussed with General Huebner how best to handle the
situation. The city lay in a bowl, partly surrounded by hills, chiefly on
the south side. Though not a walled city, nor organized as a fortress,
it was within the two bands of the West Wall obstacles. Like all ancient European cities, it was a jumble of solid stone houses, through
which meandered narrow cobbled streets. It could be a tough proposition if the Germans chose to defend it. Huebner was reluctant to get
involved in what could be a costly street battle. He argued that if we
were to seize and hold the bordering hills on the south side we could
dominate the city, prevent passage of any German reinforcements,
and yet have some of his 1st Division available to assist the 3rd Armored in breaking through the corridor between Aachen and Hürtgen.
The city could be taken whenever necessary after the XIX Corps came
abreast. I agreed and decided to limit the 1st Division's operations to
seizing the southern rim of hills, while bypassing the city to the south.
Later intelligence indicated that at that time Aachen was only lightly
held and might have fallen to the 1st Division without a bitter fight,
but there was no way of knowing this.

The 9th Division was given the task of clearing the northern section of the Hürtgen Forest to prevent its use by the enemy as a base
from which to counterattack or place fire against the south flank of
the 3rd Armored as it drove head-on against the West Wall.

The probing reconnaissance commenced on September 12 as the
VII Corps began crossing the border into Germany. Not much prog-

ress was made, though the 16th Infantry of the 1st Division got through the initial row of obstacles on the south side of Aachen and Combat Command Boudinot reached Rötgen. A coordinated attack was launched the following day, with better results. One of Boudinot's battalion task forces led by Lieutenant Colonel William B. Lovelady —an unlikely name for a tough, able tanker—cracked a hole in the front line of the dragon's teeth and reached the village of Rott, while farther north a task force of Combat Command Hickey, under Colonel Doan, after a tough fight broke through the first band of obstacles, the "Scharnhorst Line," to the village of Neutheim.

The advances were followed up during the next two days, and by noon of the fifteenth the 16th Infantry had entered Eilendorf and the 1st Division had accomplished its mission of ringing Aachen on the hills south and east of the city. This permitted Hickey, with a battalion of the 16th Infantry, to batter his way through most of the pillboxes blocking the road to Stolberg. Lovelady did even better, driving through Kornelimünster, and by evening of September 15 he had broken through the "Schill Line," the second row of the West Wall.

Assisting the 3rd Armored on its right, the 9th Division took Zweifall, in the northern edge of the Hürtgen Forest, with little trouble, but when George Smythe's 47th Infantry entered the forest to outflank the town of Vicht it ran into small groups of enemy stubbornly defending pillboxes of the Schill Line, partly hidden in the dense woods. The morning of the sixteenth the 47th Infantry sliced through these defenses, took Vicht, and advanced on Shevenhütte.

Buoyed by these successes, I had high hopes of reaching Düren, the objective of the "reconnaissance" attack. On September 15 the Corps CP moved into a building in Kornelimünster used as Nazi party headquarters for the Aachen area. We found food on the dining table and other evidence of its hasty evacuation. Stiffening resistance inside the Hürtgen Forest and in the open country along the Scharnhorst Line boded ill for the 9th Division. And the 3rd Armored was hit with heavy tank losses by fire from the high ground on either side of Stolberg and was stopped on a line halfway through the town.

Even though the forces manning the West Wall were depleted remnants of the Seventh Army and hastily organized secondary troops, they clung tenaciously to their heavily fortified positions, taking a toll of American tanks and infantry. Foul weather settled over the battle zone, robbing the VII Corps of the excellent close air support to which we had become accustomed and making more difficult the supply of artillery and tank ammunition. When the Germans finally were able to bring in their fresh, full-strength 12th Division I called off the attack of the 3rd Armored on September 18 and directed General Craig to shorten the Corps front between Shevenhütte and Monshau and secure it from infiltration and counterattack. This turned out to be one of the tougher assignments for the 9th Division. For the remainder of September and most of October the Division doggedly battled the German 353rd Division and part of the 12th Division in a series of attacks and counterattacks in the thickets and mud of the Hürtgen Forest, made cold and sodden by heavy autumn rains. Neither side could make much headway, though the 9th did penetrate the Schill Line between Lammersdorf and the key town of Shevenhütte, which was captured and held against repeated counterattacks.

Plagued by the same logistical problems as the VII Corps, Gerow's V Corps had no better success with its probe of the West Wall in the Eifel region. Gerow stopped his attack on September 16 after shallow penetrations of the West Wall in two narrow zones.

It was now clear to all concerned that the frontage of the First Army would have to be reduced before it could break through the West Wall. With conclusion of the Brest peninsula campaign in France, General Bradley brought up Middleton's VIII Corps from Brest to take over part of the V Corps front in the Ardennes, which permitted Hodges to reduce the VII Corps' front to about twenty miles. These changes were accomplished by September 25.

Hodges was now ready to renew his drive to the Roer River, but first had to get Corlett's XIX Corps through the West Wall north of Aachen, then complete the encirclement of that city by the XIX and VII Corps, after which the VII Corps would clean out Aachen. Aachen had little military significance to either the Americans or Germans now that the XIX Corps, as well as our VII Corps, could bypass it on the way to the Rhine, but it did have great political and psychological importance to Hitler and the Nazi party. Hitler at times fancied himself as a sec-

ond Charlemagne, and was well aware that Aachen had been the capital of the Holy Roman Empire, which he and his more ardent follow-
ers had hoped to duplicate as a secular Nazi German empire. Hitler
had ordered that Aachen be held at all costs.

The Fall of Aachen

The 1st Division had long been in position to attack Aachen, and I left
the details of the operation in Huebner's capable hands. The 30th Division of the XIX Corps signaled the attack of the 1st Division when
it occupied Alsdorf, north of Aachen on October 7. For the next three
days the 1st and 30th Divisions fought to close the ring about the city.
Following capture of Verlautenheide by the 18th Infantry, von Rundstedt released the 1st Panzer Corps to counterattack against the 16th
and 18th Regiments. But the panzers were beaten off by those veteran
1st Division regiments, greatly aided at a critical moment on October
15 by the timely arrival of the 492nd Squadron of P-47 fighter-bombers.

When the 30th Division broke through to a junction with the 1st
Division south of Würselin on October 16 the fate of Aachen was
sealed, and Huebner did not wait to send into the city a demand for its
surrender, hoping he could avoid further destruction of the city, which
had been bombed frequently by the British, reportedly in reprisal for
the German bombing of Coventry. Huebner's twenty-four-hour ultimatum was rejected on October 10, and it remained for Colonel John
F. R. Seitz's 26th Infantry to carry out the onerous task of reducing
the inner city.

In compliance with Hitler's orders, the German garrison took cover
in the cellars and even in the sewers, and fought every step of the way
along the winding streets lined with stone houses and apartments.
Our troops soon learned that these buildings could withstand the fire
of tanks and the 90-mm guns of tank destroyers. One of the infantry
battalion commanders, Lieutenant Colonel John T. Corley (one of the
best of a fabulous group of battalion leaders in the 1st Division), used
an attached 155-mm gun as a direct-fire weapon to batter down the
heavy walls of buildings such as the Quellenhof Hotel, where Colonel
Gerhard Wilck, the garrison commander, was thought to be holding
out. To speed Seitz's task I sent him a task force of the 3rd Armored

Division under Lieutenant Colonel Samuel L. Hogan, and by October 19 the critical high ground in a city park where Wilck was holed up in a concrete bunker was seized by Corley's and Hogan's men. Despite urgings by Hitler to "hold this venerable city to the last man, and . . . if necessary allow himself to be buried in its ruins," Wilck surrendered when Corley blasted his bunker with a 155-mm rifle. The fighting at Aachen was over, the 1st Panzer Corps having been directed by Rundstedt to call off its attempts to rescue the city.

I went into the city a few days later and found it a shambles, with far greater destruction than I had seen in any other city. There was scarcely a building with its roof intact. Fortunately the cathedral was relatively undamaged, particularly the older octagonal section with the reputed throne of Charlemagne, which had been bricked over to protect it. Aachen was a sad tribute to Hitler's maniacal delusions.

During the fighting in Aachen and the Stolberg corridor in September, the 9th Division had secured the western section of the Hürtgen Forest to protect the right flank of the VII Corps, but the Corps and division frontage was too great to attempt to clear the southeastern half of the forest northeast of Lammersdorf. In early October, after the First Army was able to narrow the VII Corps front, I was directed to renew the attack to break through the remainder of the forest and seize the town of Schmidt, north of the upper reaches of the Roer River. No mention was made of the two major dams on the Roer and its Urft tributary south of Schmidt, nor were they assigned as objectives of the VII Corps. They had been built years before to control floods downstream and to provide hydroelectric power for Düren.

In light of subsequent developments, there seems to have been no excuse for the lapse in intelligence with respect to the potential threat to our operations posed by these dams if they should be destroyed, or their floodgates opened, whenever the First Army opposite Düren, or the Ninth Army farther north, should attempt to force a crossing of the Roer in their drive to the Rhine. No terrain analysis or intelligence estimate of this danger had been made by Supreme Headquarters, Allied Expeditionary Force (SHAEF), XII Army Group, or First Army, and for the first and only time my able G-2 and Corps Engineer failed to provide me with such an analysis or estimate.

Apparently the only responsible officer who noted the danger was the 9th Division G-2, Major Jack A. Houston, who noted in his G-2 report dated October 2, 1944: "Bank overflows and destructive flood waves can be produced (on the Roer River) by regulating the discharge from the various dams. By demolition of some of them great destructive waves can be produced which would destroy everything in the populated industrial valley (of the Roer) as far as the Meuse and into Holland." The G-2 First Army discounted this estimate.

There was little that General Craig's 9th Division, which had the mission of capturing Schmidt, could have done about the Roer dams if we had been apprised of their importance. Despite heroic efforts, in almost three weeks of fierce fighting in the mud and dense woods the 9th Division was unable to break through to Schmidt. On October 25 the division was relieved by the 28th Division of the V Corps, which on orders from General Hodges took over responsibility for the Roer dams. The 9th Division was given a well-earned rest in a nearby camp.

The High Command Plans for the Drive to the Rhine

At a meeting in Brussels with Bradley and Montgomery on October 18, 1944, General Eisenhower decided to give the Germans no respite, but to continue the Allied drive to the Rhine through the fall and winter, if necessary. The American First Army was directed to attack in early November with the object of establishing a bridgehead beyond the Rhine south of Cologne. On October 21, as Aachen fell, Bradley outlined his plan for attack by the First and Ninth Armies, with the First Army making the main effort. In turn Hodges advised me that the VII Corps would make the main effort of the First Army, for which I was to submit a plan.

About the same time I had a telephone call from Bill Kean, Hodges' Chief of Staff, asking if I would like to have the 104th Division, commanded by Major General Terry de la Mesa Allen, which had been helping the Canadian Army open Antwerp. I replied that I would be glad to have him. Allen had a reputation of being hard to handle and had been relieved of command of the 1st Division at the end of the Sicilian campaign. I had known him at the Infantry School as a rambunctious man but possessing great qualities of leadership. When relieved of his division he was reported to have sworn that he would make his new 104th Division the equal of the 1st. With a view to stimulating both divisions I placed the 104th in the line adjacent to the 1st.

The 104th increased VII Corps to four divisions, deployed on a twenty-mile front in order from the north: the 104th, 3rd Armored, 1st, and 4th Divisions, the latter having replaced the 9th Division. As approved by General Hodges, the VII Corps plan called for the 104th to seize the high ground east of Stolberg and clear the Eschweiler industrial area, which would open the way to the Roer plain. The 1st Division, assisted by Combat Command Boudinot of the 3rd Armored, was to make the main effort of the Corps astride the Hamich ridge, along the western edge of the Hürtgen Forest, with a view to turning the north corner of the forest. Farther south the 4th Division was to break through along the Gemeter–Hürtgen–Kleinhau axis to outflank the Hürtgen Forest on the south.

The VII Corps November Attack

Bradley had arranged for a massive air bombardment along the front of the First and Ninth Armies (the latter, under General William H. Simpson, had moved up to the German border from the south of France) prior to the attack scheduled for November 5. Foul weather forced postponement until the sixteenth, by which time the ground attack found the German positions well dug in, thoroughly mined, and heavily supported by additional artillery.

Terry Allen's 104th Division was slow showing its mettle in its first action under VII Corps, until I made clear to Allen that I expected better results. But it took four days of heavy fighting before the 104th captured the high ground east of Stolberg. Boudinot's Combat Command cleared the area between Eschweiler and the Hamich ridge, and then reverted to Corps reserve along with the remainder of the 3rd Armored.

Meanwhile the 1st Division, which had turned the 26th Infantry into the Hürtgen northeast of Shevenhütte, was making little progress either in the woods or along the Hamich ridge. For several days the 16th and 18th Regiments fought their way along the ridge under heavy artillery fire controlled from hill 187 north of Sherpenseel. I intervened on November 21 to have Willie Palmer arrange a concentration of twenty battalions of artillery on hill 187 for three minutes, probably the heaviest concentration on a single target during the war. It helped clear the way for an advance into open country, where we threw in a task force from the 3rd Armored, which helped carry the main drive of the 1st Division past the northern tip of the Hürtgen Forest.

Within the forest the 26th Infantry and the 4th Division farther south were encountering the same deadly combination of concealed pillboxes, fallen trees, mud, and dogged German resistance that earlier confronted the 9th Division. It was not until November 29 that Jeff Seitz's 26th Regiment penetrated the eastern edge of the woods opposite Merode. The 1st Division had accomplished its chief mission of breaking out of the Stolberg corridor and turning the northern corner of the Hürtgen Forest. It had been in action almost constantly since D day. I could ask no more of it, and on December 5 the 1st Division was relieved by the 9th Division, which returned to VII Corps after a well-earned rest.

While the 1st Division was fighting its way through and around the north tip of the forest, Tubby Barton's 4th division was struggling with the fastnesses of the Hürtgen farther south and attempting to break out around its southern end through the more open country bordering the Hürtgen–Kleinhau–Gey road that led to Düren. "Buck" Lanham's 22nd Infantry drew the major role of driving through the southern section of the forest on Kleinhau and Gey. Using clever, imaginative tactics, Lanham was able to inject some maneuver into his attack but it was not until the end of November—after the 5th Armored Division, under Major General Lunsford E. Oliver, was assigned to the VII Corps—that the 22nd Infantry, with help from the 5th Armored, was able to clear the southern tip of the Hürtgen Forest overlooking Gey. I authorized the 4th Division to dig in there. In early December the First Army replaced the 4th division—which, like the 1st Division, had been in almost continuous action since D day—with Bob Macon's 83rd Division.

Terry Allen Makes Good on His Boast

While the 1st and 4th Divisions were slugging their way in and around the Hürtgen Forest, Terry Allen's 104th Division was making hay in the north section of the VII Corps zone. After capture of the high ground east of Stolberg on November 20, against increasing resistance from the German 12th Division, it moved quickly to Eschweiler, which it occupied on November 22. Thus far the operations of the 104th were largely on its right in support of the 1st Division. As the action opened up on the Roer plain, emphasis in the 104th zone shifted to its left in conjunction with the XIX Corps, to whose command Major General Raymond S. McLain had acceded when General Corlett had been invalided home. I sometimes had difficulties arranging Corps boundaries and supporting fires with Corlett, who was not well. This all disappeared when Ray McLain took command of the XIX Corps. Our two Corps ran alongside one another most of the way for the remainder of the war. McLain and I became close friends and established collaboration between the VII and XIX corps to the benefit of our troops.

Following the fall of Eschweiler, General Allen's left regiment, the 413th, under the able leadership of Colonel Welcome P. Waltz, pushed forward almost eight miles from Verlautenheide through the remainder of the West Wall, now largely abandoned, to the town of Pützlohn, which it reached November 22. Allen then began a series of night attacks that became the hallmark of his division. Night attacks are difficult to control and require well-trained troops. I always gave a large measure of credit for their success in the 104th Division to Brigadier General Briant E. Moore, Terry's Assistant Division Commander, who had "cut his teeth" with the Americal Division on Guadalcanal, and whose skill as a tactician and trainer complemented perfectly Allen's flamboyant leadership. Pützlohn fell to a well-organized night attack as did Weisweiler, putting the 104th in advance of the 1st Division, which at that time was still battling, against heavier opposition, on the Hamich ridge. By November 29 the 104th had driven the 3rd Panzer Grenadier Division from Lamersdorf, Inden, and Lucheberg and was across the Inde.

While the 1st Division was being relieved by Craig's refreshened 9th Division and the 4th Division by the 83rd, I suspended offensive operations within the VII Corps. When realignment of troops was completed, we renewed the attack on December 10. The 104th resumed its night marauding, and by December 13 had reached the Roer along its entire front.

South of the 104th, in the zone of the 9th Division, we employed a combination of armor and infantry under a uniquely cooperative command arrangement. I wanted to avoid getting Rose's 3rd Armored too involved in action west of the Roer, hoping to keep it at full strength for exploitation beyond the Roer to the Rhine. Yet some armor could be helpful to the 9th Division in the open plain between the Hürtgen Forest and the Roer. Although I have always been a firm believer in unity of command and responsibility, I departed from this doctrine in planning the attack of the 9th Division.

Knowing and respecting General Rose's objections to having his combat commands attached to infantry divisions, I consulted with Craig and Rose and decided to divide responsibility for the initial action in the 9th Division zone between the 3rd Armored and the 9th. I directed Rose to make a limited-objective attack with one combat command to capture three towns (Obergeich, Geich, and Echtz) in the left half of the 9th Division zone, after which the armor would be relieved by the 9th Division and would return to corps reserve. A concurrent attack of the 9th on the right was to be conducted in close conjunction with the 3rd Armored. I would not recommend this arrangement as a normal procedure, but it worked well in this instance. By the end of the first day all three villages were secured.

Farther south Bob Macon's 83rd Division, greatly improved since its first combat experience in Normandy, and Oliver's 5th Armored Division, joined the advance. By the night of December 16 the VII Corps was in control of the entire west bank of the Roer in its zone except for two towns south of Düren. But before we could attack across the Roer the VII Corps headquarters was shifted seventy-five miles to the southwest to help stop Hitler's counteroffensive in the Ardennes "Bulge."

Retrospect

As I look back now after thirty-five years, the Aachen–Stolberg–Hürtgen campaign looms as the toughest, most costly of the VII Corps' operations in Europe. As the able Army historian Charles E. MacDonald, who has been quite critical of the First Army's operations in the Aachen area, has written, "Perhaps the real difficulty lay in the fact that the First Army fought in the Aachen area in the first place." But the First Army had no choice as to where it was to fight, and whatever force was sent through the "Aachen gap" would have confronted the same terrain, the same city, the same West Wall, the same Hürtgen Forest, the same Roer dams, none of which could have been avoided.

As far as concerned the VII Corps, it might have been better to have concentrated at the start on clearing Aachen, instead of first attempting to break through the West Wall via the Stolberg corridor. But it must be remembered that Aachen was almost on the boundary between the VII and XIX Corps, and that when the VII Corps approached the city in September, the XIX Corps was some distance back and had not yet crossed the Meuse. It was not until October 1 that the XIX Corps was in position to assist the VII Corps in the capture of Aachen. If the 1st Division had become embroiled in Aachen, it would not have been able to help the 3rd Armored crack the West Wall at Stolberg in September. While it took two weeks, October 7–21, for the 1st and 30th Divisions to capture Aachen, it required until December 9 for the VII Corps to clear the Hürtgen Forest, an essential preliminary to the seizure of the Roer dams, which in turn would determine when the Roer would be safe to cross. The time "lost" in taking Aachen was but a fraction of the sixteen weeks (September 12–December 16) required to clear the Stolberg corridor and the series of forests west of the Roer dams, which the Americans have called the Hürtgen Forest.

Costly as was the Aachen–Stolberg–Hürtgen battle to the First Army in casualties, ammunition, and equipment, it cost the Germans far more, and forced Rundstedt to employ divisions, tanks, and gasoline intended for the Ardennes counteroffensive, weakening that supreme German effort and the subsequent defense of the Rhine.

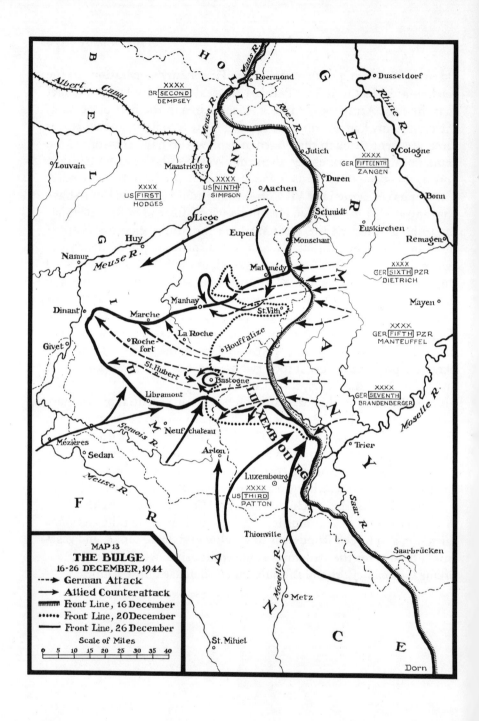

XXXX
BR SECOND
DEMPSEY

Roermond

Dusseldorf

Julich

XXXX
GER FIFTEENTH PZR
ZANGEN

Cologne

Duren

Bonn

Maastricht

XXXX
US NINTH
SIMPSON

Aachen

XXXX
US FIRST
HODGES

Schmidt

Euskirchen

Liege

Eupen

Monschau

Remagen

Louvain

Huy

Namur

Meuse R.

Malmedy

XXXX
GER SIXTH PZR
DIETRICH

Mayen

Manhay

St.Vith

Dinant

Marche

La Roche

Houffalize

XXXX
GER FIFTH PZR
MANTEUFFEL

Givet

Roche fort

St.Hubert

Bastogne

Libramont

XXXX
GER SEVENTH
BRANDENBERGER

Mézières

Sedan

Semois R.

Neufchateau

Arlon

Trier

Moselle R.

Luxembourg

XXXX
US THIRD
PATTON

Saar R.

Thionville

Saarbrücken

St. Mihiel

Metz

Dorn

MAP 13
THE BULGE
16-26 DECEMBER, 1944
- - -▶ German Attack
——▶ Allied Counterattack
▭▭▭▭ Front Line, 16 December
•••••• Front Line, 20 December
—— Front Line, 26 December

Scale of Miles
0 5 10 15 20 25 30 35 40

CHAPTER XIV

The Bulge—Battle of The Ardennes

While Bradley's 12th Army Group, plagued by adverse weather and shortage of gasoline and ammunition, was battling its way through the West Wall against determined German resistance, Hitler had assumed direct command of the Wehrmacht and was readying his forces for an all-out counteroffensive, the objective of which was to split the British and American Armies in the West, capture the port of Antwerp, and, presumably, force the Western Allies to sue for an armistice. Hitler's Field Marshalls, Rundstedt and Model, realizing that Germany no longer had the capacity to force such a "big solution," favored a so-called "small solution," limiting the attack to the area east of the Meuse, with the object of destroying the Allied forces threatening Cologne and the Ruhr. Hitler stuck to his original plan. Perhaps it was indicative of a lack of clarity on his part as to the object of his big solution, or lack of faith in its outcome on the part of his military leaders, that there was no provision in the approved plan for any operations that might follow the fall of Antwerp.

The German Sixth SS Panzer Army, under General Josef "Sepp" Dietrich, and the Fifth Panzer Army, commanded by General Hasso-Eccard von Manteuffel, consisting of seven armored and four infantry divisions, assembled with great secrecy in the Eifel region south of Cologne in early December, 1944. Supported by the Fifteenth Army on the north and the Seventh Army on the south, they were to be the main striking force against the V and VIII American Corps in the Ardennes. On the morning of December 16 the eleven divisions of the two panzer armies struck the 99th Division, the south flank division of the V Corps, and the 106th and 28th Divisions of the VIII Corps.

The 99th and 106th Divisions were in combat for the first time and the 28th Division had suffered heavy casualties in the Hürtgen Forest and Roer dams fighting. By December 20 a breakthrough had been made by the Fifth and Sixth Panzer Armies, punching a bulge through the fronts of the 106th and 28th Divisions, cutting direct communication across the break.

General Eisenhower consulted Montgomery and Bradley and on December 20 decided to place Montgomery temporarily in command of all Allied forces north of the Bulge; Bradley would retain command to the south. At the same time the 82nd and 101st Airborne Divisions and other reinforcements were being rushed to stem the German attack.

We in the VII Corps had reports of a concentration of German armor somewhere south of Cologne, which First Army Headquarters and I both feared would threaten the right flank of the Corps in its drive on Cologne after we crossed the Roer River. When the German counteroffensive began, we had followed reports of the action but continued our attack toward Düren. I had no intimation that the VII Corps would join the Ardennes battle until the afternoon of December 20, when I was informed by First Army that as soon as possible we were to move south to the vicinity of Marche in Belgium, south of Liège, after turning over the Corps zone to Ray McLain's XIX Corps of the Ninth Army.* Generals Simpson and McLain, with members of their staffs, arrived early in the evening at my CP in Kornelimünster. We worked well into the night to give them a picture of our tactical and administrative procedures so that our headquarters might slip away in the morning without alerting the enemy. Our divisions would continue their attack under XIX Corps, but our corps troops would displace south gradually. The Corps Chief of Staff, Colonel Partridge, and a few staff officers were off at 10:00 P.M. to be in the Marche area at first light to select a new CP.

I left Kornelimünster by jeep with my aide, Captain Walsh, the following morning to report to General Hodges at Chaudfontaine, a suburb of Liège, for instructions. After being stopped several times by

*I learned later that Montgomery had specified that he wanted me to command the counterattack force he was assembling north of Marche.

wary MPs on the lookout for German parachutists, said to have been dropped back of our lines, we arrived at Chaudfontaine as Hodges' headquarters was moving to Tongres, west of the Meuse. I was told that the VII Corps would consist of the 84th Division, then en route to Marche from the Ninth Army; the 75th Division, just arrived from the States; and the 2nd Armored, which would be brought down from the Ninth Army on December 22. Also I learned that part of the 3rd Armored Division, which had joined the XVIII Airborne (AB) Corps on December 18, might be available later. The VII Corps Artillery and other Corps troops were already en route from the Aachen area. We were to take over a sector from the Ourthe River, on the left, to the junction of the Lesse and the Meuse, a fifty-mile front, by midnight, December 23, prepared to launch a counterattack on Army order to the south, southeast, east, or northeast. The assembly of the VII Corps would be screened by Matt Ridgway's XVIII Airborne Corps, then made up of the 82nd Airborne Division and the 3rd Armored Division. The 84th Divison would operate under Ridgway's command until VII Corps was prepared to take over on the twenty-third.

I proceeded at once to Marche to the CP of the 84th Division, commanded by Brigadier General Alexander R. Bolling, where we arrived in the late afternoon. An ominous quiet hung over the small road-center town near the western end of the Ardennes Forest. Alex Bolling met me on the sidewalk outside his command post. I did not know him well but was struck by his air of calm confidence in himself and his troops, some of which had not yet arrived in the area. He was not sure where the nearest enemy troops were but knew he was astride their main route of approach to the Meuse from Bastogne, twenty-eight miles to the southeast, where Tony McAuliffe and his 101st Airborne Division were holding out against Manteuffel's Fifth Panzer Army. Bolling had posted his leading regiment in a perimeter defense around Marche while awaiting arrival of the rest of the division. That morning he had dispatched part of the regiment to Hotten, six miles to the northeast, to assist the 51st Engineer Combat Battalion defend a key bridge over the Ourthe, and shortly after noon had received reports of enemy infantry and tanks to the southeast. But he was confident that with the imminent arrival of the rest of his division, including an attached tank battalion, he could hold the line Hotten–Marche, as directed by First Army. I left Alex Bolling to his lonely vigil in the gathering dusk, with admiration for his courage and his quiet acceptance of responsibility. The 84th Division was in good hands.

From Marche, Captain Walsh and I were driven by Sergeant Davis back north to the village of Mean where Colonel Partridge had located our new CP in the Chateau de Bassines. I badgered Dick Partridge for this selection, because the only means of entering or leaving the chateau was over a narrow causeway, which could readily have been blocked by small groups of marauding enemy paratroopers reported to be in the area. Luckily we had no difficulty during the night.

Next morning, December 22, while the 75th Division, Major General Fay B. Prickett commanding, was moving into its assembly area back of the 3rd Armored, and the 2nd Armored was en route to its area east of Dinant, I visited Army Headquarters to express my concern that the 2nd Panzer Division, the leading unit of Manteuffel's Fifth Panzer Army, might slip south of Marche and thus endanger the assembly of the VII Corps. Hodges directed Ridgway to have Bolling block all roads southwest of Marche to Rochefort. Later in the day Montgomery arrived at First Army with word that the 59th Armored Brigade of Lieutenant General Brian G. Horrocks' 30 British Corps had taken over the defenses of the Meuse bridges between Namur and Givet and the next day would reconnoiter the area southwest of the VII Corps assembly area and clean out any enemy groups that might have infiltrated there. Montgomery and Hodges agreed that the counterattack by the VII Corps would go off on the twenty-fourth. Meanwhile we were not to get involved in the defensive operations.

I visited General Ridgway at his CP at Werbomont, south of Liège, on the morning of the twenty-third. I had not seen Matt since the Cherbourg campaign, and found him in fine fettle, as dynamic as ever. I was glad to have his corps on my left flank. At the moment he was concerned with a critical situation involving part of the 3rd Armored Division east of the Ourthe River. I agreed to let him have a battalion of the 75th Division and a battalion of 155-mm howitzers for attachment to the 3rd Armored.

I returned to my headquarters in time to meet General Hodges to plan for the counterattack of the VII Corps, postponed until Christmas Day. Courtney had invited General Horrocks to be present. I remembered him from Monty's pre–D-day exercise at St. Paul's school in London and liked him, as did all Americans who knew him. He was anxious to get in the fight. I told him I would appreciate it most if he would have his artillery tie in with Willie Palmer's corps artillery. I brought Courtney Hodges up to date on our situation, and undoubtedly told him I would assume command of the VII Corps, as newly constituted, including the 3rd Armored Division, later in the afternoon. Reports had begun to come in of increased activity on the front of the 84th Division, and I advised Hodges that it might be necessary to commit part of the 2nd Armored Division to prevent any enemy penetration toward Dinant.

VII Corps Joins the Defensive Battle—December 23

After they left, reports began to pour in of enemy tanks moving toward Ciney and Buissonville, northwest and west of Marche, and of an armored attack on a battalion task force that Bolling had posted at Rochefort. Without waiting for orders Major General Ernest N. Harmon—a veteran of the North African and Sicilian campaigns, and a 1917 classmate of mine at West Point, who had succeeded Ted Brooks in command of the 2nd Armored—with characteristic initiative and drive had dispatched Combat Command A, under Brigadier General John "Pee Wee" Collier, to Ciney to clean out any enemy tanks found there. These turned out to be British armored patrols from Dinant.

By now it was clear that the VII Corps could not remain aloof from the defensive battle, and I directed Harmon to attack at once to clear any enemy from the area Ciney–Buissonville–Rochefort. Harmon started his entire division forward to the west of the 84th Division and instructed Collier to secure Buissonville and continue on to Rochefort to relieve the task force of the 84th Division, hard pressed by our old antagonist Fritz Bayerlein and his Panzer Lehr Division. Alex Bolling's 84th was living up to my expectations, but needed help east of Marche as well as at Rochefort, so I attached Task Force Doan of the 3rd Armored to the 84th Division.

Farther east the 3rd Armored Division, which passed to my command in the late afternoon of the twenty-third, was heavily engaged west of St. Vith, the town having been evacuated by Brigadier General Robert W. Hasbrouck's 7th Armored Division on December 22–23, after its gallant defense had dealt a crippling delay to Dietrich's Sixth SS Panzer Army's drive on Liège—as important an action as Tony McAuliffe's disruption of Manteuffel's Fifth Army at Bastogne, though not as dramatic.

My first opportunity to check in with General Rose was on the morning of December 24 as I began a round of our divisions. Knowing that under the fluid situation it would be difficult to maintain wire communications between our various headquarters, I had authorized General Palmer, who served as deputy corps commander in my absence, to take any action he deemed necessary if I could not be reached.

I was delighted to have Maurice Rose back in VII Corps again. As was usually the case, his division, heavy in armor, needed additional infantry. The 75th Division, in corps reserve, was close at hand, but neither it nor its commander, Major General Prickett, had seen any action as yet. I decided to attach temporarily two of its RCTs (regimental combat teams) to the battle-tested 3rd Armored, which I also reinforced with heavy corps artillery and tank destroyers. Rose was to defend a sector along the Aisne River between the 84th Division and the 82nd Airborne. The 75th Division, less detachments, would remain in corps reserve.

From Rose's CP, I moved on to the headquarters of the 75th Division, north of Hotten, and there renewed my acquaintance with Fay Prickett, whom I had known as a cadet in the class ahead of me at the Point. I explained to him my reasons for attaching the bulk of his division to the 3rd Armored.

I then stopped in to see Bolling in Marche. Alex had lost none of his confidence, but was grateful for the help of Task Force Doan and the 2nd Armored. Hard fighting had developed east of Marche when German tanks and infantry, which prisoners revealed were part of the 116th Panzer Division, penetrated close to the Marche–Hotten road. I wished for my armored car as Captain Walsh and I cautiously felt our way in our jeep to Harmon's CP north of Celles. It was bitterly cold but the sky was clearing, which gave hope that Pete Quesada's fighter-bombers would be out in force in the morning. Another bright omen was that the German panzers, frustrated by the stiffened resistance of the Americans and well behind schedule in their drive to the Meuse, were beginning to run out of gas, both figuratively and actually.

Crisis at Celles—Christmas Day

It was midafternoon by the time I reached Ernie Harmon's CP. Somewhat earlier, 2nd Armored reconnaissance had discovered elements of the 2nd Panzer Division, apparently short of gas, in a wooded area near Celles southwest of Ciney. Harmon had called VII Corps and requested release from the "strings" imposed by Montgomery and Hodges on becoming involved in action prior to the planned counterattack. Willie Palmer advised Ernie to wait for my imminent arrival. Fearful of losing the opportunity to wreck the 2nd Panzers, Harmon called Palmer again urgently requesting clearance to attack. Palmer still demurred but authorized preparations for attack pending my arrival.

Meanwhile Montgomery at First Army Headquarters on his customary afternoon visit reviewed with Hodges the threatening situation developing on the VII Corps' open west flank. There is no record of their discussion, but we have the following from a statement of Hodges' Chief of Staff, General Kean, quoting from memory, in an article in the May, 1947, issue of the *Infantry Journal*:

(1) Marshal Montgomery . . . had directed that plans be made for the protection of the right flank and the lines of communication of the First Army.

[Paragraphs (2) and (3) dealt with British troops of Horrocks' 30 Corps.]

(4) General Collins would at once prepare plans to hold at all costs the line Hotten–Andenne in the event he was forced back.

(5) That in the event VII Corps was forced back, he [General Collins] would make the actual decision, relative to the implementation of his plan.

The above-quoted purported instructions were never received by me or my headquarters, and evidently were not clear to the staff of the First Army. After Montgomery left Army Headquarters, Hodges, Kean, and members of their staff discussed Monty's instructions. They decided to send Colonel R. F. "Red" Akers, an assistant G-3, to my CP to ensure that I understood Montgomery's wishes. After being briefed personally by General Hodges, Akers set out after dark on his long, cold jeep drive from Tongres, north of Liège, to our CP.

Since it would be hours before Akers could arrive, Kean telephoned Willie Palmer, about 3:30 P.M., shortly after Harmon's second call. Here is Palmer's account of what transpired, as told subsequently to Hansen Baldwin and printed in the *Infantry Journal* of May, 1947:

> (1) Colonel Akers was enroute to our Headquarters with important instructions.
> (2) CG VII Corps was given unrestricted use of all of his troops. (Kean emphasized this.)
> (3) CG VII Corps was authorized to change his defensive line. (As we looked at our respective maps, Kean tried to explain in guarded double talk, asking me if I saw a town A and a town H which at that time I identified as two villages, both of which were more or less in the no-man's land that Harmon wanted to invade anyhow.)
> All this fitted nicely with Harmon's plan and my conception of the tactical situation. I dictated a memorandum for General Collins (reproduced herewith) giving Kean's message, with my interpretation of "town A and town H," all very encouraging to Harmon's desire, and dispatched my aide, Lieutenant Carson, to deliver it to General Collins personally at Harmon's CP.
> About 1630, just after Carson had left, Kean telephoned again to say that on reflection he doubted whether I had understood him. He then repeated that Akers was enroute and that Collins was granted complete freedom to use *all* his troops, and then said: "Now get this. I'm only going to say it once. Roll with the punch."
> Looking at the map, and hearing this, I instantly spotted Andenne and Huy as very prominent "towns A and H," but about 30 miles in rear of the tiny villages I had spotted in our earlier double talk; I felt sure Andenne and Huy were more consistent with rolling with the punch.
> On the carbon copy of my earlier message to General Collins I wrote a footnote explaining how badly my first message to him had missed Kean's meaning, and that I now took Andenne and Huy to be towns A and H— which coupled with the "roll with the punch" meant a serious withdrawal. I added, "I think you had better come home," and dispatched a liaison officer to deliver the annotated message to General Collins personally at Harmon's CP

Palmer's first message reached me shortly after I had arrived at Harmon's headquarters. I had heartily approved Harmon's plan to attack with Brigadier General I. D. White's Combat Command the following morning, Christmas Day, because the early winter darkness had forced a delay. We were finishing final details when the second message arrived. I told Harmon to hold everything, but made clear he was to go ahead with the attack unless I specifically directed otherwise.

Back at my CP, as we waited for the arrival of Akers, I discussed the situation with key members of the staff—Willie Palmer, Dick Partridge, "Trixie" Troxel, the G-3, and Leslie Carter, my fine G-2. There was no question in their minds, and none in mine, but that we should attack. It was late evening when Akers did arrive, his lips blue with cold and his face almost frozen after his long ride in an open jeep. We gave him a hot toddy and then listened, a bit aghast, as he confirmed the tenor of Kean's guarded hint to Palmer of a possible withdrawal by the VII Corps to the line *A*ndenne–*H*otten. But such a withdrawal was *authorized*, not ordered. I was given full control of all units assigned to the Corps, which was released from its former counter-offensive mission and would assume the defensive role of stabilizing the right flank of the First Army.

As I listened to Akers' recital my mind went back to an incident in the First Battle of the Marne in World War I, with which I was thoroughly familiar, having lectured on the battle to Reserve officers in Birmingham and Anniston while an instructor at Benning. During that battle von Kluge's First Army, as it turned the flank of the French Sixth Army near Paris, had itself been outflanked by Joffre's "Taxicab Army," which had been rushed to the front in Paris cabs. But von Kluge by some deft maneuvering had righted his situation and was poised again to strike Joffre's flank when a staff officer, Lieutenant Colonel Hentsch, arrived from von Moltke's Supreme Command Headquarters with oral instructions from von Moltke, which Hentsch interpreted to require von Kluge to withdraw. Kluge reluctantly accepted this interpretation, thus leading to a great French victory in one of the decisive battles of World War I.

I had already decided to go ahead with Harmon's attack, but I did not want to have this action, which bade fair to becoming one of the decisive engagements of the Battle of the Bulge, to rest on *oral* instructions. I asked Akers to state in writing his understanding of General Hodges' instructions, which he did, as reproduced herewith.

HEADQUARTERS FIRST U.S. ARMY
A.P.O. #230,   U.S. ARMY

24 December 1944

SUBJECT: Confirmation of Oral Instructions.

TO: Commanding General, VII Corps, APO #307, United States Army

1. In compliance with instructions received from Field Marshal Montgomery, C-in-C 21st Army Group, Commanding General, First United States Army, is endeavoring to shorten the line now held by First Army units to halt the advance of the enemy and stabilize the line.

2. For the time being, the VII Corps is released from all offensive missions and will go on the defensive with the objective of stabilizing the right flank of First United States Army. Commanding General, VII Corps, is hereby authorized to use all forces at his disposal to accomplish this job. Commanding General, VII Corps, is authorized, whenever in his opinion he considers it necessary, to drop back to the general line: Andenne–Hotton–Monhay. In the event that the line drops back this far, the bridge at Andenne will be secured. Firm contact on the left will be maintained with XVIII Airborne Corps in the vicinity of Monhay.

By command of Lieutenant General HODGES:

R. F. AKERS, JR.,
Colonel, G. S. C.,
G-3 (Ops)

I called Harmon at once and directed him to attack as planned. This he did on Christmas morning with devastating success, resulting over the next two days in destruction of the bulk of the 2nd Panzers. In contrast with Christmas Eve, we relaxed Christmas evening with a fine turkey dinner, with bachelor Willie Palmer, under heavy coaching from our married staff, carving the turkey.

While I. D. White's CC "B" was mopping up the Celles pocket, "Pee Wee" Collier's CC "A," with the VII Corps' 4th Cavalry Group, was engaged with Panzer Lehr and the fresh Ninth Panzer Division at Humain, southwest of Marche. To clinch that fight Harmon committed his Reserve Combat Command under Colonel Sidney R. Hinds, who was greatly aided, as were all units of the VII corps during the critical

Christmas week of fighting, by Quesada's wonderful fighter-bombers and by the great flexibility and accuracy of our massed artillery fires. By December 28 the advance of von Manteuffel's Fifth Army to the Meuse, disrupted and stalled by the 101st Airborne at Bastogne, had been stopped cold by the 2nd Armored, the 84th Division, and part of the 3rd Armored, backed up by Brian Horrocks' 30 British Corps. The line Celles–Marche–Hotten became the high-water mark of Hitler's drive on Antwerp.

Fighting on the North Flank of the Bulge

From December 26 on I had to devote most of my attention to the east wing of the corps front between Hotten and Manhay where the 3rd Armored, supported by the 75th Division, in conjunction with Ridgway's XVIII Airborne Corps, was battling stoutly to checkmate Sepp Dietrich's desperate attempt to salvage something of the mission of his Sixth Panzer Army, the main effort of the Ardennes offensive. Having been stopped at St. Vith, Dietrich again had tried to turn north toward Liège through the 82nd Airborne and 3rd Armored Divisions, striking as usual at the junction of the two divisions and the XVIII Airborne and VII Corps. Fortunately Ridgway and I knew one another well, and were able to make the complicated adjustments of troops and boundaries to thwart Dietrich's final drive.

During the next week, while Ridgway and I fretted at Montgomery's delay in launching the counterattack of the VII Corps, Monty came every other day to my CP, where Matt Ridgway would join us for a review of the situation. More than once I told Monty that I should be positioned farther east opposite St. Vith and that a counterattack near the point of the German salient would force the enemy out of the Bulge —as he had done at the Falaise pocket—rather than cutting off escape near its base. Ridgway agreed. Monty's contention was that the northern front had not yet been stabilized, a requisite under traditional tactical concepts before a counterattack should be launched. Monty was still fearful that the Sixth Panzer Army might break through the First Army's northern front. I insisted that the situation was totally different from that at the opening of the German counteroffensive when the inexperienced 99th and 106th Divisions and the worn-out 28th and 4th Divisions had been struck by five armored and twelve infantry divisions.

"Nobody is going to break such top-flight divisions as the 1st, 2nd, and 30th Infantry Divisions or the 82nd Airborne or the 3rd Armored Divisions," I said.

But Monty replied in a non sequitur: "Joe, you can't supply a corps over a single road," referring to the highway from Liège to St. Vith.

At that I countered—I will admit in disrespectful exasperation: "Well Monty, maybe you British can't but we can."

As always happens in such cases, the umpire, Monty, won that argument. But there were no hard feelings.

I had submitted three plans to First Army for the VII Corps counterattack, two aimed at a junction in the vicinity of Bastogne with Patton's III Corps commanded by Major General John Milliken, driving up from the south to the relief of Bastogne; and one with St. Vith as the objective. I can find no record of the details of these plans, but General Hodges apparently (according to Major Sylvan's unpublished diary) favored the most conservative and westerly of the three, and aimed at Bastogne.

After some delay, during which Hodges, Ridgway, and I continued to press Montgomery to launch the First Army's attack as soon, and from as far east, as possible, Bradley was as anxious as we were to get an attack going and had suggested to General Eisenhower on December 27 that the corresponding attack of the Third Army be directed from Bastogne toward St. Vith. Ike approved and the Third Army drive began on December 30, with Middleton's VIII Corps' objective the high ground just south of Houffalize, northeast of Bastogne. Milliken's III Corps joined the attack the following day, headed for St. Vith.

Montgomery finally decided on December 31, with Hodges' concurrence, to direct the VII Corps on Houffalize, and the XVIIIth on St. Vith, but we were not to jump off until January 3. In compliance with this decision Hodges called in Kean, Thorson, Ridgway, and me to to make final plans for the offensive. The VII Corps, to consist of the 75th, 83rd, and 84th Infantry Divisions and the 2nd and 3rd Armored Divisions, with twelve corps artillery battalions and other supporting troops, totaling close to 100,000 men, was to attack east of the Ourthe

River toward Houffalize. Ridgway was to protect the left flank of the VII Corps and on Hodges' order was to drive toward St. Vith. Horrock's 30 British Corps would take over Bolling's 84th Division sector, while the 84th and 3rd Armored sideslipped to the east and Bob Macon's 83rd Division assembled north of the 3rd Armored. The 75th Division was to become First Army reserve. Montgomery approved these plans and fixed the time of attack as 8:30 A.M., January 3, 1945.

VII Corps Counterattacks, January 3, 1945

Three panzer divisions of the II SS Panzer Corps opposed the VII Corps. I started the attack with the 2nd and 3rd Armored Divisions, in order from the right, hoping for a quick penetration of their front, in order to trap as many as possible of the Fifth Panzer Army still in the tip of the Bulge. The 84th Division was to mop up any residual opposition back of Harmon's 2nd Armored and the 83rd was to do the same behind Rose's 3rd Armored. A heavy bombardment by the Ninth Air Force was to precede the attack.

Snow and thick fog that swirled through the treetops on the morning of the 3rd prevented air support and coated the narrow, steep roads with ice, making them hazardous for tanks, even those with rubber treads. It was bitterly cold, freezing not only the ground but the hands and ears of advancing troops. For the next fortnight snow piled up in drifts several feet deep, concealing mine fields and tank obstacles. Weather and the rough terrain of the Ardennes offered more resistance initially than the lightly held enemy outposts, but as the weather worsened on January 7 and continued foul, the infantry accompanying and following the tankers had to bear more of the fighting. We found, as the panzers did before us (and as Patton's armor did south of Bastogne), that the Ardennes was "lousy" tank country, particularly in freezing weather. Our corps artillery, especially the 8-inch howitzers, remarkably accurate weapons, did much to pinch-hit for our fighter-bombers. One day I watched a task force of the 2nd Armored, which was forced to attack frontally through a village on a narrow ridge, the steep, icy slopes preventing any flanking maneuver. German infantry with Panzerfausts, effective bazooka-type antitank weapons, were holed up in the basements of the houses. It was only after observers methodically sent 8-inch howitzer shells with delayed fuses crashing down through the roofs of these houses to the basements, one house at a time, that our tanks were able to advance.

That same afternoon a tank destroyer with broad, steel caterpillar treads, just ahead of our jeep, going slowly down a side-hill slope, and unable to check its massive momentum, slid off the icy road and tumbled downhill, carrying its helpless driver to his death. This was but one of several such incidents, some involving pileups of vehicles, with resultant traffic jams and casualties.

Under such conditions, progress against the veteran German SS divisions was slow and costly, especially on the front of the 2nd Armored Division, and for the first and only time I had to put some pressure on my good friend and great fighter, Ernie Harmon, to keep his "Hell on Wheels" Division moving. Farther east the 83rd Division ran into stiff opposition on the watershed between the Salm and the Ourthe Rivers, east of Houffalize, until the 3rd Armored managed to cut the highway between Houffalize and St. Vith, blocking the last major escape route of the Germans from Houffalize north of the Ourthe.

The weather cleared temporarily on January 14 on the front of the 2nd Armored, permitting fighter-bomber support to the armor and the 84th Division. Despite some intense fighting, the 2nd Armored entered Houffalize the following day, and on January 17 the Third Army's 11th Armored Division reached the southern exits of the town, ending the disruption of communications between the First and Third Armies created by Hitler's counteroffensive. It also terminated the subordination of the First Army to Montgomery's 21st Army Group. Commencing January 16 the V Corps, to the right of the XVIII Airborne, joined the offensive, belatedly in my judgment, and met stiff resistance from the Germans, skillfully withdrawing from the Bulge. The VII Corps, having reached its objectives, was pinched out on January 22 between the XVIII Airborne and Patton's III Corps west of St. Vith, which, appropriately, Bob Hasbrouch's 7th Armored Division reentered on January 23. While some fighting, chiefly by the Third Army of the southern shoulder of the Bulge, continued until January 28, the Battle of the Bulge was over.

An Evaluation of the Ardennes Battle

Hitler's gamble for a breakthrough in the West thus ended in complete failure. At the start it obtained almost complete surprise, overwhelmed two American divisions on the lightly held Ardennes front, created a salient in the First Army lines, and severed communications between the north and south halves of the Bulge. But from the first I felt that it never really had a chance of reaching its objective of Antwerp, much less achieving its probable political objective of forcing the Allies to sue for an armistice in the West. That I was not alone in this estimate is attested by Field Marshal Model's reported comment: "This plan hasn't got a damned leg to stand on," and by von Rundstedt, who opposed the plan initially and later testified at his trial: "All, absolutely all, conditions for the possible success of such an offensive were lacking."

A dangerous break in the front had been opened, which would have made it difficult if not impossible for Bradley to have controlled operations north of the Bulge from his headquarters in Luxembourg. Eisenhower was right, in my judgment, in placing Montgomery temporarily in command of all troops on the north side. But I never doubted that as soon as we could reinforce the flanks of the Bulge with experienced troops we would stop the German drive east of the Meuse. With the Russians threatening on the Eastern Front, the Germans would not dare draw many more troops from the East, and they did not have sufficient reserves in the West to initiate a second offensive north of Aachen, or in the Saar region, to pin down units of the Ninth or Third Armies that might be moved against the Bulge. The two fine airborne divisions of Ridgway's XVIII AB Corps were immediately available, and it was only a question of time before powerful counterattacks, overwhelmingly supported from the air once the weather improved, would drive the enemy back to the West Wall.

All these things were accomplished in a little over a month in what was probably the most effective Allied cooperation of the war. For the Army's part of this success Monty deserves much credit, though the same results could have been achieved sooner and with more devastating losses to the enemy if he had acted boldly and with greater confidence in the ability of American troops and their combat leaders. In spite of his later protestations of admiration for the fighting qualities of American troops, he unduly prolonged the anxiety at SHAEF, and among the British Chiefs of Staff, that the Germans might penetrate beyond the Meuse. In a succession of messages to General Eisenhower in mid-December he expressed his doubts. On the twenty-second he wrote, "I am not optimistic that the attack of the Third Army will be strong enough to do what is needed and I suggest Seventh German Army will possibly hold off Patton from interfering with the progress westward of Fifth Panzer Army." He added, "In this case I will have to deal unaided with both Fifth and Sixth Panzer Armies." As late as the twenty-fifth he wrote Ike that if the Allies intended to take the initiative they would need more troops, and indicated that they could be found only by withdrawing American forces from salients and holding shorter fronts. Bradley, Hodges, Ridgway, and I all expressed strong disagreement. Ridgway and I were much closer to our own troops and had far more accurate knowledge of conditions than Montgomery, who placed too much faith in the daily reports of "phantom" observers, junior British staff officers, whom he placed at our headquarters. Bradley protested Montgomery's delay in launching the counterattack of the VII Corps, but to no avail.

Meanwhile the British press had again taken up the cudgels for the appointment of Montgomery as a single ground-force commander in the West, to which was added criticism of Eisenhower as Supreme Commander. In a belated and mishandled attempt to turn off the British press, Monty held a press conference that created the impression it was largely his masterly handling of the situation and the timely interposition of British troops that saved the north flank of the Bulge. There is no question that it was reassuring to Courtney Hodges to know that Horrocks' 30 Corps was immediately available as a backup for the First Army, but only one division actually participated in the fighting, when the 53rd Division relieved Bolling's 84th Division so that the 84th could join the counterattack of the VII Corps. That press conference so irritated Bradley and Patton, and many of us who fought on the northern front of the Bulge, that it left a sour note to what actually was a great cooperative Allied Army and Air effort.

Worse than the great losses in men and material sustained by the Germans was the blow to the morale of the Nazi military and political machine. The German will to win ended with The Bulge. The net result of Hitler's gamble was assurance of Allied victory and the shortening of the war by at least six months.

CHAPTER XV

From the Roer to the Ruhr

When the VII Corps was squeezed out near St. Vith by the convergence of the XVIII A.B. and III Corps on January 22, it was out of action for the first time since D day. With approval of Courtney Hodges, I sent most of the key members of our staff to Paris and London, and accompanied by Jack Walsh, flew off on January 27 for a week's rest on the French Riviera at Cannes. In contrast to the snow and cold of the Ardennes, the Mediterranean was bathed in warm sunshine. We returned to our CP in Kornelimünster on February 5 greatly refreshed and ready for another crack at the Fifth Panzer Army.

Following elimination of the Bulge, Montgomery's 21st Army Group was to launch a new Allied drive to the Rhine north of Cologne. General Simpson's American Ninth Army, consisting of the XIII and XIX Corps, had been assigned by Eisenhower to Monty's command. The Ninth was concentrated on the south flank of the 21st Army Group, north of Düren, along the Roer River, which it was scheduled to cross on February 10. Futile efforts had been made to bomb out the Roer River dams, so as to prevent the Germans from flooding the stream after the attack started. On February 9 the enemy destroyed the discharge valves on the dams, turning the upper reaches of the normally placid Roer into a raging torrent and flooding areas downstream to a mile in width. Simpson had postponed his attack until February 23, a day before the reservoirs were calculated to run dry, hoping thereby to gain some surprise.

The VII Corps, now consisting of the 104th and the 8th Infantry Divisions, Brigadier General Briant E. Moore commanding the latter, and the 3rd Armored, was to attack across the Roer in conjunction with the XIX Corps on its left, seize Düren, and protect the right flank of the Ninth Army on the drive to the Rhine. The two infantry divisions abreast, 8th Division on the right, led off the attack at 3:30 A.M., February 23, astride the Aachen–Düren–Cologne autobahn. The Germans had blown the Roer bridge at Düren and the current was so swift that the initial crossings had to be made in assault boats. In the 8th Division zone south and upstream from Düren, where the stream was a vicious torrent, the boats were to have been powered by motors, but in the cold dampness few of the motors would start and the men had to paddle or row across. A few boats managed to get across but others capsized or were swamped. Fortunately the Germans were surprised and offered little resistance to the 3rd Battalion of the 28th Infantry Regiment. But as soon as the crossings were discovered, the enemy opened up with prearranged artillery fires which, after daylight, were joined with direct machine-gun fire from the high banks beyond the river and from the open upstream flank. The only feasible way to cross in the 13th Infantry zone was by ferries. Despite heroic efforts by corps and division engineers to keep the ferries operating, all were shot away by noon. Heavy counter-battery fire and fighter-bomber support could not blast out the concealed and dug-in enemy artillery, mortars, and machine guns. They prevented any successful bridge construction in the 8th Division zone until after dark, when a vehicular bridge was built across the concrete piers of the autobahn bridge at Düren. But it was not until the night of February 25 that the southern half of Düren was cleared.

The 104th Division, farther downstream where the current was not as swift, had better luck. Initial waves of the two leading regiments got across the Roer with little opposition, but as soon as daylight came enemy artillery fire made bridge-building almost impossible. Just north of Düren, in spite of heavy shelling, the engineers had almost completed a light ponton bridge by early afternoon, when a single hidden artillery piece got the range and destroyed much of the bridge with direct hits. At other bridge sites construction could not even start until after dark, and except for the one bridge at the autobahn site, no bridge was open to traffic until the twenty-fifth. The engineers of the VII Corps, under the personal direction of Colonel Mason Young, finally succeeded in constructing nine bridges for the 8th and 104th Divisions, but took 154 casualties in doing so.

Fortunately the 12th Volks Grenadier Division, its morale probably

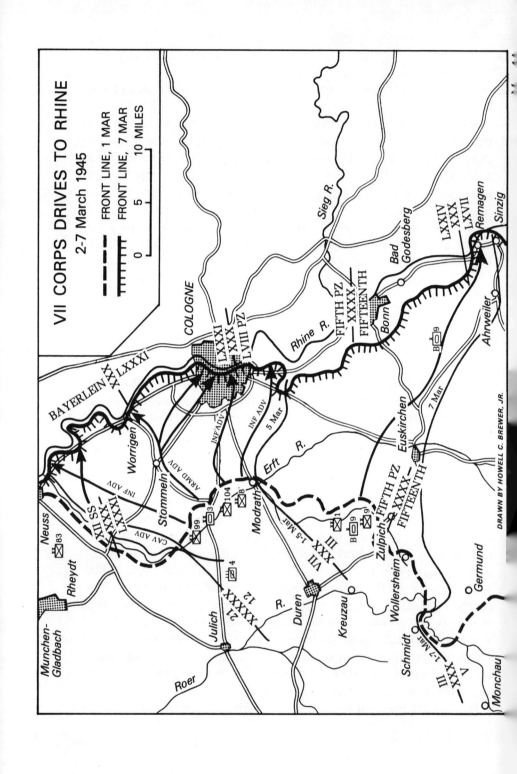

VII CORPS DRIVES TO RHINE
2-7 March 1945

FRONT LINE, 1 MAR
FRONT LINE, 7 MAR

0   5   10 MILES

DRAWN BY HOWELL C. BREWER, JR.

COLOGNE

Sieg R.

Rhine R.

Bad Godesberg

Bonn

Remagen
Sinzig
Ahrweiler

LXXIV
XXX
LXVII

FIFTH PZ
XXXX
FIFTEENTH

BAYERLEIN
XXX LXXXI

LXXXI
XXX
LVIII PZ

Worrigen

Stommeln

INF ADV

INF ADV

ARMD ADV

5 Mar

Erft   R.

Euskirchen

7 Mar

B 9

Neuss

83

INF ADV

CAV ADV

XII SS
XXX
LXXXI

99

33

104

8

Modrath

1-5 Mar

VII
XXX
III

B 9

11

Zulpich
FIFTH PZ
XXXX
FIFTEENTH

Wollersheim

Germund

Schmidt

1-7 Mar

V
XXX
III

Monchau

Rheydt

Munchen-
Gladbach

Roer

Julich

21
XXXXX
12

4

Duren   R.

Kreuzau

shattered by the punishment it received in the Bulge, failed to counterattack against the weak American toehold, and by February 26, VII Corps had a firm bridgehead around Düren which was linked up with McLain's XIX Corps front east of Jülich. I directed Rose's 3rd Armored to move into the Düren bridgehead on the night of the twenty-fifth, prepared to attack on the twenty-sixth in the first phase of the VII Corps drive on Cologne.

VII Corps Drives on Cologne

The checkerboard pattern of towns on the Cologne plain, most of which were organized for defense by the Germans, suited perfectly the organization and tactics employed by General Rose in spearheading the attack of the Corps. By now I made a standard practice of attaching an infantry regiment from one of our infantry divisions to the 3rd Armored Division. This enabled Rose to form six task forces, each consisting of a battalion of tanks and a battalion of infantry, each task force usually reinforced with artillery, engineers, and tank destroyers. The Division Reconnaissance Battalion, reinforced, was often used as a seventh task force. Rose normally attacked in four columns, pitting one or two task forces against each town in turn, permitting variation in maneuver and providing some rest for those not actively engaged. The task force commanders, Doan, Kane, Welborn, Lovelady, Hogan, and Richardson were all great combat leaders, as were the combat commanders, Hickey, Boudinot, Howze, and, of course, Maurice Rose.

At this stage of the campaign we usually had two or more infantry divisions, which followed up the armor, protecting the flanks and cleaning out any resistance bypassed by the armor. As we approached the Erft River, ten miles from Cologne, the 8th, 104th, and 99th Divisions took over the assault mission of breaking across that river. They had accomplished this task against light resistance by the evening of March 1. The 99th Infantry Division, Major General Walter E. Lauer commanding, had been added to the VII Corps when we took over responsibility from the XIX Corps for the zone north of Cologne between the Erft and the Rhine.

The city of Cologne was guarded on the west by a low, flat ridge, the Vorgebirge, which provided excellent observation over the flat land west of the city. This land was potted with open-pit lignite mines, intermingled with flooded areas, slag piles, factories, and small towns. To the northwest of Cologne the countryside was flat and pastoral with no major obstacles. I decided to pass the 3rd Armored around the north end of the Vorgebirge and attack Cologne from the northwest, with the 99th Division on its left flank, while the 104th and 8th Divisions moved on the city from the west and southwest.

The 3rd Armored attacked before dawn on March 2 and made some progress, but the 9th Panzer Division, fighting stubbornly behind a series of antitank ditches and field fortifications, prevented a breakthrough. The following morning, in another predawn attack, Combat Command Hickey caught the Germans by surprise and drove to the edge of Stommeln, cutting the main road north of the city, while the 104th cleared the crest of the Vorgebirge along the Düren–Cologne highway. It was now only a question of time before the city would be surrounded up to the Rhine. This was accomplished on March 4 when Boudinot drove on to the Rhine at Worringen.

I got quite a thrill as I crossed the Vorgebirge with Jack Walsh the following morning and saw the great city, the fourth largest in Germany, spread out before us. Smoke hung over the city from the factories, many of which were still operating. The great cathedral towered above the smoke, seemingly undamaged despite its nearness to the main railway station, which was an empty shell from the many bombings, and to the Hohenzollern bridge over the Rhine, two spans of which had been blown by the Germans a day or so before. As we drove into the outskirts in search of Rose's CP, I was relieved to find that, while sporadic fighting was still going on, no effort was being made to turn Cologne into a Stalingrad. Rose was confident that in a couple of days he would have the city cleared.

It was unsafe to aproach the cathedral at that time but I returned a few days after to show "Beetle" Smith and Air Marshal Tedder around. We entered the Dom and talked to one of the priests who had stayed throughout the war. The floor of the nave was littered with rubble from the interior ceiling, which the priest said had finally collapsed only a few days before. Even in this unkempt condition the nave was awe inspiring in its soaring gothic height. The cathedral had not been bombed but the north tower had been nicked near its base by a small stray bomb, which caused no structural damage. As at Aachen, the escape was almost miraculous, for the cathedral was circled with gutted ruins. The china shop on the Domplatz where Gladys had bought her fine Rosenthal dinner service in 1921 was obliterated. But none of this could take away the majesty of the magnificent twin spires of the cathedral, which towered above the surrounding destruction.

Rose's time estimate proved correct. By noon, March 7, the city was in our hands and Briant Moore's 8th Division had sliced around its south side to the Rhine, completing its encirclement. Capture of Cologne marked another major phase of our operations since D day. We had come well over six hundred miles from Utah beach, and the day before had captured our 140,000th prisoner, better than half the number taken by the First Army, and more than the entire Third Army had captured to that date. This last show had been one of our most successful, netting over 13,000 prisoneres, almost 1,000 per day.

In the middle of all this activity General Eisenhower came through on a quick swing round the front. He stopped by my CP west of Cologne long enough to say hello and express pleasure at how things were going. Before leaving he surprised me by asking to speak to me privately for a moment. He said he thought I was entitled to know how highly he regarded the work I had been doing, that I had been the ace corps commander since D day. He said that this came not only from his own observations but from Monty, Brad, and Courtney. He went on to say that Gerow had been selected in January to head the new Fifteenth Army, then intended for postwar occupation duty in Germany, because he also had a fine record and was much senior to me, but that if the opportunity for an army command ever arose again, I would be nominated. I had given no thought to an army command and would have hated to give up the VII Corps at that time. I felt certain that the war in Europe was nearing its end and that the Fifteenth Army would never see any real action. Having commanded the VII Corps from D day, I wanted to have the privilege of leading it all the way to Berlin or wherever we were to meet the Russians. But I did appreciate Ike's words of esteem for what the Corps had accomplished.

To share with our troops the thrill of our capture of Cologne, as I had followed the fall of Cherbourg, I had a flag-raising ceremony on March 11, in the city stadium where I imagine many Nazi ceremonies had been held. This time, instead of glorifying Hitler, we would be raising an American flag on the Rhine for the first time since World War I, as a mark of his folly. I wrote to Mrs. Collins on March 11, 1945:

> Our ceremony was brief and simple. . . . A platoon from each major unit in the Corps acted as a guard of honor for the massed colors of all units. After this formation had been presented to me, the massed colors were marched to the front. I then presented an American flag to the color bearers and spoke briefly on the significance of our assembly and our purpose in again raising our flag on the Rhine. . . . The massed colors then marched to the flag pole which was at one end of the field. Arms were presented and as the band played "The Star Spangled Banner" the flag was run up and a squadron of fighter bombers, which had been furnishing us cover, wheeled by overhead. Twenty-five hundred men were in the stadium as spectators and I believe they will always remember that brief picture.

I am equally sure that the ceremony was not lost on the Germans passing by outside.

III Corps Captures the Remagen Bridge

The day Cologne fell, March 7, the First Army's III Corps on our right scored an even greater coup. A task force of the 9th Armored Division, commanded by Lieutenant Colonel Leonard Engeman and led by 1st Lieutenant Carl H. Timmerman, seized the planked-over railway bridge at Remagen, ten miles south of Bonn, before the Germans could destroy it. My old friend from the Philippines, Major General William H. "Bill" Hoge, commanding the CC "B," 9th Armored, rushed reinforcements to Remagen, where by dark a tenuous little bridgehead had been established by the gallant men of Engeman's task force.

Word of the bridge seizure was rapidly telephoned up the chain of command, each headquarters anxious to capitalize on the unexpected break, and General Hodges ordered engineers and boats to Remagen even before calling Bradley at 12th Army Group for approval to reinforce Engeman's toehold. Brad enthusiastically approved, despite a demurral from the SHAEF G-3, Major General Harold ("Pinky") Bull, who happened to be at Bradley's CP and who feared that a buildup at Remagen would lead nowhere and would detract from Montgomery's elaborately planned main effort north of the Ruhr. Ike's reaction was quick and decisive: "Well, Brad, we expected to have that many divisions [four] tied up around Cologne and now those are free. Go ahead and shove over at least five divisions instantly, and anything else that is necessary to make certain of our hold."

A hole in the flooring of the bridge from a last-second German demolition charge, which failed to demolish but did damage the structure, was repaired by the handful of engineers with Engeman's force, who while braving machine-gun and rifle fire finally patched the hole by midnight. Nine tanks managed to get across to furnish support for the 27th Armored Infantry Battalion, which fought off several platoon-sized counterattacks throughout the night. In the next twenty-four hours almost 8,000 men of the 9th Armored and 78th Infantry Divisions moved into the bridgehead.

Eisenhower's initial enthusiasm over the seizure of the Remagen bridge began to cool under pressure from his combined British-American staff, still intent on furnishing maximum support to Montgomery's attack north of the Ruhr. Over the protests of Bradley and Hodges, and to the distress of everyone in the First Army, SHAEF decreed that the bridgehead force was to be limited to five divisions and daily advances limited to one thousand yards. Furthermore, when the Cologne –Frankfurt autobahn was reached, only six miles from the Rhine, the First Army was to halt until Eisenhower gave the order to advance in conjunction with the 21st Army Group under Monty, which was not scheduled to cross the Rhine until March 23.

Hodges Expands the Remagen Bridgehead

But Courtney Hodges did not delay in reinforcing the bridgehead. As soon as VII Corps cleared Cologne he sideslipped the Corps to the south and directed me to take over from the III Corps the responsibility for capturing Bonn, which the 1st Division was attacking. The 1st Division, now commanded by Brigadier General Cliff Andrus, who had succeeded Huebner when the latter took over the Vth Corps in January, passed to my command. Though Bonn was strongly contested by elements of the German 3rd Parachute Division in a "last ditch" stand, I was happy that Andrus' men were able to clear Bonn without much damage to the famous university and with none to Beethoven's birthplace, which I had visited from Coblenz in 1919.

By March 14 the III Corps, with some urging from Hodges, had crossed the 9th Division into the bridgehead and made room there for the 1st Division, the leading unit of the VII corps. I crossed the Rhine on the fourteenth, on reconnaissance, over a ponton bridge built by the III Corps while the Remagen bridge was undergoing much-needed repairs. As I wrote Mrs. Collins at the time:

> The river was as green and as swift as I remembered it, and its terraced vine-clad hills and placid villages as charming as ever. I had intended, like most American soldiers, to at least spit in the Rhine, but I was too lost in memories to remember such rudeness. In a minute we were pulling up the far bank and running along the river road past a carefully trimmed double row of shade trees, not yet in leaf, with their accompanying benches. Only now there were no quiet German burghers sitting on these benches, sipping beer from brown mugs as they half-dozed in complacent contemplaction of their beloved Rhine. If they had only had sense enough to sit tight on their benches when the neurotic Hitler awoke them to illusions of grandeur! In their place on Rhine Anlangen were antiaircraft gunners, tankers, engineers and doughboys rushing about with characteristic American dash, too busy to take in much of the beauty but bent upon the task of preserving and enlarging their precious bridgehead.

The 1st Division began crossing the river the next day with no opposition, using III Corps bridges and ferries. The Division completed its crossing on March 16, taking position to the right of the 78th Division, commanded by Major General Edwin P. Parker, which passed to control of the VII Corps as I assumed command of the northern sector of the bridgehead.

During the next five days the VII Corps Engineers built three floating bridges across the Rhine. To stimulate interest and enhance morale among our fine engineers, I told the commander Mason Young that I wanted them to break the time record of about 24 hours for bridging the Rhine, established by the 1st Division engineers after World War I at the site of Caesar's bridge near Coblenz, known to every high school student of Latin. Mason's men broke that record, completing the first two bridges in 22 and 17:45 hours respectively. I then cajoled him into accepting a challenge to bridge the river in 10 hours, a record

I felt might stand for all time. He demurred at first but when I said I would buy beer for the whole battalion if they succeeded, his owl-like face lit up and he accepted. On March 21, a short distance south of Bonn, the 237th Combat Engineer Battalion, commanded by Lieutenant Colonel Hershel Lynn, assisted by Company E, 23rd Armored Engineer Battalion and a company of the 238th Combat Engineer Battalion, completed our last bridge, measuring 1,308 feet, in 10:11 hours. I of course ignored the extra eleven minutes. Then we had to scour the adjacent towns along the Rhine to find enough beer to quench the thirst of the jubilant engineers at the party I gave for them. They posted a sign on the bridge: "The Beer Bridge—Short Cut to the C.B.I." The C.B.I. was the China–Burma–India theater. General Eisenhower was so impressed with this engineering feat that he referred to it in a letter to General Marshall on March 26, 1945, only in telling the story he raised my ante from beer to champagne. I could not have afforded champagne and the men would have preferred beer anyway.

On the morning of March 17, I again crossed into the bridgehead on a ponton bridge, this time to check on the operations of the 78th and 1st Divisions moving up the Seig River, which was to be used as a protective barrier for the north flank against counterattacks from the Ruhr. The German Fifteenth Army under General Bayerlein had moved into the area north of the Seig, from where Bayerlein wanted to counterattack. Field Marshal Model, commander of Army Group B, feared that the Americans would make their main effort to the north across the Seig in their attack against the Ruhr, so held up Bayerlein until the Seig defenses could be strengthened. I was favorably impressed by General Parker and his division, serving with the VII Corps for the first time. Cliff Andrus, who had been Huebner's artillery commander in the 1st Division, was proving a good successor to Huebner.

I had intended to return across the Rhine on foot, by way of the Remagen bridge, which had been closed to vehicles since the thirteenth while the engineers, who said the bridge was hanging by its teeth, tried valiantly to save it. Unfortunately the cumulative effect of the initial demolition charge, the heavy vibration from our tanks and infantry, a few hits from long-range artillery, and the blasts of nearby bombs, combined with the weight of heavy engineer equipment, finally caused the bridge to collapse. The end came without warning during a quiet period, crushing or dropping into the river many of our engineers working on the bridge. Twenty-eight men were killed and ninety-three injured. It was a tragic loss but we now had enough ponton bridges to sustain our attack.

I Revisit Coblenz am Rhein

I took advantage of a lull in the action on the twenty-third to run up to Coblenz, in the Third Army area, to see what had happened to my post–World War I "home town." Sergeant Davis drove Jack Walsh, Brigadier General Thomas North, a visitor from the War Department, and me through the lovely countryside I knew well. Because Coblenz was an important rail center at the confluence of the Moselle and the Rhine, the city had been heavily bombed. Our 8th Infantry Stein Strasse barracks was a blackened shell, as was the Festhalle, our billets on Mainzer Strasse, and the palace where Gladys and I were married. As we sped past the Festhalle, we came under observation from the town of Pfaffendorf, across the Rhine, and without any warning a burst of machine-fun fire splattered around us. Luckily none of us was hit, but I did feel annoyed at being shot at in my "home town." I felt better when the thought occurred to me to see if there was any wine left in the Dienhart cellars, off Jesuiten Platz. Thanks to a heavy guard of MPs, there was still a goodly supply. When the old German caretakers learned that I had been stationed in Coblenz, they got out their keys and opened a barred section of the cellars where the best Rhine and Moselle wines were stored. They loaded our jeep with Bernkasteler Doktor and Rudesheimer Riesling and a case of fine champagne.

Next day our Chief of Staff, Dick Partridge, who loved German wine, persuaded me to allow him to risk a second poaching of the Third Army territory. But I did whittle him down from a two-and-a-half-ton truck to a three-quarter-tonner. Amazingly, he came back alive with a truckload of the best German wines, which set up our mess for the rest of the war.

First Army Prepares to Outflank the Ruhr

When the VII Corps first moved across the Rhine, General Bradley had discussed the situation with me. Considering the limited number of divisions then allowed to the First Army in the bridgehead, I had suggested that we attack to the north without delay, before the enemy could build up his defenses north of the Seig River, while resting our left flank along the river until we knew more as to when and how Montgomery's attack north of the Ruhr would develop. Brad was right in turning down this suggestion and projecting a deeper penetration to the east, south of the Seig, before beginning the envelopment of the Ruhr. But this would require more troops than was initially authorized by SHAEF.

Hodges on March 19 received from General Bradley an authorization for four additional divisions in the First Army, plus a directive to be prepared, from March 23 on, to break out of the bridgehead toward Limburg in the Lahn valley, to form a junction with the Third Army, once Patton was across the Rhine. The two armies were then to attack astride the Lahn to Kassel, where the First Army was to turn north to form the south pincer of a double envelopment of the Ruhr, in conjunction with the Ninth Army under Montgomery.

By March 22 the VII Corps troops east of the Rhine, now consisting of the 78th and 1st Infantry Divisions and Combat Command "Howze," 3rd Armored, had reached the limiting line imposed on the First Army by SHAEF, a limitation that neither Hodges nor I could ever understand.

Patton in characteristic fashion made his surprise move across the Rhine near Mainz under cover of darkness on the night of March 22–23, beating Montgomery over by approximately twenty-four hours, much to Patton's delight. Bradley was now ready to launch the First Army's breakout drive, with the VII Corps on the north flank; the III Corps—now commanded by Major General Van Fleet, who had succeeded Milliken on March 17—in the center; and Huebner's V Corps on the right.

The "Spearhead" 3rd Armored Division, with the 414th Infantry (104th Division) attached, was to lead the attack of VII Corps, passing through the 104th Division—which had crossed the Rhine on the twenty-second—and the 1st Division. Minor opposition would be bypassed by the armor, and eliminated by the infantry troops. The initial

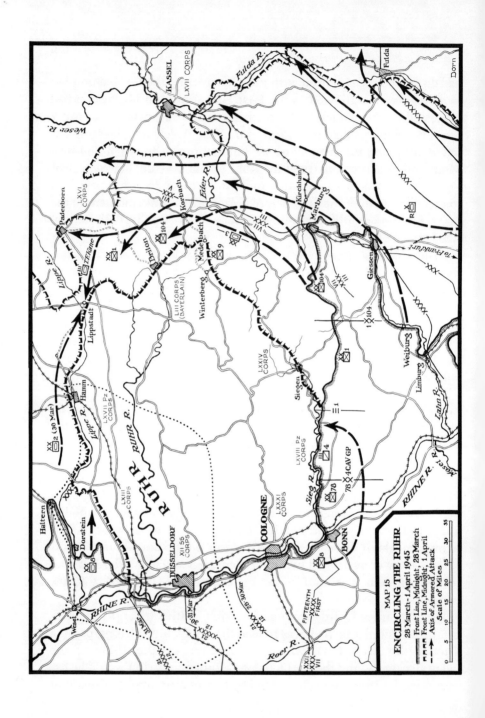

MAP 15

ENCIRCLING THE RUHR

28 March–1 April 1945

Front Line, Midnight, 28 March
Front Line, Midnight, 1 April
Axis of Armored Attack

Scale of Miles

0   5   10   15   20   25   30   35

Corps objective was the high ground and road center at Altenkirchen, but the 3rd Armored was to be prepared to exploit toward Marburg on the upper Lahn. The 78th Division was to protect the left flank of the corps along the Seig River, relieving elements of the 1st Division as far east as Merten, thirteen miles from the Rhine, as the attack of the 1st progressed. The 8th Division and the 4th Cavalry Group, which were patroling the west bank of the Rhine between Cologne and Remagen, were to be relieved by the 88th Division, whereupon they were to assemble in the vicinity of Bonn in Corps reserve. The Cavalry was to be prepared to cross the Rhine and take over the defense of the north flank of the corps east of Merten, progressively, as the 1st Division advanced.

The First Army Attacks March 25, 1945

The attack of the First Army went off on March 25 against only light resistance except along the Seig, where the 1st Division repulsed a series of counterattacks. By the twenty-eighth the 3rd Armored had blazed ahead to Marburg, capturing that medical and cultural center of 25,000 people with virtually no damage to the thirteenth-century cathedral or the famed unversity, founded in 1527. As an indication of how surprised the Germans were at the arrival of our troops, a trainload of civilians and convalescent soldiers being brought to Marburg for rest and rehabilitation was halted just outside the city by our tanks.

With the fall of Marburg, General Bradley decided the time had come to turn the First Army to the north to link up with the Ninth Army in the Kassel–Paderborn area, completing the encirclement of the Ruhr, after which the Ninth Army would revert to Bradley's command. Again the VII was to make the First Army's main effort. Our east flank would be protected by the III and V Corps, but we would be responsible for our inside (left) flank, which included our sector along the west bank of the Rhine south of Cologne and extended almost two hundred miles as we neared Paderborn.

VII Corps Turns North on Paderborn

The 3rd Armored Division led off the VII Corps drive on Paderborn with Combat Commands Boudinot and Howze abreast, Boudinot on the right, each CC in two columns, separated by from three to five miles, preceded by the division Reconnaissance Battalion. CC Hickey followed in the center, prepared to assist either flank. General Rose, accompanied by his aide, Major Robert Bellinger, rode in a jeep close behind the leading elements. The artillery commander, Colonel Frederick Brown, and Lieutenant Colonel Wesley A. Sweat, the G-3, in another jeep, and an armored car with radio communications, completed Rose's party.

CC Howze, normally the reserve command, did not often get an opportunity to lead a major attack. Its commander, Bobby Howze, was bent on making the most of it. His orders to his two task forces, Hogan and Richardson, were "Just go like hell!" Hogan on the left flank ran into some stiff roadblocks, but Richardson drove headlong until his force reportedly discovered in Brilon a warehouse full of champagne, which naturally slowed it down. Richardson pushed on until near midnight when, concerned about reports of tanks moving south from an SS training center near Paderborn, he halted for the night short of Paderborn. Task Force Hogan, like the turtle in Aesop's fable, had fought through the night, passing Richardson, to within five miles of the town, after covering almost ninety miles over twisting country roads, the longest day's advance of the war. Comparable advances were made by CC Boudinot. To protect our west flank I inserted the 8th Division between the 4th Cavalry group and the 1st Division. I kept shifting the 1st Division northward because I wanted it immediately available to turn east after we reached Paderborn.

During the drive east from the Remagen bridgehead and north to Paderborn the only way I could keep in touch with our widely separated units was by cub airplane. I spent a large part of my time flying from one CP to the next, consulting division commanders and giving them direct oral instructions, while Dick Partridge "kept store" at the Corps CP, with which I was in constant touch by radio.

The second day of the move north from Marburg, all columns began to run into small groups of enemy tanks and foot soldiers armed with panzerfausts in advance of a hastily organized defensive line manned by students from the training center in Paderborn and an SS tank replacement battalion of some sixty Tiger and Panther tanks.

Some of these tanks apparently were manned by instructors from the training center. They and their students fought with skill and fanatic fervor, slowing the advance of our tankers.

Late on the afternoon of the thirtieth, I had landed in a pasture alongside one of Boudinot's columns south of Korbach. I flagged down a jeep to drive me into Korbach, where I joined Boudinot. He had just had a brush with one of the delaying enemy groups and his aide had been badly wounded in the jeep seat next to him. Unperturbed as always, this quiet, highly competent leader invited me to ride with him. By the time Korbach was cleared it was getting dark and Boudinot wisely decided to coil his columns for the night. I radioed back to my CP, which had moved up to Marburg, that I would remain overnight on the road with Boudinot. We had halted in a sunken part of the road, above which, one of the young enemy soldiers who had manned a panzerfaust and had been shot through the head, was slowly dying. One of our medics had examined him and said there was nothing that could be done to save him. Our minds were temporarily diverted from the wayside tragedy by the unexpected crunch of artillery fire off to our left. We crawled up the bank and were relieved to find that the explosions were coming from a German ammunition train, which our next column to the west had set afire. The ruddy glow from the burning train lit up the lowering clouds, brightened from time to time as an exploding shell rocketed skyward, so that as we came back down the embankment we could see that death had come mercifully to the wounded German, whose crumpled body lay at the foot of the opposite bank.

Death of General Rose

At the same time, unknown to us, tragedy was striking again not far from us to the northwest, this time at the very heart of the 3rd Armored Division. Boudinot's left task force, commanded by Colonel John C. Welborn, followed closely by General Rose's party, had tried to bypass Paderborn on a secondary road. Dusk was falling when enemy small arms and tank fire cut off Rose's party from Welborn's task force. Rose radioed to CC Hickey, which was following Welborn, to have Task Force Doan come up and clean out this opposition, but before Doan could arrive, four enemy tanks appeared, coming up the road from the south. Rose had General Brown call for artillery fire on them, then led his party in a dash to get by the tanks. Brown succeeded in getting by in his jeep, but one of the tanks suddenly swerved, pinning Rose's jeep against a tree. The German commander motioned with a "Burp" gun to the occupants to dismount with their arms up. They had no alternative. Then he shouted something about "Pistolen." Major Bellinger and the jeep driver, Tech. 5 Glen H. Shounce, who like most officers carried their weapons in shoulder holsters, dropped their holsters without lowering their arms. Rose, who habitually wore a pistol belt, dropped his arms, presumably to remove his belt. But the tank commander, evidently thinking that Maurice was reaching for his revolver, fired a stream of bullets at point-blank range. Rose, killed instantly, pitched forward in the dusty road. Bellinger and Shounce dived for the ditches and in the confusion managed to escape. Colonel Sweat and the crew of the armored car were taken prisoner.* The following morning Rose's body was found where he fell, his pistol still in its belt, and the abandoned jeep untouched. The German force had withdrawn without knowing that it had killed a division commander.

Maurice Rose was the top armored commader in the Army when he was killed. Tall, handsome, always dressed immaculately, even in combat, he was a commanding figure who claimed instant respect from officers and men alike. Somewhat stern, and wholly dedicated to defeating the Nazis, perhaps because of his Jewish origin, which I learned about only after his death, he was not given to easy comradeship. Yet I came to have great respect and affection for him. I will always remember him as he met me one day on the Cologne plain, outside his CP located in an exposed house at the very end of a small town.

"Maurice," I said, "do you *always* have to have your CP in the last house in town?"

He drew himself up as he replied: "General, there is only one way I know to lead this division, and that's at the head of it!"

*A few days later Bellinger made his way to our CP and gave me a detailed account of what happened.

And that is how he died, at the head of his Spearhead Division. God rest his soul.

Ruhr Encirclement Completed

As the 3rd Armored neared Paderborn, Field Marshal Model realized that his entire army group would soon be trapped in the Ruhr industrial complex unless he was permitted to withdraw or could receive help from outside. The reserves necessary for counteratack from outside were nonexistent, and Hitler's edicts precluded withdrawal. Model decided to attempt to break out of the Ruhr by having Bayerlein's LIII Corps, his only reserve, attack from Winterberg, south of Paderborn, against the west flank of the First Army. We began to get reports from prisoners of preparations for a counterattack from that area.

To meet this threat, which was made more serious because the 1st Division was vacating the area as it moved north following the left of the 3rd Armored, I had the 104th Division take responsibility for the Winterberg sector. Then as the 104th moved north to plug another threatened escape route via Brilon, General Hodges transferred the 9th Division from the III Corps to the VII Corps. I inserted Craig's 9th Division into line opposite Winterberg, behind the 104th. I now had five infantry divisions, the 78th, 8th, 9th, 104th, and 1st, plus our 4th Cavalry Group, strung out in a 175-mile arc from Remagen to the outskirts of Paderborn, boxing in Model's Army Group B. We were thinly spread, even though the 9th and 104th had beaten back Bayerlein's efforts to break through. But an escape route was still open on the north side of the Ruhr, west of Paderborn, on the front of the Ninth Army, which, as far as I then knew, was still under Montgomery's control.

Anxious to close this gap, as well as relieve pressure on my 9th and 104th Division, I went outside normal command channels on the evening of March 31 and telephoned, around three sides of the Ruhr, direct to General Simpson's Ninth Army headquarters. Thanks to our fine Signal Corps field communications, I got a clear connection with Simpson, whom I knew well from our service together as instructors at the Army War College. I explained the situation to him and said, "For God's sake, Bill, get Monty to let you release the 2nd Armored

Division for a drive on Paderborn. I will send a combat command of the 3rd Armored across to meet the 2nd at Lippstadt. We will then have the Ruhr wrapped up." Simpson agreed. The 2nd Armored actually had already started east and had advanced close to Beckum, thirty-five miles west of Paderborn. The next morning, on Easter Sunday, to match our previous Christmas Day defeat of the 2nd Panzer Division in the Bulge, CC "B" of the 2nd Armored and Task Force Kane of the 3rd Armored met at Lippstadt, completing the encirclement of the Ruhr, which we in the VII Corps proudly named the "Rose pocket." Though we did not know it at the time, we had trapped over 300,000 men of Model's Army Group B, including its commander, who committed suicide.

Doyle Hickey Takes Over the 3rd Armored Division

When word of General Rose's death reached Courtney Hodges he called Bradley at once, and, apparently feeling that only a man of the caliber of Ernie Harmon could take Rose's place, asked Brad for Harmon, who was then commanding the XXII Corps in Gerow's newly formed Fifteenth Army. Bradley approved. I had not been consulted, unusual in such a case, and was not informed of Harmon's assignment until two days later. Meanwhile, Doyle Hickey, the senior Combat Command leader, had assumed command of the 3rd Armored Division. When I learned that Harmon had reported to take over the 3rd Armored, I protested to General Hodges. Hickey had been with the Division for three years and had commanded CC "A" with distinction in all its campaigns under the VIIth Corps. Though he did not have the magnetic personality or drive of Maurice Rose, he was highly esteemed throughout the 3rd Armored, and I had full confidence in his ability to lead the division. I told Courtney that, much as I admired Ernie Harmon, I felt that in fairness to Hickey, Doyle was entitled to a shot at command of the division. Rose had instilled a fierce pride within all ranks of the 3rd Armored. There had been a subtle rivalry between the two big divisions, which had twice served together in the VII Corps, and I knew that placing a 2nd Armored man in command of the 3rd Division right after Rose's death, would not sit too well with the men of the 3rd. Harmon felt as I did, and Hodges, after hearing my argument, agreed, as did Brad. Harmon returned to his former post without any loss of prestige, and Hickey continued his command of the 3rd Armored with great success.

Hickey still had a tough fight with the hard-core Nazis of the SS Panzer training center in Paderborn, hastily organized as the Ersatzbrigade Westfalen, but Paderborn had fallen by April 1 and all efforts of the Germans to break out of the Ruhr had been repulsed. By April 5, VII Corps had shifted its front to the east and was ready for a final drive, leading to a meeting with the Russians in or near Berlin.

CHAPTER XVI

We Meet the Russians on the Elbe

As forces of the Western Allies headed east after the encirclement of the Ruhr, General Eisenhower's plan for the final major campaign on the Western Front consisted essentially of three parts. First, a thrust by Bradley's 1st Army Group straight across central Germany on the axis Erfurt–Leipzig–Dresden to a junction with the Russians on the Elbe River. Bradley's drive would be supported on the north by Montgomery's 21st Army Group, now consisting of the Second British and the First Canadian Armies, and assisted on the south by General Devers' 6th Army Group, comprising the American Seventh Army and the French First Army. Bradley's junction with the Russians would split Germany in two. The second and third parts of Eisenhower's plan called for concurrent advances by Montgomery to the north to cut off Denmark, and by Devers into Austria and the mountainous area to the south. After reaching the Elbe, Bradley would aid Montgomery and Devers as necessary.

Eisenhower's plan excluded any attempt to capture Berlin before the Russians could reach the city. This greatly upset Churchill, who now placed primary emphasis on the political influence that would accrue, in the postwar period, to the side that occupied Berlin. Eisenhower felt that it was a bit late to raise this political argument after the Western Allies had agreed at Yalta that the Russian occupation zone would include Berlin, and that the demarcation line separating the American and British zones from the Russians would be two hundred miles west of Berlin. Eisenhower had further irritated Churchill by advising Stalin of his plans, without first getting approval of the American-British Combined Chiefs of Staff.

The British, including their press, protested vigorously that Ike's plan should have reinforced Montgomery with American troops for one massive drive to capture Berlin ahead of the Russians, but instead had relegated British troops to a secondary role well to the north of Berlin. Eisenhower refused to change his plan and was backed by President Roosevelt and the American JCS.

When Bradley was asked by Eisenhower shortly after March 28 what it might cost to break through from the Elbe to Berlin, he had estimated 100,000 casualties. "A pretty stiff price for a prestige objective," Bradley had added, "especially when we've got to fall back and let the other fellow take over." So he had agreed with Eisenhower's decision not to attempt to race the Russians to Berlin. Yet in his letter of instructions to his army commanders, dated April 24, 1945, Bradley had directed the Ninth Army, which was nearest to the Elbe, to exploit any opportunity for seizing a bridgehead over the Elbe River and be prepared to continue the advance to the east on Berlin or to the northeast. In explaining this seeming contradiction of views as to Berlin, Bradley wrote later in his *Soldier's Story*, "This was not in preparation for an advance on Berlin . . . but only to establish a threat that might draw off German resistance from east of Berlin in front of the Russians." I suspect that there was more to it than that, that Brad wanted to be prepared to move on Berlin if the Germans had succeeded in holding off the Russians. He could afford some leeway in implementing Eisenhower's plans because, with return of the Ninth Army to the 12th Army Group, he now had under his command 4 armies comprising 12 corps and 48 divisions, totaling over 1,300,000 men, the largest American field force under a single commander in American history.*

Under Bradley's directive No. 20, the First Army, consisting of the VII Corps and Huebner's V Corps, was to advance east "along the axis Kassel–Leipzig to gain contact with the Soviet forces." As with the Ninth Army, the First was to "exploit any opportunity for seizing a bridgehead over the Elbe River and be prepared to continue the advance to the east thereof."

---

*On January 1, 1865, in the American Civil War, the entire Federal Army had 590,000 soldiers. Pershing's army in the Meuse–Argonne offensive of World War I totaled 1,200,000 combat troops.

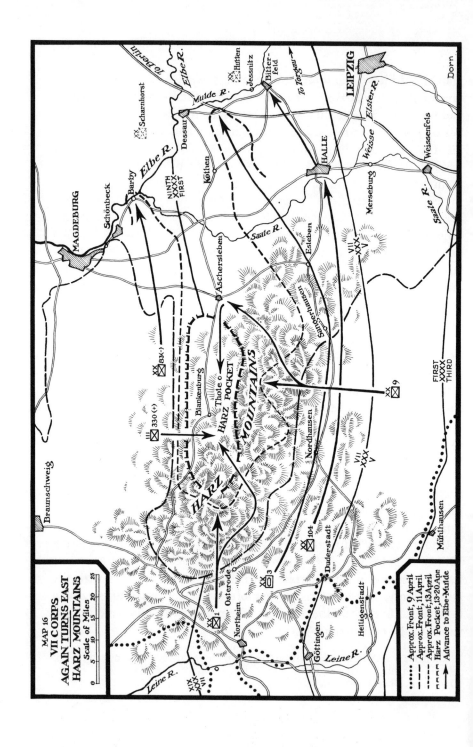

MAP 16
VII CORPS
AGAIN TURNS EAST
HARZ MOUNTAINS
Scale of Miles
0   5   10   15   20   25

LEIPZIG

MAGDEBURG

Braunschweig

Schönbeck

Barby

Schönbeck

Scharnhorst

To Berlin

Elbe R.

Mulde R.

Dessau

Köthen

NINTH
XXXX
FIRST

Aschersleben

Saale R.

Eisleben

Sangerhausen

HALLE

Merseburg

Weissenfels

Weisse

Elster R.

Saale R.

Jessnitz

Bitter-
feld

Hütten

To Torgau

Dorn

VII
XXX
V

FIRST
XXXX
THIRD

9

Thole

Blankenburg

HARZ POCKET

MOUNTAINS

Nordhausen

HARZ

Osterode

Northeim

Duderstadt

104

3

1

Göttingen

Heiligenstadt

Leine R.

Leine R.

Mühlhausen

VII
XXX
V

330 (+)

83 (-)

VII
XX

•••••• Approx. Front, 9 April
—·—·— Approx. Front, 11 April
— — — Approx. Front, 13 April
‒ ‒ ‒ Harz Pocket, 13-20 Apr
⟶ Advance to Elbe-Mulde

As the VII Corps moved north from Marburg in its envelopment of the Ruhr, I had kept the 1st and 104th Divisions positioned so that they could quickly follow the 3rd Armored Division in our anticipated drive to the east. We were set to go April 5th.

VII Corps Turns Again to the East

The 3rd Armored at once ran into stubborn resistance from remnants of Ersatzbrigade Westfalen that had withdrawn from Paderborn. The division, now under command of Doyle Hickey, did not reach the Weser River until April 7, by which time all bridges over that broad stream were destroyed, halting the armor. But I was glad to note, as I drove up to a point overlooking the Weser, that little or no enemy fire was coming from the hills on the far bank. The 104th Division, using ferries and a bridge in the adjacent V Corps zone, established footholds across the river, covering construction of six bridges by VII Corps engineers, thus enabling the 1st Division and tanks and artillery to cross. The 3rd Armored renewed its advance on April 9, passing through the two infantry divisions. The Leine River, east of the Weser, was crossed without difficulty, and the 3rd Armored, followed by Terry Allen's 104th, sped on to the east, south of the Harz Mountains. As they moved forward, they began to overtake hundreds of emaciated laborers, mostly Polish Jews, Russians, and other East Europeans in their black and white prison garb, hobbling along the roadsides from their liberated slave farms and factories. They were a pitiful sight to behold.

We were deeply saddened also by the news of President Roosevelt's death April 12. It was tragic that he could not have lived to see the Allies clinch the victory that he had done so much to help achieve.

The northern boundary of VII Corps, which separated it from Ray McLain's XIX Corps of the Ninth Army, back again on the left of the First Army, ran through the northwest corner of the Harz Mountains to the junction of Mulde and Elbe Rivers at Dessau. This placed the bulk of the Harz Mountains in the VII Corps zone of action. The mountains, with heights up to 3,700 feet, run generally eastward between the Leine and Salle Rivers. Hitler, in another of his grandiose aberrations, had directed Field Marshal von Kesselring to have the newly formed Eleventh Army organize and hold the Harz as a base from which the inchoate Twelfth Army was to counterattack to relieve Model's already doomed Army Group B in the Ruhr. We knew nothing of this impossible scheme at the time, but the Harz Mountains, sitting menacingly on the flank of Hickey's 3rd Armored and Terry Allen's 104th Division, could not be ignored. We were fortunate in having Cliff Andrus' 1st Division immediately available to take on the 70,000-man Eleventh Army that Kesselring had managed to assemble in the Harz under General Walter Lucht.

A veteran corps commander, Lucht made skillful use of the rough, heavily wooded terrain of the mountains, which the 1st Division later described, with some exaggeration, as "tougher than the Hürtgen Forest." While the Eleventh Army was made up largely of the remnants of units, it did contain some experienced soldiers as well as rabid young Nazis from nearby military schools and training centers. Using roadblocks, demolitions, and the many caves and mines in the heavy forests, they fought stubbornly against the steady advance of the Americans. The 9th Division had returned from the Ruhr pocket to VII Corps on April 14. I moved it into the eastern half of the Harz to put a triple squeeze on the enemy now trapped between the 1st and 9th Divisions on the west, south, and east, and 83rd Division of the Ninth Army on the north. General Hodges was not altogether satisfied with the methodical advance of the VII Corps troops, but, knowing that there was no escape for the Eleventh Army, I was loath to put undue pressure on our veteran 1st and 9th Divisions in the waning days of the war. The German commander, Lucht, evidently felt much the same about his troops. Though duty-bound to fight, he forswore a scorched-earth campaign and spared his troops and the civilian population as much as possible.

After six days of tough delaying actions, the end was in sight on April 19, when the 1st Division captured hill 1142, the dominant height in the mountains. Resistance ended the next day as units began to surrender en masse. On that day the 9th Division took over 8,000 prisoners and the 1st Division a like number, including the 100,000th PW captured by the 1st Division in World War II. Altogether, VII Corps accounted for over 80,000 PWs from the Harz, including 11,000 hospital patients. Fittingly for the great 1st and 9th Divisions, which had battled Hitler's armies from North Africa and Sicily, through France and across Germany, the end of their campaign came on April 20, Hitler's birthday.

April 20 happened to be a red-letter day for me for that and other reasons. It marked the twenty-eighth anniversary of my graduation from West Point, when I received the shiny gold bar of a 2nd Lieutenant, and on the same day that the fighting ended in the Harz Mountains I received word that I had been nominated by President Truman to be a Lieutenant General. I am not sure which elevation I prized more.

Word of confirmation by the Senate did not come until several days later. I happened to be at First Army headquarters when the confirmation cable arrived, including Hodges' promotion to General. Courtney and I exchanged congratulations. When I arrived back at our airport the entire Corps staff was there to greet me. There was a spontaneity to their greeting that touched me. I was even more pleased that many enlisted men individually stopped me in the next few days to add their congratulations.

3rd Armored Overruns Nordhausen

While the Harz Mountains were being cleared, Doyle Hickey's 3rd Armored Division was speeding by their southern fringe. On April 12, as our CP was moving into Nordhausen, in the Harz foothills, Doyle came to my headquarters and said his troops had just discovered a prison labor camp so ghastly that I would have to see it before I would believe its horrible condition. I went with him at once to the railway yards on the far edge of town. Alongside the tracks were nine or ten large warehouses in which slave laborers from a nearby underground factory were held, apparently when they rebelled or were too sick to work. There they were left, to starve to death or die of illness. Not knowing the nature of the warehouses, our bombers, a few days before Nordhausen was captured, had attacked these buildings as well as the railway. When our troops arrived most of the Nazi guards had fled, leaving the wounded and sick to their own devices.

The one building Hickey and I entered, which had not been hit by bombs, was a scene of utter horror. Hundreds of men in their striped prison uniforms were scattered about on the damp dirt floor, the dead and dying intermingled in straw, the only cover afforded them. As we looked in with a medical officer to weigh the problem that confronted us, wails and piteous pleas for food came from the living, while the stench of the dead filled the air. As I wrote home at the time:

> We took out about six hundred and fifty prisoners still alive but in such miserable stages of starvation that scores of them have since died. Almost three thousand dead were found in the buildings, most of whom had died of starvation or disease prior to the bombing. I directed our military government officer to collect German civilians, including the so-called "best people" of the town, members of the Hitler Jugend and German prisoners of war, to remove the bodies and inter them. We had the Burgomeister set aside a plot of ground overlooking the town, and these people were required to dig graves and carry every one of the dead up the hill and bury them. The local officials disclaimed any knowledge of the camp which, of course, was pure tommyrot. We are going to require them to erect a monument in this cemetery as a memorial to these dead.

A few days later I visited the underground factory where these prisoners had worked. This tremendous plant was contained in two enormous tunnels cut through a limestone ridge. Thirty or forty cross tunnels linked the two main shafts, each of which housed an assembly line, one for V-1 bombs, the other for the newer V-2s. The cross tunnels were filled with machine tools, component parts, and raw materials for the bombs, which were in all stages of production. Later, many of them were shipped back to the States, where I understand they were used for our first experimental rockets.

VII Corps Reaches the Mulde and Elbe

Stopping at Nordhausen only long enough to replenish supplies of gasoline and oil, the 3rd Armored resumed its advance early on April 12 and in two days had covered forty-five miles, clearing Sangerhausen and seizing crossings of the Saal River northwest of Halle, the objective of the 104th Division. The enemy had destroyed all bridges over the Saal on the direct approaches to the city, but Terry Allen, teaming well with Doyle Hickey, crossed the river on the assault bridges built by the Armored's engineers and attacked the city from the north. He penetrated the fringe defenses at once.

With the 3rd Armored already past Halle to the north, it was apparent that the city was doomed, but the hard-nosed commander of the hastily formed mixture of SS remnants, school troops, and antiaircraft gunners refused to surrender. After costly house-to-house fighting had broken out, he did agree to limit his defense to the industrial section of Halle so as to spare Allied and German patients in the city's hospitals. Even so, it took three days of senseless fighting to clear the city on April 19. Meanwhile the remainder of the division continued east through the next town to the Mulde, which it reached on April 21.

The 3rd Armored ran into tougher opposition east of the Salle River from two new divisions, Schornhorst and Ulrich von Hutton, formed from officer candidate schools of the army, and from the navy and Hitler Jugend organizations, containing a goodly proportion of experienced personnel. Hitler was said to have taken a personal interest in formation of these divisions, which may have accounted for their stubborn defense of the approaches to Dessau. They were endeavoring to hold a bridgehead west of the Elbe as a base from which the Twelfth Army, under Hitler's plan, was to have launched its effort to join the Eleventh in the Harz. Despite their skillful defense, they could not hold for long against the task forces of Hogan, Richardson, Welborn, and Lovelady that had handled the tougher SS and Panzer units in the past. But the 3rd Armored, operating on a front of twenty-five miles, was missing the back-up infantry divisions to which it had grown accustomed. The 1st and 9th Divisions were still winding up the Harz Mountains battle, and the 104th Division had its own broad front to cover south of Dessau. Still the organic infantry regiment of the 3rd Armored and attached infantry battalions had their hands full doubling back to the rear to wipe out enemy groups that had been bypassed by the armor, or had infiltrated into the rear areas. It was only after Hickey had sent patrols through each village back to the Saale to warn each Burgomeister to turn in all military personnel in or out of uniform and all arms, or face severe reprisal, that resistance ceased in rear of forward units.

Welborn reached the autobahn crossing of the Mulde two miles south of Dessau on April 15, though not before the bridge had been dropped into the broad shallow stream. Some infantrymen scrambled across the wreckage and established a small bridgehead, but spasmodic shelling, and a lack of immediately available equipment, delayed construction of a bridge until the following day when the decision of General Eisenhower not to attempt to seize Berlin caused Bradley to withdraw all bridgeheads across the Mulde.

On April 18, Task Force Hogan took the town of Aken on the Elbe west of Dessau, linking up there with Bill Simpson's Ninth Army. The 3rd Armored spent the next few days cleaning out the small towns along the Mulde before attacking Dessau. Task Forces Boles, Orr, Richardson, and Welborn, representing each of the three Combat Commands Doan, Boudinot, and Howze, which had done such splendid fighting from Normandy to the Elbe, closed in on Dessau and put an end to the house-to-house combat on April 22. Two days later I was able to report to Courtney Hodges that enemy resistance in the VII Corps zone was over.

During its 221 days of combat in Europe, practically all of which was with the VII Corps, the 3rd Armored distinguished itself as one of the finest armored divisions in the Army. From the Seine to the Elbe, the division led practically every attack of the Corps, richly earning its by-name as the Spearhead Division.

We Meet the Russians on the Elbe and Mulde

When Stalin learned from Eisenhower on March 31 that the Western Allies were planning to meet the Russians on the Elbe, instead of driving on Berlin, he at once regrouped his forces on the eastern front for a drive on Berlin. With resistance practically over throughout the First Army zone, the game now was to see which American unit would be the first to make contact with the Russians. During the next week large numbers of Allied PWs, individual German soldiers and civilians, fearful of the Russians, kept trying to cross the Mulde to our side. General Hodges issued instructions that only Allied PWs and German soldiers wishing to surrender would be permitted to cross. By the end of May the number of such Germans taken by the VII Corps alone had risen to over 75,000.

The Russian encirclement of Berlin was completed on April 25, and the same day the 173rd Regiment of the Russian 58th Guards Division of the XXXIV Corps, which had passed south of Berlin, met elements of the 69th Division of Huebner's V Corps, on our right, at Torgau on the Elbe. Two days later the 104th Division of VII Corps contacted the Soviet 118th Regiment at Pretzsch, also on the Elbe, north of Torgau. On April 29, VII Corps took over responsibility for the V Corps zone including the 69th and 2nd Infantry Divisions and the 9th Armored Division.

Shortly thereafter, in the course of a visit to the 69th Division, I received word that a Russian officer in Torgau wanted to see an American general. Curious as to what was going on at Torgau, I jeeped there with Jack Walsh. We had trouble finding the Russian, but finally locating him in a Wirtschaft. He was a chunky, powerfully built man, dressed in a rumpled field uniform and customary Russian boots that showed signs of rough campaigning. He looked more like a tough noncom than an officer, but he had "fighter" written all over him. We had no interpreter with us, but fortunately his English was understandable. Unfortunately I have no record of his name or rank, but he must have been the commander of the regiment opposite Torgau. He greeted us warmly and invited us into the cafe for the inevitable toasts. He first raised his glass to President Roosevelt, whom he praised as a friend of Russia, to which I replied, of course, in a toast to Marshal Stalin. Eisenhower, Koniev, Montgomery, and others were drunk to in turn. Each time my Russian host would jump to his feet and deliver an impassioned speech. What interested me was that he paid tribute to our military aid, particularly to our trucks, without which he said the Soviet army would never have reached the Elbe. There was no political commissar present to dampen his enthusiasm for our military assistance.

When we had finished our many toasts we drove up to the Elbe, where I watched in amazement as a group of Russian soldiers, using a hand-operated pile-driver, drove freshly cut logs into the muddy river bottom to serve as pilings for a foot bridge. No wonder the Russians were slow in closing on Berlin. As we stood watching this primitive bridge building—and a woman MP efficiently directing traffic on the far bank—I asked him about the disposition of his troops. With no sign of the secrecy usually associated with the Russians, he did not hesitate an instant, but pulled a wrinkled map from inside his tunic and pointed out the location of his troops along the east bank of the river, which he said they had orders not to cross. After I outlined our dispositions, he asked, "Are you digging in?" I replied, "Of course not." He turned to an aide and said, "Tell them not to dig in!" I wish that all Russians might have remained as open and friendly as he was.

A few days later General Baklanov, commanding the Russian XXXII Corps opposite us, accompanied by one of his division commanders and members of his staff, called on me in Leipzig, where I had moved our headquarters on April 30. I had a luncheon for them, to which I invited our division commanders and principal staff officers. Baklanov was a handsome young man, I would guess not over thirty-five. He had risen from the ranks to corps commander, which proved his ability. He could speak no English or French, so we had to converse through a Russian interpreter, which probably accounted for his stodginess. But after a few drinks of straight gin, the nearest thing to vodka that we could offer the Russians, Baklanov relaxed and was more at ease. He and his people were appreciative of our friendliness and I am sure were anxious to reciprocate. He repeatedly said how glad he was to be in Leipzig and how he had scarcely believed it possible a week before. The Russians still had some fighting to do, but I was invited to a return luncheon at his CP as soon as this was over.

Peace at Last

The war was now rapidly moving to an end, generating rumors and speculation as to when we were going home and what was to happen to the First Army. On May 1 the death of Hitler was announced and the same day word was received that Headquarters First Army had been accepted by General MacArthur for service in the Pacific. On the sixth, as Hodges prepared to return to the States, VII Corps passed to control of the Ninth Army, the first time we were out of the First Army since D day. Then on April 7 in General Eisenhower's headquarters in Reims, Field Marshal Keitel signed the unconditional surrender of the German forces, to become effective at 11:01, May 8.

The announcement was anticlimactic for us, because we had not been fighting since the fall of Dessau. We did get a thrill on the afternoon of the eighth when a group gathered at Corps headquarters to listen to the emotion-filled voice of the doughty Prime Minister of the United Kingdom make the first official announcement of the end of the war. Courtney Hodges had come by to say a word of appreciation, and I had our division commanders in to bid goodbye to him. We crowded around the radio to hear Churchill speak. Tired as he undoubtedly was, his voice had a triumphant ring that made his brief speech a stirring statement of victory. As he ended, I felt a keen sense of loss that President Roosevelt had not lived to speak for America in the glowing words that only he could have added to Churchill's announcement.

General Hodges and his staff left for the States shortly thereafter. I had to pinch-hit for Courtney in presenting decorations to a group of about sixty Russians in commemoration of the historic meeting of the First American and Fifth Guards Armies. The decorations ceremony and its aftermath had some interesting and amusing aspects. Arrangements had been agreed upon for the Russians to fly into the Leipzig airport, where I had a band and guard of honor to greet them. The commander of the Fifth Guards Army, General Jadov, and the Corps commander, Baklanov, were to be among them. But at the appointed hour of 10:00 A.M., there was no sign or word of the Ruskies. We waited and waited. Finally a light plane arrived with word that our guests were on their way, or ways, by automobile, in several organizational groups.

The officer courier estimated that they should all be in by 4:30 P.M., so we set a new ceremony for that hour in a square in front of the main hotel in Leipzig. We had planned a luncheon, which we now changed to dinner, and again lined up the band and guard of honor. Again, no Russians came. It was late afternoon before they began to arrive in driblets. Darkness was beginning to fall when Jadov and Baklanov appeared. We went ahead with the ceremony, though not all the Russians were present. I presented appropriate decorations, mostly Legions of Merit or Bronze Stars, according to the rank of the recipients, as was always the case with such ceremonial awards. General Jadov reciprocated with medals for our staff.

Some groups of Russians, probably coming from units located farthest from Leipzig, were still arriving when we went into the hotel for dinner. We had collected all the gin we could find for the myriad toasts, and filled in with Scotch, which our guests seemed to take to with no pain, as they did the fine dinner that the German cooks had prepared.

We were weary from the long drawn-out ceremony but enjoyed the dinner and the opportunity to talk, despite the necessity of interpreters, with these extraordinary people. I liked General Jadov and appreciated Baklanov more than I had at our luncheon meeting. Both had relaxed with a few drinks and acted more naturally after their initial self-consciousness. The trouble was that after dinner was over none of the Russians wanted to leave. When Jadov and Baklanov rose to go, our guests paid no attention to them. I did not want the generals to get away and leave us with the problem of persuading the rest of the company to follow. I asked Baklanov for help. He stood on a chair, and after rapping for order, shouted something in Russian, which must have meant "Charge!," for our guests took off pell-mell for the entrance door, sweeping the generals out to the sidewalk.

We had Jadov's and Baklanov's cars parked at the hotel entrance and had arranged an MP motorcycle escort to lead them out of town. There wasn't a chance. The crowd of Russians piled into their autos, parked around the square and adjacent streets, surged past the cars of the generals and drove off wildly into the night. We could only stand in amazement on the sidewalk and wave goodbye, wondering how such an outfit ever licked the Germans. Equally amazing, they all managed to find their way back across the Mulde and Elbe, without any serious accidents.

A few days later I drove with Jack Walsh to Baklanov's headquarters near Pilsen in Czechoslovakia for a luncheon. Elaborate preparations had been made for our visit. I sensed that a deliberate effort had been made to impress the townspeople of Russian-American friendship. After reviewing an honor guard, we walked several blocks to an inn, past small groups of Czechs who seemed wary of showing any enthusiasm. There was a staged welcoming committee of citizens at the inn, complete with a pretty little girl in native costume to present me with a bouquet of red roses, wrapped tightly in cellophane.

The excellent lunch was followed by a sparkling program of acrobatics, singing, and dancing by a professional troupe of Soviet artists who must have been brought in for this occasion. I was more impressed with this theatrical performance than with the Soviet staff work connected with the Russian visit to Leipzig. It is indeed sad that these friendly exchanges of visits between American and Soviet military forces right after World War II could not have been followed by equally friendly political exchanges.

Home Again—Briefly

Rumors of VII Corps' going to the Pacific began to firm up in early June. At the same time General Marshall developed a plan to bring home from Europe some of the Army's combat commanders to make them better known to the American public. He arranged a series of public receptions in several cities for groups of officers and noncoms whose homes were in the adjacent states. I was among the group, headed by General "Sandy" Patch, that flew into San Antonio, Texas. We were given a rousing welcome and feted by the city. The best part of these arrangements was that our wives were brought in to meet us, and we were given thirty days leave following the festivities. Gladys flew down to join me and returned with me to Washington.

On June 30, 1945, Headquarters and Headquarters Company, VII Corps, departed Le Havre en route via Camp San Luis Obispo, California, for assignment to the Pacific Theater. Meanwhile General Hodges had stopped in Washington to call on the President and General Marshall and to arrange with the Operations Division of the War Department (OPD) for the transfer to the Pacific of the headquarters of the First Army and five corps, including VII Corps. Apparently Hodges had asked especially for me, remarking that "Collins is the outstanding Corps commander." Perhaps thinking of MacArthur's earlier rejection of me as "too young" for corps command, and MacArthur's known preference for older men, General Marshall on May 28 instructed General Hull, acting head of OPD: "As stated this morning, I do not wish to ask General MacArthur's opinion at this time as to what particular corps commanders he desires. . . . Inform General Hodges that when you and he have reached an agreement, we will notify General MacArthur that these corps commanders are coming out with the First Army, and if General MacArthur objects to any individual we can reconsider the matter on that basis." In the cable, sent

"Personal to MacArthur from Marshall," Van Fleet was listed to command III Corps; Huebner, V Corps; Collins, VII Corps; Major General Alvan C. Gillem, XIII Corps; and Ridgway, XVIII Corps. All of us, except for Van Gillem, were younger than most of the corps commanders then in the Pacific. I have been unable to find a reply to that cable.

I left Washington after a refreshing month's leave, two wonderful weeks of which Gladys and I spent at a convalescent hospital at Lake Placid, New York, where General Marshall, thoughtful as ever, had sent us. We rode horseback every day in the lovely woods and hills around Lake Placid. It was hard to leave home again. Fortunately, the Japanese decided they had enough of war shortly after the atomic bombs were dropped on Hiroshima and Nagasaki. I got out as far as San Luis Obispo, but was there only a few days when I had a telephone call from General Jacob L. Devers, who had taken command of the Army Ground Forces, directing me to return to Washington to be his Chief of Staff.

CHAPTER XVII

Back to Washington, 1945–1948

Chief of Staff, Army Ground Forces

I had no desire to return to staff duty in Washington, but life in our capital city is always exciting and there was joy in the prospect of having our family together again at Fort McNair, where General Devers had his headquarters. Gladys and the children had remained in Washington throughout the war, and the children were glad to remain in the same schools with their friends.

I reported to General Devers early in September, 1945. We had served together only once, after World War I, while we were instructors at West Point. I did not know him well but always liked "Jakie" Devers, who had been a star baseball player in the class of 1929 at the Point and an enthusiastic horseman in the Field Artillery. General Marshall thought well of him and had picked him early for high command in World War II. At the end of the war Devers was commanding the 6th Army Group on the south flank of the allied front in western Europe.

The Army Ground Forces were then engaged in trying to maintain some sense of unity and combat readiness in the Army that was being torn apart by public and congressional pressure to demobilize as rapidly as possible and to "bring the boys home" from the combat theaters abroad. It was a challenging task. Before I became involved, however, I was diverted by General Marshall to another challenging problem to which Marshall had given considerable thought during World War II: the unification of the War and Navy Departments into a single department. He was anxious to initiate some movement to effect unification before he retired from active duty.

Two great wars had ended America's political and military isolation and had brought home the need to reorganize our military establishment to meet the broadened responsibilities inherent in our new

333

role of leadership in international affairs. Pearl Harbor had demonstrated the lack of coordination of plans and operations of the Army and Navy, and the tremendous growth of air power during World War II had forced its integration into the strategic and tactical operations of the older services. Better coordination had been achieved during the war by expanding the Joint Chiefs of Staff to include a Chief of Staff for the President and a representative of the Army Air Forces, and by establishment of unified field commands in each theater of operations, such as that in Europe under Eisenhower and in the Pacific under Nimitz.

First steps toward giving air power equal status with land and sea forces had been taken on March 2, 1942, when the Army Air Forces was made semi-independent of the Army Ground Forces and its commander, General Henry A. "Hap" Arnold, became a member of the JCS on an equal footing with General Marshall, Admiral Ernest J. King, CNO, and Admiral William D. Leahy, Chief of Staff to President Roosevelt. But these organizational and operational changes were accomplished under the war powers of the President. Their permanent status would have to be confirmed by legislation.

General Marshall in 1943 had initiated studies on postwar organization of the armed services by the Special Plans Division (SPD) of the War Department under Brigadier General William F. Tompkins. SPD recommended a single Department of War under a civil Secretary, with four subdepartments of Army, Navy, Air, and Common Supply, each headed by an Under Secretary. A single Chief of Staff would supervise a Joint General Staff, which would consist of the Chiefs of Staff of the three combat services and a Chief of Staff for Supply. General Marshall approved the study and sent it to Admiral King for consideration by the JCS. The latter appointed a special committee of Army, Navy, and Air officers to study the subject. The senior member, Admiral James O. Richardson, was designated chairman.

Ten months later, April 1, 1945, after visiting all theaters of operations and consulting most senior combat commanders, the committee recommended a single defense department. Admiral Richardson submitted a lone dissenting opinion, a dissent that set a pattern for all subsequent Navy testimony on unification, despite the fact that Nimitz and Halsey, along with Eisenhower and MacArthur, had testified before the Richardson Committee in favor of a unified department.

The JCS split on the Richardson report, Marshall favoring and King opposing unification. Finally on October 2, 1945, the JCS agreed to send the report, together with Marshall's and King's views, to the President for decision.

Meanwhile, congressional concern over the need for unification was growing. In January, 1945, bills had been introduced in the Senate by Senator Lister Hill of Alabama and in the House by Representative Jennings Randolph of West Virginia, to consolidate the War and Navy Departments into a single department. In the following October a second unification bill had been submitted in the Senate jointly by Senators Edwin C. Johnson of Colorado and Harley M. Kilgore of West Virginia. Hearings on the two bills were scheduled for mid-October by the Senate Committee on Military Affairs.

Shortly after I arrived in Washington in September, General Marshall asked me to serve as spokesman for the Army in presenting to the Senate Committee a plan for unification of the military departments developed during the past two years, based on the studies of SPD and the Richardson Committee report. He outlined the plan, generally along the lines recommended by SPD.

The main point that he emphasized had to do with the submission to the President of budget recommendations of the JCS. He said that prior to World War II recommendations of the Army Chief of Staff and the Chief of Naval Operations with respect to the budget rarely, if ever, actually reached the President. They had always been modified by budgetary reviews within the War and Navy Departments and by the Bureau of the Budget, so that the Commander in Chief never learned the real military needs of the services as estimated by responsible military leaders. Marshall wanted the Army's plan to specify that budget recommendations of the Chiefs of Staff, based on their recommended strategic plans, should be submitted annually through the Secretary of the Armed Forces to the President, without modification, but with any comments or recommendations the Secretary cared to make. I reported to General Tompkins and assisted in writing the final version of the Army proposal.

The Navy Organizes to Oppose Unification

Realizing that it was inadvisable for the Navy to maintain a solely negative approach to unification, James V. Forrestal, who had moved up to be Secretary of the Navy in June, 1945, requested Ferdinand Eberstadt, former Vice Chairman of the War Production Board, to conduct a special investigation. A large staff of naval officers and civilian specialists was assembled.

The following September, 1945, Eberstadt reported against a unified defense department, recommending three separate departments, Army, Navy, and Air. No provision was made for a single secretary to supervise the three departments. The Eberstadt plan by-passed this key element of unification but provided for a complex superstructure of councils and boards that would link the military departments to almost every other agency of the federal government. Some of the boards, such as the National Security Council, would probably be required whether or not the military departments were unified. Surprisingly Eberstadt placed the JCS under the National Security Council, with no provision for a chairman or a Chief of Staff for the President, which would have removed the JCS from any direct contact with the Commander in Chief.

Hearings began on October 17, 1945, with testimony by Secretary of War Robert P. Patterson, who had succeeded Stimson, and by Generals Marshall and Arnold. The three men cited the need for unification, based on their long experience, and Patterson spelled out in some detail the key provisions of the SPD study he had approved. General Marshall put the basic problem in a nutshell when he said:

> During the war, time was the compelling factor—not money. In peace, money will be the dominating factor. . . . Under the present system, or lack of system, two separate executive departments compete for annual appropriations. Each asserts its independent viewpoint before separate committees and subcommittees of the Congress. And each tends to seek the maximum appropriations for itself. Such a procedure offers no assurance that each dollar appropriated buys the largest measure of protection for the Nation.

Forrestal then presented the essentials of the Eberstadt plan, except that he disagreed with a separate department for Air. Forrestal was followed by Admiral King and General Alexander A. Vandegrift, the Commandant of the Marine Corps, both of whom opposed unification. I appeared next and presented the War Department plan, essentially as developed by SPD, shown in outline form below, which I explained in detail to the committee.*

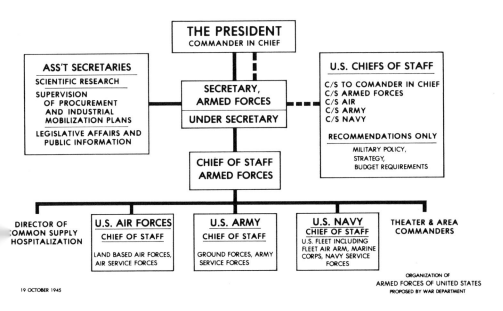

At the outset I emphasized that this was not a plan to merge the Army, Navy, and Air Forces into a single service but to integrate the management of the three autonomous services: "We are looking now only into the internal organization of the Department of the Armed Forces." The Navy would retain its Fleet Air Arm and Marine Corps, but the land-based Air Forces would achieve parity with the Army and Navy for the first time.

Coordination of military policy, strategy, and budget, under the Secretary of the Armed Forces, would be charged to the Chiefs of Staff. The Chiefs of Staff would not be an operating agency but would be

*See Hearings on S.84 and S.1482, Committee on Military Affairs, United States Senate, 79th Congress, First Session.

limited to recommendations on military policy, strategy, and budget.

A Chief of Staff of the Armed Forces would be the military advisor to the Secretary. Though not shown on the chart, so as not to clutter it with a multiplicity of lines, the Secretary, his Deputy, and the Assistant Secretaries would have direct access to the operating services and to the Director of Common Supply and Hospitalization.

Navy Objections to the "Collins Plan"

There would be no point here in reviewing in detail the Navy's objections to parity to the Air Forces, or in rehashing the need for eliminating duplication in the procedures of the War and Navy Departments. The chief Navy spokesman in opposition to unification was Assistant Secretary of the Navy H. Struve Hensel. Though it was well known that the plan I presented was prepared by the staff of the War Department, and had the personal support of General Marshall, Hensel shrewdly dubbed it the "Collins Plan." He concentrated his heaviest fire on the charge that it would put an end to civil control of the military, particularly in the budgetary procedures, which he implied were designed to bypass the Secretary.

Most of Hensel's charges were refuted in later testimony by John J. McCloy, Assistant Secretary of War, who disclosed that Marshall was responsible for the Army's recommendations on the budget, not with a view to bypassing the Secretary but to ensure that the views of our top military leaders reached the Commander in Chief. But we all, including General Marshall, were naïve in thinking that this budget provision would survive the latent American distrust of professional military men, rekindled by Navy arguments against unification.

After weeks of arguments in which the Army and Navy protagonists stuck to their positions, the Senate Committee adjourned in December, 1945, without reaching any conclusions. My direct connection with unification ended with these committee hearings, though in my later assignments I was indirectly involved, and I constantly supported unification.

Additional hearings were held during the next year and a half, culminating in the National Security Act of 1947, which provided for a National Defense Establishment of three co-equal departments of the Army, Navy, and Air Forces, with Forrestal as the first Secretary of Defense. The Defense Establishment was hampered by structural weakness, stemming largely from the fact that while the Secretary was charged with responsibility for coordinating the military services, he was given inadequate authority and staff assistance. Some of the Navy's and Forrestal's own objections to unification had come back to thwart him. Forrestal accepted a full measure of blame. In a forthright statement to a Senate committee in 1949 he acknowledged: "After having viewed the problem at close range for the past 18 months, I must admit to you quite frankly that my position on the question has changed. I am now convinced that there are adequate checks and balances in our governmental structure to prevent missuse of the broad authority which I feel must be vested in the Secretary of Defense."

After almost two years of further delay the weakness of the Act of 1947 were corrected by amendments in 1949. The changes clarified the authority of the Secretary of Defense to direct the military departments, provided the Secretary with the staff required for his increased authority, authorized a Chairman for the JCS to expedite its business and help the Secretary and the President resolve differences in its judgments, and reestablished the Munitions Board and Research and Development Boards.

Despite the dire warnings of the opponents of unification, there has been no lessening of civil control of the military, nor has a military "man on horseback" risen from the ranks of the dedicated Americans who make up the armed forces of the United States.

Chief of Information, War Department

General Marshall retired as Army Chief of Staff in October, 1945, and was succeeded by General Eisenhower. Shortly thereafter I learned that I was being considered for the new post of Chief of Information of the War Department, and I went to see Eisenhower to try to head off this assignment. The General greeted me with a friendly grin but his expressive face changed to a frown as I fired my opening gun:

"I've been hearing rumors that you are considering recommending me to be Chief of Information of the War Department, but I would like you to know that I don't want any part of it." I paused for a moment, as his frown quickly became a scowl, then added:

"I thought my métier was commanding troops."

Ike growled at me: "Joe, what in the hell have you been doing for the past two years!" Whereupon I beat a hasty retreat. Next day, December 16, 1945, orders were issued appointing me Chief of Information of the War Department

The Army was being subjected to a barrage of criticism from the press and Congress during the transition period from active fighting to the cold war, and there was some dissatisfaction within the Army itself with respect to postwar problems. Some of this criticism was warranted and called for prompt corrective action, but much of it was based on erroneous information and was detrimental to the orderly process of demobilization. Walter Page, Vice President in charge of Public Relations for the American Telephone and Telegraph Company, who was a consultant to the Secretary of War, suggested that an experienced senior officer be appointed to attend all staff meetings at the Secretary or Chief of Staff level, at which major policy or procedural matters were to be decided. It was to this post that I was assigned.

It was my function at these meetings to raise such questions as: "Have we considered the reaction of the public, or the Congress, to this proposed action?" or "What will be the impact of this procedure on the morale of our troops?" Then, after a decision had been made, it was my duty to follow it up. To do this, I had three information agencies, each headed by a talented officer: Public Relations, under Major General Floyd L. Parks; Congressional Relations, Major General Wilton B. "Jerry" Persons; and Troop Information and Education, Major General Charles T. Lanham. They kept me alerted to any possible difficulty, and I was responsible for coordination of appropriate action in event anything untoward developed. They alerted me to problems and I arranged for action by the War Department staff.

On one occasion Floyd Parks learned that Drew Pearson was preparing one of his typical exposés—a charge that the Army was guilty of malfeasance, or at best bureaucratic bungling, in failing to procure coffins of acceptable quality for use in returning our war dead. If the allegation was true, I believed that the Army should acknowledge it and take corrective action. If false, it should be headed off to spare needless heartache among the families of the dead.

I asked the Quartermaster General to get the facts. After a flurry of overnight transoceanic phone calls and cables, I was able to present to Eisenhower the next day a full account, and I suggested that I meet Pearson, give him the facts, and ask him not to publish his charge. Ike agreed. In fact he offered to accompany me, but I dissuaded him.

After I laid the facts before Pearson at a meeting in my quarters, he decided to drop the story. During our talk I told him that General Eisenhower and I were determined to see that the Army did an honest, forthright job during this difficult time of demobilization, and I offered to cooperate with him in running down any future alleged delinquencies, an offer Eisenhower had approved. Pearson accepted our offer, and as long as I remained Chief of Information he lived up to our agreement.

I hold no brief for the Pearsons and their fellow scandal-mongers, who make a living off the foibles and mistakes of men bearing heavy responsibilities in public office. But he and his ilk do keep some crooks "honest," for fear of disclosure, and thus do a certain amount of good; and the public loves the Pearsons. I sat next to a dowager at a Washington dinner party during this period, on a day when Pearson had broken a particularly juicy story. My dinner partner exclaimed as I seated her: "Isn't Drew Pearson terrible!"

I said, "Yes, he is terrible."

"Isn't there anything we can do about him?" she asked.

"Certainly."

"What?"

"Just don't read him!"

If the lady had had a dagger in her purse, she would have run me through as she glared at me. She would no more have foregone Pearson's breakfast dish of scandal than she would have missed a meeting of her bridge foursome.

The barrage of press and congressional criticism continued at home as we went through the sad task of tearing apart the finest military force ever assembled. Meanwhile the Soviets, their military power intact, took political control of Poland, threatened Iran, Turkey, and Greece, and supported Yugoslav demands on Trieste.

I had attended one or more of the semiannual meetings of the managing editors of the Associated Press and was familiar with the format of having panel discussions of national problems at these meetings. I suggested to Robert McLean, publisher of the Philadelphia *Bulletin*, who was then president of the AP, that he arrange a panel discussion on "The Responsibility of the Press in the Cold War." I raised this proposition with McLean at his office in Philadelphia, where he re-received me cordially. But he refused even to consider whether the press had any responsibility in the cold war period, other than to abide by its own tenets of good journalism.

McLean did arrange for me to address a session of the managing editors of the AP at their next meeting. This happened to be at the peak of the furor over the Army's procedure for determining the order in which men who had been drafted for service overseas in World War II would be brought home. Admittedly imperfect, the procedure was as equitable as the Army could devise, though it could never meet the demands for early return of every mother's son. It was inevitable that disgruntled soldiers or parents would write to congressmen with pleas for preferential treatment, and that newspapers would feature such stories, with resultant pressure to bring the boys home at all costs.

The furor reached the height of absurdity in Washington just before my scheduled address to the AP. I had accompanied Eisenhower to Capitol Hill, where he was to testify before the House Military Affairs Committee. When he arrived he was handed a message from the committee chairman, Andrew Jackson May of Kentucky, to the effect that May first would like to see the General in the Chairman's office. As we opened his door, cameras clicked and light bulbs flashed, revealing Chairman May poised in front of a table, beyond which a bevy of middle-aged women, with a banner that proclaimed them members of the "Bring-the-Boys-Home Mothers Club," gazed wistfully at a pile of baby shoes in the center of the table! That picture of a startled and furious Eisenhower, glowering across the stack of baby shoes at the smug-faced Chairman, with the "mothers" as a backdrop, went all over the United States.

Blown up to life size, it was displayed prominently near the dais when I addressed the managing editors. I seized on it as exemplifying the problem of the Army in trying to overcome the irrational approach of a large segment of Congress and the press, to the Army's complex problems of demobilizing over a million men, scattered around the globe, while trying to maintain some semblance of ability to check the Soviets' ruthless takeover of much of Eastern Europe. I pointed out the destructive effect on our combat units, which in addition to being stripped of key personnel were forced to leave much of their equipment, worth billions of dollars, untended in open fields in Europe and in the jungles of the Pacific Islands, to rust and rot. But all the efforts of the Army, even with some belated support from some of the press, could not slow the incessant demands to bring the drafted men home.

During the next year I received many a lesson in public relations. I was fortunate in establishing friendly contacts with the editors of the Washington *Post*, the *Star*, the *Herald*, and the Pentagon reporters, but ran afoul—temporarily at least—of reporters assigned to our occupation forces in Germany. General Eisenhower had sent me to Europe, where for a variety of reasons we were getting a bad press, to make clear to all senior troop commanders the importance of maintaining high standards of conduct on their part and that of their troops. At a press conference at Army headquarters in Frankfurt I was asked by a reporter if I thought the American people were aware of the complex problems of the occupation. I replied "No," and when asked "Why not?" I said, "Because you fellows spend most of your time concentrating on scandal instead of the important aspects of the cold war being fought between the Russian and Allied forces of occupation."

My statement was reported by all the wire services and understandably raised the ire of American reporters in Germany. They were waiting for me with sharpened pencils when I went to Berlin. There, on August 19, 1946, I was the guest of the Berlin Press Club at an unusual dinner. Attendance was limited to club members, myself, and one aide. After a pleasant round of cocktails and an excellent meal, I was subjected to an attack by Kendal Foss, Chairman of the Correspondents Association of Berlin, and others, who made the point that as long as there was scandalous conduct among the officers and men of our occupation forces, it would be reported in the press. I agreed that it should be, but stuck to my guns that the scandal reports were far out of balance with the general character of the Army's performance, and overshadowed the real problems of the occupation.

Finally one man spoke up and said he agreed with me to some extent, but that I should talk to the city editors at home. He said he had been sending reports for months on our difficulties with the Russians, without any response. Then he wired a story on pregnant nurses and immediately received a reply, "Send us more of the same."

I wound up the discussion by saying that the whole object of my trip was to emphasize to our commanders that they would get no better reports from the press than their performance deserved, to which the reporters chorused "Amen!" It may have been wishful thinking, but I felt my give-and-take exchange with the Berlin press had a salutory effect on them and our officer corps.

In retrospect, much as I had objected to my assignment as Chief of Information, if I had deliberately chosen a position in which to school myself to be Army Chief of Staff, I could not possibly have picked a better one. It gave me insight to the problems of congressional, public, and Army information relations that I could not have gotten any other way.

Deputy Chief of Staff to Eisenhower

As Chief of Information I saw Eisenhower almost daily and we came to know one another on a more personal basis, which probably accounted for his telling me one day, in the autumn of 1947, that he wished to make me his Deputy. This came out of the blue. I said, of course, that I would be delighted, but wondered if we might not think too much alike on most matters, and if he would not be better served by someone less outspoken—a remark that Ike simply waved aside. So on September 1, 1947, I became Deputy Chief of Staff of the Army. As Deputy, I relieved the Chief of most of the routine business of his office. The worsening situation in Europe following Soviet pressure on Yugoslavia required more of his time and attention on JCS matters.

When Eisenhower retired on February 7, 1948, he was succeeded by Omar Bradley, who had been serving as head of the Veterans Administration. I remained as Bradley's Deputy. We thus began another long period of close association, always a source of great satisfaction for me. General Bradley asked me to reorganize his office to meet the demands placed on it by the continued Soviet aggression. Secretary Gordon Gray and Bradley approved my recommendation for establishment of positions of Vice Chief of Staff and two Deputy Chiefs, one for Plans and the other for Administration and Operations. These posts were later authorized by the Congress. I took over the job of Vice Chief, becoming Bradley's alter ego, working closely with him and Secretary Gray in the day-in, day-out business of the Army, and in absence of the Chief representing him on the JCS. I also pinch-hit for him occasionally by making inspections of troops at home and abroad, and by acting as spokesman on such matters as universal military training, UMT.

Efforts to Establish Universal Military Training

For years our country had relied on small military forces, backed by the National Guard. The Guard and the Organized Reserves were inadequately trained for immediate combat service under a system of week-end flying and armory drills and summer encampments. In both world wars our allies had been able to hold off the enemy until our Regulars could be strengthened and the Reserves given months of hard field training to prepare them for combat. After World War II we could no longer count on such a respite.

To correct this situation President Truman called Congress into extraordinary joint session on March 17, 1948, shortly before the Soviet blockade of Berlin, to consider his recommendations for an extension of the selective service "draft," which was about to expire, and initiation of UMT. The draft was required to maintain the Regulars at full authorized strength, while UMT was to supply the Reserves with soldiers sufficiently well-trained that these units would require only a little more training after being mobilized.

During the next three years I was involved in the Defense Department's effort to persuade the public and Congress to support UMT and the draft. Outbreak of the Korean War in 1950 swung support to extension of selective service, but UMT had much harder sledding. Though supported unanimously by a special presidential advisory committee of distinguished citizens, headed by Karl T. Compton, President of the Massachusetts Institute of Technology, and backed by Secretary Forrestal, the three Secretaries of the Army, Navy, and

Air Force, and the JCS, UMT met a wall of opposition from religious and educational organizations. No amount of argument, however logical, could overcome the effect of this largely emotional opposition of the Eightieth Congress.

This was epitomized for me by Congressman Dewey Short, a member of the House Committee on Armed Services, before which I was testifying at one stage in support of UMT. I had gotten to know and respect Short as one of the most knowledgeable members of the committee. In the middle of my testimony Dewey abruptly rose from his chair and left the committee room. Afterward he apologized: "Lightnin' Joe, you were about to convince me, so I *had* to walk out on you." He and other members of Congress simply could not swallow their inherent distaste for any form of compulsory military service in peacetime. The Eightieth Congress adjourned without any action on UMT.

A year after outbreak of the war in Korea, Congress in 1951 passed a combined selective service and UMT act that provided for a National Training Corps. The act contained complicated restrictions that tied initiation of UMT to a reduction in strength of the active services, not feasible as long as the Korean War lasted. UMT died aborning. But in these hearings I learned a lot about Congress and, in turn, became well known to the Armed Services Committees, which was helpful in my next assignment.

CHAPTER XVIII

Chief of Staff, United States Army, 1949–1953

The National Security Act of 1949 established the post of Chairman of the Joint Chiefs of Staff, to which General Bradley was appointed by President Truman, effective August 16, 1949. At the same time I was nominated to succeed Bradley as Army Chief of Staff.

I have little knowledge of the circumstances surrounding my appointment. I assume that Louis A. Johnson, then Secretary of Defense, and Gordon Gray, Secretary of the Army, recommended me to the President, but I do not recall that either of them ever discussed the matter with me. I do know that, as is always the case, a canvass of my qualifications was made. After my appointment was announced, Colonel Thomas W. Mattingly, Jr., Chief of Cardiology at Walter Reed Hospital, told me that he had been queried at the time by General Eisenhower as to my physical condition. Mattingly advised the General that I had a "bundle branch block," a heart condition the doctor did not consider serious. Mattingly said that Ike replied, "There's nothing the matter with his *head*, is there?"

I chose as Vice Chief General Wade Hampton "Ham" Haislip, an able administrator whom I had known since our service together in Coblenz. The two deputies were also well known to me: "Matt" Ridgway for Operations and Alfred M. Gruenther for Plans. When Haislip retired on July 1, 1951, I picked as his successor a fellow staff officer from the VII Corps in Birmingham, General John E. "Ed" Hull. As Ridgway and Gruenther were shifted to other key assignments, they were succeeded by other top-flight former associates, Maxwell D. Taylor and Charles L. Bolté. My tasks were greatly lightened by such able assistants.

My fellow members of the JCS during most of my tour as Chief, in addition to General Bradley, were Admiral Forrest P. Sherman, Chief of Naval Operations (CNO) and General Hoyt S. Vandenberg, Chief of Staff, U.S. Air Force. Sherman, a 1917 graduate of the Naval Academy, had been a naval aviator. He had served with distinction in the Pacific in World War II and as Deputy to Admiral Nimitz in Washington. After a tour in command of the Sixth Fleet in the Mediterranean, he succeeded Admiral Louis Denfeld as CNO in 1949. I had met Sherman during the fight over unification of the Defense Department and had recognized him as a formidable opponent. We had no ill will over the fight, and I came to admire him. We worked together on the JCS until his untimely death in 1951. He was succeeded by Admiral William L. Fechteler. Vandenberg, the youngest of the chiefs, had graduated from West Point in 1923. I had gotten to know and like him while he was a student at the Army War College during my tour as instructor there. During World War II he had commanded the Ninth Air Force, which provided fine support to the 12th Army Group.

The years 1949–1953, which encompassed my time as Army Chief of Staff, were a critical period in the diplomatic and military history of the United States. On April 19, 1949, shortly before I took office, we joined the North Atlantic Treaty Organization (NATO) and on June 29, 1950, a little over a year after I became Chief, we entered the Korean War. The Korean War ended July 27, 1953, after spanning almost all of my tour as Chief of Staff. Though it was the dominant military event of that period and required the major share of my time and attention, I remained the JCS executive agent for the NATO area throughout the war, and was responsible still for the Army's morale, training, and readiness to fight.

I Call on General MacArthur in Japan

A week after I became Chief, I flew out to Japan to call on General Mac-Arthur and to inspect the troops of the Eighth Army under his command. No member of the JCS had visited the Far East since General Eisenhower's trip in 1946. I sensed that MacArthur might have been a bit put out by this seeming slight on the part of the current Chiefs. Since I had left the Pacific area to serve in Europe during the war, I wanted MacArthur to know that I still had great interest in the Far East.

The General received me most cordially, emphasizing his welcome with a magnificent military review in my honor on the broad open expanse surrounding the emperor's palace in Tokyo. He billeted our small party in the sumptuous guest house adjacent to his quarters in the high-walled American compound, and he and Mrs. MacArthur graciously entertained us. We were given a full briefing on the current situation by the General and by members of his staff, most of whom I had known in prior service, including the Chief of Staff, Major General Edward M. Almond, and the G-2, Major General Charles A. Willoughby.

B-36 Congressional Inquiry

Unfortunately my stay in Japan was cut short by a call to return to Washington to testify before the Committee on the Armed Services of the House of Representatives, on the conflict between the Navy and the Air Force over allocation of funds in the 1951 budget. This was precipitated by Navy complaints of unfair treatment when Secretary of Defense Johnson, with concurrence of the JCS, terminated a Navy project to build the super carrier *United States*, while at the same time authorizing procurement of additional B-36 intercontinental bombers. Underlying the complaints was the Navy's continued opposition to unification of the armed services, as testified by Johnson and Secretary of the Navy Francis P. Matthews, who had succeeded Secretary John L. Sullivan when the latter resigned in protest over Johnson's action on the *United States*. Navy complaints had not ended until after Matthews relieved Admiral Denfeld as Chief of Naval Operations in May, 1949.

I was not a member of the JCS when Secretary Johnson made the allocation of funds between the B-36 bomber and the super carrier, so offered no testimony on this controversy. But during the hearings the Commandant of the Marine Corps, my friend from Army War College days, General Clifton B. Cates, made several erroneous statements about the "Collins Plan" and added a serious charge that in World War II "xxxx troops from the Fleet Marine Force occupied Iceland because no others were prepared to move, and later defeated the Japanese at Guadalcanal at a time when Army divisions, although present in the Pacific, were not ready to undertake an offensive mission."

I could not let such statements go unchallenged. With reference to

Iceland, I reminded the committee that the Army then was prohibited by law from sending outside the United States any men drafted under the Selective Service Act, or any Reserve officers, except in an emergency declared by Congress. The law did not apply to the marines, so marines were sent until Regular Army personnel could replace them.

As to Guadalcanal, I pointed out that I was familiar with the situation in the Pacific following the attack on Pearl Harbor, having arrived in Hawaii a few days after the attack. Two Army divisions, including the 25th Infantry Division, which I later had the privilege of commanding, were assigned to the defenses of Hawaii. Since the Navy became the executive agent of the JCS in the Pacific, the allocation of units for operations thereafter became the responsibility of the Commander in Chief of the Pacific Fleet. Admiral Nimitz naturally chose to send to Guadalcanal the 1st Marine Division, uncommitted at the time. But, if he had chosen to send the 25th Division I knew it would have given a good account of itself, as it did later when he sent it into Guadalcanal to relieve the 1st Marines.

In refuting Cates's charges I did so without rancor, which changed the tone of preceding testimony, as was attested by Carl Vinson, Chairman of the unified Committee on the Armed Services. Long an opponent of unification while chairman of the old Naval Affairs Committee, Vinson congratulated me on the "calmness, the carefulness, and the broad outlook set forth in your paper." Other members joined in this accolade, notably Sterling Cole, one of the strongest Navy advocates.

Army Organization Act—1950

An aftermath of unification of the War and Navy Departments was passage of the Army Organization Act of 1950, a statutory basis for the new Department of the Army still governed by regulations authorized by the President under his war powers. Upon expiration of these powers the Army would have reverted virtually to its pre–World War II organization. Many outmoded provisions, long since discarded, would have come back into effect. Two years before, the Secretary of the Army, Kenneth C. Royall, had directed a study of legislation needed to place the Army on a sound statutory basis. Gordon Gray, then Under Secretary, acted for the Secretary in overseeing the preparation of the Army's draft of the proposed legislation, and I did the same for General Bradley. An excellent job of codifying the old laws and drafting the new was done by Colonel Kilbourn Johnston and Archibald King of the Judge Advocate General's Corps and Lieutenant Colonel G. Emery Baya of the Army Comptroller's office. After careful staff review and some modifications by Secretary Royall, the new code was finally approved by the Secretary of Defense for submission to Congress as H.R. 5794.

Hearings on H.R. 5794 before Subcommittee No. 2 of the Armed Services Committee of the House were conducted from March 1 through March 20, 1950. Gray, who had succeeded Royall as Army Secretary, was the first witness and testified at three of the eight sessions of the committee. I accompanied him, along with Colonels Johnston, King, and Baya, and testified at all sessions.

In accord with recommendations of the Hoover Commission for Reorganization of the Executive Branch, the principal proposed changes from the old statutes were intended to clarify the authority and responsibility of the Secretary of the Army and the Chief of Staff, to give them greater flexibility in managing the Army. Such details as tables of organization of Army units were to be omitted; the offices of the Chiefs of Infantry, Cavalry, and Artillery eliminated; the new branches of Armor, Transportation Corps, and Military Police Corps authorized; and, importantly, the post–Civil War authorization of four black regiments eliminated.

No real problems arose in the hearings until we reached Section 204, which spelled out the duties of the Chief of Staff. It had always been the clear intent of Congress and the Army to preserve civil control of all aspects of Army organization and operations. Ever since the Army reorganization of 1903 under Elihu Root, the Army Chief of Staff had been solely a staff officer. He commanded nothing. This was in marked contrast to the status of the Chief of Naval Operations, and the Air Force Chief of Staff, who commanded respectively the "operating forces of the Navy" and "the United States Air Force."

This difference was noted by Representatives Carl Vinson and Sterling Cole and after some discussion they suggested to me, in the absence of Secretary Gray, away on a short vacation, that I should have the Army staff, working with the staff of the committee, draft new wording for Section 204 so that the Chief of Staff should have some specific responsibility for combat readiness of the Army. The applicable subparagraphs of Section 204 were reworded as follows:

> (b) The Chief of Staff shall preside over the Army Staff. He shall be directly responsible to the Secretary of the Army for the efficiency of the Army, its state of preparation for military operations, and plans therefor. He shall transmit to the Secretary of the Army the plans and recommendations prepared by the Army Staff, shall advise him in regard thereto, and, upon the approval of such plans and recommendations by the Secretary of the Army, he shall act as the agent of the Secretary of the Army in carrying the same into effect.
>
> (c) Except as otherwise prescribed by law, by the President, or by the Secretary of Defense, the Chief of Staff shall perform his duties under the direction of the Secretary of the Army.

Wording of (b) had not been cleared with Gray because of his absence from Washington. On his return I called the wording to his attention, whereupon he asked to be heard as a witness on March 20. Gray said he would have preferred omitting Section 204 (b). But Vinson strongly supported the section, saying "I think it strengthens the office of the Chief of Staff. I think it strengthens the hand of the Secretary. The Secretary has someone fixed by statute who has certain responsibilities, and he looks to him for plans and readiness for combat use of the Army. He can hold him by statute as well as by Department orders." After some discussion, Gray withdrew his objection to 204 (b) as long as (c) was retained.

When the House bill came before the Senate Committee on the Armed Services, May 24–25, 1950, Gray had retired as army secretary, but asked to appear before the Committee to object to the wording of Section 204 (b) as passed by the House. He now made clear that his objections were twofold. First, to provide that the Chief of Staff shall be directly responsible to the Secretary for the efficiency of the Army and its state of preparation for military operations would duplicate and thereby weaken the responsibility of the Secretary, because Section 101 (a) of the same act stated that the Secretary of the Army shall be responsible for and shall have the authority to conduct all affairs of the Army Establishment including those necessary or appropriate for the training, operations, preparedness, and effectiveness of the Army. Second, to prescribe in Section 204 (b), quoted above, that the Chief of Staff would be *directly* responsible to the Secretary might some day allow a Chief of Staff to challenge the authority of the Secretary to delegate responsibilities to one or more of his Assistant Secretaries.

Questioned as to this point, I said that in the day-in, day-out business of the Army I had no objection to such delegation—in fact it was done all the time. But as long as Congress wished to spell out responsibility to the Chief of Staff for efficiency of the Army and its readiness for combat, responsibility should be directly to the Secretary and not through any Under Secretary or Assistant Secretary.

My view was supported by the Chairman, Senator Millard E. Tydings of Maryland, and other members of the Committee. But to satisfy Gray's first objection as to duplication of responsibility, Section 204 was finally modified and adopted as follows:

> (b) The Chief of Staff shall preside over the Army Staff. Subject to the provisions of section 101 of this Act, and of subsection (c) of this section, he shall be directly responsible to the Secretary of the Army for the efficiency of the Army, its state of preparation for military operations, and plans therefor. He shall transmit to the Secretary of the Army the plans and recommendations of the Army Staff, shall advise him in regard thereto, and upon approval of such plans and recommendations by the Secretary of the Army, he shall act as the agent of the Secretary of the Army in carrying the same into effect.
>
> (c) Except as otherwise prescribed by law, the Chief of Staff shall perform his duties under direction of the Secretary of the Army.

The exception in (c) has to do principally with duties of the Chief of Staff as a member of the JCS. Aside from responsibility to the President as Commander in Chief, each of the Chiefs has a dual role. He is responsible to his Secretary—Army, Navy, or Air—for efficiency of his service and its readiness for combat; and as a member of the JCS he has joint responsibility, along with his fellow Chiefs, to the Secretary of Defense for strategic war plans and, in time of war, execution of those plans by theater or task-force commanders.

Objections have been raised that this dual role does not allow a Chief sufficient time for his duties on the JCS. It has been suggested that a separate group of distinguished retired officers, or senior men on their last active duty assignments, should constitute the JCS. I do not agree. I know from my own experience that it is difficult for a retired officer to keep abreast of developments in weapons and their effects on tactics and strategy. I believe also that the men responsible for preparation and the carrying out of such plans should have responsibility for the readiness of the troops and selection of the commanders of major units.

There have been changes in recent years in the internal structure of the Army, but the broad authority granted the Secretary of the Army under the Army Organization Act of 1950 has permitted the changes. I am proud of the part I played, along with Gordon Gray and members of the armed services committees of Congress, in establishing a clear congressional record on the relations of the Secretary of the Army and his Chief of Staff.

Segregation

One of the most difficult problems all the military services faced during my time as Chief of Staff was elimination of segregation. Army units made up wholly of blacks had fought in the Union Army during the Civil War, and Congress thereafter had authorized four black Regular Army regiments, the 24th and 25th Infantry and the 9th and 10th Cavalry. By federal law, segregation became established in the armed services. My first contact with black troops was at Fort Benning, where the 24th Infantry, though organized as a combat regiment, was employed almost exclusively as service troops for maintenance of the post.

My experience with black troops of the National Guard, all of which were organized in northern states, has been recounted in Chapter VII. I had no black combat units under my command in World War II, but black logistical units attached to the VII Corps did well, and late in 1944 when the need for replacements in Europe became critical, Lieutenant General John C. H. Lee, commanding the Communications Zone, organized platoons of black volunteers from service units to fight as combat infantrymen. Each platoon had one white officer and one white noncom, and was given six weeks of combat training before being assigned to infantry or armored divisions in the First and Seventh Armies. Reports of this first experimental integration of combat troops in action wre uniformly favorable. Though on a small scale, and limited to volunteers of higher-than-average educational qualifications, results augured well for the future. The most encouraging sign to me was that while many white enlisted men initially were reluctant to serve alongside blacks in combat, the great majority found that the blacks performed competently in action when mixed in units with whites. Whites and blacks soon developed mutual respect and confidence.

The attitude of most senior officials of the Army, both civil and military, during World War II and in the early postwar period, was that the Army was not designed or intended as an instrument to accomplish social and political changes in American society. Its mission was to provide for the military security of the United States. Many senior officers, and I was one of them, felt that the military services should move ahead to provide equal opportunity to all soldiers for training and advancement, but that the lead in eliminating segregation, as distinct from discrimination in the ranks, and in the social aspects of Army life, should be political and accord with state and federal laws and customs. Most of the Army was stationed in the South, which undoubtedly accounted for this attitude. When we look about us now and see the effect of military control of civil governments in many areas of the world, we can be grateful that American military leaders have generally kept to their responsibilities.

President Truman took the first real step toward providing political leadership with the issuance of Executive Order 9981 on July 26, 1948, which declared the policy of the President, as Commander in Chief, to provide "equality of treatment and opportunity for all persons in the armed services without regard to race, color, religion or national origin." Recognizing many difficulties, the President added, "This policy shall be put in effect as rapidly as possible, having due regard to the time required to effectuate any necessary changes without impairing efficiency or morale."

To ensure progress, President Truman appointed a Committee on Equality of Treatment and Opportunity in the Armed Forces under the chairmanship of Charles Fahy of Georgia, a former Solicitor General. All executive departments and agencies of the Federal Government were to cooperate with the Committee, and furnish such personnel, documents, and testimony as the Committee might require.

Under prodding by the Fahy Committee, supported by pressure from prominent black activists and the liberal press, opposition to integration slowly began to diminish. In April, 1950, shortly after Gray succeeded Royall as Secretary of the Army and I became Chief of Staff, Gray and I agreed with Fahy to eliminate the quota system—long opposed by black activists and the Fahy Committee—of limiting the percentage of black draftees assigned to the Army to 10 percent, the approximate percentage of blacks in the American population.

The outbreak of the Korean War quickly increased this ratio. The Army doubled by December, 1950. To meet this increase, draft boards, no longer limited by quotas, upped the percentage of black draftees furnished the Army, while the percentage of black voluntary enlistments tripled. This produced an overstrength in the Army's segregated units in the United States. Combat casualties in Korea in the all-white divisions there created an increasing demand for replacements, which could be met only by tapping the excess black strength in stateside units and among incoming draftees. By June, 1951, blacks among replacements arriving in Korea rose to 22 percent. Without any mandate from Washington, the Eighth Army began to integrate blacks into combat units without regard to ratios. It was no surprise to those of us who were familiar with the success of integrated black platoons in World War II that the integrated units performed well.

This was in marked contrast to the experience in Korea of the all-black 24th Infantry Regiment, which had replaced the 161st Infantry in my old 25th Division. There were many individual acts of heroism in the 24th Infantry, but the regiment as a unit performed poorly. Investigation disclosed that 62 percent of the regiment's personnel were below average or inferior under the Army General Classification Test (AGCT), compared to an average of 43 percent in the two white regiments of the Division. The Division commander, Major General William B. Kean, concluded that segregated black units would not work in combat, and recommended that the 24th Infantry should be withdrawn and its soldiers reassigned throughout the Eighth Army to white companies at a ratio not to exceed 10 percent. General Ridgway, who had succeeded to command of the Eighth Army after the death of General Walton Walker, agreed, but as the Eighth Army was in the midst of a major offensive he was unable to take any action then.

When President Truman recalled General MacArthur on April 11, 1951, and appointed Ridgway to succeed him, Ridgway promptly requested authority to abolish segregation in his command starting with the 24th Infantry, the statutory requirement for four black regiments in the Army having been eliminated by the Army Organization Act of 1950. Secretary Frank Pace, Jr., and I approved his recommendation. I outlined the plan to the chairmen of the appropriate congressional committees, who offered no objection, and Pace informed the President. The deactivation of the 24th Infantry and integration of the Far East Command was announced on July 26, 1951, the third anniversary of President Truman's Executive Order 9981, but it took several months longer to complete the program.

For a variety of reasons, including some opposition in Congress, integration in the Army in the United States and in Europe proceeded at a slower pace. I had agreed with the Army Inspector General, Louis A. Craig, in August, 1950, that the Army's segregation policy was not in line with the outlook of younger Americans, and that the Army would eventually have to integrate. But I did not wish to speed up integration until the Navy and Air Force, which were able to obtain more highly qualified volunteers, were required to take a fair share of the poorly educated blacks being caught in the draft and funneled into the Army. Otherwise the percentage of less-qualified soldiers in the Army might rise to an intolerable 30 percent. The Secretary of Defense allayed these fears when in April, 1951, he directed that all military personnel must be distributed among the services on a qualitative basis. On December 29, 1951, I ordered all major commanders to prepare plans for full integration of their commands in orderly stages. I had to push SACEUR General Thomas T. Handy to get moving on these plans, but by July, 1954, shortly after my tour as Chief expired, integration throughout the Army was essentially completed.

It is interesting to me that Army integration was accomplished under two southerners, Secretary Frank Pace, Jr., of Arkansas, and J. Lawton Collins of Louisiana.

NATO and the Development of Nuclear Artillery

Though the greater part of my time and attention during the Korean War had to be given to that conflict, I was still JCS executive agent for the European theater and concerned with the Soviet threat to that area. There was always the possibility that the Communists might take advantage of our involvement in Korea, and their preponderance of strength in Europe, to launch an attack there.

To most senior military men at the time it seemed clear that NATO ground forces would be no match for the powerful Soviet armies unless nuclear weapons were made available to bolster NATO defenses. We and our allies would be loath to employ the large nuclear bombs, whose broad destructive effect would be likely to overlap friend and foe alike. But if NATO forces could be deployed to hold key areas to prevent the rapid overrunning of Allied defensive positions, the Soviets would be forced to concentrate their attacking troops and thus present targets for nuclear artillery. Fire on such targets, registered in advance with normal high-explosive shells, could be delivered accurately even if an enemy attack was launched at night or in weather that would prevent employment of our spotter planes.

Uranium 235, the explosive isotope of uranium essential for a nuclear weapon in the 1950s, was still in short supply. Most of a "charge" could be exploded in a large bomb of the Nagasaki type, but not in a small bomb or artillery shell. The Atomic Energy Commission (AEC) was unwilling to authorize such "wasteful" small bombs that might be carried in the bomb bays of Navy carrier-based aircraft or fired from Army artillery. It was not until April, 1950, that need for such smaller, lighter nuclear weapons was agreed to by the JCS. Development of an artillery shell then proved unexpectedly difficult. The largest artillery piece at that time was a 240-mm gun. Not only would the bomb have to be squeezed down to fit into a ten-to-twelve-inch gun barrel; it would have to be rugged enough to withstand the shock of being propelled from the gun without premature explosion. The Air Force and, to a lesser extent, my Navy colleagues on the JCS, opposed the "waste" of uranium 235 on the Army project. I argued that NATO forces, supported by nuclear artillery, could prevent the rapid overrunning of Western Europe and might thus dissuade the Soviets from ever undertaking such a costly adventure. As to the feasibility of a safe nuclear shell, I was constantly encouraged by Robert LeBaron, then Deputy to the Secretary of Defense for Atomic Energy, who assured me that before long such shells could be produced in small calibers.

The problem of designing a safe and effective nuclear shell was solved in 1949 by a brilliant young Army ordnance officer, Major Angelo R. Del Campo, with the assistance of Robert Schwartz, an expert shell-design engineer from the Army's Picatinny Arsenal. Del Campo presented his design to Marshall Holloway, head of the Weapons Design Division of the AEC's Los Alamos laboratory, who was favorably impressed. But Holloway's staff felt that the shell would have to be larger than 240-mm. In ten days Bob Schwartz redesigned the 240-mm shell to a caliber of 280-mm, which would produce a fissionable yield equivalent to 10 to 20 kilotons of TNT. Del Campo, accompanied by Holloway, presented the project to the Advisory Board of the AEC, and won approval.

Three years of development was required before the 280-mm gun, mobile carriage, and ammunition were ready for test firing. This was done successfully at the AEC's Proving Grounds on Frenchman Flats, north of Las Vegas, on May 25, 1953.

Fortunately it has not been necessary to fire any of the 280-mm cannon or the smaller 155-mm guns now available in Europe. But there is no question in my mind that the presence there of our nuclear guns has contributed greatly as a deterrent to any offensive by the Soviets.

Outbreak of the Korean War

Our participation in the undeclared war in Korea followed the surprise attack on June 25, 1950, by North Korea across the 38th Parallel, which marked its boundary with South Korea. This attack by forces armed by the Soviet Union and trained by the Russians for offensive operations was in flagrant violation of the Cairo Declaration of 1943, in which Roosevelt, Churchill, and Chiang Kai-shek, later joined by Stalin, pledged a unified and independent Korea. Following the attack, the United Nations Security Council, in the absence of the Soviet delegate, Jacob Malik, approved a resolution condemning the attack, demanding withdrawal of the attackers, and calling on all members "to render every assistance to the United Nations in the execution of this resolution."

The North Korean Army paid no attention to the UN resolution, but continued its attack, driving before it the South Korean Army, which only a short while before had been converted from a constabulary force, trained and equipped for internal police duty. On June 27, Syngman Rhee, President of the Republic of Korea, appealed to the United Nations for assistance. The same day the Security Council, with the Soviet delegate still absent, again condemned the attack, but this time called on members of the United Nations to furnish assistance to the Republic of Korea to repel the attack and restore peace and security. This resolution laid the groundwork for participation by the United States and other UN members in support of the Republic of Korea.

North Korean troops broke through the last organized resistance north of Seoul on June 28. The following morning President Truman reviewed the situation with Secretaries Dean Acheson and Louis Johnson, the JCS, and other top advisers in State and Defense. With the complete agreement of those present, the President authorized MacArthur to use U.S. Army combat troops to secure a port and air base in the Pusan area at the southern tip of Korea and undertake other measures, including the employment of naval and air forces in North Korea, with the hope of preventing the overrunning of all Republic of Korea (ROK) territory. That morning MacArthur had flown to Korea to gauge personally the seriousness of the situation. His report, which I received for the JCS about midnight of June 29–30, stated that the only assurance that ROK forces would be able to check the North Koreans would be introduction of U.S. combat ground forces. He concluded that if authorized he intended to send immediately to Korea a U.S. Army RCT and to provide for a possible counteroffensive by two divisions from his troops in Japan.

Greatly concerned by the critical situation as MacArthur had drawn it, I arranged for a teleconference with the General at about 3:00 A.M.

Washington time June 30 (5:00 P.M. same date, Tokyo time). With me in the Pentagon telecon room were General Gruenther and the heads of the Army General Staff; Dean Rusk, Assistant Secretary of State for Far Eastern Affairs; and the Korean desk officer, Neil W. Bond. Present with MacArthur at his headquarters in Tokyo were his Chief of Staff, Ned Almond, and his principal staff officers.

In a succession of televised messages I advised MacArthur that he had been authorized in an earlier JCS message to send an RCT to the Pusan base area, but that presidential authority would be required to move it to the battle zone, and that I was sure that Truman would wish to consult with his top advisers before deciding on any buildup of American forces. MacArthur protested that although the authorization to dispatch an RCT to Pusan established the principle that U.S. ground combat troops could be used in Korea, it did not give "sufficient latitude for efficient operation in present situation," and did not cover his proposal for a buildup to two divisions. He concluded that "time is of the essence and a clear-cut decision is imperative."

After discussion with Rusk and Bond and my staff officers, I called Secretary Pace at his house and gave him the gist of our telecon exchange. There was no time to consult with other members of the JCS, but as their executive agent for Korea, I recommended that the Secretary consult President Truman at once to secure authority to send the RCT to the battle zone. Pace agreed, and woke the President by a call to his bedside phone. A few minutes later Pace telephoned me that the President had given prompt approval for movement of the RCT to the combat area and that a decision on possible reinforcement would be made later in the day. I relayed this information immediately to MacArthur.

At 8:30 that morning President Truman assembled his senior advisers, told them of his earlier decision to send an RCT to Korea, and asked for advice as to possible reinforcements. It was quickly agreed that MacArthur's request for two divisions should be approved. On Admiral Sherman's recommendation, supported by the JCS, the President authorized a blockade of North Korea. By dark the following day, July 1, a combat team of the 1st Battalion, 21st Infantry, commanded by Lieutenant Colonel Charles B. Smith, had landed at Pusan, and

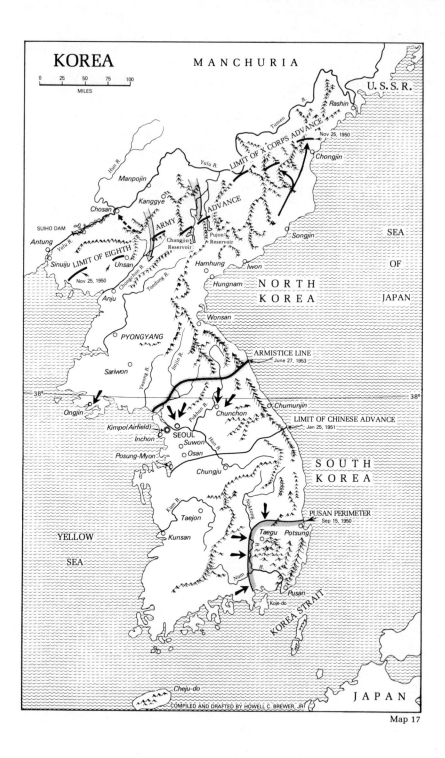

KOREA

MANCHURIA

U.S.S.R.

0   25   50   75   100
MILES

Tumen R.

Rashin

LIMIT OF X CORPS ADVANCE
Nov 25, 1950

Yalu R.

Hun R.

Manpojin

Chongjin

Kanggye

ADVANCE

Chosan

SUIHO DAM

ARMY

Songjin

Antung

Yalu R.

Changjin
Reservoir

Pujon
Reservoir

SEA

Sinuiju   LIMIT OF EIGHTH

Unsan

Chongchon R.

Hamhung

Iwon

OF

Nov 25, 1950

Toedong R.

Hungnam

NORTH

JAPAN

Anju

KOREA

Wonsan

PYONGYANG

Imjin R.

ARMISTICE LINE
June 27, 1953

Sariwon

Yesong R.

38°   38°

Ongjin

Pukhan R.

Chunchon

Chumunjin

LIMIT OF CHINESE ADVANCE
Jan 25, 1951

Kimpo (Airfield)

SEOUL

Inchon

Suwon

Han R.

Posung-Myon

Osan

Chungju

SOUTH

KOREA

Kum R.

Naktong

Taejon

PUSAN PERIMETER
Sep 15, 1950

YELLOW

Kunsan

Taegu Potsung
R.

SEA

Nam R.

Pusan

Koje-do

KOREA STRAIT

Cheju-do

JAPAN

COMPILED AND DRAFTED BY HOWELL C. BREWER, JR

Map 17

MacArthur had issued orders for movement of the 24th Division to Korea.

On July 7, 1950, the UN Security Council adopted a third resolution, of which the chief provisions were:

3. Recommends that all members providing military forces and other assistance pursuant to the aforesaid Security Council resolutions [of June 25 and 27] make such forces and other assistance available to a unified command under the United States.
4. Requests the United States to designate the commander of such forces.
5. Authorizes the unified command at its discretion to use the United Nations flag in the course of operations against North Korean forces concurrently with the flags of the various nations participating.

MacArthur was designated Commander in Chief, United Nations Command, by President Truman on July 8, and a week later President Rhee placed all ROK forces under MacArthur's command. Thus, for the first time in our history, the United States embarked in peacetime on a major war in a far-off country that many Americans had never heard of, a war that began without a congressional declaration and ended without a peace treaty. It was unique also because, though the United States furnished the bulk of the troops, equipment, supplies, and leadership, it was fought by an international force under the aegis of the United Nations. Consequently the United States did not have complete freedom of action in the conduct of the war.

A few years ago, writing from the viewpoint of the American Joint Chiefs of Staff, I recounted the experience of the United Nations Command in Korea in my book *War in Peacetime* (Boston: Houghton Mifflin, 1969). It is possible here to give only a brief summary of principal events of the war.

The UN Command Holds North of Pusan

Following the fall of Seoul on June 28, the first thing that had to be done was to stop the onrushing North Korean (NK) forces north of the port of Pusan. This task was assigned to Lieutenant General Walton H. "Johnny" Walker, commander of the U.S. Eighth Army in Japan, three divisions of which were moved to Korea as rapidly as possible. They were joined in August by the 1st Marine Brigade and 2nd Infantry Division from the States and by the British 27th Infantry Brigade, the first non-American United Nations reinforcement. In mid-July, President Rhee placed the ROK Army under the operational control of the Eighth Army. Thereafter, Walker wisely issued his instructions to the ROK forces through General Chung Il Kwon, Chief of Staff, ROK Army. Walker set up his headquarters in Taegu, sixty miles north of Pusan.

Walker checkmated each successive NK probing advance by the skillful shifting of his scant reserves, chiefly Colonel John H. Michaelis' 27th RCT and Brigadier General Edward A. Craig's 1st Marine Brigade. They were supported by the U.S. Fifth Air Force, without which Johnny Walker said, "we would not have been able to stay in Korea." By September 12 the NK Army had been halted along the UN perimeter defenses north of Pusan.

During the withdrawal south to Pusan, I had made two trips to Tokyo and Korea, the first with General Vandenberg in July before the NK advance had been halted. At that time Vandenberg and I conferred with MacArthur and his staff in Tokyo and visited Walker at his CP at Taegu. We reviewed with them the need for reinforcements and supplies and promised full support from the JCS within the resources of men and material then available.

MacArthur Plans a Counteroffensive

Even before the NK attack had been halted north of Pusan, MacArthur was planning for a counteroffensive against the west flank and rear of the NK Army to be initiated by a landing on the west coast of Korea at Inchon. Before leaving Washington with Vandenberg, we had been briefed by the CNO's staff on possible landing sites on the Korean west coast and, while in Tokyo, we had heard MacArthur's staff outline the plan then being developed to land the 1st Marine Division at Inchon by mid-September, when tidal conditions would be best for a landing there. In conjunction with this amphibious attack, the Eighth and ROK Armies were to break out of the Pusan bridgehead and attack to the north. I reported the gist of the plan to the JCS upon our arrival back in Washington.

The JCS raised no question about the concept of a flanking maneuver against the west coast of Korea, but the Navy and Marine Corps were skeptical about the feasibility of a landing at Inchon because of the tides, running as high as thirty-six feet, the narrow tortuous channel leading from the Yellow Sea to Inchon, and the vast mud flats at low tide in the harbor, which would require that the approach and landing be made in daylight. There were other possible landing areas on the west coast, notably at Kunsan, about a hundred miles south of Inchon, and at Posung-Myon, thirty miles south of Inchon. At Posung-Myon underwater naval reconnaissance teams had made several undetected landings and found deep water that would permit landings day or night, unrestricted by the tide.

Inchon, however, had several important advantages over either of these areas. It was close to the capital city of Seoul and the Kimpo airfield, the best in South Korea, both of which might fall to a quick drive from Inchon. In addition to the psychological effect of the fall of Seoul, its capture would cut all of the NK supply routes leading to the Pusan perimeter.

The JCS had received no details of the plan for a landing at Inchon since my oral report in July. In considering the pros and cons of a landing there, the JCS had to weigh our responsibilities to the President as well as to the commander of the United Nations Command. We could have asked no questions of MacArthur, raised no challenge to the plans as we knew them, and allowed the General to assume full responsibility for the outcome, which he was perfectly willing to do. But we could not have washed our hands of any responsibility for Inchon as long as we had real doubts about its success. We were not prepared to do this. Furthermore, since Truman had not asked Congress to approve his actions in entering the war, he was deeply committed personally and wished to be kept fully informed as to military operations.

The JCS decided to send two representatives, Admiral Sherman and me—Sherman as its member most directly concerned with the amphibious phase, and I as executive agent for the Far East—to review directly with MacArthur and his staff the detailed plans for Inchon and its followup. We arrived in Tokyo on August 21 and were greeted cordially by General MacArthur, who had arranged for a brief visit to Korea and a full discussion of the Inchon plans. The next day Sherman and I flew to General Walker's CP at Taegu, where we were assured that the Pusan bridgehead would be held. The next morning we accompanied Walker on a quick aerial survey of the front, stopping at all division headquarters, and the CP of the 1st Marine Brigade, before returning to Tokyo.

That afternoon we had a full-scale discussion of the Inchon plans, which were outlined by Almond and his staff. In early August, Sherman had suggested that the Pacific Fleet Marine Force in Honolulu, commanded by the experienced Marine Lieutenant General Lemuel C. Shepherd, should furnish the headquarters and staff of the landing force. Instead MacArthur had designated his Chief of Staff, Ned Almond, to command a newly formed X Corps, to consist of the 1st Marine Division and the Army's 7th Infantry Division, fresh from the States, which would constitute the landing force. Almond selected his staff largely from GHQ in Tokyo. It was headed by Brigadier General Edwin K. Wright with Rear Admiral James H. Doyle as his chief Navy planner.

After a brief introduction by General MacArthur, Wright outlined the plan to land the 1st Marine Division, under Major General Oliver P. Smith, directly at Inchon. After capture of the port the division was to seize Kimpo airfield and storm Seoul. The 7th Division, commanded by Major General David G. Barr, was to follow the 1st Marines ashore, secure the high ground north of Suwon, and form the anvil on which the Eighth Army, after breaking out of the Pusan perimeter, would pound the NK Army to pieces. Next, Doyle and his naval and marine planners spelled out the amphibious phase, emphasizing its difficulties and dangers. They were frankly pessimistic. Doyle ended the presentation by stating that though the operation was not impossible he did not recommend it. I questioned the ability of the Eighth Army to make an early junction with the X Corps south of Inchon and made the suggestion that further consideration be given to landing at Kunsan, which was seconded by Sherman.

MacArthur had listened quietly to the discussion. He continued silently for a few moments to puff on his corncob pipe while we waited for his concluding remarks. He then spoke in a matter-of-fact tone at first, gradually building up emphasis with consummate skill. He admitted the difficulties and hazards pointed out by the Navy and Marines, but was confident that problems would be overcome. He insisted that any landing south of Inchon would fail to outflank the NK Army, and that our fears that the X Corps might be overwhelmed before it could be joined by the Eighth Army were ill founded. By attacking, as Wolfe did at Quebec, where the enemy thought it impossible, he would gain surprise and a decisive victory. He closed with a dramatic peroration in which he staked his reputation that Inchon would not fail. I was favorably impressed, but still had some reservations, as did Sherman and a number of the senior Marine officers. There was more at stake than General MacArthur's reputation, great as that was. The General did not ask us to approve his plans, which, of course, we had no authority to do.

On our return to Washington we briefed the President, the Secretary of Defense, and the other Chiefs. For the first time Washington was well informed about the attack plans, the risks involved and MacArthur's personal confidence in the outcome. After some further questioning the JCS radioed MacArthur that they had approved his plans, and had so informed the President. As is well known, Inchon was spectacularly successful, as was the counteroffensive that recaptured Seoul and drove the NK Army back across the 38th parallel. As I wrote in *War in Peacetime*, "The success of Inchon was so great, and the subsequent prestige of General MacArthur was so overpowering, that the Chiefs hesitated thereafter to question later plans and decisions of the general which should have been. In this we must share with General MacArthur some of the responsibility for actions that led to defeats in North Korea."

MacArthur Plans Advance into North Korea

Much debate had been going on between the State and Defense Departments and in the National Security Council as to whether and how far the UN Command should pursue the NK Army. The JCS supported MacArthur's intention not merely to drive that army north of the border, but to destroy it. Only by doing so could international peace and security in Korea be restored, as required by the UN resolution of June

27. But it was not until September 25 that the JCS was authorized by President Truman, as recommended finally by the National Security Council, to send a dispatch to General MacArthur stating, in part:

> Your military objective is the destruction of the North Korean armed forces. . . . You are authorized to conduct military operations . . . north of the 38th Parallel in Korea, provided that at the time of such operations there has been no entry into North Korea by major Soviet or Chinese Communist Forces. . . . Under no circumstances will your forces cross the Manchurian or USSR borders of Korea and, as matter of policy, no non-Korean ground forces will be used in the northeast provinces bordering the Soviet Union or in the area along the Manchurian border.

Meanwhile questions related to carrying the war into North Korea were being debated in Congress and the press. Public opinion, and political considerations, domestic and within the United Nations, under whose aegis the war was being fought, had to be weighed by the President and his advisers. By and large the news media indicated strong support of continuing military operations to eliminate the Communist government of North Korea and thus prevent a recurrence of the war. President Truman insisted on a mandate from the United Nations to authorize operations in North Korea. On October 8, 1950, the General Assembly adopted a resolution recommending that "(a) All appropriate steps be taken to ensure conditions of stability throughout Korea, and (b) All constituent acts be taken . . . for the establishment of a unified, independent, and democratic government in the sovereign state of Korea."

Although no directive to unify Korea was ever included in the missions assigned MacArthur, there was no question but that the General Assembly, President Truman, the Secretaries of State and Defense, the JCS, and the bulk of American and non-Communist world opinion approved the crossing of the 38th parallel. Most of the debate concerning the wisdom of this action came after the event.

MacArthur advised the JCS of his plan for the North Korean campaign. According to the plan the X Corps would be withdrawn to Inchon and Pusan, from which ports it would move up in convoy to Wonsan for an amphibious landing there. Meanwhile the Eighth and ROK Armies would be restocked with food, fuel, and ammunition, after which the Eighth Army would resume its advance on Pyongyang. The ROK Army, less its I Corps, was to concentrate in the central highlands east of the Eighth Army. The ROK I Corps was to move up the east-coast road prepared to attack toward Wonsan. After the capture of Pyongyang and Wonsan by the Eighth Army and X Corps respectively, they were to join forces via the Wonsan-Pyongyang corridor, hoping thereby to trap and destroy the remnants of the North Korean Army that had escaped into North Korea. MacArthur would control the combined operations from GHQ in Tokyo. Perhaps awed by the stunning success of the Inchon operation, the JCS, Secretary of Defense Marshall, and President Truman approved the plan in spite of some doubt about the command arrangements.

A brief analysis of the terrain of North Korea is essential to understanding the operations there. North Korea is largely a jumble of high mountains and tortuous steep valleys. The dominant feature is the Taebaek mountain range, with peaks up to 7,400 feet, which parallels the east coast from the Manchurian border to Pusan. Except for a single-track railroad and a highway between the port of Wonsan and Pyongyang, the Taebaeks are a formidable barrier to east-west travel, particularly in the snowbound winter months. The western half of the country is cut by a succession of rivers which drain the western slopes of the Taebaeks into the Yellow Sea. The most important of these rivers is the broad Yalu, which forms the northwest boundary with Manchuria.

For some time the JCS had been concerned with the possibility of Chinese intervention. On occasion in late September and early October the Chinese foreign minister, Chou En-lai, had indicated that if United Nations troops entered North Korea, China would send in forces from Manchuria to support the NK Army. MacArthur had been informed of these threats, and he had been directed to stay clear of the border. Unfortunately this precluded any ground or air reconnaissance beyond the Yalu or close to it, and thus there was no way for him to determine Chinese intentions or capabilities.

Without awaiting any resolution of this intelligence question, or replenishment of supplies, the ROK Army under instructions from President Rhee and contrary to General MacArthur's orders continued its advance into North Korea following the Inchon-Seoul campaign. The ROK I Corps on the east coast drove across the border at Chumunjin, captured Wonsan, and by October 17 occupied Hungnam. In seventeen days the ROK I Corps had advanced over 160 miles and captured two valuable ports—a splendid job.

Eighth Army Crosses the Chongchon River

General Walker obtained clearance from GHQ to advance on October 9, and by the nineteenth his troops entered Pyongyang. Meanwhile, because of logistical difficulties in moving X Corps by water from Inchon and Pusan as planned by MacArthur, to Wonsan, and in clearing the sea approaches to Wonsan of enemy mines, delayed the landing there of X Corps until October 25. Thus Wonsan and Pyongyang had fallen to the ROK and Eighth Armies under Walker's command before the X Corps landed at Wonsan. Walker moved his CP to Pyongyang.

With the hope of cutting off the enemy troops withdrawing in front of the Eighth Army, the 187th Airborne RCT was dropped by parachute north of Pyongyang on October 20. After witnessing the drop MacArthur announced "This closes the trap on the enemy," and from Tokyo the next day added, "The war is definitely coming to an end very shortly." Unfortunately these optimistic forecasts were far from the facts. The paratroopers did trap and destroy one NK regiment, but the bulk of MacArthur's estimated thirty thousand enemy troops had already escaped to the mountain fastnesses in the north. Buoyed by the seeming success of the aerial drop, and discounting the increasing reports of Chinese troop concentrations along the Yalu border, MacArthur on October 24 removed all restriction on the use of non-Korean ground troops close to the Manchurian border, and directed his commanders to press forward to the northern limits of the country, using all their forces. When the JCS received word of this order we at once notified MacArthur that it was contrary to the JCS instructions of September 27. MacArthur's reply justified his action as a military necessity because the ROK forces lacked sufficient strength and experienced leadership to seize and hold critical areas along the border. The JCS tacitly accepted MacArthur's reply and made no move to countermand the order, for which it must bear some responsibility for the debacle which followed.

The Eighth Army had moved out of Pyongyang on October 20. Little resistance was encountered, and by October 25 the bulk of its troops had crossed the Chongchon River. The ROK 6th Division on the right of the ROK II Corps had the easiest going. On the morning of October 25 one of its reconnaissance platoons reached Chosan, overlooking the Yalu, and fired on NK troops fleeing across the river on a ponton bridge. It then withdrew for the night. It turned out to be the only unit under Eighth Army command to reach the Yalu.

Commencing the following morning, undiscovered Chinese forces, which earlier had crossed the Yalu, struck the ROK II Corps. The inexperienced South Koreans were no match for the Chinese veterans, battle hardened in numerous campaigns against the forces of Chiang Kai-shek. The ROKs were routed and driven back to the Chongchon River. This exposed the right flank of the U.S. I Corps, manned by the ROK 1st Division, which was swarmed over by additional Chinese forces north of Unsan. Fearful that this division might break like the II Corps, Walker replaced it with the 1st Cavalry Division, commanded by Major General Hobart R. Gay, Patton's former Chief of Staff. Not even this fine division could fill all the gaps in the extended front, into which elements of two Chinese divisions poured. A battalion of the 8th Cavalry was surrounded and decimated at Unsan, in spite of heroic efforts to save it. The Eighth Army held off repeated efforts by the Chinese to break through the Chongchon bridgehead. On November 6 the Chinese withdrew into the hills to the north, but it should have been clear that they would be back. In Tokyo, four hundred miles away, MacArthur still discounted the threat of Chinese intervention, and made the critical mistake of directing Walker to continue the attack.

Concurrently the ROK I Corps and U.S. X Corps east of the Taebaek mountain range had advanced north of Hamhung against scattered NK resistance. The ROK I Corps captured Chongjin, sixty-five miles south of the Siberian border, on November 26. The U.S. 7th Division, under Dave Barr, having landed at Iwon, advanced into the mountains toward the Pujon Reservoir, driving off a battalion of Chinese troops from Paeksan Mountain. Despite this indication of Chinese reinforcements east of the Taebaeks, Almond ordered Barr to continue his attack toward Hyesanjin on the Yalu, which was reached on November 21, drawing plaudits from Almond and MacArthur. West of the 7th

Division, the 7th Regiment of the 1st Marine Division, moving up a steep mountain pass en route to the Changjin reservoir, beat off a strong attack by a Chinese regiment and entered Hagaruri on November 14.

The Chinese Counteroffensive

It is unnecessary here to recount the sad events that transpired in Korea after the Chinese Fourth Field Army, led by the redoubtable General Lin Piao, launched its counteroffensive on November 25. Walker's UN Command of four U.S. divisions, three ROK divisions, and the British and Turkish Brigades, was slashed by eighteen divisions of the Chinese Communist Forces (CCF) XIII Army Group. Similarly, Almond's X Corps was hit by twelve divisions of the CCF IX Army Group. By November 28 these massive forces, totaling almost 300,000 infantrymen, supported by cavalry, artillery, and service units, had crushed the ROK II Corps, forcing a roll-back of the Eighth Army's right flank, and had cut the main supply lines of the X Corps east of the Taebaeks. Realizing for the first time the seriousness of the threat to the UN Command, MacArthur radioed to the JCS, "We face an entirely new war," and said he was passing to the defensive. He ordered Walker to withdraw as far as necessary to prevent the CCF from outflanking the Eighth Army, and directed Almond to protect the withdrawal of the Marine Division and the 7th Division and to concentrate his X Corps in the Hamhung–Hungnam area.

On November 30, MacArthur reported that the Eighth Army would not be able to halt the Chinese in the foreseeable future but would have to withdraw by successive stages, and that unless massive ground reinforcements were sent him promptly the United Nations Command would face steady attrition and possible destruction. In light of this dire turnabout in CINUNC's* forecasts, President Truman authorized the JCS to direct MacArthur to give first priority to the safety of the UN Command and to concentrate the Eighth Army and attached units in beachheads based on Inchon and Pusan, and the X Corps in the Hungnam–Wonsan area.

---

*Commander in Chief United Nations Command.

To get a clearer picture of the situation, State and Defense with the President's approval decided that I should go to Korea to consult with MacArthur and see the situation firsthand. I flew to Tokyo, arriving there on December 4, and after checking in with MacArthur I flew over to General Walker's headquarters, which had been moved back to Seoul. That evening Johnny Walker outlined to me the events since the Chinese attack. He said that the Turkish Brigade, which had done a fine job covering the poorly handled withdrawal of the U.S. 2nd Division, had been badly hurt, along with the 2nd Division, but that the other units of the Eighth Army were in good shape. If the Chinese were to drive across the 38th parallel in full strength it would be doubtful that he could hold Seoul and the adjacent area north of the Han River. A forced withdrawal by way of Inchon would be very costly, but if the Eighth Army was reinforced by the X Corps, Walker was confident that Pusan could be held indefinitely. Throughout my visit he appeared undismayed. While the situation was tight, I saw no signs of panic and left the next morning for the X Corps reassured that the Eighth Army could take care of itself. Almond met me at an airstrip near Hungnam and we drove to his nearby CP for a review of the action in his zone, then visited the command posts of the 3rd and 7th Divisions in the Hungnam area. Almond assured me that the X Corps could hold the Hungnam beachhead as long as desired. I was impressed with his estimate and agreed with it.

I spent most of the next day in Tokyo with General MacArthur and his staff, trying to sort out their views of the options available to the UN Command. MacArthur's chief point was that unless his Command was given substantial reinforcements very shortly it should be withdrawn from Korea. I did not argue the point but I did not agree, basing my opinion on my discussions with the field commanders who were confident that they would hold off the Chinese. I so reported to the JCS and the President. Shortly thereafter, on the recommendation of General Wright, CINUNC's G-3, who had shown good judgment throughout, MacArthur authorized the X Corps to withdraw from the Hungnam area, and reluctantly passed control of the X Corps to the Eighth Army. The Chinese did not attempt to interfere with the withdrawal of the X Corps, but a cruel fate stepped in as Johnny Walker was about to take command of a united Eighth Army, which rightly should have been his long before. On a road north of Seoul on December 23 he was killed instantly when the jeep in which he was riding was struck by a truck. It was a sad and inglorious end for a fine, gallant field commander.

Ridgway Turns the War Around

When MacArthur learned of Walker's death he personally advised me and asked that Ridgway, who was then serving as my Deputy for Operations, be sent over at once. I informed the President, Secretaries Marshall and Pace, and the JCS, recommending approval. The President promptly designated General Ridgway as Commander of the Eighth Army. I telephoned Matt at once, giving him the word. Great soldier that he always was, without waiting to spend Christmas with his family he left Washington the next morning and arrived in Tokyo shortly before midnight, Christmas Day, 1950.

Matt Ridgway's qualifications for his new command were unexcelled. Within the past year he had visited Japan and Korea and had kept abreast of the situation. He had all the confidence, drive, and aggressive spirit to revive the flagging morale of the Eighth and ROK Armies after the reversals they had suffered from the massive Chinese forces. Fortunately, also, MacArthur was now ready to give Ridgway a free hand in command of UN forces in the field. No longer would they be controlled from Tokyo.

The combat operations of the Korean War need no further recounting here. Ridgway's brilliant success in stopping the Chinese forces and then driving them back north of the 38th parallel are well documented in the official histories published by the Chief of Military History of the Department of the Army, in my *War in Peacetime*, and in other personal accounts.

Similarly, the dismissal of General MacArthur by President Truman on April 11, 1951, which was supported unanimously by the members of the JCS and by the Secretary of Defense, General Marshall, has been fully publicized, especially in the report of the hearings of the Senate Committees on Foreign Relations and Armed Services, *Military Situation in the Far East*, 66th Congress, 1st Session, 1951.

I recommended, and Secretaries Pace and Marshall approved, the appointment of Lieutenant General James A. Van Fleet to command the Eighth Army, as President Truman designated Ridgway to head the United Nations Command. Van Fleet was of the same tough mold as Ridgway and his success as chief of our military aid group in training the Greek Army had fully qualified him for the task of rehabilitating the ROK Army.

Stalemate and Armistice

It became apparent in the spring of 1951 that neither the UN Command nor the Chinese–North Korean forces could gain any substantial advantage by continued fighting. In Washington, political leaders within the administration and Congress, sensitive to waning public interest in the war, began to consider a negotiated settlement. Following a meeting with the Secretaries of State and Defense, the JCS recommended that the current operations in Korea be continued until a satisfactory political settlement; they urged that dependable South Korean forces be developed as rapidly as possible to take over the major share of the defense of the country, and that preparation be made immediately for action by naval and air forces against the Chinese mainland in the event of a broadening of the war by the Communists. These recommendations were embodied in a National Security Policy Statement on May 17, 1951, which confirmed the intent of the United States to solve the Korean impasse primarily by political negotiations rather than by military action alone. This policy limited the operations of the UN Command during the two long years of stalemate before the signing of an armistice on July 27, 1953.

Some historians in recent years have described the Korean War as a defeat for the United States, likening it to the war in Vietnam. I thoroughly disagree. It must be remembered that we went into Korea under the aegis of the United Nations to prevent the takeover of South Korea by naked aggression from the north. This we achieved. If we had not done so, the United Nations might well have followed the League of Nations into oblivion. In spite of the obvious weaknesses of the United Nations today, it still serves a valuable purpose in helping to maintain peace in many areas of the world.

U.S. Representative, NATO Standing Group

When my four-year tour as Army Chief of Staff was up in August, 1953, President Eisenhower, who had taken office on January 20 of the same year, asked me to remain on active duty as the United States Representative on the Military Committee and Standing Group of NATO. The twelve member states of NATO were Norway, Denmark, the Netherlands, Belgium, Luxembourg, France, Portugal, Italy, the United Kingdom, Iceland, Canada, and the United States.

The top organization in NATO was the Council of Ministers, consisting of the foreign ministers of the member countries, who determined the political objectives and policies of NATO. Below the Council was the Defense Committee, made up of the defense ministers, who advised the Council as to their countries' contributions to the common defense. In turn the Defense Committee was advised with respect to military plans and requirements by the Military Committee, usually consisting of the military attachés of embassies located in Washington. A smaller "Standing Group" of senior, experienced officers representing France, the United Kingdom, and the United States, serving on a full-time basis, acted as executive agent for the Military Committee. The French representative at that time was General Paul Ely, with whom I would later be associated in Vietnam; the United Kingdom was represented by General Sir John Whiteley. I agreed to serve on the Military Committee and the Standing Group for two years.

While General Bradley was Chairman of the JCS, 1949–1953, he also had served as the U.S. representative on the Standing Group. During part of this period General Eisenhower had been NATO Supreme Commander in Europe (SACEUR). Apparently he had not been satisfied with the support he had received from the Standing Group. Bradley had his hands full as the first Chairman of the JCS in the newly organized Department of Defense. President Eisenhower wished me to serve full time on the Military Committee and Standing Group and wanted to have more drive put into the Standing Group "to get things done." He was concerned especially with the slow progress of some member countries in meeting their troop commitments to NATO. In announcing my appointment Secretary of Defense Charles E. Wilson said the Chairman of the JCS should be "relieved as much as possible of any duties that would take him outside of the country for any extended period of time or that would require his particular attention on matters not directly connected with his primary duties."

I attended the NATO Council meetings in Paris and visited each member country that was falling behind on its NATO commitments and used what influence I had with the defense ministers and their chiefs of staff to step up their military preparations. I was fairly well known to most of these men from my service in World War II but I had little real influence with them. Defense ministers usually answered my appeals for fuller support of NATO by pointing out the economic difficulties of their countries resulting from World War II. We had made some progress when the President sent me off to Vietnam in November, 1954, to survey the situation there following the French defeat at Dien Bien Phu, and to recommend what might be done to bolster the regime of Ngo Dinh Diem. My deputy, Brigadier General Karl Truesdell, Jr., took over during my seven-month absence.

I doubt that the Standing Group or the Military Committee were ever of much real help to SACEUR in holding the NATO ministers to their commitments. Such obligations were determined more by political and economic than by military considerations. SACEUR himself, particularly while General Eisenhower held that position, was much more influential with the NATO Council and Defense Committee than the less prestigious and more distant members of the Standing Group in Washington. When in 1967 the NATO headquarters was moved from Paris to Brussels after DeGaulle withdrew France from active participation in NATO, the Standing Group was abolished. I doubt that it was greatly missed.

CHAPTER **XIX**

Mission to Vietnam, 1954–1955

A Surprise Assignment

On the evening of Saturday, October 30, 1954, I was at the home of General and Mrs. Ray McLain in Oklahoma City, where I had given a luncheon talk to a civic group, when a telephone call came from one of President Eisenhower's aides at the White House. He said I was to return to Washington the following day and report to Secretary Dulles, then added in guarded words that I would be going shortly on a special mission to a country where "Iron Mike" was located. I knew this would be Vietnam, where Lieutenant General John W. (Mike) O'Daniel was head of a military assistance group.

On my arrival at Bolling Field in Washington on Sunday morning word was awaiting me that I was to join Dulles in a conference at his house with representatives of agencies involved with the situation in Vietnam. The conference was already underway when Colonel John E. Kelly and I arrived. Present in addition to Secretary Dulles were Robert Anderson, Deputy Secretary of Defense; Walter Robertson, Assistant Secretary of State for Far Eastern Affairs; Douglas MacArthur III, State Department Counselor; Kenneth T. Young, Jr., who headed a special State Department task force on Vietnam; Admiral Radford, Chairman of the JCS; and Colonel Andrew J. Goodpaster, Staff Secretary to the President.

I had met Dulles before but had only slight contacts with him. He greeted me graciously and introduced me to those present, all of whom I knew. The Secretary outlined the critical situation in Vietnam following the defeat of French colonial forces by the insurgent Viet Minh under Ho Chi Minh at Dien Bien Phu in May, 1954, and the Geneva Conference, which formally ended the fighting. He emphasized the growing distrust between the French and Ngo Dinh Diem, whom the

378

Emperor Bao Dai, living in France, had appointed president of a council of ministers to govern Vietnam. An impasse was developing between the French and Diem over the Geneva Accords, which divided Vietnam temporarily into two zones at the 17th parallel, subject to a plebiscite in two years that would determine whether the country would be reunited. Dulles said he had discussed the situation with the President and pointed out that our ambassador in Saigon, Donald R. Heath, was due for a change of station but that his intended replacement, Julian F. Harrington, then Minister to Hong Kong, had not been announced. The President—who knew I had visited Vietnam in 1951 while a member of the JCS and had kept in touch with developments there—had suggested that I be sent to Vietnam on a temporary mission, to take a fresh look at the situation and recommend a program of assistance to reinforce the political and economic stability of the government of Diem and the internal security of the country. Dulles agreed. On this assignment I would have the personal rank of ambassador, which would not require Senate confirmation nor endanger my commission in the Army. I would temporarily relinquish my membership on the Standing Group of NATO.

The Secretary did not minimize the difficulties with Diem or with the continuing French regime in Vietnam, though he was aware that I had close relations with General Paul Ely, the French Commissioner General in Saigon, while Ely had been French representative on the NATO Standing Group. He stated frankly that the chance of success of my mission was only one in ten, but that the importance of checking the spread of communism in Southeast Asia was worth the effort.

Discussion followed, ending with a consensus that I should leave for Vietnam as soon as possible and that Ambassador Heath should return to the States shortly after my arrival. It was estimated that my mission would require sixty to ninety days. Meanwhile Harrington should not proceed to Saigon until its completion. Dulles said I could take with me, if I desired, representatives from State, Defense, and the Foreign Operations Administration (FOA), which administered all our economic aid programs. No one asked if I would accept the assignment, taking for granted that I would comply with the wishes of the President

From the Dulles residence Walter Robertson, Ken Young, Doug

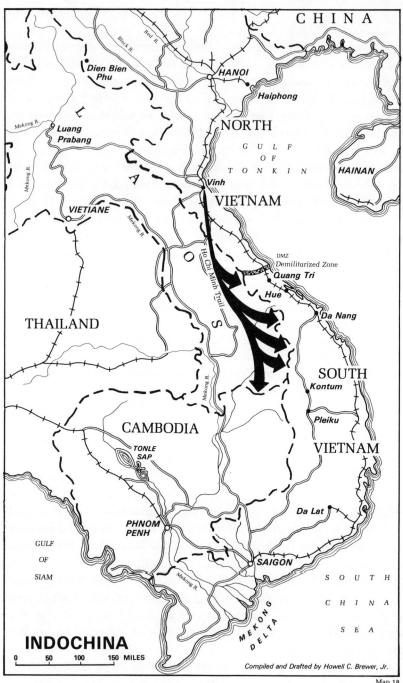

CHINA

Red R.

Black R.

Dien Bien
Phu

HANOI

Haiphong

Mekong R.

NORTH

Luang
Prabang

G U L F
O F
T O N K I N

HAINAN

L
A
O
S

Vinh

VIETNAM

VIETIANE

Mekong R.

Ho Chi Minh Trail

DMZ
Demilitarized Zone

Quang Tri

Hue

THAILAND

Da Nang

SOUTH

Kontum

Mekong R.

CAMBODIA

Pleiku

TONLE
SAP

VIETNAM

PHNOM
PENH

Da Lat

GULF

OF

SIAM

Mekong R.

SAIGON

S O U T H

C H I N A

S E A

MEKONG
DELTA

INDOCHINA

0   50   100   150 MILES

Compiled and Drafted by Howell C. Brewer, Jr.

Map 18

MacArthur, Jack Kelly, and I went to Robertson's house, where we discussed details of timing, my terms of reference, notification of French Premier Pierre Mendès–France, Donald Heath, and Julian Harrington and arrangements for briefings by representatives of State, Defense, and other government agencies involved with Vietnam, and a call on President Eisenhower.

The next three days were filled with consultations with Dulles and Robertson on matters of policy and my terms of reference and with further briefings by the Defense Department, the Foreign Operations Administration, the United States Information Agency (USIA), and the Central Intelligence Agency, then headed by Allen W. Dulles. While Secretary Dulles was not critical of Ambassador Heath, he did indicate that there was need for closer coordination and direction of the operating branches of the agencies in Saigon.

Harold Stassen, head of the FOA, and his staff brought me up to date on current and projected economic aid programs and the Army did the same for military aid programs. Paul Sturm, a Foreign Service officer of the State Department—who had spent some time in Vietnam—along with Robertson, Young, and MacArthur, reviewed the political situation and the status of relations between Diem and the French authorities. By November 3 the briefings were completed and I had a final session with the JCS covering the Vietnamese military forces we might be able to support.

At noon I accompanied Dulles to the White House for the signing by the President of my letter of instructions, prepared in the State Department and evidently already reviewed by the President. After reading the letter aloud to me he commented that it was the best directive he had seen since taking office. He was particularly pleased that I was given broad authority to direct, utilize, and control all agencies and resources of the United States in Vietnam. I was authorized to speak with frankness and the full authority of the United States in support of our objective of maintaining a free, noncommunist government in Vietnam. We would assist the Vietnamese to develop and maintain forces solely for its internal security. While not mentioned in my directive, I understood that protection against any potential external aggression would ultimately be provided by the newly organized

Southeast Asia Treaty Organization (SEATO) but meanwhile the French Expeditionary Corps (FEC) under General Ely would be responsible. The President and Dulles assured me of their full confidence and support. I was sure that I would need both.

At 8:30 P.M. on November 3 the members of my mission, consisting of Paul Sturm from State, Colonel Kelly who would serve as my executive, Lieutenant Colonel John E. Dwan from the office of the Secretary of Defense, Lieutenant Colonel Thomas H. Farnsworth, aide-de-camp, and Master Sergeant Frederick W. Bodemer, secretary, assembled at Bolling Field for departure for Saigon. Because the mission was expected to be of short duration, none of our wives was to accompany us. En route we stopped overnight in Hawaii and in Manila. In Hawaii I was met by Admiral Felix Stump, Commander in Chief of U. S. Forces in the Pacific. I was glad to get the Admiral's assurances of support of our mission. Even more important was my meeting in Manila with President Ramon Magsaysay, who said that his government was ready to assist in training the Vietnamese, who confronted problems similar to those encountered by the Philippines during the Huk rebellions and in resettlement of displaced persons. I was most favorably impressed by Magsaysay.

We arrived Saigon in midmorning, November 8, and were met by Ambassador Heath, the Embassy Counselor Randolph A. Kidder, who would serve as chargé d'affaires after Heath's departure, Mike O'Daniel, and members of the Embassy staff. The Foreign Minister, Tran Van Do, represented Diem. I was a bit surprised that General Ely was not present. His representative explained that the General was in Dalat, the summer residence of the French High Commissioner in the mountains 150 miles northeast of Saigon. It was the first indication I had that the French were not happy over my mission.

I met with the Ambassador and senior members of the Embassy staff before lunch at the Kidders' residence, which was followed by a political briefing at the Embassy. Then I called on Diem at the Norodom Palace, where Mrs. Collins and I had stayed as guests of Marshal DeLattre in 1951. Diem met me at the head of the marble steps on the second floor, as he did many times thereafter. Dressed in an American-style white sharkskin suit, he greeted me in French, smilingly welcoming me to his country. My first impression was of a pleasant, pudgy little man, self-conscious and not quite sure of himself. The tenacity and stubborness that I later learned to know did not show in his round placid face, topped by a head of thick black hair. I gave him greetings from President Eisenhower and expressed my pleasure in being back in Vietnam, after which we had a cup of tea before my call on the Foreign Minister, Tran Van Do.

That ascetic-looking, painfully thin, sallow-faced Vietnamese had apparently represented his country well at Geneva. He was composed and at ease. While we did not then delve into any of his country's problems, we did have opportunities to do so in subsequent weeks and I came to have considerable respect for him.

A dinner at the Embassy residence by Ambassador Heath and his attractive wife brought the busy day to a pleasant conclusion. Kidder had kindly arranged to put me up at his residence until the Embassy was cleared of Heath's belongings. I saw the Heaths off for the States on November 14.

France had agreed on March 6, 1946, to recognize Vietnam as a "free state with its own government, parliament, army, and finances" and as an associated state of the French Union consisting of Laos, Cambodia, and Vietnam. This was confirmed by the Élysée Agreement of March 8, 1949, which gave Vietnam "independence," except that defense and foreign relations were to remain in French hands. When I arrived in Saigon in 1954, French influence still pervaded every organ of the government and the armed forces, after half a century of colonial rule. Many government officials still had dual citizenship in France and Vietnam, and a number of high-ranking officers in the armed forces, including the Chief of Staff, General Nguyen Van Hinh, retained French as well as Vietnamese commissions. Many French officers and noncoms exercised command of Vietnamese units. Training of the Vietnamese forces was entirely in the hands of the French and responsibility for security of Vietnam against external aggression —including possible further attacks by the Viet Minh from north of the 17th parallel—was the responsibility of the FEC under command of General Ely.

United States military and economic aid to Vietnam since its beginning in 1950 by President Truman had been extended directly to the French colonial authorities, with virtually no control of its use by Vietnam or the United States. Following the Geneva Conference the American JCS recommended that if military aid was to be given to Vietnam, the French should relinquish overall command of the armed forces of Vietnam as soon as the National Army was capable of exercising command, and that this capability should be developed by intensive training and progressive promotion of native officers to posts of higher command and responsibility. These recommendations were approved by the National Security Council.

If I was to attain these objectives it was essential that I establish friendly relations with General Ely without delay. I sensed that Ely had avoided being present in Saigon when I arrived. Instead he sent an invitation to me for lunch in Dalat. Disregarding any niceties of protocol, I flew the next day to Dalat to lunch with him. Despite the cordial relations we had while members of the NATO Standing Group, he received me with cool formality. But he did have a band and an honor guard of native troops at the Dalat air strip, and at lunch he relaxed and became again the friendly man I knew.

He said frankly that his first reaction to my coming had been adverse because he feared the Viet Minh might seize on it as a pretext for agitation, but that there had been no such development and he had noted no untoward reaction among the Vietnamese people. I explained that my directive called for the fostering of a friendly, noncommunist government in Vietnam and in particular for support of Diem. Ely replied that he was sorry that my instructions specified support of Diem so explicitly. I answered that we felt more could be done to assist Diem and that he should be given every possible chance to succeed.

Ely said the first things that needed to be done were to end the feud between the Chief of Staff, General Hinh, and Diem, and to build up a strong Ministry of the Interior to bolster the unsteady government. I said I intended to do something about Hinh, and hoped to persuade Diem to broaden and strengthen his cabinet, which caused Ely to say that he could support Diem with more confidence if this were done.

With respect to the French Expeditionary Corps, Ely pointed out that in agreement with the United States France was committed to maintain the FEC to protect Vietnam from the Viet Minh. In addition, maintenance of a sizable FEC would be necessary for the security of sixty thousand French nationals in the country. I agreed that French forces would be required for some time but that it would be difficult to persuade the American Congress to help support sizable French forces in Vietnam for any length of time. Ely doubted that reliance could be placed in SEATO to protect Vietnam's internal security without specific treaty arrangements within the framework of the Manila pact, which I had to admit would be difficult to secure. More heartening from an immediate point of view was Ely's statement that he opposed weakening the National Army by any support of independent and often rival forces, which I took to mean the forces of the pseudo-religious sects that controlled goodly portions of Vietnam south of Saigon. He agreed that the National Army should be subordinate to the government of Diem. Altogether, our meeting pointed up serious differences in views but established a more cordial basis for the tough negotiations that we both knew lay ahead.

The uncertain state of affairs in Vietnam was brought home to me on the day of my arrival when the Chief of Staff, General Hinh, attacked President Diem over a government radio supported in part by U.S. funds. Diem informed me on November 10 that Bao Dai had ordered Hinh to report to him in France. Hinh had told Diem he could not obey the orders for a week. Ely and I had decided that each of us should urge Hinh to comply at once.

Accordingly I invited Hinh to see me the next day. He spoke forthrightly of the impasse between himself and Diem, whom he regarded as utterly incompetent to lead the country and would have to be removed. There were two ways to do this: Bao Dai could dismiss Diem or he, Hinh, could execute a coup d'état. I assured him that if he attempted a coup it would mean the end of military aid to Vietnam. He said he realized this, but that the question was whether Vietnam was better off with Diem and American aid, or without Diem and without U.S. aid. He said he would make up his mind within forty-eight hours. I thanked him for his frankness but urged him to comply with Bao Dai's orders. I did not take seriously his threat to attempt a coup.

A few days later, at the request of American and Vietnamese report-

ers, I held a press conference in which I made clear that the United
States intended to support the government of Diem and a National
Army as long as it was loyal to President Diem. This word was publicized in the native press and was gratefully acknowledged to me by
Diem as strengthening his hand. It may have had a part in convincing
Hinh to leave for Paris, which he did on November 29, never to return.
While getting acquainted with the embassy staff and the chiefs of our
missions, I concentrated on two initial objectives: first, an agreement
with General Ely on the strength and organization of the Vietnamese
armed forces that the United States might support and arrangements
for their training and control; and, second, initiation of steps by which
we might help strengthen and stabilize Diem's government.

The Embassy staff, while not exceptional, was generally competent
and certainly cooperative. The Chargé, Randy Kidder, knew Vietnam
and its chief officials quite well and was a big help, as were Gardner
Palmer, the economic counselor, and Francis E. Meloy, Jr., chief of the
political section. But I came to rely chiefly on Mike O'Daniel and Leland Barrows, of the United States Operations Mission (USOM), in
developing our assistance programs. I consulted with the knowledgeable representatives of the United Kingdom, Australia, and Canada
and found them always sympathetic to our cause and fully cooperative.

Collins-Ely Agreement on Vietnam Armed Forces

General Ely and I proceeded without delay on our negotiations in reference to the Vietnamese armed forces. These required some tough
discussions extending over a considerable period. At these sessions,
conducted either in Ely's office or mine, I was always accompanied by
Paul Sturm and my executive Jack Kelly. Ely was quite fluent in English but preferred to speak French. My French was fair, but I never
trusted my understanding of any important point without verification by Sturm.

On December 13, 1954, Ely and I finally signed an agreement, subject to the approval of our and the Vietnam government, substantially
as follows:

a. I agreed to recommend U.S. support of a Vietnamese National
Army of three combat divisions and three territorial (local defense) di-

visions, totaling approximately 80,000 at an estimated annual cost of $172,500,000; a Navy of small craft, totaling 3,250 men; and an Air Force of two liaison squadrons and one transport squadron of 3,150 men. The total strength of the armed forces for the first year was to be approximately 88,000, at a cost of about $193,000,000. The estimated cost of MAAG (Military Assistance Advisory Group) operations, $8,500,000.

b. The above force structure, requiring a reduction of about 50 percent of the existing strengths, was to be accomplished by the gradual elimination of the least effective men.

c. Full autonomy would be granted the Vietnamese forces by July 1, 1955, with all units commanded and staffed by Vietnam personnel.

d. Full responsibility for the development and training of the Vietnamese forces would be assumed by O'Daniel's MAAG by January, 1955, under the overall authority of General Ely. Ely would remain responsible for the strategic direction of French and Vietnamese forces against external aggression and internal subversion.

e. United States and French training personnel assigned to Vietnamese forces would operate under the direction of MAAG. As the Vietnamese personnel developed proficiency, both American and French trainers would be eliminated.

French approval of the Collins-Ely agreement was held up by the Premier of France, Mendès-France, ostensibly to ensure that it did not violate the Geneva accords. Mendès' real difficulty was in agreeing to phase out French instructors. The Vietnamese feared the economic and morale effects of discharging almost 100,000 men. The United States finally agreed on January 20, 1955, to raise the Vietnamese force levels that we would support in December, 1955, to 100,000 at a cost of $214,500,000. The French held out until February 11, 1955, before accepting the original agreement. The following day Mike O'Daniel assumed responsibility for the training of the Vietnamese. A major hurdle to the accomplishment of my mission was behind me.

Concurrently with the negotiations with Ely I was searching for ways to assist Diem in strengthening his government. I had been attracted to him from the beginning of our acquaintance; he was so beset with problems that I could not help being sympathetic. The re-

moval of Hinh had been a help but I soon realized that Diem's difficulties went far beyond Hinh.

To start with, Diem was a strange anomaly in Vietnam: a devout
Roman Catholic, a man of integrity and lofty ideals, at the head of a
people almost wholly Buddhist and of easy-going standards. He came
of a high mandarin family, his father having been Court Chamberlain
to the emperor Than Thai. As a youngster he had spent some time in
a monastery with the idea of becoming a Catholic priest but decided
against it because, according to his brother Archbishop Thuc, "the
church was too worldly for him." Instead, at the age of twenty he graduated at the top of his class at the French-run School for Law and Administration in Hanoi. In 1929 he was appointed Governor of Quang
Tri province and at age thirty-two became the Interior Minister and
Secretary of the Commission on Reform of Annam. He resigned after
becoming convinced that the French opposed reforms, and he publicly
accused Bao Dai of being "nothing but an instrument in the hands of
the French authorities."

Thereafter Diem and Thuc traveled extensively in Belgium and the
United States, staying mostly in Catholic monasteries while enlisting support for an independent Vietnam from such powerful men as
Senators Mike Mansfield and John F. Kennedy, Congressman Walter
Judd, and Cardinal Spellman. After having twice refused the premier-
ship, Diem finally accepted appointment from Bao Dai to be President of the governing Council of Ministers on June 16, 1954.

The real power back of Diem as he took over the presidency of the
Council of Ministers—he was usually addressed as "Mr. President"—
was not Bao Dai, but the Ngo family. Brother Nhu was Diem's closest
political adviser and operator behind the scenes. I rarely saw him but
was always conscious of his influence in the background and I instinctively did not like or trust him or his highly visible and personable
wife, who acted as Diem's official hostess. She founded the Women's
Solidarity Movement, constantly meddled in politics, and became a
member of the Assembly. She was such a vixen that her father, Tran
Van Chung, whom I knew in Washington as the Vietnamese Ambassador, later turned against her and her husband Nhu. Nhu and brother
Can, who held no public office but was said to be the political boss of

Annam, organized the National Revolutionary Movement (NRM), made up chiefly of government employees, which became the majority party in the National Assembly. Another brother, Archbishop Thuc, quietly marshaled Catholic support for the administration, and a fourth brother Luyen was appointed Ambassador to the United Kingdom and was an adviser on foreign affairs. Ambassador Chung's brother, Tran Van Do, was the respected Foreign Minister, and a third brother of the related Tran family, Bac, was Minister of Public Works, while two other in-laws held important subcabinet posts.

As with his over-reliance on Ngo family ties, Diem's Catholicism was a detriment to him in the minds of many Buddhists and other non-Christian Vietnamese. Diem never realized this, or else ignored it. When Cardinal Spellman visited Saigon in January, 1955, much ado was made in the native press of his influence on Diem. Spellman was followed in March by Cardinal Gilroy and Archbishop O'Brien from Australia. They came at the suggestion of Foreign Minister Casey of Australia, according to Diem's brother Bishop Thuc, as a demonstration of Australia's interest in the refugees. The streets near the palace and the cathedral were hung with the signs of welcome to them, as was the case during Spellman's visit. These banners, which carried such slogans as "Long Live the Catholic Church," in French, Latin, English, and Vietnamese were put up by over-zealous refugees, but inevitably were attributed to Diem's "Catholic government" or "Catholic party." I suggested to Bishop Thuc that a moratorium on visits by Catholic cardinals or bishops be called for at least six months. Any advantages that might have been gained from such visits would have been outweighed by the opportunities afforded the sects and the Viet Minh for anti-Diem propaganda.

Diem's first cabinet was fairly representative of the diverse segments of the population of South Vietnam, but it was also illustrative of Diem's problems. It contained few strong men other than the leaders of two pseudoreligious sects who ruled extensive fiefs, largely independent of the central government, in the rich, rice-growing provinces of the Mekong Delta west and south of Saigon. Each group had its own army, subsidized by the French, and collected its own taxes. The Cao Dai ("Cow die") led by General Nguyen Than Phuong operated a powerful political party under the cloak of a synthetic religion that combined elements of Buddhism, Catholicism, Confucianism, and Taoism, which did have an appeal to the simple peasant farmers. The Cao Dai had their own pope, Pham Cong Tac; a gaudy cathedral; and a holy mountain in Tay Ninh. The Hoa-Hao ("Wha-how"!) sect, headed by the wax-mustachioed General Tran Van Soai, likewise appealed to the peasants with a veneer of Buddhism and a protective paternalism comparable to that of New York's Tammany Hall. To win support of the powerful sects, at least temporarily, Diem offered the Cao Dai and the Hoa Hao three positions each in the cabinet.

Another armed group with extensive power, though not represented in the government, was the Binh Xuyen ("Bean Zuyen"), made up of former river pirates, which manned the police force, including the secret police. It was headed by a gangster, Bay Vien, who would have been at home in the Chicago underworld of the 1920s. The Binh Xuyen didn't bother with a religious cover. Their Saigon headquarters was in a corner of the square facing the French cathedral, in a building surrounded by sandbagged and barbed-wired machine-gun and mortar emplacements. From the second-story windows heavy machine guns jutted out menacingly. The Binh Xuyen had their main base in a fortified area in the suburb of Cholon, on the west side of Saigon, from which they controlled the gambling casinos and brothels of Cholon.

One of my major objectives was to strengthen Diem's government. Diem had retained for himself two of the most important ministries, Defense and Interior, each a full-time job. Dr. Phan Huy Quat, whom I came to know and respect as potentially one of the ablest Vietnamese leaders, had been Defense Minister at one time but was forced out of office by the sects when he tried to bring their private armies under government control. Paul Sturm knew him well and held him in high regard, as did Ely. I did my best to persuade Diem to appoint Quat either as deputy prime minister in charge of both Defense and Interior, or as minister in either post. Diem would not consider making Quat his deputy but more than once assured me that he would appoint Quat to Defense, only to have brother Luyen or Nhu persuade Diem that Quat's appointment would antagonize the sects, which undoubtedly would have been the case. After weeks of indecision, Diem told me in mid-December that his Deputy Defense Minister, Ho Thong Minh, objected to serving under Quat. Unable to get Minh to change his mind, Diem said he had decided to promote Minh to the Ministry and that he would give Minh a free hand to run the armed services.

Dulles was scheduled in mid-December to meet in Paris with Mendès-France and Anthony Eden to discuss developments in Vietnam since Geneva. The time had arrived for me to advise the State Department of my growing doubts as to Diem's capacity to unite the divisive factions of his country. I cabled Dulles on December 13, outlining the situation and reporting that I had become convinced that Diem and brothers Luyen and Nhu were unwilling to turn over control of the armed services to Quat or any other strong man, and that they probably feared Quat as a potential successor to Diem. I doubted that Diem would delegate real authority to Minh but would continue to meddle in the ministry, to the detriment of O'Daniel's mission and the development of effective forces.

I said we should begin to consider alternatives to Diem, even including the possible return of Bao Dai, or the gradual withdrawal of support from Vietnam. I realized that abandonment of Diem would embarrass our government but added, "I believe it would be better to take a slight loss of prestige in the near future while time to attempt other solutions remains, rather than continue to support Diem should failure appear relatively certain. We have not reached this point, though I have grave misgivings re Diem's chances of success."

At the Paris tripartite meeting, Mendès, supported by Eden, pressed Dulles to consider alternatives to Diem, including the appointment by Bao Dai of a "viceroy" who would act for Bao Dai in settling disputes between Diem and the factions. Dulles objected strongly but did agree that Ely and I should consider alternatives if the situation was not improved by mid-January.

I Submit a Seven-Point Aid Program

While the State Department was mulling over these matters, I submitted a seven-point program that I had been developing with our

Embassy staff and missions, on which I intended to concentrate during the remainder of my stay in Vietnam. I had discussed this program with Ely who had agreed to cooperate.

1. *Vietnamese armed forces*. Implementation of the Collins-Ely agreement.

2. *Strengthening and stabilizing the Diem government*. Though stymied in getting Diem to appoint Quat as defense minister, I still hoped to persuade Diem to employ Quat in the Interior Ministry or elsewhere in the government. Meanwhile, Mike O'Daniel and I would continue to press Diem to give Minh a free hand in running the armed forces.

3. *Resettlement of refugees and displaced persons*. This would be a long-range process requiring considerable American aid and economic reorientation. Such a program would have to be supported by USOM for economic assistance, under Leland Barrows, who had already initiated discussion with French and Vietnamese authorities.

4. *Land reform*. Another long-range program in connection with the resettlement program on which USOM and the Embassy staff had initiated studies dealing with land ownership and use.

5. *Creation of a national assembly*. It was imperative that some form of national assembly be created by the government to give Diem democratic support and develop political leaders. I directed the Embassy staff to expedite its study of this program.

6. *Financial and economic aid*. A team of representatives of the Embassy and other U.S. missions in Vietnam was already working on means and methods of extending U.S. aid directly to Vietnam as announced on October 23, 1954, by President Eisenhower. This would be broadened to assist the Vietnamese Ministry of Information in development of a program in support of U.S. aid.

7. *A program for Vietnamese administrative personnel*. Selection, education, and training, and related educational and cultural matters.

I did not ask for formal approval of this program by any of the agencies in Washington, but received the tacit approval of State, Defense, and the FOA as we moved along.

In trying to carry out the above points I soon learned that one of

Diem's great faults was his inability to delegate responsibility. With O'Daniel's strong backing, Minh wished to appoint a General Vy as the new Chief of Staff, a man whom they both regarded as the ablest available combat-type officer. Reportedly on urging of Diem's brother Nhu—who was beginning to assert great influence on Diem—over Minh's protest the President appointed General Le Van Ty, a man whom O'Daniel regarded has having few traits of leadership and no backbone. This was but the first of a series of incidents in which Diem went over Minh's head to make even minor appointments and promotions, which in any well-ordered military ministry would be the prerogative and responsibility of the Minister of Defense. In subsequent crises Ty proved a weakling and Vy later participated in an abortive coup against Diem.

To help Diem develop some popular support among his people, I and the chief of our United States Information Agency urged Diem to get out in the provinces to make himself known. This was contrary to his mandarin heritage, which made it unseemly for him thus to appeal for popular support. We did persuade him to visit his home province in Annam in mid-January, 1955. This trip was a great success; Diem was surprised and delighted with the reception he received. I cannot recall his venturing forth again. He turned more and more to autocratic rule and dependence on his family.

The Geneva accords provisionally divided the country along the 17th parallel, roughly 50 miles north of Hué. Any civilian who desired to move from one zone to another was to be permitted to do so prior to May 18, 1955. Close to 900,000 northerners chose to move south from the communist-controlled zone, though this meant giving up their ancestral land, their houses, and practically all their belongings. They were moved south by French and American ships and planes.

Resettlement of refugees was well handled by the Diem government, but the fact that they were northerners, and were settled chiefly in new Catholic communities under their village priests, did not sit well with the natives of Cochin China, particularly the Buddhist majority. The refugees were looked on somewhat as intruders unduly favored by the "Catholic government" of Diem, much as the carpetbaggers who moved south from our northern states after the American Civil

War were disliked by the "rebel" South. Instead of becoming a political asset to Diem, as they should have been, they remained isolated in their Catholic villages and were never really assimilated into the Cochin Chinese population.

Linked with settlement of refugees was the program of agrarian reform. For a variety of bureaucratic reasons Diem was slow in implementing any program to correct abuses of landlord-tenant relations, or provisions of distributing land abandoned by owners or otherwise not in use. It was not until January, 1955, after considerable prodding from me and Barrows, that two basic decrees were issued aimed at reduction of land rents, protection of the rights of tenants through tenancy contracts, and provision for resettlement of refugees from the north. Other decrees followed, but actual implementation of these reforms, particularly the distribution to peasant farmers of unused and undeveloped land, did not begin until long after I had left Vietnam in May, 1955.

Little progress was made toward creation of a national assembly before then. Members of the politial section of the Embassy staff, headed by the able Meloy, had assisted Vietnamese officials of the Foreign Ministry in drafting a decree establishing such an assembly, but Diem took no action while awaiting the outcome of his confrontation with the sects and a determination of the future role of Emperor Bao Dai.

Financial advisors to Burrows in USOM, and Embassy staff members headed by Gardner Palmer, Counselor for Economic Affairs, worked with Vietnamese officials to establish procedures acceptable to the United States with regard to foreign exchange, import controls, and related matters. The French government had agreed at a Franco-American conference in Washington in September, 1954, to permit Vietnam to issue its own currency. A national bank of Vietnam was established by decree on December 3, 1954, in time to receive American aid money, which after January 1, 1955, was to be paid directly to the Vietnamese government as provided in the Collins-Ely agreement of December 13, 1954.

One of Diem's earliest and staunchest backers was Wesley R. Fishel, professor of political science at Michigan State University where Diem had lectured once while visiting the United States in the 1930s. When

Diem became Premier in 1954 he arranged for a group of professors, headed by Fishel, to go to Vietnam, independently of the FOA mission headed by Leland Barrows. Not long after I arrived Professor Fishel submitted his recommendations to the FOA that, if approved, would have transferred to Michigan State, from USOM, responsibility for all categories of United States aid except the military programs. On Barrows' recommendation, which I fully supported, we limited the contract with the university to the establishment and training of a national police force and the establishment and supervision of a National Institute of Administration. The latter institution served a highly useful purpose in training Vietnamese to fill the civil service positions in the government vacated by the French as the latter withdrew.

I Report to the National Security Council, January 24, 1955

In December of 1954 when Dulles met with Mendès-France and Anthony Eden in Paris it was agreed that General Ely and I should review the situation in mid-January. Accordingly, on January 20, I submitted to Dulles a status report, highlighting the following factors that would determine the outcome of our efforts in Vietnam.

Free Vietnam could not match the military power of the Viet Minh, which would retain the capability of overrunning all of Vietnam. Free Vietnam's ultimate security would lie in the military and moral support it might receive from the signatories of the Southeast Asia Treaty Organization (SEATO). A clear affirmation from them that they would react if hostilities were renewed might be essential to deter the Viet Minh from an open attack and would greatly strengthen the Diem government.

There was considerable doubt in my mind as to the real intentions and objectives of France in Indochina. A French mission, under Jean Sainteny, was being maintained in Hanoi to look after French interests. While I had no doubt about Ely's honesty and integrity in his dealings with me, Sainteny's instructions sometimes ran counter to those sent Ely, indicating that the French were preparing to preserve their interests in Vietnam, whether or not a free government survived in the South. Without the unequivocal support of the French, neither Diem, nor any other anticommunist leader, would succeed in establishing a viable government in South Vietnam. I suggested that Secretary Dulles have this out with Mendès-France.

While the sects were anticommunist in orientation, they were feudalistic and self-centered in every other respect. They would continue to hold an effective veto over any government action that might threaten their preferred military, economic, and political status until the Vietnamese armed forces became strong enough to neutralize them.

The reorganization of the Vietnamese armed forces and their training under American supervision had strengthened the national forces and given them renewed confidence. Diem had a fair measure of control over the armed forces but it was too early to say whether all elements were fully subordinate to the central government.

Free Vietnam was capable of maintaining a viable economy at modest levels. It was self-sufficient in food. Export of rice and rubber, the former chief sources of Vietnamese foreign exchange, should again become profitable as internal security increased.

But the key factor in the outcome of our efforts in Vietnam would be the ability of Diem to establish broad support for his government, about which I still had serious doubts. He still had much to learn about practical politics and public relations, but had recently shown greater flexibility in handling people and increased confidence in dealing with his ministers and with public issues. I had failed thus far to induce Diem to broaden the base of his government by bringing in other able leaders such as Dr. Quat. However, on balance, I felt that Diem's personal integrity, strong nationalism, tenacity, and moral qualities made him the best available head of government and that with continued American support he might succeed. I therefore recommended that we continue to support Diem, while keeping our options open. Accompanying the report were cost estimates for FY 1956 of approximately $258 million.

I was summoned to Washington on January 22, 1955, for meetings with State, Defense, FOA, and the JCS while the National Security Council reviewed my report and approved my recommendation for continued assistance to Vietnam and the Diem government. I called on President Eisenhower and brought him up to date on the situation in Vietnam, in which he was greatly interested. Unknown to me, Diem had written the President asking that my mission be extended. The President discussed this with me and on February 3 replied to Diem that he was asking me to stay another two months.

It is interesting that when Secretary Dulles passed through Saigon near the end of February en route to Washington from Europe, he stopped off for a few days while calling on Diem and the French High Commissioner. He was accompanied by Douglas MacArthur III, counselor of the State Department, and Walter Robertson. They were all enthusiastic about the job I was doing in Saigon, so much so that Doug MacArthur suggested that I transfer to the Foreign Service, as Brigadier General Henry A. Byroade, later ambassador to Burma and the Philippines, had done a short while before, and remain on in Vietnam as ambassador. I don't know that the Secretary was aware of this suggestion, but in any event I had had enough of government service for a while and was more interested in other fields. I urged instead that an experienced Foreign Service officer be selected as my successor, as soon as convenient after the two-month extension of my assignment.

Diem Puts a Squeeze on the Sects

Meanwhile I returned to Saigon, but not before getting in a much-needed rest with my family at our cottage on the Chesapeake. I returned on February 9, as Diem began to put a squeeze on the sects and the Binh Xuyen. Diem's conspiratorial nature warned him that the only way he could defeat the sects was to attack them piecemeal, first by cutting their financial support, then by setting them against each other. He aimed first at the Binh Xuyen by refusing to renew their license for the Grande Monde, the principal gambling casino in Cholon, and one of their major sources of revenue. Then, as the French subsidies to the sect armies expired in February, Diem refused to meet the sects' demands for financial assistance or the large-scale induction, or "rallying," of their forces into the Vietnamese National Army, except on a selective basis. He used the age-old device of bribery to persuade dissident minor leaders among the Hoa Hao and the Cao Dai to "rally" to the government. For the handling of these astute moves, Diem relied chiefly on brother Nhu, assisted by Colonel Edward G. Lansdale, an "unconventional warfare" Air Force office They duty with the CIA, who was attached to Mike O'Daniel's training group.

Alarmed by these defections, representatives of the Cao Dai, Hoa Hao, and the Binh Xuyen met in Tay Ninh on March 3–4, under sponsorship of the Cao Dai "Pope," Pham Cong Tac, and formed a National Front in opposition to Diem. They were joined by other smaller dissident groups. On March 21 the front issued an ultimatum demanding that Diem form a "government of national union" within five days, subject to approval of the National Front. At the same time the six representatives of the sects withdrew from the cabinet.

During the next few days I met almost continuously, in turn, with Diem, representatives of the sects, cabinet ministers, and, in absence of General Ely—who was in Paris conferring with the new French Premier, Edgar Faure—with Ely's Deputy High Commissioner Jean Daridan and Generals Jacquet and Gambiez, in order to prevent any violent action by the sects. Jacquet and Gambiez acknowledged responsibility of the FEC to maintain security in Saigon, but refused to say flatly that they would block any move by the Binh Xuyen to strengthen their forces in Saigon–Cholon.

Diem was relatively cool and confident when I called on him on March 22. He had brought into the Saigon area three battalions of "Nung," mountain tribesmen, part of his loyal militia from Tonkin, and two battalions of paratroopers, also from Tonkin. These troops had no ties to the Cochin China sects. Diem said he had reached agreement with Minh whereby, in case of disturbances, the Vietnamese army would intervene. I suggested he seek to avoid such a confrontation by calling in the sect leaders and explaining his plans for integrating some of their forces and, through the agricultural and resettlement programs, assisting those who would be discharged. He said he had asked his ministers to draw up such a statement for him, but as usual nothing had been done. I told him that such lack of action, particularly in not moving to broaden his government, was making it difficult for me to support him. Nevertheless I assured him that American policy with regard to his government remained unchanged, and I urged him to stand firm against the sects' demands.

Continuing his pressure on the Binh Xuyen, Diem issued a decree on March 26 establishing a separate police force for the Saigon–Cholon area, independent of the Binh Xuyen, but not affecting their hold on the national sureté or police.

I met with General Ely on March 27 following his return from Paris. After some inconclusive discussion of the sect problem, Ely said it could be solved only by the return of Bao Dai under conditions carefully stipulated in advance by the French and United States governments. When I asked how precisely this would solve the sect crisis, Ely said Bao Dai could get the sects to accept many things that no one else could impose on them. I replied that I doubted Diem would remain in office unless Bao Dai returned as a constitutional monarch. The only heartening item I got from our meeting was that the Faure government would not play a double game with Sainteny being able to go over Ely's head.

Around noon on March 29 I had word from General O'Daniel that Defense Minister Minh had resigned. I invited Minh to my office at once and was given the following story: That morning Minh and his Chief of Staff, General Ty, had been summoned by Diem to his office and informed that effective at once Colonel Nguyen Le would replace Lai Huu Sang as Chief of the National Police and Sureté and that at 1:30 P.M. the National Army would take over Sureté headquarters at the corner of the cathedral square, guarded by Binh Xuyen commandos, in the heart of Saigon. Apparently this was the first time Minh or Ty had heard of the plan. Minh said he had advised the President to delay until he could secure cabinet approval. Diem replied that he had thought the matter through, that he had full power to act. Minh declared he had no alternative but to resign, whereupon at the President's invitation Minh wrote out his resignation, which Diem accepted. I urged Minh to withdraw his resignation, but he would consider doing so only if Diem asked him and if a better working relation could be established between them. I told Minh I would urge the President to return Minh's resignation and to come to an understanding.

Shortly thereafter I had a call from Ely's office that Diem had notified Ely of his proposed action against the Binh Xuyen. Ely had sent his deputy Wintrebert and General Jacquot to Diem to urge him not to use any army troops to take over Sureté headquarters. According to their report, Diem shuttled back and forth between them and brother Luyen off-stage, who they were convinced was the prime mover behind the proposed operation. I was told they had succeeded in persuading Diem to postpone action.

I was just drifting off to sleep that night, March 29, when Jack Kelly knocked at my door to say that machine-gun fire had broken out in Cholon a few moments before and at the same time mortar shells began to explode at or near the Norodom Palace, only a few blocks from the Embassy residence. We went out on the upper porch to watch and hear. Tracer bullets were ricocheting and lighting the sky over Cholon, and a few mortar shells were exploding in or near the palace grounds. Reports from our intelligence people began to arrive in a few minutes and continued for the next hour or so until the firing finally died away.

First thing the following morning I had a report from James Cooley, whom I had gotten Allen Dulles to send out to serve as evaluator of the sometimes conflicting reports I received daily from the military services and the CIA. The account was in essence as follows: At the stroke of midnight approximately eighty Binh Xuyen attacked the police headquarters in Cholon, which had been taken over by Vietnamese Army paratroopers. By 1:30 A.M. March 30 the troopers, reinforced by the army, had driven off the attackers. Total casualties were reported as ten killed and forty wounded. The Binh Xuyen had also attacked VN Army headquarters in Cholon, but been repulsed; five army soldiers had been killed and twenty-one wounded. At the same midnight hour, intermittent 81-mm mortar shelling of the presidential palace had begun. Two rounds hit a wing of the palace and others landed in the palace grounds and nearby, wounding several VN soldiers.

Ely phoned me later that Foreign Minister Tran Van Do and the Ministers of Social Action and Public Health, all members of the independent Tinh-Than party, had resigned from the cabinet. I was distressed at this news, since Do was the one stabilizing influence left in the government. I invited Do to see me at the Embassy residence, which he did that afternoon. He was greatly depressed over the turn of events, as he confirmed the resignations. I expressed my sympathy but said I wondered if he realized the full implications of his action. I asked if he and his colleagues were trying to bring about the fall of the government. Do seemed shocked at this query and quickly denied such such an intention, saying their object was to force Diem to adopt a "reasonable policy." I then urged him and his group to withdraw their resignations, which he agreed to do, but only if Diem asked him to do so. Knowing how rapidly rumor spread in Saigon, I sent an officer from the Embassy to see the President with a message from me earnestly suggesting that he call the Foreign Minister to the palace that evening.

The staff officer reported back a little later. Diem had said he doubted that Do would come to the palace for fear of another Binh Xuyen attack. Then the President launched a long tirade, attacking Do and his colleagues. He finally said he would telephone Do and invite him and his group to the palace early the following morning, March 31. Diem stressed that he would request that they withdraw their resignations "because they would be committing stupidity" at this critical juncture. He said also that he would emphasize that they must accept his judgment and be obedient, since he was Commander in Chief and had full powers both civil and military.

A Truce is Arranged

A shaky truce between the Binh Xuyen and the VN Army had been arranged by the French on March 31 in order to avoid the possibility of widespread destruction in the heart of the city surrounding the Binh Xuyen police headquarters and adjacent to the cathedral, and not far from the French hospital, barracks, and communications center. When firing again broke out in Cholon, on April 19–20, the FEC took control of this area, precluding any direct attack by the VN Army. The next three weeks were spent in a succession of futile efforts by Ely and me to persuade Diem to reorganize his government, while our staffs drafted a plan gradually to eliminate the sect forces by integrating certain numbers of them into the National Army, along with a proposal of severance pay for all men not integrated who would surrender their arms.

Ely finally suggested that Bao Dai should proclaim a ten-day extension of the truce, at the same time summoning Diem, the sect leaders, and such political leaders as Quat to Paris to work out a solution.

Bao Dai would be advised in advance as to what our governments wished him to achieve, which I said would have to include Bao Dai's support of Diem's removal of Sang. I doubted that the State Department would agree to Ely's plan but cabled Washington that it was the only new proposal to date and had the advantage of being a French plan. If it failed, the French might be more amenable to any alternative we might suggest, and it would at least provide further time for negotiations.

Stalemate

As I expected, the State Department turned down Ely's proposal. However, Washington could do no better than we in Saigon in suggesting an alternative solution but simply repeated its stand that we should continue to support Diem unequivocally, while urging him to broaden his government. I accepted the Department's stand but pointed out the danger of rigid support of Diem, leaving no maneuver room if Bao Dai should relieve Diem, or if Diem should resign.

In my reply to State, I summed up the situation as I then saw it: Diem was now with the support only of brothers Luyen and Nhu. Though Do and his group had returned to the cabinet, this was only because of my persuasion, and they had no influence. Both Do and Justice Minister Bui Van Thinh, an independent supporter of Diem, said no able man would join the government unless Diem changed his methods and delegated some authority. I had not been in Vietnam long enough to challenge Ely's conviction that while Diem might be able to overthrow the Binh Xuyen in Saigon, this would cause them, and some of the sect forces, to engage in guerrilla warfare with which, in Ely's opinion, the Vietnamese Army would not be able to cope.

On April 7, Ely asked to speak to me privately with only Paul Sturm present. He said that he wished to inform me, even before advising his own government, that after much "soul-searching" he could no longer support Diem. He reviewed our problems in endeavoring to get Diem to broaden his government and concluded that Diem was supported only by the two of us, and Diem's family. He felt that Vietnam could still be saved from the Viet Minh under good leadership; the economic situation was favorable, the population was still neutral; the Vietnamese Army, while raw, was making progress under O'Daniel's training group; and our seven-point program needed only management to make it successful. But he was convinced that unless Diem was replaced while these general conditions were still favorable, Vietnam would be lost to the communist Viet Minh.

Ely said this was his final judgment. In reply to my questions he said he had no one specifically in mind as a successor to Diem, but Quat, Do, Minh, or the Minister of Plans, Nguyen Van Thoai, an independent relative of the Ngo family, would be acceptable.

I said I would have to consider his statement but doubted that Washington would consider supporting anyone other than Diem until maximum U.S.–French pressure was brought to bear on Bao Dai to back Diem fully in relieving the Binh Xuyen of all responsibility for the police and Sureté. Ely agreed that the Binh Xuyen should be so relieved but felt that this should be done as part of an overall reorganization of the government. I said I would report his views to the State Department while restricting any dissemination within the Embassy. I made no commitment as to my judgment.

About this time I received a message from Secretary Dulles expressing regret that the French had "prevented" Diem from attacking the Binh Xuyen by restricting their supply of ammunition and gasoline (a report vigorously denied by Ely) and preventing the Vietnamese Army from storming the Sureté and police station in Saigon. He said he had thought when he had visited Saigon in February that we had agreed that our support of Diem was irreversible. He had discussed the situation with President Eisenhower, who felt the same. They realized they were a long way from the action and had great confidence in Ely and me. They faced the practical difficulty that Congress was not likely to authorize funds for support of any successor to Diem chosen by Bao Dai with French sponsorship.

This cable, following on the heels of Ely's denouement, caused me to conclude that the time had come for me to make my own judgment as to whether we should continue our all-out support of Diem. I could not escape my responsibility. I had wrestled with this decision for weeks, torn between our commitment to Diem—along with my personal agreement with his objectives—and my growing conviction that despite Diem's many admirable attributes he did not have the leadership and political know-how to unite the divisive forces of Vietnam in the face of the unity and tough efficiency of the communists under Ho Chi Minh. That was the judgment that I transmitted, with deep regret, to Secretary Dulles on April 7, 1955. I had come to admire Diem's spiritual qualities, his personal incorruptability, dogged patriotism, and tenacity, but these very qualities, linked with his stubborn reliance on the venal ambitions of his brothers, his lack of political sense, his inability to compromise, and his distrust of anyone who disagreed with him, convinced me he would never make the grade as leader of his country. I felt Diem was not indispensable, and that it would be better to support a change in the presidency before we became wedded to him. Other men would be able, with our support, to carry out the constructive program Ely and I had developed for Diem. I told Dulles I fully realized the gravity of my recommendations, which I made with a heavy heart but with conviction that Vietnam could still be saved from communism.

My message naturally caused quite a stir in the highest circles. Senator Mansfield adamantly opposed the replacement of Diem, and Secretary Dulles was still hopeful that "other elements" could be brought into the government that "would assure real delegation of authority" —something we had tried to achieve without success. Finally, on April 17, I was advised to return to Washington, ostensibly to review the budget for aid to Vietnam, actually to discuss with the State Department and other appropriate agencies what should be done about my recommendation.

Before leaving I called on Diem to advise him of my summons to Washington. In discussing the possibility of changes in his cabinet Diem said he would select only men having the same political concepts as himself. He made clear that this would rule out men like Do, Quat, Thoai, and Minh. This remark confirmed my judgment that there was no worthwhile alternative to our supporting the replacement of Diem.

As the final call of the day, I saw Ely and told him that I had been called to Washington for consultation. There had been some desultory firing in Cholon during the afternoon and I wondered if I should delay my departure. Ely felt there would be no immediate blow-up between the VNA and the Binh Xuyen and urged me to go, as he was anxious to get a decision from Washington.

Accompanied by Sturm, Colonels Dwan and Farnsworth—Jack Kelly had gone home earlier for medical treatment—we flew from Saigon on April 19, 1955, leaving our Embassy in the competent hands of Randy Kidder.

Back in Washington on April 21, I had lunch with the President and a series of meetings with Secretary Dulles and a long session with staff representatives of State, Defense, and the CIA. It was obvious that several of the State Department people, including especially Ken Young and Robert D. Murphy, for whom I had considerable respect, did not agree with my assessment of Diem. Despite this staff opposition Dulles decided on April 27 to cable Ambassador Douglas Dillon in Paris and Chargé Kidder in Saigon that, while continuing to support Diem, the department was giving serious consideration to his replacement if the Vietnamese leaders developed a plan acceptable to Bao Dai.

Fighting Erupts in Saigon

While Washington wavered, Diem published an edict on April 27 dismissing Sang as head of the police and secret service. The Binh Xuyen responded by shelling the Norodom Palace grounds and automatic weapons fire erupted in Cholon. Diem notified Ely that he would employ the Vietnamese Army against the Binh Xuyen if the firing continued. The French had no troops in Cholon with which to interpose and made no move from their restricted area in Saigon to stop the shelling, whereupon Diem ordered the VNA to attack. The Army responded, quickly gaining the upper hand in skirmishing in the streets bordering Cholon and Saigon. Fires raged in the Binh Xuyen area of Cholon as the Binh Xuyen troops were slowly forced from their fortified areas.

When word of Diem's bold action and the army's initial success reached Washington, whatever influence I might have had either with the congressional committees I had briefed, or the State Department, was quickly dissipated. Senator Mansfield announced that if Diem were replaced he would oppose any further military aid to Vietnam, and Congresswoman Edna F. Kelly of New York, speaking for a group of House committee members, informed the State Department to the same effect. The combination of successful action by Diem and powerful support in Congress caused Dulles to cable Dillon in Paris and Kidder in Saigon to suspend action on earlier cables advising them that consideration was being given to the possible replacement of Diem. I was directed to return to Saigon to await the arrival of G. Frederick Reinhart, whose nomination as ambassador already had been submitted to the Senate.

I Return to Saigon

Back in Saigon on May 2, I was glad to learn that the VNA action was progressing favorably. By May 5 the Binh Xuyen forces had been driven from Cholon into a swampy area to the south. Unfortunately the VNA made no real effort to round up the outmanned and defeated Binh Xuyen troops, and permitted Bay Vien, former Police Chief Sang, and other rebel leaders to escape. The sects failed to aid the Binh Xuyen and the army remained loyal to Diem and, generally, conducted itself well.

At this juncture Bao Dai ordered Diem to appoint Vy as chief of staff of the army, replacing Ty, and summoned Diem to report to him in France. He also made the mistake of dispatching the discredited General Hinh to Vietnam as his personal mediator. Diem refused to relieve Ty or to permit Hinh, who had been stopped in Cambodia, to enter the country, and he ignored the summons to report to Bao Dai.

As a counter to these moves by Bao Dai, the National Revolutionary Congress, which purported to represent all political parties but was undoubtedly sponsored by Diem's brother Nhu, convened in Saigon. It was backed by Cao Dai Generals Phuong and Thé, Hoa Hao General Ngo, and a group of minor politicians. The Congress issued a declaration repudiating Bao Dai as chief of state and calling for the formation of a new administration by Diem and election of a national congress to determine the form of government. When the Congress dissolved after passing a variety of resolutions to the above effect, a continuing Revolutionary Committee was formed to follow up on the resolutions of the Congress.

Diem prepared to capitalize on the action of the Revolutionary Congress. When I called on him shortly after my return to Saigon, he said the Revolutionary Committee was determined to overthrow Bao Dai and indicated clearly that he favored such action. I warned Diem that the committee had no legal standing whatever, was made up of some undependable people, and if successful in toppling Bao Dai might next turn against him. I urged him not to support the program of the Revolutionary Committee. At the same time I cabled the State Department and asked for guidance. A prompt reply came back from Dulles backing my stand and directing me to so inform Diem.

Diem's position definitely had been strengthened by his action against the Binh Xuyen, and the prestige of the French, whom many Vietnamese believed had supported the Binh Xuyen, correspondingly weakened. The Revolutionary Committee stepped up its anti-Bao Dai and anti-French propaganda, which had a strong appeal to large segments of the population. This infuriated Ely and the French Commissariat to the point that they lost much of their objectivity as to popular reaction to Diem's recent moves. They tended to blame the United States for worsening French-Vietnamese relations, which in turn affected French-American cooperation, so essential to support of Vietnam against the Viet Minh communists.

My Final Estimate of the Situation

In the light of these developments, I submitted to the State Department, on May 5, 1955, my estimate of the situation with conclusions, in essence as follows:

The Diem government should be fully supported in bringing to a final and quick solution its conflict with the Binh Xuyen.

This will require on the part of the French, not only in Paris, but more importantly in Saigon, that genuine assistance rather than passive obstruction be offered to the Vietnamese government and armed forces.

Specifically, General Ely should be directed to take active steps to persuade the Binh Xuyen to withdraw their forces from three police posts remaining in the French security zone in Saigon, or if the Binh Xuyen refuse, then to permit the VNA to reduce these posts with minimum casualties. . . .

The French garrison in Saigon should be reduced without delay.

There should be a public announcement by appropriate French authorities of their full support of the Diem government in its present conflict with the Binh Xuyen.

On the American side, the U.S. MAAG should step up its ongoing efforts to assist in the establishment and training of essential logistical services for the VNA to make it independent of the FEC.

As soon as the current crisis is over, decisive efforts must be made to persuade or otherwise force Diem to reorganize his government and to establish a cabinet competent to implement the broad programs of reform covered by the Collins-Ely seven-point program, plus a program for integration of the sects into the normal life of Vietnam.

If, after a reasonable period of trial, Diem is unable to constitute a government capable of implementing these programs, the United States should join with France and Bao Dai in assisting liberal Vietnamese nationalists to establish a competent government.

I recognize that General Ely may be irrevocably opposed to supporting any Diem government. If this proves to be true, I would suggest we urge the Faure government to replace him. . . .

I recognize also that it may be difficult politically to withdraw U.S. support from Diem even if a period of trial proves he is incapable of establishing an effective government. I still feel that even if Diem manages to suppress the Binh Xuyen, this will not change his own basic incapacity to manage the affairs of government. His present successes may even make it harder for us to persuade Diem to take competent men into the government, to decentralize authority to his ministers, and to establish sound procedures for the implementation of reform programs. I am still convinced that Diem does not have the knack of handling men nor the executive capacity truly to unify the country and establish an effective government. If this should become evident, we should either withdraw from Vietnam, because our money will be wasted, or we should take such steps as can be legitimately taken to secure an effective new premier. . . . No matter who heads the government here, free Vietnam will not be saved [from communism] unless sound political, economic and military programs are promptly and effectively put into action. This will require whole hearted agreement and coordination between the Vietnamese, Americans, and French. Difficult as this may be to achieve, it is possible, in my judgment. If this tripartite approach is not secured, we should withdraw from Vietnam.

Tri-Partite Conference in Paris

This report reached Dulles as he, Faure, and Harold Macmillan, Foreign Secretary of Britain, met in Paris on May 8 to consider problems of European defense. The more pressing situation in Vietnam quickly preempted the discussion. After some heated statements by lesser

French officials critical of American support of Diem, Faure said that if the Americans insisted on continued backing of Diem in spite of French objections he would consider withdrawal of the FEC and French retirement from Vietnam if the United States would assume responsibility for protection of French civilians and the Vietnamese refugees from the north.

Dulles replied that the worst aspect of the Vietnam situation was the differences it created between France and the United States. He said that "Vietnam is not worth a quarrel with France." He then matched Faure's offer of withdrawal by saying that the United States was prepared to withdraw from Vietnam if that would solve the problem, but warned that United States financial support could not be expected for any solution which he could think of as an alternative to Diem. The conferees decided to adjourn while canvassing the situation further.

Our embassy in Saigon had been kept advised of the Paris negotiations. When Faure offered to withdraw the FEC, Dulles cabled the JCS and me for our judgments as to the effects of such a withdrawal. I replied that the presence of the FEC was essential for the security of Vietnam, for the further training and logistical support of the VNA, and as a stabilizing influence on Vietnamese politics. The JCS likewise opposed precipitate withdrawal of the FEC.

Influenced by these judgments when the Paris negotiators met again on May 11, Dulles softened somewhat his approach to Faure. He urged Faure to continue French support of the Diem government at least until a National Assembly could be elected, which would determine the ultimate form and composition of a government that might not include Diem. Reluctantly, Faure agreed, subject to certain face-saving stipulations to which neither side could agree. Thereafter the days of joint French-American policy were over.

When on May 11, I advised General Ely that I would be leaving shortly after the arrival of Ambassador Reinhardt, Ely confided that he expected to be recalled by the end of the month but, in any event, intended to resign if not transferred to another post. While I disagreed with French colonial policies in Vietnam, I had a good deal of sympathy for Paul Ely, who had been given an impossible task by his government. His mission ended on June 2, 1955.

I Return to my NATO Assignment

G. Frederick Reinhardt's nomination as ambassador to Vietnam was confirmed by the Senate on April 20, 1955, but he did not arrive in Saigon until mid-May. On May 11 I began the round of receptions, luncheons, and dinners that mark the departure of officials from any post. Many are dull, routine affairs. The somewhat strained relations between the French and Vietnamese and uncertainty as to what my departure might signify to future French, American, and Vietnamese cooperation, lent an air of tension to these parties. But the latent animosity of some of the French toward Diem and his official hostess, the vixenish Madame Nhu, which I feared once or twice might break into the open, was discreetly held under control.

I did appreciate the warm farewell reception extended to me by General Ely and his wife, and the final state dinner in my honor given by President Diem at the Norodom Palace. The note of strain carried over to that evening. When someone proposed a toast to Bao Dai, I found myself raising my glass instead, sotto voce, "To the Vietnamese people," as was later noted by an alert observer. Fortunately, no one took umbrage and the evening went off well.

The following day I made my farewell calls on British Ambassador Stephenson, Foreign Minister Vu Van Mao, who had succeeded Do, General Ely, and Diem. Despite our many differences Diem and I had grown to have a certain respect for one another, as was attested, on his part, by the inscription he wrote on his photograph that he shyly presented to me:

> To General J. Lawton Collins
> In appreciation of his unstinting and
> sincere efforts to assist us in our
> struggle for independence and democracy.
>
> Ngodinhdiem

Saigon, May 1955

On the evening of May 14, 1955, I and the small staff I had brought with me six and a half months before left by military air transport for home. Back in Washington, Secretary Dulles did me the courtesy of accompanying me to the White House for a brief call on President Eisenhower, who greeted me, as always, with his friendly grin.

I said, "I hope, Mr. President, that you and Secretary Dulles do not feel that I have let you down in Vietnam." The Secretary quickly interjected, "By no means, Joe. When we sent you out, we thought there was a 10 percent chance of saving Vietnam from Communism. You have raised that figure to at least 50 percent." The President added his generous agreement and congratulations.

Next day I was back on the job as U.S. Representative on the Standing Group of NATO.

Postscript

Unfortunately, my forecast of Diem's inability to overcome the vast obstacles that beset him proved to be largely correct. Despite his, and our, failures in Vietnam, he was a dedicated Vietnamese patriot whose brutal murder was despicable and wholly unwarranted. He deserved a better fate at the hands of his countrymen.

CHAPTER **XX**

Return to
Civilian Life

On March 31, 1956, after forty-three years of service, I retired from the United States Army. Retirement after so many years away from one's original home base is a more drastic change than retirement from most civil occupations. It usually involves finding not only a place of residence but a new locale and a new mode of life. Gladys and I were inclined to remain in Washington, where my brother James and two of my sisters were living, and where we had many friends. But before settling down, I wanted to make a clean break from the military service. Both Gladys and I needed a change of scene and a period of relaxation. We decided to take a six-month vacation in Europe. Although Gladys was not enthusiastic about going off at once, we wanted to reach Europe in springtime, and I feared that something might turn up that would delay our departure indefinitely. In fact, after our plans were made, Secretary of Defense Charles E. Wilson belatedly asked me to remain on duty for another year, which I declined.

So on April 2, 1956, we sailed from New York for Bremerhaven. In years past we had traveled over much of Europe, but this time we wanted to visit areas with which we were not familiar, especially Spain, Provence, the Italian lakes, and the Dolomites. On my last trip to Paris I had bought a small Renault sedan which I had left with Gladys' brother Major General Ernest Easterbrook, then stationed at Fontainebleau. After a pleasant visit with Ernie and his attractive wife Nancy, "Vinegar Joe" Stilwell's eldest daughter, we were off to Spain where we spent the first two months.

Spain was refreshingly new to us. Perhaps from reading about the Spanish custom of long afternoon siestas, when everyone stops work for two hours, we had gotten the impression that Spaniards are lazy and indolent. Not so. We found them an industrious, hardworking people who have sensibly adjusted their working hours to the climate and their temperament. Daily we drove past whole families spring planting in the fields until dark, and when Gladys had to have some dental work done in Madrid, the only appointment she could get was 8:00 P.M. We quickly accustomed ourselves to siestas, and to Spanish meal hours: breakfast at 10:00 A.M.; lunch, 2:30 P.M.; dinner 9 or 10:00 P.M. Instead of driving 250 or more miles a day, we were content to do 100, or less, with the minimum of advance reservations, and no rigid itinerary. Before leaving Washington, I had taken a short refresher course in Spanish so that I had little difficulty with the language. We had brought with us Henry C. V. Morton's excellent *A Stranger in Spain*, which gave the historical background and points of interest for the places we planned to visit, running from San Sebastián on the French border via Salamanca, Avila, Segovia, Madrid, Toledo, Cordoba, Sevilla, Gibraltar, Granada, to Valencia. Timing our trip so as to be in Madrid and Sevilla for their fiesta weeks, we had gay times in each city. Except for Madrid's great Prado and fiesta, we enjoyed most in Spain the charming cities of Segovia and Sevilla and the exotic beauty of Granada.

From Valencia we ferried the Renault overnight to Majorca, which, lovely as it was, did not measure up in our eyes to the Hawaiian islands. A steamer took us from the city of Palma to Barcelona, where we left Spain reluctantly on June 20, after a wonderful stay. We were amazed to find that we had averaged less than sixteen dollars a day total expenses, much less than if we had stayed at home.

From Spain we drove across the Pyrenees to the ancient walled city of Carcassonne, thence via Nimes to les Baux, near the center of Provence, which we made our base for the next four days while visiting the surrounding Roman towns of Arles, Avignon, Orange, and Aix with their well-preserved arenas, theaters, and temples. Interesting as they were, none could rival the magnificent aqueduct-bridge, the Pont du Gard.

From Provence we drove up the Rhone valley to Mentone on Lake Annecy, thence to Geneva and Chamonix at the foot of Mont Blanc. The sun was warm and the skies clear as we drove up the valley of

Chamonix. We had refilled our wine bottle with good local wine, bought fruit, a loaf of crisp French bread, and a generous slice of cheese for our customary picnic lunch. I spotted a hillside meadow, high above the road, looking directly toward Mont Blanc. As we spread out our blanket, there in all its glory was the sparkling mountain resplendent before us, seemingly so near that we had only to reach out to touch it.

We meandered back south via the route taken, in reverse, by Napoleon on his return to France from Elba, to St. Paul de Vence, overlooking the French Riviera between Cannes and Nice. We were charmed by this sequestered little town, from whose narrow streets and alleys all vehicles are barred. But we found even lovelier the delicate Chapel of the Rosary in nearby Vence, designed late in his life by Henri Matisse for the Dominican nuns of Vence, and described by himself as his masterpiece. It was only a short way to Monte Carlo, but we took a quick look into the Casino and drove on via the spectacular Grand Corniche Route, high above the Mediterranean, to the Italian Riviera.

Our main stops in Italy were in Florence and Siena, which was as far south as we cared to go in the increasing summer heat, particularly since we had both visited Rome. In Siena we came upon the splendor of the Piazza del Campo unexpectedly, following a rain shower. Centered at the junction of three gentle hills, it is shell-shaped, paved in soft red with nine radial strips of stone leading down to the base of the shell from which rises the magnificent gothic town hall and campanile. The fresh rain brought out the soft two-toned pink coloring of the stone-and-brick facade of the broad hall and the campanile towering alongside. The effect was breathtaking.

We renewed our affection for Florence, which we had visited separately before we married. One evening we happened by chance on a rare performance of the oratorio *The Conversion of Magdalen*, by Giovanni Bononcini. We had gone up to Fiesole for dinner, after which we were strolling through the square when we heard music coming from the modest cathedral. We sat outside on the steps until the loveliness of the solo voices and chorus enticed us inside. The oratorio was an unexpected delight.

San Martino di Castrozza, high up in the Dolomites, brought welcome relief from the heat along with spectacular views of jagged peaks and fang-like projections of pink or orange-colored bare dolomite rock. Enthralled with the strange beauty of the region, we spent a week before moving on to Bellagio, which rests serenely in the notch of Lake Como. From Bellagio we toured the surrounding Italian lakes before moving on to Milan for another visit to the great cathedral and a period of contemplation before Leonardo da Vinci's poignant *Last Supper* on the wall of the refectory of Sta. Maria Delle Grazie.

We entered Switzerland on August 26, via the St. Gotthard Pass to Interlaken, the ideal center from which to tour that gorgeous country where we spent the next ten days. The quaint city of Vaduz in Liechtenstein was our next stop before ending our trip with a final two weeks at the American Army recreation area at Garmisch in the fringe of the Austrian Alps south of Munich. I was most rewarded for our wonderful nine-thousand mile journey when at its end Glad allowed that she was ready to start all over again.

Hungarian Refugee Relief

We returned to Washington on October 13, 1956, and moved into 4000 Massachusetts Avenue. N.W., as one of its first occupants. It was our first experience in apartment living. We would never have been content with it if we did not have our cottage, "Jayhawk Rest," at Scientists Cliffs, an idyllic spot on Chesapeake Bay, where we can dig in the ground. This combination of city apartment and Bay cottage has worked admirably.

We had barely settled down to retired life when on the morning of December 12, 1956, I heard a radio report that President Eisenhower had established a committee of prominent citizens to supervise a program for the admission of thousands of Hungarians who had rebelled against the Soviet invasion of their country. Many thousands had fled to Austria, where they awaited transportation to countries that would accept them. Tracy S. Voorhees, former Under Secretary of the Army, was appointed to organize the committee and serve as its chairman. I went directly to the phone, called Tracy, and volunteered my services in any capacity he might desire. He accepted at once, and I reported to him that morning as vice chairman and director, in effect his chief of staff.

Tracy Voorhees set up the head office in Washington, where at its first meeting the committee recommended that all refugees coming to America would be brought in via Camp Kilmer, a World War II cantonment in New Jersey near the port of New York. Brigadier General Sidney C. Wooten was appointed Commander of the Joyce Kilmer Refugee Reception Center. This was the committee's first bit of good fortune, for Wooten proved to be a versatile, top-flight commander. The second was equally fortunate. Leo Beebe, Director of Public Relations of the Ford Motor Company, and a personnel expert, was made available to the committee by Henry Ford. Voorhees made him a vice chairman and assigned him to Kilmer to provide administrative assistance to Sid Wooten. William H. Tuck became a third vice chairman and served as committee liaison with the American Ambassador to Austria, Llewellyn E. Thompson. The committee's Washington office consisted simply of Voorhees, Ugo Carusi, a retired immigration officer, Mrs. Florence Philip, secretary, a clerk or two, and me.

The President's committee had no operational authority but with the backing of the president, and the persuasive power of its members, was to coordinate the activities of twenty volunteer and government agencies in the reception and settlement in the United States of the thousands of refugees destined to come here. Tracy Voorhees and I worked closely with the government agencies involved, principally the State and Defense Departments, the Immigration Service, and the American Red Cross. As is always the case in such emergencies, the military services were called upon for much of the work of transporting, receiving, housing, and caring for the refugees. The bulk of the airlift was furnished by U.S. Air Force and Navy aircraft through the Military Air Transportation Service, and ocean-lift by Navy transports. But the major task of housing, feeding, providing medical care, and arranging for resettlement throughout the United States was handled by the Army and the sponsoring agencies, which set up offices at Kilmer. Before entry into the United States each refugee had to be sponsored by an agency, which assumed responsibility for setting him in an agreed community. The great majority of refugees were sponsored by the three largest religious agencies: the National Catholic Welfare Conference, represented by Monsignor Edward E. Swanson; the Church World Service, R. Norris Wilson; and the Hebrew Immigrant Aid Society, Moses A. Levitt. The Lutheran Refugee Service, United Ukranian-American Relief Committee, and the International Rescue Committee also gave yeoman service.

The President's committee neither solicited nor received any funds but did obtain invaluable help from several business organizations, the press, and many communities throughout the country that accepted refugees for resettlement. In addition to Leo Beebe, Henry Ford provided two personnel experts and a secretary. Standard Oil of New Jersey supplied a member of Beebe's staff, as did Seagram Distilleries. Beebe reported to me and I kept in close touch with him and Sid Wooten by phone and periodic visits to Kilmer; Beebe worked directly with Wooten, and soon became his right-hand man. Upon arrival each refugee was given a physical exam by a doctor from the Public Health Service; he was interviewed by inspectors from U.S. Customs and the Immigration and Naturalization Service, who determined occupational experience, education, skills, family status, and housing requirements. This information was recorded on business machine cards. Since the Hungarian language has no Latin or Greek roots, and few of the refugees spoke English, the interrogators had difficulties until the Army came to the rescue. Military units throughout the States, including the Language School at Monterey, California, were canvassed for persons fluent in Hungarian.

After watching the personnel screening process during his first few days at Kilmer, Leo Beebe suggested that a film strip be produced, showing the procedure in detail. Ford provided the necessary script, camera crew, and equipment and produced a twenty-minute movie that was shown to all refugees shortly after their arrival. It helped solve the language problem and speeded up the interrogation process.

The Red Cross, in the words of General Wooten, was "of tremendous assistance. They came in at the very beginning and went right to work, relieving the Army of many problems, and doing their job without presenting problems of their own." A major contribution was the formation of a Red Cross motor corps at Kilmer, which ran errands and escorted small groups of refugees to the nearby rail and air terminals. Under the supervision of Henry Bloss, local director, the Red

Cross set up a consultation service, answering thousands of refugee inquiries, placing over nine thousand long-distance telephone calls and sending an equal number of telegrams to various parts of the country to relatives or friends of the refugees. It also received, sorted, and distributed great quantities of clothing, toiletries, and toys. The enthusiasm of the women volunteers was exemplified by one woman who arrived at the clothing center, took off her coat, rolled up her sleeves, and went to work with a vengeance, to find at the end of an arduous day that she had issued out her own coat, with her car keys in one of its pockets.

During its five months of operation Kilmer processed more than 32,000 refugees, comprising one of the finest groups of immigrants ever to be admitted to the United States. Almost half were skilled workers, including engineers, technicians, teachers, physicians, musicians, lawyers, and craftsmen. With the cooperation of American labor, there was no difficulty fitting them into our labor force. The great success of the entire operation was a tribute to the skill and readiness of the armed services, particularly the Army, to transport, house, feed, and care for the thousands of refugees on such short notice; also to the effective cooperation of the religious and other agencies that handled the resettlement; and to the quality of the refugees themselves. Special credit was due three men: Tracy Voorhees, Leo Beebe, and Sidney Wooten, whom I recommended for promotion to major general.

On May 14, 1957, Tracy Voorhees, speaking for the committee assembled at the White House, reported to the President that its work was completed. The committee's last act was worthy of its performance. It recommended its own dissolution, which President Eisenhower accepted with grateful thanks.

Work with Volunteer Civic Agencies

With the close-out of the Hungarian relief program I had more time to work with a number of volunteer agencies. My eldest sister May had been active for years in our home town of New Orleans in the Society for the Prevention of Blindness and the Lighthouse for the Blind. After the death of her husband, Allen L. Vories, she moved to Washington,

D.C., where she was shocked to find that there was no organization dedicated to the prevention of blindness, over half of which can be prevented. May enlisted the support of Dr. William H. Wilmer, a leading opthalmologist, and in 1936 together they founded the Society for the Prevention of Blindness of Metropolitan Washington, a private organization of volunteers. Dr. Wilmer died within a few months and May was left to shepherd the young society until she was able in 1947 to enlist the services of Helen Curtis Demary, a trained professional executive. Since that time, under Helen Demary's expert guidance, the society has flourished, to the great benefit of the people of Washington, especially with its programs for the early detection of glaucoma, the principal cause of blindness. I have actively supported its work and have been privileged to serve on its board of directors for a number of years.

The rise of the United States as a world power following World War II led to great interest abroad in American institutions, particularly in the fields of government and education. Thousands of foreign students began flocking to Washington to attend the local universities or to consult with government agencies. There was then no central agency to provide information or assistance to these students. To fill this void, a group of interested citizens of the District of Columbia met in the fall of 1956 with the foreign student advisers of the five universities in the area, with representatives of the Pan American Union and the New York-based Institute of International Education (IIE), and founded the Foreign Student Service Council (FSSC) of greater Washington. On September 11, 1956, President Eisenhower called a "people-to-people" conference in Washington at which he advocated a broadening of international contacts on a personal basis, rather than solely through government-to-government negotiations, as a means of reducing international tensions and thereby lessening the chance of wars. While the conference produced no program, it did create considerable interest and its concept appealed to me. Consequently when I was called on in January, 1957, by representatives of the FSSC and asked if I would accept election as its first chairman I readily agreed.

The purpose of the FSSC is to furnish to foreign students coming to Washington information about the city, to assist them in finding lodgings, arrange occasional hospitality in private homes, plan individual or group appointments with government officials, including members of Congress, and in general help them gain an understanding of the community and the American way of life. No financial assistance is offered to students or visitors, and FSSC has relied wholly on donations from foundations, private organizations, and individuals, and occasional benefit affairs sponsored by individuals or foreign embassies. From its inception FSSC has worked in close cooperation with IIE, its initial sponsor, with the Bureau of Cultural Affairs of the State Department, and agencies of the federal government with interests in international education.

As a result of my association with the Foreign Student Service Council of Washington, I was invited in January, 1957, to become a member of the board of trustees of the Institute of International Education (IIE), then headed by Kenneth Holland. IIE is a private nonprofit organization that develops and administers programs of educational exchange for foundations, private organizations, governments, corporations, and colleges and universities in the United States and abroad. In 1957 about 7,500 students, teachers, technicians, and specialists from about 125 countries were studying or training under these programs. Headquarters of IIE is in New York City with several regional offices in the United States and abroad, one of which is located in Washington, D.C. In 1958, I assumed the chairmanship of the advisory committee of the Washington regional office. I remained on the parent board until 1965. I finally had to resign from the board because of business commitments.

I Join Chas. Pfizer & Company

Worthwhile as these volunteer activities were, they added nothing to the family coffers. Gladys and I had already acquired six grandchildren, with more in prospect, who someday would need help with their education. So my ears pricked up when I received a telephone call in mid-January, 1957, from General Ed Hull, then president of the Chemical Manufacturers Association, inquiring if I would be interested in joining the board of directors of Chas. Pfizer & Co., a leading producer of pharmaceuticals and fine chemicals. Ed Hull had given my name to the president of Pfizer, John E. McKeen, who was looking for a senior retired military officer who had considerable experience abroad, to serve on Pfizer's board. Ed said he told McKeen, "You are talking about Joe Collins," which led to my meeting at Pfizer's headquarters in Brooklyn with John McKeen and John J. Powers, Jr., senior Vice President and head of Pfizer's international subsidiaries.

Tracy Voorhees, a native of Brooklyn, knew Pfizer well, so before meeting with McKeen and Powers I consulted with Tracy, who vouched for the excellence of Pfizer products and its management. He also gave me good legal advice as to certain stipulations I wished to make with respect to my possible employment.

I was received most cordially by Messrs. McKeen and Powers, but it was clear that they had been thinking simply of my joining the boards of the parent company and the international subsidiaries. Their interest increased as I explained that I was looking beyond membership on the boards to full-time employment with the company for the remainder of my active career. I outlined the scope of my experience not only as a combat commander but as a senior staff officer in positions of considerable management responsibility both at home and abroad. All of the directors had grown up in the company, and Powers, particularly, seemed to sense that I might bring a fresh point of view to the company management.

After lunch with some members of the Pfizer boards, we resumed our discussions. McKeen and Powers said they wanted to explore further the conditions under which I might join Pfizer. They readily agreed that I would do no lobbying of any kind, nor do any business with the Department of Defense in matters of supply or procurement. I added that I would have no hesitancy in dealing with other branches of the government or testifying before committees of the Congress on any matters on which I was competent. I said I would like to continue living in Washington, and that as Mrs. Collins and I had been separated much of the time in recent years, I hoped that she might accompany me occasionally on business trips abroad to company branch offices and installations, to all of which McKeen and Powers promptly agreed. We parted with mutual expressions of confidence that we could work out a definite agreement to our mutual benefit. We signed a contract on April 1, 1957, and I was duly elected to the board of directors at the shareholders meeting on April 15, 1957, and to the boards of the international subsidiaries later in the month, with the title of vice chairman of the international division. I thus began twelve fascinating years of close association with this splendid company.

After I had been with Pfizer for some time, many of my friends in Washington would ask if I didn't find life strange in the business world. My reply always was, "Not with Pfizer." I quickly discovered that Pfizer ran its international business on the same cardinal principle as the Army, *i.e.*, authority and responsibility should be decentralized but never separated; and Pfizer and the Army alike followed the corollary: while decentralization is a sound general rule, there have to be some centralized controls. I was glad to find that Pfizer had an international procedures manual to govern normal business operations, corresponding to the Army's standing operations procedures, "SOP." Pfizer's management organization abroad was similar to the Army's field commands: each country had a country manager, comparable to a division commander; countries were grouped by regions, or "theaters" in military terms, such as Europe or the Far East, each under a regional manager, or "theater commander" in military parlance. Pfizer's international budget was built up much as in the military service, starting with the country budgets, based on country managers' forecasts of sales and expenses; then it was assembled, reviewed, and modified by regional managers, and then consolidated for submission to international headquarters in New York. There they were reviewed, by regions, by Jack Powers and his staff in conjunction with the regional managers and their comptrollers. Finally, the international budget was consolidated with the domestic company budget for review and approval by the board of directors, much as is done by the Secretary of Defense.

The final techniques in controlling decentralized operations abroad in Pfizer and in the Army were identical: frequent visits by top management, including members of the board, not only to major subordinate headquarters but down to the operating units—plants, depots, and distribution centers.

I took over supervision of the Washington office of Pfizer, which

was expanded to include a representative to handle congressional relations, and to assist me in public relations and contacts with other
government agencies. I began a series of visits to all of our plants in
the United States and to our research installations in Groton, Con-
necticut, and Maywood, New Jersey, to become acquainted with management personnel and all phases of our domestic operations. I was
immediately impressed with the company's wise and generous personnel policies and the close and cordial relationship of management
with the workers. John McKeen, a chemical engineer who had risen
from the ranks of the company, knew every wrinkle in the production
processes and called every plant foreman by his first name. Stock op-
tion rights were extended to all levels of workers throughout the company, a rare practice in those days. I frequently queried men in the
plants as to whether they owned any company stock and invariably
received a reply, "Yes, I have ten (or more shares) and intend to buy
more." I felt right at home and knew that I would enjoy my stay with
Pfizer.

The same was true with the international division, presided over by
Jack Powers, who was young, able, and always receptive to new ideas.
After a tour of our major European subsidiaries, headed by Dick Fen-
ton, a sharp, competent Englishman, I began to take over a role of ne-
gotiator and troubleshooter for Powers abroad. Many of our problems
overseas were involved in getting import licenses, payments for imported goods, or permits for the construction and operation of local
plants and other facilities. I was soon convinced that many of these
problems could be solved if we could get the active cooperation of our
embassies and other government agencies abroad. But when I would
ask one of our country managers if he had taken up a problem with
the American embassy, I was usually told that the embassy was not
interested or that our manager could not get to see the ambassador.
There was some validity to this charge, but we were pouring economic
aid into Europe under the Marshall Plan and it was to our interest, as
well as Europe's, to further American business there. Being well known
to most of the senior officials in the State and Commerce Departments
and to many of our ambassadors abroad, I discussed this situation with
them and received assurances that they would instruct their repre-

sentatives overseas to assist our people in every legitimate way. Each time thereafter when I visited a European country—and this was extended later around the world—I called on the ambassador and brought along our country manager, usually for the first meeting with the ambassador. We outlined our business, our specific problem, and the importance of Pfizer's contribution to our nation's balance of payments. We were always cordially received by the ambassador and appropriate members of his staff, and promised their active assistance. We first put these assurances to the test in Turkey.

Belgium had extended considerable credits to Turkey to pay for imports from Belgium. Turkey then had practically no domestic production of antibiotics, which it needed badly. These requirements were met by production from Pfizer's plant in Brussels, imported through our Turkish subsidiary, Pfizer Ilaçlari. Turkey had fallen far behind in payments for imports from Belgium including large amounts due Ilaçlari. Jack Powers learned of a move by the Agency for International Development to help Belgium collect its debts from Turkey. Powers asked me to look into the situation to see if the Turkish debt to Ilaçlari could be included in the overall settlement of Turkey's Belgian debts. Calls on some of my acquaintances in the State Department and the Agency for International Development (AID) furnished valuable information warranting a trip to Turkey. I brought along to Ankara a young lawyer, Jack Humbert, from our New York office, and we camped for six weeks at the Ankara Palace Hotel—which was no palace—while negotiations with the Turkish government dragged on. With the help of the American Ambassador, Fletcher Warren, and of Pfizer's Turkish manager, Mussafer Turhan, and his influential relatives, we finally succeeded in including Pfizer Ilaçlari in the Belgium settlement—the only American-based company so included—which netted a substantial sum to Pfizer.

As a result of this success, early in 1958 I was given an even more complicated assignment in Turkey, which was continuing to have trouble with its balance of payments, including debts to Pfizer. One of Pfizer's major chemical products is citric acid, made by fermenting beet sugar or sugar cane molasses. Turkey had few natural products other than tobacco with which to earn foreign exchange. But it did have a surplus of sugar beets and was capable of producing a goodly amount of molasses. Pfizer purchased most of its molasses from domestic sources or from France. French molasses was of high purity but very expensive. Mr. McKeen thought he saw an opportunity to solve our continuing financial problems with Turkey, if we could arrange a quasi-barter agreement whereby Pfizer would exchange pharmaceuticals for Turkish molasses. I was asked to essay the Pfizer side of the arrangement, and at the same time to complete negotiations with our Turkish associates in Pfizer Ilaçlari—Mussafer Turhan, his father, and uncle Ishan Duruk—for the construction of a pharmaceutical plant on the outskirts of Istanbul.

Accompanied by Allen Debevoise, our Middle East manager, and by Jacques Humbert, I was back in Istanbul on February 7, 1958. Negotiations for the plant construction proceeded satisfactorily, subject to final approval after completion of the molasses arrangements. Debevoise returned to his Rome headquarters. Then after thorough briefings by our Turkish partners on the intricacies of the pharmaceutical-molasses proposal, my party, including Mussafer, Ishan Duruk, and Pfizer's Turkish lawyer Ali Nur, an astute, suave multilingual Turk, moved up to Ankara for the molasses talks.

There was no waterfront storage facility in Turkey to which molasses could be shipped by railroad tank cars from the several sugar refineries, which were located east of the Sea of Marmara. A terminal would have to be built, including storage tanks, a railroad siding where tank cars could be parked while the molasses was being pumped into storage tanks, and a pier for mooring tanker ships. Such facilities can readily be found or built in any modern port, but each element presented difficulties in Turkey at that time. Molasses is a sticky, viscous substance, which tends to solidify in cold weather. Storage tanks, railroad tank cars, pumps, and transmission lines all had to be steam-heated, and all were in short supply in Turkey, as were steel rails for the car siding. Their availability for our terminal, under the government-controlled economy of Turkey, would have to be cleared with the ministers of finance, commerce, industry, and health and the heads of the Sugar Monopoly and the government-owned railroads. Since Pfizer Ilaçlari was an international company the Minister of Foreign Affairs and ultimately the Prime Minister would have to approve construction of the terminal at Yarimça on the Sea of Marmara, as well as all elements of the antibiotics-molasses deal.

Our negotiating team had two principal objectives: (1) authorization to build the terminal under the terms of a Turkish law designed to encourage foreign investments, which would permit remittances to New York of Pfizer's share of any profits from the operation; (2) authority to import $1,000,000 of antibiotics, in bulk, to be packaged in dosage forms at Ilaçlari's Istanbul plant, and paid for by the molasses exported from Yarimça. Our Turkish partners would handle most of the negotiations with the ministries and the Sugar Monopoly, while I concentrated largely on construction of the molasses terminal. My acquaintance with many of the Turkish military men who now held important positions in the government was helpful. The Minister of Transportation was General Uçaner, former Chief of the Turkish Air Force, whom I had known in Washington. He greeted me with open arms and promised to issue instructions to the Director General of Railways to get our rail siding at Yarimça under way without delay. Similarly, we were helped by Admiral Ulusan, a former associate on the NATO Military Committee, with the special mooring that would be required for a tanker at Yarimça. The lone pier there did not extend out into deep water, so it would be necessary to moor an ocean-going molasses tanker head-on at the end of the pier. A special rig, using three anchors, would be required to hold a tanker in place against the strong current from the Bosporus. A personal call on Ulusan, then stationed at a nearby Turkish naval base, resulted in our obtaining the necessary technical information for procurement of the proper mooring gear.

Meanwhile, Mussafer's uncle Ishan Duruk was finalizing the details of the molasses-antibiotics deal with the several ministers involved. Apparently he had cleared the way when one of the ministers countered with a proposal to convert practically all of the molasses into alcohol for transfer to Germany in exchange for certain machinery. This despite our signed agreement with the Sugar Monopoly for all surplus molasses not required for domestic use. If this counterproposal had been approved Pfizer Ilaçlari would have been forced out

of business, because Pfizer could not have afforded to continue sending millions of dollars worth of drugs into Turkey with no early prospect of payment. Ishan Duruk quickly prepared a memorandum pointing out this possibility, arguing that Turkey needed antibiotics more
than the German machinery and emphasizing the political impact of
the loss of jobs, if our plant were closed. He also arranged an appointment for me to present the memorandum to Emin Kalafat, an influential deputy to Prime Minister Menderes. I reinforced Duruk's points
and stressed the importance to Turkey as well as Pfizer of our inter-
related molasses and pharmaceutical arrangement.

Our combined intercession with Kalafat put an end to the German
machinery proposal by early March, but Humbert and Ali Nur still
had considerable work to do preparing the necessary legal documents
for formal approval by the government, which would be handled by
Mussafer. This would take a week or more, during which time I would
have nothing to do. I had long wanted to visit the Holy Land, but could
never do so while on military duty. By chance, Robert McClintock,
U.S. Ambassador to Cambodia while I was in Viet Nam, and Charles
W. Yost, who was Ambassador to Laos, were then our ambassadors to
Lebanon and Syria respectively. We had worked closely together in
Indochina and had become firm friends. I cabled each of them and received quick replies urging me to fly down for a visit, which I did on
March 9, 1958. During the next eight days, thanks to the McClintocks
and Yosts, I was able to visit the ancient cities of Tyre, Sidon, Biblus,
Beirut, Damascus, the magnificent Roman ruins at Ba'albek, and Jerusalem, Jerico, and the Dead Sea. Damascus was somewhat disappointing to me, but Ba'albek, Jerusalem, and the Holy Land were fascinating and measured up to my expectations. I was saddened, however, by
the maze of chapels, representing the conflicting claims of the various
Christian communities that have grown up around Christ's birthplace
in Bethlehem and his crucification on Calvary, which detract from
the simple majesty of Christ's birth, crucifixion, and resurrection.

Arrangements had been made for me to enter the Israeli half of Jerusalem through the Mandelbaum gate where Otto Preminger, Pfizer's
representative in Israel, met me with his car and drove me down to
Tel Aviv. Pfizer had no plant in Israel but was doing business through

a distributor. Tel Aviv, with its stereotyped rows of apartment houses that lined every street, appeared drab after the ineradicable charm of old Jerusalem, though I admired the energy and determination of the Jews who had built this bustling city from the sandy wastes adjoining the port of Jaffa. The countryside bore further evidence of the industriousness of these people, offering pleasant vistas of terracing, reforestation, and carefully cultivated fields. I enjoyed a drive the next day to Haifa, Nazareth, and the Sea of Galilee. Fortunately this was nine years before the war of 1967 and all was peaceful at Galilee, where we paused while I tried to recapture in my mind's eye the scenes that transpired there in the life of Christ. Our long day ended with a pleasant dinner in Tel Aviv with the Premingers and Pfizer's distributor Alex Aizenberg and his wife.

I flew back to Istanbul in time to check with Jacques Humbert and Mussafer on the arrangements for construction of the Istanbul plant, upon which they had agreed, subject to approval by the Pfizer board, which I recommended. John McKeen's plan of using Turkish molasses to offset sales of pharmaceuticals to Turkey did not work out well at first. Because of some technical difficulty in separating the beet sugar from the by-product molasses, the latter became too viscous to be pumped easily into or out of the molasses tankers. The first tanker load was lost when the tanker captain, irate over his inability to pump the molasses out of the tanker's hold, flushed it out with live steam. The Turkish Sugar Monopoly was finally persuaded to accept the advice of a technical expert from Germany on how to operate their evaporating pans properly, which solved the viscosity problem. Pfizer finally sold the Yarimça terminal to the Sugar Monopoly, which has since operated it successfully, while Pfizer in turn has received adequate import licenses to warrant operating its completed Istanbul plant.

During the remainder of my service with Pfizer I visited all of our overseas plants around the world, including Europe, the Middle East, the Far East, Australia, New Zealand, much of Africa, practically all of South and Central America, and Canada. On these visits I traveled sometimes with Jack Powers but usually with the various area and country managers, chiefly to discover their problems and find out how

New York might help them, while at the same time gauging their strengths and weaknesses. They all realized that I was not seeking any advancement in the company at their expense, and were frank and open with me in discussing their problems. At the end of each trip I submitted a written report to Jack Powers.

I particularly enjoyed my several trips with Robert Middlebrook, our Middle East manager, including visits to Afghanistan, Pakistan, India, and Ceylon. Bob Middlebrook's interests extended beyond the particular business problems at hand, encompassing the economic, historical, and cultural backgrounds of peoples of the area. Without sacrificing any of our management responsibilities, we never missed an opportunity to visit points of interest along our way, whether it was to run up to the Khyber Pass between Afghanistan and Pakistan or drive down the spectacular gorge of the Kabul River between Kabul and Rawalpindi, or a visit in the moonlight to the impeccable Taj Mahal.

Our most important and memorable trip together was to India in 1958. Pfizer's plant in India was located in a congested area of Bombay, which allowed no expansion. Bob Middlebrook had been negotiating for almost three years with Manabai Sha, Under Secretary of Commerce, for a permit to build a plant in an industrial park in Chandigarh, the new capital of the Punjab, whose modern government buildings, designed by the French architect Corbusier, had attracted world attention but few bidders for space in the industrial park. Manabai Sha had refused Pfizer's request to build there, saying that India had no need for another antibiotics plant because the Soviets were going to build a major pharmaceutical complex in India, which would be owned and operated by the Indian government. We knew from a similar Russian-built complex in Egypt, which I had visited, that the Russian plant would be inefficient and would take a long time to build. Bob Middlebrook had promised the Minister of Industry, L. K. Jha, that if Pfizer was permitted to build in Chandigarh the plant would be completed within a year, thus assuring India of an early and reliable source of badly needed antibiotics. But neither Sha nor Jha, both of whom were wedded to the concept of government ownership of manufacturing facilities, would yield to Middlebrook's request. Middlebrook finally arranged an appointment through Pfizer's public relations man in Bombay, K. G. Pillai, a cousin of Prime Minister Nehru's principal secretary, for Middlebrook and me to present our case directly to the Prime Minister.

We were graciously received by Mr. Nehru, but he showed no sign of interest as we outlined our project until I said we were planning to build the new plant in Chandigarh, when his face lit up.

"Chandigarh," he repeated. "Why Chandigarh?" We explained that the city had laid out an industrial park there, complete with sewage and electric power connections, but thus far had no tenants. Pfizer had purchased a section of the park, was prepared to initiate construction without delay, and the city and Punjab state authorities were anxious to have us as the first tenants. I spoke of the interest generated in Chandigarh by Corbusier's innovative architecture, and that we would complement the architecture with a modern plant, which under Pfizer's management policies would be operated almost exclusively by Indians, thus helping reduce unemployment in the Punjab. Nehru asked a number of questions, thanked us, and said he would consider the project.

We were scarcely seated in his secretary's anteroom when the door to Nehru's office was opened by the Prime Minister, who stood for a moment with our calling cards in his hand and asked Secretary Pillai to come in to his office. Pillai returned in a few minutes to say that Mr. Nehru had been well impressed by our proposal and had asked him to look into it. A few days later the project was approved. There was no doubt in my mind that Nehru, whose family had originated in Kashmir, adjacent to the Punjab, was influenced in Pfizer's favor as much by his sentimental ties to that region—accentuated by the 1947 dispute with Pakistan over Kashmir, when the British withdrew from India—as by our economic arguments. He reacted to our proposal as a good politician would anywhere in the world. But never one to mix sentiment with hard business considerations, L. K. Jha insisted on our giving India the right to manufacture Pfizer's patented tetracycline in the Russian plant when it would be built. Our plant was completed within a year and was a success both for India and Pfizer. My only regret was that on two trips to Chandigarh bad weather in Kashmir prevented me from visiting that fabulously beautiful state.

One of the last and perhaps most important task I performed for

Pfizer was to "discover" Edmund T. Pratt and help Jack Powers persuade him to join Pfizer. Powers obviously was heir apparent to succeed John McKeen as head of Pfizer, and in 1964 he asked me to be on the lookout for an experienced man leaving government service during the change of administrations following the assassination of President Kennedy, since we would be needing a replacement for Ed Smith, our controller, whom Jack was planning to make a vice president with responsibility for finance. I had gotten to know Robert McNamara, Secretary of Defense, well enough to call on him for help. I explained our situation and asked if there was anyone among his assistants whom he might recommend for Pfizer's post. Without hesitating a moment he replied, "Yes, the Assistant Secretary of the Army for financial matters, Ed Pratt. If I were going back to Ford, I would be glad to have Pratt as top financial man in the company." That was sufficient recommendation for me. McNamara suggested two or three others and gave me permission to speak to them, but I decided to go after Ed Pratt. Stephen Ailes, Secretary of the Army, like McNamara, said he would hate to lose Pratt, but recommended him highly and said he had no objection to my talking to him.

I knew Pratt slightly, having met him only occasionally at Army functions, but had liked his modest, friendly manner. When I called on him at his office he was frankly surprised at Pfizer's interest. He had been on the job about a year, was thoroughly enjoying his assignment with the Army, and expected to remain for the normal two to four years. He did admit that my enthusiasm for Pfizer, its high-caliber people, progressive operating policies, and possibilities for dynamic world-wide growth, intrigued him. I was impressed with Pratt's searching questions, his quiet self-confidence, and balanced outlook. I urged him to give our proposition serious thought. I suggested to Jack Powers that he concentrate on getting Ed Pratt. This he did, with the result that Pratt joined Pfizer on December 1, 1964, as controller, a post he held until February, 1967, by which time Powers had followed John McKeen as president. Pratt then succeeded Powers as president in September, 1971, and when Powers retired the following year Ed Pratt was elected chairman of the board and chief executive officer, a post he has filled superbly ever since.

The company had no fixed retirement age, but in 1966 I advised

Jack Powers, then chairman of the board, that I was approaching seventy and that I was ready to retire if he wished me to do so. His ready reply was, "Joe, if you are happy, we are. So what?" But I realized that at the rate Pfizer was growing—sales exceeded $621 million in 1966 —Powers would want to strengthen the Pfizer board with more experienced financial men, so again offered to retire in 1966. Jack Powers accepted, but asked me to remain on the boards of Pfizer's international subsidiaries, which I did until April, 1969, when I fully retired.

CHAPTER XXI

Retrospect: The Role of the Military in American Society

Forty-eight years ago, with my eyes open, I decided to forego the possibilities of a career as a lawyer and to stick to the profession of soldier which I had chosen as a youngster in 1913. I have thought over that decision many times since, always with the same result—I have no regrets, though I have had to make some philosophical adjustments along the way. The lack of roots in a permanent home community, which I and my wife have felt, has been compensated for by our association with the wonderful, dedicated people who make up the corps of officers of the United States Army. But I had to reconcile myself also to the fact that military service is distasteful, at best, to most Americans, many of whom have a traditional distrust of the military as a potential threat to their personal freedom. This has been manifested ever since the American Revolution, when militiamen quit the Army at the end of their very short terms of service, no matter how critical the military situation at the time. It took strenuous efforts on

the part of General Washington and dire warnings of defeat before the Continental Congress, fearful of the mere thought of a standing army, agreed to extra pay for officers and men to serve to the end of the war. As soon as the war was over Congress virtually disbanded the army, limiting it to eighty men to guard ammunition and equipment stored at West Point. This attitude continued until 1801 when the United States Military Academy was authorized at West Point, with two engineer cadets. It took the threat of war with Great Britain to persuade Congress on April 29, 1812, to authorize the attendance at West Point of cadets appointed in the infantry, cavalry, and artillery. This act marked the real beginning of the professional army.

I was well aware of the latent distrust of the military by many Amer-

433

icans that continued in the interval between World Wars I and II, even as Hitler and his Nazis grew more and more threatening, and it became apparent that we would have to rebuild our armed forces —which could be done only with the aid of compulsory military service. The House of Representatives extended on August 13, 1941, the Selective Service Act beyond its initial year by the margin of a single vote. This was just a few months before the Japanese attack on Pearl Harbor.

Along with this antimilitary attitude on the part of a large segment of the Congress in 1940–41 was the carping criticism of some elements in the academic community, and members of the press, with their sniping references to the "military mind." But these relatively minor drawbacks, which to some extent exist even today, have been far outweighed by the fascinating challenges of my military service, which have caused me to give considerable thought to the role of the military in our society in relation to the President, the civilian Secretaries, the Congress, and to the public at large, to all of whom we in the armed forces have such deep obligations. Fortunately, I never had any problem subscribing fully to the basic thesis governing these relationships, *i.e.*, that our military personnel and institutions must be under civil control.

The Constitution makes the President Commander in Chief of the Army, Navy, and Air Force of the United States. This places more direct responsibility on the President for the operations of the armed forces than is the case with any other operating agency of the government. Since passage of the National Security Act of 1947, the President has exercised his command responsibility through the Secretary of Defense. The 1947 act failed to provide the Secretary with the necessary authority to meet his great responsibilities. It took eleven years of operating under eight successive Secretaries before the Department of Defense Reorganization Act of 1958 finally gave the Secretary full authority and responsibility for operation of the Department.

Since then, the Departments of the Army, Navy, and Air Force are no longer executive departments with cabinet status. These "military departments" still have major responsibilities, under direction of the Secretary of Defense, to organize, equip, and train their Services, but have no role in the operations of these forces. Units of the Army, Navy (including the Marine Corps), and Air Force are assigned to eight combatant commands, each under a senior military commander who is directly responsible to the Secretary of Defense and the President. At present, five of the combatant commands made up of Army, Navy, and Air Force units have regional assignments: Atlantic Command, European Command, Pacific Command, Southern Command (Central and South America, except Mexico), and the Readiness Command, which includes all Army and Air Force units in the United States not assigned to regional or specified commands but available to reinforce them.

Three combatant commands are classified as "specified commands": Strategic Air Command (SAC), Military Airlift Command (MAC), and Aerospace Defense Command (ADCOM). SAC is made up of Air Force units only and does not include the long-range ballistic-missile submarines of Navy units assigned to the Pacific, Atlantic, or European Commands. MAC's chief mission is to provide airlift support to the unified and specified commands. Like SAC, it contains only Air Force units. ADCOM's mission is to provide early warning and defense to the United States against aerospace attack. It includes antiaircraft missile units of the Army and Air Force. ADCOM's operations are coordinated with those of a comparable Canadian command.

Although the combatant commands are established by the President, through the Secretary of Defense, with the advice of the Joint Chiefs of Staff, they are not in the chain of command from the President. Full operational control of the forces assigned to the combatant commands has been transferred directly to their commanders, making the latter responsible in event of emergency for prompt initial action, within their assigned missions. This delegation of responsibility to theater commanders does not include authority for the employment of nuclear weapons, which still requires specific authorization from the President. It does obviate the necessity for clearance from the JCS or the Secretary of Defense by combatant commanders to initiate action in situations such as General MacArthur faced when South Korea was invaded in 1950. There is danger, of course, of a mistake in judgment by a combatant commander that might commit the country to action contrary to the wishes of the Commander in Chief. However, the JCS is apparently well prepared to handle such contingencies, to counter promptly any unwarranted action, keep the Secretary of Defense and the President informed, recommend remedial courses of action, and issue the necessary orders to implement the decisions of the Secretary and the President. Procedures for carrying out these actions have been tested in several international crises, notably following the capture of the USS *Pueblo* by the North Koreans in 1968 and the seizure of the SS *Mayaguez* in 1975.

Because of the cancellation of the system whereby the JCS designated one of its members as executive agent for each theater of operations, there is presently no established procedure for on-the-spot verification of the execution of orders, which is essential to the success of any military operation. Lacking an executive agent to check on the preparations for possible action against Cuba in 1962, the JCS designated each Chief to act as its representative in supervising his service in its share of the preparations. In addition, the Chiefs had frequent sessions in Washington with Admiral Robert Dennison, Commander in Chief of the Atlantic Command, the unified command with headquarters in nearby Norfolk that would have conducted the invasion of Cuba if such action had been directed by the President. But a committee is a poor substitute for a responsible individual to check on actual conditions in the field, as I did as executive agent for the JCS during the Korean War. It would be impossible for the JCS as a body to make such checks if a conflict should break out in the Middle East. The Secretary of Defense hence should designate the Chairman of the JCS as his executive agent, or delegate authority to the Chairman to designate another one of the Chiefs to follow up on the execution of instructions from the Secretary to SACEUR or whoever might be assigned by the President to handle the situation. Staff support for the executive agent should come from the Joint Staff of the JCS.

The position of the Chairman of the JCS has been strengthened by the 1958 amendments, but his authority and responsibility for assisting the Secretary in evaluating JCS recommendations should be increased and clarified. One of the remaining weaknesses of the JCS shows up when there is a divergence of views among the Chiefs on any important problem. At times in the past, pressure to obtain unanimous agreement has resulted in watered-down solutions that failed to solve a problem. Or if no agreement was reached, the Secretary of Defense, a civilian, was forced to resolve the views of military experts without the objective recommendation of a top military man responsible directly to the Secretary. While I was Army Chief of Staff, I suggested to the Nelson Rockefeller Commission, appointed by Secretary Charles Wilson in 1953 to study the organization of the Department of Defense, that in case of disagreement among the Chiefs on any issue, the Chairman should be required to present to the Secretary his own recommendation along with those of the other Chiefs. This suggestion was not adopted. I feel more than ever that it should be.

The Chiefs of Staff of the Army, Navy, and Air Force "wear two hats," in their dual roles, (1) as members of the Joint Chiefs of Staff, joint advisers to the Secretary of Defense in the formulation of strategic plans and in monitoring the implementation of such plans by unified combatant forces, and (2) as Chiefs of their individual services, responsible to their service Secretaries for the organization, training, equipment, and preparedness of their troops. A Service Chief's duties as a member of the JCS take precedence over his role as Chief of his individual service. This dual responsibility has been studied by several commissions and debated at length by the military affairs committees of Congress. Study groups have at times proposed eliminating the dual roles by replacing the Joint Chiefs by a group of senior retired officers from the three services who would be responsible to the Secretary of Defense for strategic plans and operations but would have no responsibilities to the Secretaries of the Army, Navy, and Air Force. These suggestions, which have a theoretical appeal to study groups, are almost universally opposed by experienced military leaders and by congressional military affairs committees familiar with the practical drawbacks of such proposals.

Like most military men, I know from my own experience that it is difficult for retired officers, divorced from their service connections, to keep abreast of new developments in tactics and weapons. Senior officers passed over for selection as Chief of Staff are likely to have biases and warped views that lessen their objectivity. Moreover, I have always felt that strategic and supporting logistical plans should be prepared under the supervision of the men who will have the responsibility of seeing that they are carried out, and who know the capabilities and limitations of the units and their commanders that will have to implement these plans. The members of the JCS as Service Chiefs have grown up with the unit commanders, followed their careers, and usually have been responsible for their selection for high command. As far as I know, officers who have served as Chiefs of Staff in recent years have proven competent to handle their dual roles. Their Vice Chiefs of Staff have properly taken over most of the duties in the day-in, day-out management of the services under the Service Secretaries. With increased authority of the Chairman of the JCS to guide the functioning of the JCS, there should be no reason for radical change in organization of the JCS.

Problems caused by the dual roles of the Chiefs of Staff do exist, but as with most personnel matters their solution lies in the personalities of the service Secretaries and their Chiefs of Staff and the ability of these men to work together in an intimate, harmonious relationship based on trust and confidence. One of the most rewarding aspects of my service as Army Chief was my association with the three Secretaries of the Army under whom I served: Gordon Gray, Frank Pace, and Robert Stevens. These men were typical of the dedicated public servants who take two or three years out of their business or professional careers, often at considerable personal sacrifice, to serve their country. Few such men are ever given any recognition, other than criticism if something within their bailiwicks goes astray. I have great admiration and respect for these men. I was particularly fortunate in having Frank Pace as Army Secretary during most of my four years as Chief of Staff. As was the case with the other Secretaries, we had adjacent offices, with a door that was never locked, leading directly from one to the other, and we were back and forth whenever a matter arose that warranted informal discussions. The latter were in addition to regular meetings of the Army Policy Council, chaired by the Secretary, and attended by the Under and Assistant Secretaries, the Vice Chief of Staff, and our principal assistants. At these meetings there was always give-and-take, but whenever a decision was called for, it was, of course, made by the Secretary. In addition to my close official association with the Secretaries, a warm friendship developed between Gladys and me and the Secretaries and their ladies that has continued to this day, and will always be a source of great pleasure.

The President has always exercised control of the armed services by means of the budget, and it is in this area that the greatest improvements have been made in recent years. While I was Chief of Staff the Department of Defense budget was simply a combination of three separate department budgets, Army, Navy, Air Force, rather than an integrated budget. Requirements for appropriated funds were computed and presented by categories such as personnel costs, construction, operation and maintenance, procurement, and other services, with little or no direct relation to JCS strategic plans. Budgets were projected only one year ahead, precluding any real long-range planning. Beginning in 1961, Secretary Robert S. McNamara, with the help of his able Assistant Secretary of Defense, Comptroller Charles J. Hitch, initiated a new "planning-programing-budgeting" system that now integrates the planning and programing of budget requirements of the unified and specified commands in accord with the objectives of JCS plans. Budgets are projected on a five-year basis, with provision for a continuous review by the office of the Comptroller rather than by the traditional annual review. Requirements to meet the objectives of the JCS are programed and cost estimates computed by the military services under ten categories of forces required: Strategic, General Purpose, Intelligence and Communications, Air and Sealift, National Guard and Reserve, Research and Development, Central Supply and Maintenance, Training, Medical and other general personnel activities, Administration, and Support of other nations.

After the Secretary has reviewed, modified, and given preliminary approval to the programs, including their dollar costs, the programs are sent back to the Service Secretaries for adjustments that may have been required by dollar ceilings determined by the Secretary of Defense under direction of the President. No one has yet succeeded in eliminating ultimate budget ceilings, which have always been the bugaboo of military men.

Congressional appropriation committees still insist on presentation of military budgets in traditional form, *i.e.*, in terms of costs of personnel, procurement of weapons, equipment and supplies, operations and maintenance and the like. After the Secretary of Defense has approved the overall budget in terms of programs and has secured the President's approval, his Comptroller's office, in October each year, converts the budget into conventional terms of costs of personnel, procurement, maintenance, research and development, and so forth, for submission to the Congress.

Establishment of unified and specified combatant commands with assigned missions in consonance with strategic plans of the JCS; the closer link of the budget to these operational plans; and the increased authority of the Chairman of the JCS have enhanced the ability of military leaders to serve the President and the Secretary of Defense. Their role could be strengthened if the combatant commanders were given a formal voice in determining the requirements of their forces, and if the Chairman of the JCS were designated as the agent of the Secretary for supervising their activities.

The question arises periodically as to what a Chief of Staff should do if, in all conscience, he cannot support the budget or other policy decisions of the President or the Secretary of Defense. In such a case he is entitled by law to appeal directly to the President, over the head of the Secretary, if necessary. I believe that in loyalty to the President as Commander in Chief, a Chief of Staff should support the President's programs unless, in a crisis, a chief is convinced that the security of the country is at stake, in which instance he should ask to be relieved. I came close to such a point shortly before the outbreak of the Korean War when I felt impelled to inform Secretary Louis Johnson at an Armed Forces policy meeting that I would be unable to accept any further cuts in the number of active divisions in the Army. If the Korean War had not intervened I might well have been relieved or forced to resign.

One of the most important and challenging duties of the Chiefs of Staff is to testify before committees of Congress with respect to military plans and programs of the Department of Defense. The Secretary of Defense and his principal Assistant Secretaries open the annual review of the budget and are always called upon first for testimony in the investigation of any military matter by Congress. Congressional committees inquire directly from the Chiefs of Staff and other military leaders as to the soundness, adequacy, and necessity of military plans, programs, and procedures. Thus, while insisting properly on subservience of the military to civil control, Congress requires military men to support or oppose publicly the policies and programs of the civilian administration. No holds are barred in the questioning, which may range from the accuracy and effectiveness of a ballistic missile to the soundness of strategic concepts and their relation to foreign policy. In spite of some inconsistency, the system has merit in providing a review of military programs and actions independent of the Defense Department, and is consistent with the responsibility of Congress under the Constitution "to raise and support armies," "to provide and maintain a navy," and "to provide for the common defense." Congress will never surrender its right to hear directly from responsible leaders, civil and military alike, their personal judgments on matters affecting national security. I usually enjoyed my many appearances before committees of Congress and always found them stimulating.

A major difficulty of this system is that it sometimes leads to involvement of the JCS in politics. During the debates in the Senate in the early 1950s, while I was a member of the JCS, over the question of stationing American troops in Europe as part of the NATO command, Senator Robert A. Taft accused General Bradley, Chairman of the JCS, of having intervened politically in support of President Truman's plan to fulfill the commitments we had made to NATO. Taft even challenged Bradley's integrity, and inferred that the Chiefs as a body were violating the unwritten code of the professional officer to place duty to country above all other considerations. There was some talk in the press that the "old" Chiefs of Staff should submit their resignations to Dwight Eisenhower, the President-elect, as has been the practice with cabinet members at changes of administration. Taft suggested that, in the interim, a standby group of prospective replacements, more amenable to the views of Taft and his adherents, be designated to review military plans and programs, including the Defense Department budget and foreign aid. As far as I know, Eisenhower never seriously entertained these suggestions, which if carried out would have injected the JCS into partisan politics. It so happened that the tours of duty of three of the four Chiefs would end in the normal course of events shortly after Eisenhower took office. Bradley and I were due to retire on August 15, 1953, and Vandenberg, who was critically ill, was retired for physical disability in May. I was surprised and disappointed that Admiral William L. Fechteler, the experienced Chief of Naval Operations, whose standard two-year term as CNO was about to expire, was not reappointed by the President, which added some credence to Navy scuttlebutt that Taft had had his way. Fortunately, this happenstance has not been repeated.

One of the great advantages stemming from unification of the Department of Defense was consolidation of the Military and Naval Affairs Committees of the Senate and House into a single Armed Service Committee in each body, and concurrent merging of subcommittees on Appropriations. Prior to unification, the Army (including the Army Air Corps) and the Navy (and Marine Corps) prepared their budgets independently and submitted them to different congressional committees. Members of these committees never had an opportunity to consider an integrated program that would show service requirements on a joint operational basis and might reveal overall deficiencies or needless duplication of capabilities. Inevitably, most members became partisan supporters of the service with which they were most familiar and lost much of their objectivity. I well remember that just before the opening of hearings on unification in 1945, I telephoned Congressman F. Edward Hebert, then a senior member of the House Naval Affairs Committee, to ask if I might discuss with him the Army's unification proposal. He cut me off at once with a snap: "General, you look after the Army. We'll look after the Navy!" Fortunately, as members of the unified committees became accustomed to considering military requirements on an integrated basis, their outlook has broadened, with resultant benefit to our military programs.

In the recent past our military forces have had to fight two unpopular wars in Korea and Vietnam, on the other side of the world. Vietnam was a traumatic experience, which adversely affected discipline and morale not only within the armed forces, especially the Army, but among the American public. The malaise among our people during the closing phases of the Vietnamese fighting, and following the withdrawal of our troops, spread throughout the academic community and the news media, and permeated the halls of Congress. The selective service system with its vital registration mechanism was dismantled, foreign aid programs were slashed indiscriminately, and "revisionist" historians seemed to vie with one another in belittling anything praiseworthy in our military past. The most serious adverse effect was that Reserve Officer Training Corps programs were canceled in a number of our top universities including Harvard, Yale, and Princeton, and such fine military schools as Virginia Military Institute and the Citadel had heavy losses. The land-grant state universities like Texas A & M, and Louisiana State, which in World War II produced many times more young officers than West Point and Annapolis, were even harder hit. During the period from 1968 to 1978, the number of ROTC graduates from Texas A & M dropped from over 1,800 annually to less than 750, and Louisiana State plummeted from almost 2,000 to less than 200. During the years from 1966 to 1973 the total ROTC enrollment fell from approximately 117,000 to 33,000. Equally serious has been the shortfall of about 20 percent in the strength of the National Guard and a shortage of almost 30 percent in the Organized Reserves, counted on to flesh out the Regular forces in event of a national emergency.

I believe that the worst part of the self-flagellation following the war in Vietnam is over. While I have some doubts about the long-term practicability of the all-volunteer Army in a major emergency, it seems to be working well so far. Enlistment quotas are being met, a good percentage of those enlisting are high-school graduates, and discipline is being maintained. Princeton has reinstituted part of its ROTC program, and with improvement in the quality of ROTC training, other top-flight universities perhaps will do likewise. I had an opportunity recently to observe some instruction in tactics at Indiana University—which should be a challenging study for any student with an analytical bent—and was impressed with the improvement in methods of instruction in this subject that has come about in the past few years.

And I am confident that the Military Academy at West Point, under the wise guidance and leadership of Lieutenant General Andrew J. Goodpaster, will continue to graduate young officers who will maintain its great traditions.

The American people rightly look to their military leaders not only to be skilled in the technical aspects of the profession of arms, but to be men of integrity who have a deep understanding of the human strengths and weaknesses that motivate soldiers under the ultimate test of war. As I look back on my military service, which comprised the major part of my life, it is this feature of the military profession that has always had the greatest appeal to me and remains the chief source of satisfaction. Only the clergy and the teaching profession offer comparable opportunities and responsibilities as I have had to assist in such activities as the rehabilitation of drug addicts from the waterfront of Brooklyn; the development of the natural qualities of leadership of a Sergeant Woodward; share the drama of heroic action of a Charlie Davis on Guadalcanal; feel the deep sadness of heavy casualties of our men in the Hürtgen Forest and the Korean War; suffer the sense of personal loss at the death of a Maurice Rose; or thrill to our victory over the legions of Hitler's menacing Nazis. These experiences all add up to my abiding admiration and affection for the Army of the United States and its men and women who, I am sure, no matter what dangers the future holds for us, will always live up to our nation's trust.

BIBLIOGRAPHY

Adams, James G. *Review of the American Forces in Germany*. Coblenz, Germany, 1921.

Allen, Henry T. *The Rhineland Occupation*. New York: Bobbs-Merrill, 1927.

"The American Breakthrough in the Direction of Avranche." On file in the office of the Chief of Military History, Washington, D.C.

Ambrose, Stephen E. *Eisenhower and Berlin 1945*. New York: Norton, 1945.

———. *The Supreme Commander*. New York: Doubleday, 1970.

Appleman, Roy E. *South to the Naktong, North to the Yalu*. Washington, D.C.: Office of the Chief of Military History (OCMH), U.S. Army, 1960.

Ayer, Leonard P. *Statistical Summary of World War I*. Washington, D.C.: Government Printing Office, 1919.

Baldwin, Hanson W. *Great Decision*. Washington, D.C.: The Infantry Journal, May, 1947.

Blumenson, Martin. *European Theater of Operations: Breakout and Pursuit*. Washington, D.C.: OCMH, U.S. Army, 1961.

Bouscaren, Anthony T. *Diem of Vietnam*. Pittsburgh: Duquesne University Press.

Bradley, Omar N. *A Soldier's Story*. New York: Henry Holt, 1951.

Bush, Vannevar. *Modern Arms and Free Men*. New York: Simon and Schuster, 1949.

Butcher, Harry C. *My Three Years with Eisenhower*. New York: Simon and Schuster, 1946.

Buttinger, Joseph. *A Dragon Embattled*. New York: Praeger, 1967.

Churchill, Winston S. *The Second World War*. 6 vols. Boston: Houghton Mifflin, 1948–53.

Clark, Mark W. *From the Danube to the Yalu*. New York: Harper, 1954.

Cole, Hugh M. *The Ardennes: Battle of the Bulge*. Washington, D.C.: OCMH, U.S. Army, 1965.

Collins, J. Lawton. *War in Peacetime*. Boston: Houghton Mifflin, 1969.

Critique of Operations of the 25th Division in the Central Solomons. Published by the 25th Division, 1943.

Critique of Operations of the 25th Division on Guadalcanal. Published by the 25th Division, 1943.

Department of Defense. *U.S.–Vietnamese Relations 1945–1967*. Washington, D.C.: Government Printing Office, 1971.

Dod, Karl C. *The Corps of Engineers: The War Against Japan*. Washington D.C.: OCMH, U.S. Army, 1966.

Draper, Theodore. *The Eighth Infantry Division in the Battle of Germany*. New York: Viking Press, 1946.

———. *84th Division in the Battle of Germany*. New York: Viking Press, 1946.

Eisenhower, Dwight D. *Papers of Dwight D. Eisenhower*. Volumes I, II, III, IV. Baltimore: Johns Hopkins, 1970.

———. *Crusade in Europe*. Garden City, N.Y.:Doubleday, 1948.

Fall, Bernard. *The Two Vietnams*. New York: Praeger, 1963.

Fiebeger, G. J. *Campaigns of the American Civil War*. West Point: USMA Printing Office, 1914.

First Army Report of Operations. Washington, D.C.: War Department, 1945.

Gravel, Mike. *Pentagon Papers*. Boston: Beacon Press, 1971.

———. *United States–Vietnam Relations* (Pentagon Papers). Washington D. C.: House Armed Services Committee, 1971.

Greenfield, Kent Roberts. *Command Decisions*. Washington, D.C.: OCMH, U.S. Army, 1960.

Harmon, Millard F., to Thomas Hardy, July 15, 1943. Letter in SOPACBACOM file, OCMH, U.S. Army.

Hanson, Chester B. Diary. On file at Army War College, Carlisle Barracks, Pa.

Harrison, Gordon A. *European Theater of Operations: Cross-Channel Attack*. Washington, D.C.: OCMH, U.S. Army, 1950.

Hechler, Kenneth W. "VII Corps in Operation COBRA." Manuscript with OCMH, U.S. Army.

Henrich, F. J. *History of the 3d Armored Division: Spearhead in the West*. Frankfurt am Main, Germany, 1945.

Hermes, Walter G. *Truce Tent and Fighting Front*. Washington, D.C.: OCMH, U.S. Army, 1966.

Hewes, James E., Jr. *From Root to McNamara: Army Organization and Administration, 1900–1963*. Washington, D.C.: OCMH, U.S. Army, 1975.

Higgins, Trumbull. *Korea and the Fall of MacArthur*. New York: Oxford University Press, 1960.

Knickerbocker, H. *Danger Forward*. Washington, D.C.: Society of the First Division, 1947.

Korb, Lawrence J. *The Joint Chiefs of Staff, The First Twenty-Five Years*. Bloomington: Indiana University Press, 1976.

Lapp, R. E. *The New Force*. New York: Harper and Row, 1953.

Lee, Ulysses. *The Employment of Negro Troops in World War II*. Washington, D.C.: OCMH. U.S. Army, 1966.

MacDonald, Charles B. *The Battle of the Huertgen Forest*. New York: Lippincott, 1963.

———. *European Theater of Operations: The Siegfried Line Campaign*. Washington, D.C.: OCMH, U.S. Army, 1963.

MacGregor, Morris J. "The Integration of the Armed Forces, 1945–1965," Part I. Manuscript done for OCMH, U.S. Army, 1973.

Marshall, George C. Correspondence File. Now filed at the George C. Marshall Research Library, Lexington, Va.

Matisse, Henri. *Chapelle de Rosaire des Dominicaines de Vence*. Paris: Meurlot Frères, 1955.

Miller, John, Jr. *Guadalcanal: The First Offensive*. Washington, D.C.: OCMH, U.S. Army, 1949.

———. *Cartwheel: The Reduction of Rabaul*. Washington, D.C.: OCMH, U.S. Army, 1959.

Mittleman, Joseph B. *Eight Stars to Victory: History of the 9th Infantry Division*. Published by 9th Infantry Association, 1948.

Montgomery, Bernard L. *Normandy to the Baltic*. Cologne, Germany: Printing and Stationery Service, British Army of the Rhine, 1946.

Montgomery, John D. *Politics of Foreign Aid*. New York: Praeger, 1961.

Morgan, Frederick Edgeworth. *Overture to Overlord*. Garden City, N.Y.: Doubleday, 1950.

Morton, C. V. *A Stranger in Spain*. New York: Dodd Mead, 1955.

National Security Act of 1947 as amended by the Department of Defense Reorganization Act of 1958.

New York *Times*, May 28, 1953.

Novick, David. *Program Budgeting*. Cambridge: Harvard University Press, 1965.

Order of Battle, U.S. Army Ground Forces, World War II, Pacific Theater of Operations. Washington, D.C.: OCMH, U.S. Army, 1959.

Palmer, Frederick. *Newton D. Baker*. Volume I. New York: Dodd Meade, 1931.

Pogue, Forrest. *The Supreme Command*. Washington, D.C.: OCMH, U.S. Army, 1954.

———. *Education of a General*. New York: Viking Press, 1963.

———. *Ordeal and Hope*. New York: Viking Press, 1966.

———. *Organizer of Victory*. New York: Viking Press, 1973.

Rees, David. *Korea: The Limited War*. London: Macmillan, 1964.

Ridgway, Matthew B. *The Korean War*. Garden City, N.Y.: Doubleday, 1967.

Ryan, Cornelius. *The Longest Day*. New York: Simon and Schuster, 1959.

Schnabel, James F. *Policy and Direction: The First Year*. Washington, D.C.: OCMH, U.S. Army, 1971.

Special Commission on United States Military Academy. Report to the Secretary of the Army. December 12, 1976.

Sylvan, William C. Diary. On file in the Office of the Chief of Military History, U.S. Army, Washington, D.C.

Taylor, Maxwell D. *Swords and Plowshares*. New York: Norton, 1972.

——. *Precarious Security*. New York: Norton, 1976.

Time, January 17, 1955.

Toland, John. *But Not in Shame*. New York: Random House, 1961.

Upton, Emory. *Military Policy of the U.S.* Washington, D.C.: Government Printing Office, 1912.

U.S. House of Representatives. 81st Congress, 1st Session. Armed Services Committee Hearings.

——. 81st Congress, 2nd Session. Subcommittee on Armed Forces Hearings. (On H.R.5794)

U.S. Senate. 79th Congress, 1st Session. Military Affairs Committee Hearings. (On S.84 and S.1482)

——. 81st Congress, 2nd Session. Committee on Armed Services on the Army Reorganization Act of 1950, Hearings.

——. 82nd Congress, 1st Session. Report of Hearings, Committee on Armed Services and Committee on Foreign Relations. (MacArthur Hearings)

Watson, Mark S. *Chief of Staff: Prewar Plans and Preparations*. Washington, D.C.: OCMH, U.S. Army, 1949.

Weber, J. J. *Mission Accomplished: Campaigns of the VII Corps in the War Against Germany*. Leipzig, Germany: J. J. Weber, 1945.

Westmoreland, William C. *A Soldier Reports*. Garden City, N.Y.: Doubleday, 1976.

Wilmot, Chester. *The Struggle for Europe*. London: Collins, 1952.

Winterbotham, F. W. *The Ultra Secret*. New York: Harper and Row, 1974.

Ziemke, Earl F. *Stalingrad to Berlin*. Washington, D.C.: OCMH, U.S. Army, 1968.

OTHER SOURCES

Records of the Department of Defense and Department of the Army on matters with which I was personally involved during World War II and the Korean War, and personal records, letters, and memoranda are filed in the National Archives, Washington, D.C. Practically all of this material has been declassified. For the benefit of scholars I have filed with the National Archives an annotated copy of my manuscript.

J. L. C.

Index

449